The Voyage of the
Northern Magic

A FAMILY ODYSSEY

DIANE STUEMER

M&S

Cloth edition published 2002
Trade paperback edition published 2004

National Library of Canada Cataloguing in Publication

Stuemer, Diane King, 1959-2003.
    The voyage of the Northern Magic : a family odyssey / Diane Stuemer.

ISBN 0-7710-8260-6 (bound).—ISBN 0-7710-8263-0 (pbk.)

1. Stuemer, Diane King, 1959-2003.   2. Stuemer family.
3. Northern Magic (Yacht)   4. Voyages around the world.   I. Title.

G440.S88A3 2002   910.4'1   C2002-902633-4

We acknowledge the financial support of the Government of Canada through the Book Publishing Industry Development Program and that of the Government of Ontario through the Ontario Media Development Corporation's Ontario Book Initiative. We further acknowledge the support of the Canada Council for the Arts and the Ontario Arts Council for our publishing program.

Typeset in Sabon by M&S, Toronto
All maps by Diane Stuemer

Designed by Blaine Herrmann
Front and back cover photos: Diane and Herbert Stuemer

Printed and bound in Canada

McClelland & Stewart Ltd.
The Canadian Publishers
481 University Ave.
Toronto, Ontario
M5G 2E9
www.mcclelland.com

1 2 3 4 5   08 07 06 05 04

Contents

 1 *Let's Do It!*   1

 2 *The Adventure Begins*   16

 3 *The First Link in Our Chain*   27

 4 *Galápagos: Wonder and Despair*   49

 5 *Facing Fear and Grief in the Vast Pacific*   59

 6 *Hopping Across Friendly Islands*   67

 7 *We Were Kings on Palmerston Island*   75

 8 *Forced to Drink Muddy Sawdust Water*   82

 9 *Life and Death in a Force Ten Storm*   90

10 *Mechanical Mutinies Down Under*   108

11 *The Land of Dragons and Smiles*   125

12 *Standing on the Front Line*   144

13 *Magic and Heartache in the Jungles of Borneo*   160

14 *Water Spouts and Lightning Strikes*   169

15 *Long Neck Ladies and Singing Apes*   177

16 *Staring Down the Wrong End of a Gun*   191

17 *Rorschach Test*   203

18 *We Place Last at the Chagos Fish Olympics*   215

19 *Africa Awakening*   234

20 *Plinking Stones Down a Mountain*   247

21 *Pirates and Terrorists in a Lawless Sea*   259

22 *Out of the Frying Pan and Into the Fire*   274

23 *The Trouble with Egypt*   294

24 *Culture Shock in Reverse*   307

25 *Captain George to the Rescue*   323

26 *Facing the North Atlantic*   332

27 *The Best Maple Doughnut Ever*   350

    Epilogue   360

    Acknowledgements   364

    Photo Credits   369

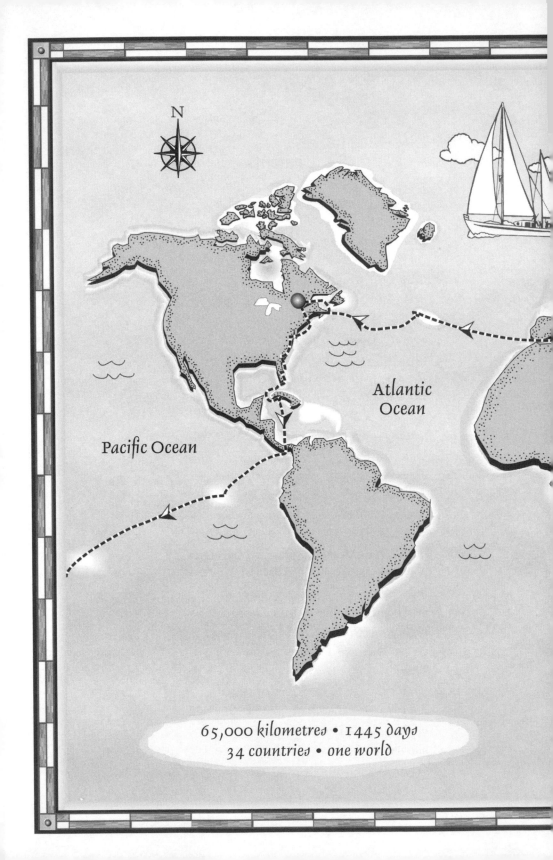

N

Atlantic Ocean

Pacific Ocean

65,000 kilometres • 1445 days
34 countries • one world

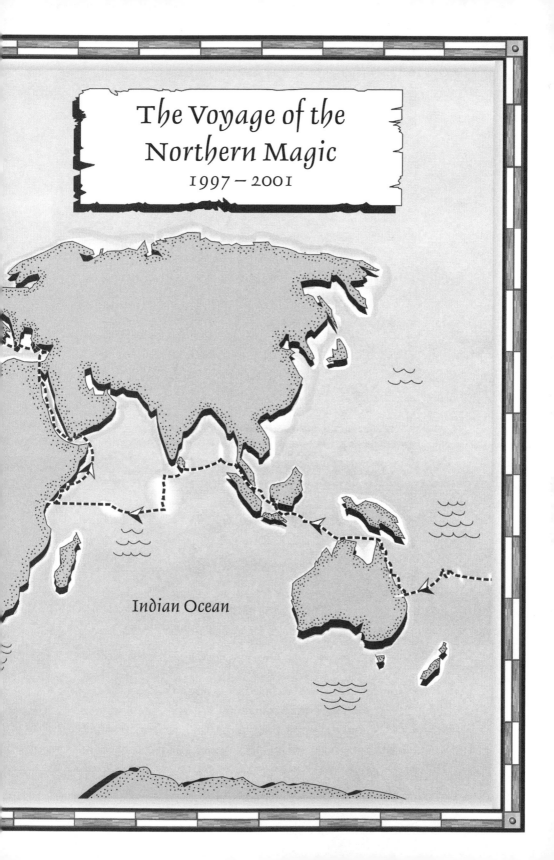

The Voyage of the Northern Magic
1997 – 2001

Indian Ocean

Northern Magic

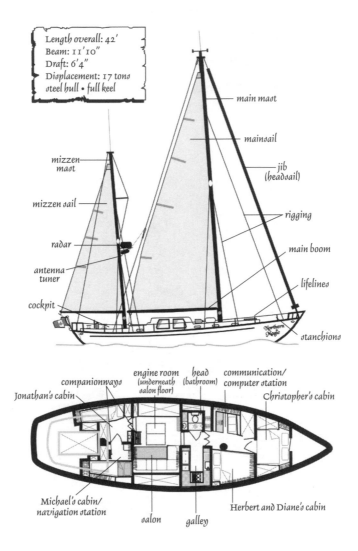

Length overall: 42'
Beam: 11'10"
Draft: 6'4"
Displacement: 17 tons
steel hull • full keel

main mast

mainsail

jib
(headsail)

mizzen-
mast

mizzen sail

rigging

radar

main boom

antenna
tuner

lifelines

cockpit

stanchions

engine room
(underneath
salon floor)

head
(bathroom)

communication/
computer station

companionways

Jonathan's cabin

Christopher's cabin

Michael's cabin/
navigation station

salon

galley

Herbert and Diane's cabin

Authors note: All references to miles are nautical miles, which are about 10 per cent longer than statute miles. Thus a nautical mile equals 1.15 statute miles, or 1.85 kilometres. Boat speeds and wind velocities are expressed in knots, or nautical miles per hour. Thus 55 knots of wind equals 63 miles per hour, or 102 kilometres per hour.

Let's Do It!

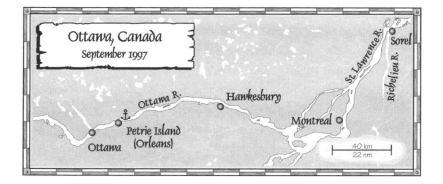

Ottawa, Canada
September 1997

St. Lawrence R.   Sorel
Richelieu R.

Ottawa R.   Hawkesbury

Petrie Island   Montreal
Ottawa   (Orleans)

40 km
22 nm

Herbert had always spoken longingly of his dream to sail around the world. Born in Berlin, Germany, my future husband grew up the son of a barge captain and spent the first six years of his life on his father's ship, travelling the inland rivers and canals of Europe. A natural genius with all things mechanical, he was capable at five years old of single-handedly piloting his father's three-hundred-ton ship into a lock. When Herbert was a teenager, his father's ship once towed a sailboat that had come all the way across the Atlantic. This boat grabbed his imagination, and from then on he secretly – and then not-so-secretly – began nurturing a dream that he, too, might one day cross oceans in his very own vessel.

In the twenty years that I'd known him, I'd often heard him describe this wish. Because I've always believed in big dreams, I never actively tried to dissuade him. I'd mumble something mildly encouraging, like, "That's a great dream, honey, and everybody should have big dreams," all the while praying he'd come to his senses and not force me to confess that I

was too chicken to accompany him. Travel around the world I'd gladly
do, but in a sailboat? Not likely. The idea of sailing across large bodies of
water was only marginally more attractive to me than spending time in a
Siberian gulag. But I humoured him as the years went by, trusting that
eventually he would give up on this crazy idea. If he really was going to
do it, my last-ditch plan was to meet him by plane at the other end.

Then all at once, everything changed. It was a positive change that
first appeared, as so often happens, disguised as calamity.

It was Mother's Day, 1994, and Herbert was, as usual in our busy
lives, taking down Christmas lights a little late. He fell off the roof,
breaking his leg and elbow. Complications from these injuries partially
disabled his right arm, forcing the sale of his thriving home renovation
business and throwing him into a depression.

Just two months later, while we were still struggling to cope with the
aftermath of his accident, we were rocked again – a suspicious spot on
my right calf turned out to be malignant melanoma, a potentially fatal
form of skin cancer. Our family, still reeling after Herbert's brush with
catastrophe, now had my very survival to contend with.

The cancer didn't kill me, but it did force a dramatic change in my
outlook on life. While surgery removed the malignancy, no scalpel could
excise the worry from my mind. At thirty-five, the thought of dying while
still a young mother shocked and terrified me. I'd always assumed, as
most people do, that I had plenty of years ahead to do the things I wanted
to do. Now I woke up crying from recurring nightmares in which I was
dead and my youngest, who was then two, was going to grow up with no
memory of me.

In the year that followed, Herbert and I both went through a period
of introspection and adjustment in which our commitment to each other
was severely tested. I found myself reviewing my life's goals and realizing that I had a long way to go before reaching them. Suddenly the quest
for more material success seemed hollow. I lost interest in the successful
advertising business I had built from a modest start in our basement ten
years earlier. Other things seemed far more important.

As a twenty-year-old, I had set myself three goals in life: to write a
book, to have children, and to travel the world. By our year of crisis, I
had achieved two of these challenges. I had written a book, the biography

of my grandfather, William Hawrelak, who had been a prominent business and political figure in western Canada. We had three wonderful boys, Michael, Jonathan, and Christopher, born in 1986, 1988, and 1992, respectively. But in the quest for more and more material success, we had completely put aside the third goal, to travel the world. We had become a very busy, materialistic, and conventional yuppie family.

Travel is what had brought Herbert and me together in the first place. I was a long-haired seventeen-year-old in platform shoes in 1976 when I first set eyes on a dark, leather-jacketed young German who was touring North America on his Honda 750 motorcycle. He was close to running out of money, and had purchased a cheap standing-room ticket to see the rodeo at the Calgary Stampede, where I was working as an usherette for the summer.

The fireworks of the midway that night paled in comparison with the sparks generated by our first meeting. If it wasn't love at first sight, it was something very close to it. Herbert followed me to Ottawa, where I received a degree in journalism at Carleton University. After years of night courses, Herbert, who was an automotive mechanic, entered teacher's college at Queen's University, becoming qualified as a technical teacher. Throughout our university years, we had continued travelling whenever we had two dollars to rub together, but as the years went on, we became trapped in the conventional pattern of home, job, and family – all of which caused us to put aside our passion for travel for almost two decades. I worked for the federal government for many years, after which I purchased a failing advertising company. Herbert, after a stint as a high-school teacher, built an award-winning renovation business. After his accident, we worked together in our now thriving advertising business, but we both still dreamed of something better.

One hot summer day, a year after the beginning of our bad times, Herbert and I went for a long walk by the river. We were still mired in despair and fear for the future. It was there that he turned to me and asked, "What would you do, if you could do anything you wanted?"

Instantly, my heart made an unaccustomed leap. An unbidden yearning jumped out of my throat. "I'd travel," I said without hesitation.

"Well then, let's do it. You pick anywhere in the world, and I'll take you there."

My heart bounded for one glorious moment before my mind attempted to squelch the seditious thought. But once liberated, that flash of joyous truth could not be suppressed. My heart knew, even if my brain didn't, where my passion lay. It was time I stopped worrying about what society expected of me and began listening to my soul. Three weeks later, the kids farmed out to camps and babysitters, we found ourselves in Egypt, a couple again for the first time in ten years.

It was there, in the shadow of the pyramids, that we rediscovered ourselves. How can I begin to describe how alive, how whole this magical place made us feel? We laughed ourselves silly as a new friend attempted to teach us the proper Muslim pre-meal blessing. I smuggled myself, giggling, inside the massive stone sarcophagus inside the Great Pyramid of Giza and crossed my arms over my chest, as if holding an imaginary crook and flail. We marched alone down the Avenue of Sphinxes at the temple of Karnak, in the ancient city of Thebes. As we walked, we felt we were the great Pharaoh Ramses himself. The hairs on my arms stood up, thrilling to the sound of drums and music throbbing from within the temple. As I write this and remember, those hairs quiver in their own recollection and stand up again. In Egypt, the world opened itself up to us, and we rediscovered the way we needed to live. Now we knew the people we wanted to be.

Oddly enough, this change was first remarked upon by two complete strangers.

"You have a good husband," a Cairo taxi driver said to me one day.

"Why do you say that?" I asked.

"Because he is quiet," was the enigmatic answer.

Quiet? My Herbert? Not many people who knew my demanding and often-difficult Prussian husband would call him quiet.

A few days later another taxi driver said exactly the same thing. "You have a good husband."

Wondering if there was a conspiracy, I pressed him for an explanation.

"Why? Because he laughs a lot," he responded knowingly.

Laughing? My Herbert? Not in a very long time. But I realized it was true; I did have a new, quiet, laughing husband. And what was more, I had become a quiet, laughing wife. The magic of the Pharaohs had worked itself on us and we returned to real life healed and renewed.

For me, the renewal meant I began spending less time at work and more with our children. I'd long been denying the feeling that I wasn't doing enough for them. For Herbert, though, it meant the revival of his old dream to sail around the world.

Not long after we returned from Egypt, Herbert made an announcement. Next summer, he said, he was going to buy a small sailboat. If we were ever going to sail around the world, we had to start somewhere. He described to me in precise terms the little boat he had in mind.

I rolled my eyes inwardly, but knowing better than to reveal my true feelings, I simply hoped he would put his plans aside as he had in the past. I shouldn't have underestimated my new quiet, laughing husband.

By next spring, *Cruising World* magazines had begun infiltrating our home. This was a bad sign. I ignored them, but they didn't go away. Herbert began babbling to me in an incomprehensible nautical language. He wanted a good starter boat – one that we'd trade up for a larger model in five or so years, finally graduating to an ocean-going boat when we retired.

As I began to see that he was serious, I confessed my doubts about the scheme. "There's nothing in this for me," I said. "I'm not supposed to be out in the sun. I don't like sailing. Every time I've ever been on the ocean I've been sick. I don't want to be away from our kids for years, even if they are grown and away." But Herbert is nothing if not tenacious, so he had an answer for each of my objections.

One day, in the spring of 1996, Herbert came home with a strange, excited look on his face. He's not an especially religious man, so what he said next was surprising.

"Something weird happened today," he began, pulling out a picture. His face was glowing. "I think God wants me to buy this boat." My eyebrows went up. *God* was in on this plan?

He had been at a sales call, and after successfully signing up a new account, the client had whipped a photograph out of his pocket. Throwing it on the table, he had asked casually, "Want to buy this?"

There it was. It was a sailboat. *The* sailboat. *Our* sailboat.

The boat in the photo was exactly what Herbert had been describing to me for months.

"I had said I was going to buy a sailboat this summer," he explained sheepishly, "but I wasn't actually doing anything to make it happen. Somehow I feel God means us to buy this sailboat. What more can He do than put it right in front of my face?"

Well, who was I to argue with the Almighty?

But before we went too far with this, I sat my new quiet, laughing husband down.

"This boat is your dream, not mine," I began sternly. "I'll support you in it, but you need to understand that I don't share it."

"I understand," he said, in a manner that was strangely – uncharacteristically – docile.

"I don't mind if you take the boys out sailing on weekends, but don't put on a long face if I don't want to come."

"Yes, dear," he said quietly.

"I don't expect you to pull weeds in my garden, so don't you expect me to swab your decks."

"Yes, dear," he said laughingly.

What choice did I have but to go with him to pick up our sailboat?

When I stepped aboard our little twenty-three-footer for the first time that July day in 1996, my previous experience with boats was scanty. Apart from two ocean trips on large ships in which I had, both times, developed an intimate and unhappy knowledge of the insides of their plumbing fixtures, most of my experience had been in renting houseboats on the Rideau Canal system, which we had done a number of times as a family.

We had, it is true, had a great time on the houseboats, but I attributed the feeling of inner peace and contentment to the bucolic surroundings. So none of my previous experiences prepared me for the feeling that overtook me as we motored our little boat down the Ottawa River to her new berth at a marina near our home. All the vibrant feelings of happiness and connectedness that we had felt in Egypt were right there. Everything around us looked bright and new and beautiful. It just felt *right*.

Suddenly, spending weekends on our boat seemed a lot more interesting than putzing around in my garden. Now, as Herbert began planning weekend outings alone with the boys, I found myself piteously bleating, "What about me?"

Finally, I managed to sign myself on as crew and we did our first overnighter on the Ottawa River – in a raging gale. Scudding along the water in our sturdy little craft under a tiny handkerchief of sail, we laughed out loud, exhilarated. The kids screamed in delight, begging to be steered into the biggest of waves. When we returned home, windblown and energized, the storm we had weathered was front-page news. The *Ottawa Citizen* newspaper quoted the head of the Nepean sailing club saying that no one in their right minds had gone out sailing that weekend.

What did that make us?

The next morning I had to face the sad reality of returning to work after this weekend of revelation. Wanting to delay the inevitable, I paused at our home computer to check for e-mail. While it was downloading, I picked up one of the ubiquitous sailing magazines that were now invading every horizontal surface in the house. The headline was "ONE FAMILY'S TERROR IN THE NORTH SEA." Did I dare read it? I did. I turned immediately to the article and devoured every word. Twice.

All I could think after I finished reading was "I could do that."

Then I spotted an article on the cost of a three-year circumnavigation. I discovered, to my surprise, that we could sail around the world for about half as much as it cost us to live three years in the suburbs. I drank it all in. The pictures the story conjured up in my mind were so vivid I simply knew this was for us. And when I put the magazine down, I knew our lives were forever changed. Not only did I want to sail around the world, I *had* to do it. This was the answer, the positive change I'd been seeking.

What did it matter that there were a thousand other perfectly valid reasons why we were crazy to be thinking about sailing around the world? All I knew was that we *had* to do it.

So I went to work, plopped myself down in front of my quiet, laughing, and soon-to-be astonished husband, and said, simply, "Let's do it."

After almost twenty years of Herbert's trying to get me to warm to the idea of sailing around the world, I had finally been convinced.

We had owned our first sailboat for all of two weeks and had sailed her once. Now we were going to sail around the world, but a mountain of preparation stood between us and that lofty goal. Yet strangely enough, we knew with absolute certainty that we could, and would, do it.

The more we investigated, the more Herbert and I became convinced that we were meant to do this as a family. Undertaking this challenge together would be an incredible gift to our boys' development, and to our relationships with them. We felt that in particular Michael, our oldest son, really needed a fresh start and the boost that would come with tackling such a lofty goal. For some reason, his self-confidence had been in a steady decline. We were certain the trip would help give him a stronger start in life.

With this as our goal, however, we had no choice but to leave immediately. In a few years Michael would be too old to want to stay cramped up in a small boat with his parents. So within days, our initial ten-year strategy evolved into a one-year plan. Considering that within that year, we would have to find a suitable boat, sell our business, rent out our house, take courses, and prepare for this monumental trip, this might have seemed an impossible goal. Yet in a strange way we knew, irrevocably, that we would move heaven and earth if need be. Somehow we would make it happen. Once the passion of this great dream had seized hold of us, we could no more fight it than we could have stopped an avalanche.

Our first priority was finding a cruising boat before the snowy Ottawa winter set in. After searching the Internet, we found a listing for a well-proven but inexpensive thirty-seven-year-old boat, named *Tarwathie*, in Beaufort, North Carolina. The very next day we were hammering down the I-95. Our eighteen hours of non-stop driving were accompanied by a definite sense of making a rendezvous with fate.

The boat was old and in poor shape cosmetically. From our years of renovating houses, however, we knew we could spruce her up. Built in 1960 in Holland, her sturdy steel hull was soft-chined and graceful. She was built along the lines of a classic bluewater cruising yacht: a deep, full keeled, heavy, and sea-kindly vessel. This was clearly the kind of boat that was meant to have a hundred fathoms of water beneath her keel.

Inside, the boat looked nothing like the sleek, apartmentlike yachts of today. This boat was unmistakably nautical: round portholes, beautiful, well-worn dark teak, gimballed brass kerosene lamps everywhere.

She was strong and proven, had been thoroughly updated, and best of all was loaded with all the heavy-duty gear we would need for cruising and a wealth of spare parts to boot. Since we were not sailors ourselves, we wanted a boat that knew more about sailing than we did. *Tarwathie*, built for the rough and stormy North Sea, was just the confidence-inspiring vessel we needed. That afternoon, subject to a professional survey, *Tarwathie* was ours.

A few weeks later, *Northern Magic*, as she would soon be named, had been trucked to Canada and safely installed at a small marina about fifty minutes away from our home. We all went there together to see her as a family for the first time. It was a moment of high expectation, like the children getting their first look at a brand-new baby brother.

"What?" exclaimed Michael, age ten, upon looking at *Northern Magic* for the first time, "We're going to sail around the world in that green piece of junk?"

She didn't look great, that is true. Her hull had been stripped and sandblasted, then painted with a coat of ugly green primer. Several welding jobs had been done afterwards, and the four or five new plates that had been welded in had rusted around the edges and left long, red stains bleeding down the belly of the boat. An ultrasonic sounding had been done to detect other weaknesses in the hull, and painted marks and lines all over the hull showed the results of this. The cabin top's stained teak was marred and peeling, its finish moulting off in giant unsightly scales.

Our future home, in which we were going to tackle the seas of the world, looked like – well, a green piece of junk.

Herbert quit coming to work in order to refurbish *Northern Magic* full time, working under a tarp with an electric heater as the snow fell two metres deep around him. He took that boat apart from stem to stern, often working in temperatures of –30° Celsius. By spring she was ready to launch and he knew her intimately, inside and out.

We also began more formal preparation: Herbert in celestial and coastal navigation and basic first aid, I in ham radio and wilderness first aid. Both of us passed our scuba certification and all ham and marine radio licences. And every spare minute we spent researching a thousand decisions about a cruising life we knew nothing about.

All this took place while we were still running and attempting to sell our business, finding a tenant for our house and a property manager for our small income property, taking care of our three children, hosting our German nephew, Marco, for six months, and me even serving as a Cub Scout leader. Those were an unbelievable eleven months, and they passed in a dizzy, tiring, and exhilarating blur. Getting a boat and ourselves ready to sail around the world in less than a year might have seemed too much to accomplish, but we never questioned whether it was doable. We just put our heads down and did it, taking energy and inspiration from the strength of our desire.

Sometimes, especially in the dark of night, we worried. Every time I saw a globe, a tremor of fear would ripple through my body. I would take a big gulp when I looked at the incredible expanse of the Pacific Ocean, that immense body of water that seemed to stretch on forever and ever. We would actually dare to sail across that? Many times I dreaded the day we would have to head off into three thousand miles of emptiness. But other people did it, I would tell myself, and if they could do it, so could we. Overcoming fear was just another challenge, another part of our growth. Still, I hated to look at that unspeakably empty gap on the globe. Even today, I still catch my breath when I see a picture of that vast ocean.

Over and over we asked ourselves whether it was right to expose our children to the dangers of the sea. Plenty of statistics were on our side, but we made a resolution that whenever we had to make a choice on our trip, we would always make it on the side of safety, for the children's sakes.

We were so busy renovating the boat, finishing up our courses and selling our business that by July, two months before we planned to leave, we hadn't had time to think too much about packing up or renting out our house. When, late in the month, a nice American army family said they needed the house in two weeks, we had no choice but to say yes.

But how could we manage to clear out the house in only fourteen days? July had already been a disaster. With all three kids out of school, we were now trying to juggle a complicated schedule of summer camps and babysitters. Often as not, I brought one, two, or the three of them into the office with me, setting them up in the meeting room with activity books, or letting them play computer games on a free workstation. Herbert was working frantically to get the boat ready. Now we had two weeks to finish the boat, pack up our large four-bedroom house, move everything we needed into the boat, and take care of the kids – all while still working full time.

My parents came to the rescue, offering to take care of the boys for three weeks at their home in Calgary. It was a generous offer, especially because the idea of us sailing around the world had to have been the last thing my Mom would ever have wanted. She hadn't said much when I first told her of our plans, hoping perhaps that the idea would go away. Dad said later he thought I was joking. But now they swallowed their objections and extended their hands in help.

Without needing to bother about the children, Herbert and I could really pick up our pace. We planned to create an area in our basement in which we would store all our worldly possessions. Aunt Gina Nichols, my mother's sister from Washington, D.C., hopped on a plane, rolled up her sleeves, and helped us from morning until midnight, getting our house put away. Friends and neighbours also came and lent a hand. Even with everyone's help, however, it seemed as if we would never get it done. Twenty-four hours before our new tenants were to arrive, every room in the house was still full of stuff.

We were in a race: could Herbert, Gina, and I clear out each room faster than the cleaning lady could clean them? She was vacuuming right behind us, nipping at our heels like a fox terrier as we frantically worked to clear the stuff out. Breathing down the neck of the cleaning lady were the carpet cleaners, who were followed hotly by Herbert and a friend with paintbrushes. Like everything else, we somehow managed to get it done before the tenants arrived. The sight of all our things, piled from floor to ceiling in a solid wall, packed so tightly you could barely fit a credit card in between, was really something, a feat worthy of the famous Inca builders of Peru. We had built Machu Picchu in our basement, a monument to consumer excess!

Ever since my cancer three years before, doctors had been keeping a very close watch on my body in case it resurfaced anywhere else. Melanoma is a strange cancer. It's easily curable, if it remains on the surface of your skin. But unlike other skin cancers, melanoma has the tendency to spread inside your body. It's simple enough to cut out a chunk of skin, as they had done on my right calf, but having malignant melanoma spread to your lungs, liver, or lymph nodes is virtually a death sentence.

A few weeks before, I had had a thorough pre-departure check-up. My doctor looked troubled as she palpated the lymph nodes in my right groin. One of the nodes felt enlarged – sometimes a sign that the cancer has spread. It was probably nothing, she said, but considering that we were going away, and she'd have no way of following up, she felt it was best to have that node removed to check whether it contained any malignant cells.

So just five days before this last twenty-four hours of frenzied packing, I had undergone minor surgery to remove a lymph node in my groin.

It was a Sword of Damocles hanging over all of us. It was impossible not to think about it as I put away all our belongings. Our business was now sold, our home rented out, so if we didn't leave on this trip we'd have nowhere to live. Herbert and I didn't talk too much about it, but from time to time we shared an anxious look as we waited to hear the results of the surgery.

The test results had been promised at eight that Friday morning, the same day our new tenants were moving in. As their moving truck arrived, I was on the phone to my doctor. The results of that conversation would decide whether I was going to sail around the world or die.

The answer: we were going to sail around the world.

I ran to the driveway in a flood of tears. All my pent-up anxiety, all the stress and rush of selling the business, packing up the house, finishing the boat, and worrying about my health came bubbling out. As our tenants stepped out of their car, I just stood there, blubbering like a baby. They must have thought I really didn't want to be leaving our home. But I felt just the opposite: I had just been given my life. Now it was up to me to make the most of it.

Soon the kids came back from Calgary, not to their old home or their own bedrooms, but to a cramped, messy boat that wasn't entirely ready to receive them. They were, especially Michael, a little disappointed. This plan to sail around the world was now disturbingly final, and Michael began wishing he hadn't agreed to it so readily the year before.

Suddenly it occurred to him that he was going to be losing his friends, his bedroom, his bicycle, everything that was important to him. More than once I know he wished we would change our minds. But it was too late to turn back now, and he adapted to his reduced circumstances with reasonably good grace.

Jonathan, nine, was more excited, probably the most enthusiastic of the three. I'll never forget when we were motoring down the Ottawa River on a beautiful summer day the year before, when Jon, sitting at the bow of the boat, had turned around, stretched, and said, "This is the best day of my *life*!"

"No, Jon," corrected Michael, "the best day is going to be when we're on the ocean." I replayed that exchange a hundred times in my mind as I imagined the luxury of endless time with my children, learning about life with them, discovering the marvels of this earth with them, and helping them grow into the kind of men we wanted them to become.

Cheerful Christopher, our five-year-old sunshine boy, was just along for the ride and had nothing much to say about it one way or the other, as long as we could reassure him that we wouldn't be going over any waterfalls or encountering any giant octopi.

By now we had sold our two cars and were running around town in a rented car. There was an unbelievable list of details to sort out before we could leave. It's a good thing I'm a list-maker. I had read and read and read, so I had everything pretty well thought out, from medical kit to books. Address changes, radio licences, consultations with doctors, sprucing up our sails, creating an extensive medical kit (even down to IV lines and catheters), setting up powers of attorney, banking, paying bills, getting inoculations, taking care of school books, these things and a million others filled page after page of lists. My list for August 26, 1997, was seventy-three items long, not including a separate shopping list. We had lists of what things we had left in our house. We had lists of instructions for our tenants. We had lists of what we had on the boat and where it was stored. What we lacked in personal experience we made up for in research. And lists. There are people in my very own family who make fun of me for these lists, but as far as I'm concerned they are what held us together.

On September 10, 1997, the last day before leaving, we set out early with one final list of the last twenty-three things we had to do before departing first thing next morning.

All day we sped from stop to stop, returning to our neighbourhood around the end of the afternoon, stressed out and exhausted. The kids were tired and complaining about being cooped up in the car without so much as a lunch break, so we drove each of them, uninvited, to his best friend's house to spend the remaining hours before departure. Each of the three families, seeing the distress on our faces, offered to keep the boys and feed them for as long as we needed. What a relief! When the mother of Christopher's best friend tried to press some dinner into my hands, I was so overwrought with stress and gratitude I burst into tears.

We returned to our house, where our tenants were still busy settling in. There was a problem: squirrels had entered the attic and chewed a hole in the corner of the roof. It had rained the night before, and water had poured in. So there we were, adding "roof repair" to our list for the day. Number twenty-four. Herbert climbed up on the roof and patched up the damage while I continued running around.

It was ten-thirty that night before Herbert and I began going from house to house to collect our kids from the kind people who had temporarily adopted them. My body sagged from stress and fatigue and my brain felt soggy.

We picked up Michael last, along with his best friend, Ian Villeneuve, whom we had invited to join us for the first week of the trip. It was almost midnight when we loaded four tired children into the dinghy and travelled in darkness over a forbiddingly black Ottawa River. We hadn't had time for a proper meal in two days.

It was cold and windy, and the waves hitting the little overloaded dinghy were choppy. We all got splashed, and were shivering and wet by the time we arrived at the place we had anchored the boat in the river. I felt ready to collapse. I've said it before, and I still believe it today: about the toughest thing we did on our trip sailing around the world was leaving.

And so, just one year after we had decided to undertake our odyssey, as the warm summer air began to take on the tang of colder days to come, we pulled up anchor and set off on our circumnavigation. We were

untried sailors, in a vessel we had never sailed. Our entire sailing experience consisted of six afternoons on the Ottawa River in a twenty-three-
foot boat. We weren't 100 per cent ready, it is true, but we were ready
enough to leave. During the next four or five months of cruising down
the eastern seaboard we would have time to sort out the myriad details
unattended to and begin learning about the craft to which we were
entrusting our family's lives.

That crazy, harried, impossible phase was behind us. Now the whole
world lay ahead.

2

The Adventure Begins

Canada ↔ United States
September 1997 – January 1998

Canada
Ottawa
Atlantic Ocean
United States
New York
Washington, D.C.
Beaufort, N.C.
Hilton Head
Ft. Lauderdale
500 km
270 nm

W̲e left Ottawa in a grey drizzle, with a dozen last-minute bags of dripping groceries leaving puddles on the freshly varnished teak floor. There was nobody there to see us off except for Wayne Cuddington, a photographer from the *Ottawa Citizen*. A few weeks earlier, I had agreed to write a weekly report about our trip for Ottawa's largest daily newspaper, and Wayne's photo of our rainy departure made the front page in Ottawa and was reprinted in many other newspapers across Canada.

Herbert and I took turns steering in the rain. In between shifts at the wheel, we continued to work away at the things that had still not been stowed away. Despite the dreary start, it felt great finally to be leaving. I found myself heaving endless sighs of relief. In the scramble of our departure I'd hardly had time to feel excited, but now that tremulous feeling of anticipation we had once felt when planning our grand adventure had returned.

I had been mentally prepared to say goodbye, and left our home for the last time without looking back. But what I had not expected was the tremendous outpouring of help and kindness from friends, family, and even strangers. Virtually everyone who knew what we were doing did something to make our preparations easier. We had been the beneficiaries of a hundred helping hands. Little did we know that this stream of helpfulness and goodwill would be a constant feature of our trip around the world, something we would experience virtually everywhere we went, and something that would change us profoundly.

Our work on the boat was far from finished, a fact that was made perfectly clear as our first day progressed, in the form of a CD player that ate up our CDs, leaky hatches we hadn't got around to fixing yet, and the realization that we had a lot more rain gear than we had hooks. Outside, we still hadn't managed to fix up all the rust spots, paint the decks, or refinish the outdoor teak. The boat, particularly the deck, was splotched with ugly rust-coloured blotches of primer paint. The teak deck, cockpit coaming, and trim were still unfinished and ugly. Somehow, we hoped to complete all these undone tasks somewhere along the way. But the weather was already starting to get cold, and soon the locks ahead of us would be closing for the winter, so we had no time to wait. In fact, it turned out to be an unseasonably cold autumn, and after Washington we had frost on our decks almost every morning, all the way down to Florida. We had left not a moment too soon.

✦

We motored down the Ottawa River with masts down, allowing us to clear under numerous bridges on the way. The kids screamed with delight at the roller-coaster ride that resulted when fast-moving motorboats crossed our path. They stayed glued to the bow of the boat, where the motion was the greatest, hoping for ever-more thrilling rides in the wake of the huge container ships and speeding tugboats that passed by. I joined them and we spent hours there in laughing, splashing, bouncing splendour, right until sundown, when we anchored for the night and realized it was already two hours past suppertime. Several times the kids remarked that if this was fun, just imagine how much fun the ocean would be, with *really* big waves. I wasn't quite as thrilled about that idea.

Soon, we began school lessons, concentrating on the basics – reading, writing, French, and mathematics. The boys studied these every day except Sunday, unless we were off the boat or conditions were too rough. They also began writing journals about the trip. Our main objective, however, was to take maximum advantage of our ever-changing surroundings, and many of their assignments reflected this. We made a decision that if there had to be a choice between the trip or doing homework, the trip would come first. Sometimes I worried that I wasn't doing a good enough job, because I had to improvise the boys' lessons on a weekly basis, depending on where we were, but on the whole I think this was the best approach for us.

It wasn't only the kids who had lessons to learn. One night, when attempting to drive in reverse out of a lock, we had a moment of excitement when the buoyed line trailing our dinghy got tangled up in the propeller, causing our engine to come to an unexpected and inopportune halt. We were forced to drop anchor hastily so that Herbert could try out his new scuba equipment, bought just the day before we left, to disentangle the offending line. In the meantime, we bumped against the lock wall, damaging our wind vane, a self-steering device operated by wind, which protruded from our stern. Mercifully, no spectators were around to see the embarrassing sight of us floundering around. Back at home in Ottawa, a large proportion of the people who'd seen the story of our departure felt we'd never make it. Even the editor assigned by the *Citizen* to handle my weekly dispatches at first declined the job. As a sailor herself, she felt there was no way we would succeed; it would be a bad career move to be associated with an effort that was clearly doomed to failure.

+

After many days of travel, we took a break in the lovely town of Saint-Denis, on the Richelieu River. The locks ahead of us were closed for the next three days, so we enjoyed an involuntary hiatus in this picturesque rural town of a thousand people.

After sailing down the Richelieu River we joined up with Lake Champlain and entered New York State. We set off early into Lake Champlain on an intemperately cold morning and found that the wind, blowing at thirty knots, made our progress slower and wetter than we expected. Without her masts to stabilize her, *Northern Magic* rolled wildly. The bucking and beating into the waves caused whomever was on deck to be drenched every fourth or fifth wave by freezing cold spray. Every time we ploughed off the top of a big wave and buried our bow into the next one, our two aluminum masts, which were lashed rather precariously to our decks, shifted ominously back and forth. With each wave, they seemed to shift and slide more. The last thing we needed was to lose our spars in the middle of Lake Champlain, so we sought refuge in a small harbour and winched the masts down more securely before continuing.

Afterwards I baked a big batch of Aunt Linda's Excellent Oatmeal Chocolate Chip Cookies, a magnificent recipe given to us by my sister, Linda. I baked them in celebration of an important milestone – the first official bout of seasickness, experienced simultaneously by Michael and Christopher, and only narrowly avoided by me. This baking of ALEOCCCs, as they became to be known, thus became entrenched as an important and oft-repeated post-barfing ritual on *Northern Magic*.

+

At Castleton-on-Hudson, a small village on the Hudson River near Troy, we said goodbye to Michael's friend, Ian, and finally stepped up our masts. It was a magnificent sight to see those clean white sails flapping up the majestic height of *Northern Magic*'s fifty-eight-foot main mast for the first time. Already several weeks into our circumnavigation, we had still never sailed our own boat. The next day we left for New York City and the Atlantic Ocean. *Northern Magic* was champing at the bit, the scent of salt water in her nose, her proud head at last held high.

Passing the Statue of Liberty and freed of narrow river channels, we ploughed into the ocean for the first time. It was just an overnight hop, but it was our maiden voyage on the ocean and felt like a momentous occasion. It was, to tell the truth, a little scary, even though we'd be no more than twelve miles from land.

The waves were small but choppy, and before too long the jerky motion began taking its toll. We were motoring into the waves, against the wind. Michael and Christopher were the lucky recipients of special wristbands that purported to reduce nausea – and indeed, the two boys fared the best. Still, Gravol began making the rounds as the afternoon turned into evening.

After bravely persevering with my attempts to provide a nutritious supper for our crew, I discovered that all the children had fallen asleep, leaving me alone with freshly cooked corn on the cob. Later, I figured out that none of us would ever have any appetite on our first day on the ocean, but I didn't know this then. Now, the normally agreeable smell of corn on the cob was more than enough to send me retching to the toilet. In the end, only Captain Ironsides ate supper, and I gratefully joined the children for a nap.

Herbert awoke me at around 10:30 p.m. for my turn at watch. My stomach was still in a state of active insurrection. Seeing that it wasn't too rough at all, I was disgusted with this betrayal by my body. What would happen when it really got wavy? What would happen on that endless Pacific?

Steering the boat in the darkness was also unexpectedly taxing. Not only did it take sustained muscle power to control *Northern Magic* in the confused waves, but when steering a compass course at night without anything else to orient yourself, it took powerful concentration. Our autopilot had broken and was back at the factory for repairs, so we were forced to steer by hand.

Your job, as helmsman, is to steer a consistent course against the forces of the waves and currents, which are trying to tear you off it. Your main tool is a large, illuminated spherical compass set in the centre of the cockpit. By watching the compass, you must keep the boat heading within a few degrees of the direction the navigator has set. Standing in the darkness of night in the open ocean, surrounded by the whooshing of passing waves and staring at the huge glowing eye of the compass, is strangely mesmerizing. As fatigue sets in, it develops into a bizarre kind of battle between you and this unblinking, unforgiving eye. Every few moments you have to will yourself away from this almost hypnotic state in order to keep watch for other passing ships. Of course, in my case, I also had to take brief sickness-breaks every ten minutes or so, but I managed to do this without ever letting go of the wheel.

Gradually, my eyelids began to get heavy and then close, opening each time with a start a few moments later to record the latest deviation from our course. With sheer willpower, I would force my leaden arms to regain control of the wheel once more. At some point, when my eyes were more closed than open, I finally tied up the wheel and went to rouse Herbert, who performed some magical calculations to determine our position and gave me permission to return to sleep.

Inside the cabin, things were quite a sight. Christopher had fallen asleep on our bunk, lying sprawled around a half-finished game of Monopoly. I returned the game pieces to their tattered box and slid my littlest one carefully under our sheets. As I did so, he woke up, smiled his angelic five-year-old smile, and said sweetly, "Mommy, I barfed!"

In the galley were the repulsive, uneaten remains of supper. My stomach heaved at the very thought of going in there. I left them untouched and put myself to bed in Michael's berth, as Michael had fallen asleep on the narrow settee behind the dining table. As I dozed off, *Northern Magic*'s motion gave me the impression of riding on the haunches of a giant cat, pouncing over and over on its prey. This image, of a jaguar with me on its back, accompanied me into a fitful sleep.

My next watch started at around 3:00 a.m., when a very tired captain woke me up and gave me our new heading. We had passed Atlantic City and were heading now for Delaware Bay. Once again I subjected myself to the relentless stare of the compass until I began spotting various lights that heralded our return to the mainland and blessed relief from seasickness. I felt miserable. Was I crazy to have signed up for years of this?

Fortunately, the kids were not as severely affected by seasickness as I was, and awoke extremely chipper as morning dawned bright, warm, and beautiful. Herbert and I took turns napping while we motored *Northern Magic* down the bay and through the D&C Canal that leads to Chesapeake Bay and Annapolis. Near suppertime we anchored in a peaceful bay, surrounded for the first time by the sounds and sights of saltwater.

We continued motoring, and occasionally sailing, down the eastern seaboard of the United States, learning as we went. We used this period as our shakedown cruise, making periodic stops to improve the boat and work the kinks out of her systems. Gradually, we began turning ourselves into sailors.

One of our stops was in Washington, D.C., where my Aunt Gina invited us to stay for a night at her house. I had been looking forward particularly to sleeping in a real bed, but in the middle of the night I half-woke, worrying about whether our anchor was dragging. Leaping out of bed, I rushed to the window and pulled the curtain aside. And there I saw, to my horror – a tree! We were hard aground!

The shock of this terrible discovery woke me up completely, and only then did I realize how silly I looked. I checked to see if any one had noticed my yell, then I slunk sheepishly back into the bed. It was a month since we had left home, but somehow, I really was becoming a sailor.

$$\text{---}\!\!+\!\!\text{---}$$

A few weeks later we arrived in Florida, just in time to watch the launch of the space shuttle *Columbia* at Cape Canaveral. The next day we had *Northern Magic* lifted out of the water and placed on stands in a boat-yard in Titusville so we could attend to some long-overdue painting.

We stayed in Titusville a month, trying to finish off the tedious and long overdue exterior work of de-rusting, sealing, and painting *Northern Magic*'s decks, and stripping and staining her teak woodwork. The obvious lack of these finishing touches had been a continuing embar-rassment. We arrived at Palm Beach, Florida, looking much improved, just three days before Christmas.

After singing Christmas carols and feasting on Christmas cake sent by Mom, one by one we hung up our stockings on the ledge beside the Christmas tree. Then, as always, I read *The Night Before Christmas*, and three excited boys climbed into their bunks to be rocked to sleep by the gentle rolling of the boat. It was the first of four Christmases we would spend on board *Northern Magic*.

It was during our stay in Florida that I learned a stern lesson in boatmanship.

I've always felt rather competent and able to quickly master most new tasks given to me. But in Florida I began to develop a suspicion that perhaps there is some masculine bond between a man and his outboard motor that is beyond the ken of the average female. Or beyond me, at least.

My adventures began one afternoon when Michael and I decided to motor over to a nearby marina to make some phone calls. I was still a little shaky about manoeuvring the dinghy, as all my instincts called for me to turn the outboard the opposite way than was actually required. As a result, I was extremely tentative about steering, first trying a little baby-turn before committing myself. No one else on *Northern Magic* seemed to have this particular disability, as both the older boys quickly became adept at handling the dinghy.

Herbert had always tried to convince me that it was easier to go at a faster speed, so that the dinghy planed. So as Michael and I left, travelling at my customary slow pace, Herbert shouted a series of instructions again – an irritating habit, I felt – and I reduced throttle to hear what he was saying. This caused the dinghy to stall, adding greatly to my annoyance.

Without power, the dinghy began drifting rapidly to shore – to the wrong shore, of course. I could see the captain of a nearby sailboat watching me curiously, but I put my head down and concentrated on starting the motor by pulling on the cord. It almost caught, but not quite. A few seconds later, the other captain was hanging over his boat with a pole, offering to secure me to his vessel.

"No thanks," I responded cheerfully, with what I hoped to be a voice of confident authority, "I'll get her going in a second." And I continued onward, yanking at the starter cord, the powerful current towing us rapidly away, my arm muscles slowly giving up. On *Northern Magic*, Herbert stood, silently watching the unfolding debacle. After a few more pulls, the motor ceased to give any sign of life. I began cursing myself for having rejected the offer of help. I looked up, pleadingly, at that maddening husband of mine, and as our eyes met I saw him begin to ready our second dinghy to come to our rescue.

In the meantime, we found ourselves entering the surf that was bringing us at a rather rapid pace to Peanut Island. Not just surf, but a rocky shore as well. *Stupid, stupid, stupid!* As soon as we came near the rocks

I had no choice but to jump overboard, fully dressed, and push us away from those menacing hazards lest we pop the inflatable dinghy. Michael giggled at me, and I did manage a rueful smile as I waited, soaked to my waist, for Herbert to row over to us. Then he lifted up the fuel line that had become disconnected from the motor, plugged it in, and effortlessly started the dinghy up again. As I said, *stupid, stupid, stupid!*

That evening we entertained the couple from the other sailboat whose help I had spurned. We chuckled about the afternoon's entertainment I had provided. Half jokingly, I used the word "incompetent" to describe my dinghy handling skills. To my horror, everyone present smirked and nodded in agreement! I went to bed in a stew. I would show them. If my children could handle a dinghy, by gum, so could I!

The next day I volunteered to ferry Herbert to shore so he could do his morning's errands. It was an extremely windy day, and the water was choppy. After Herbert got off at the dock, he again encouraged me to give a little more throttle. This time I did, heading off into the wind and back to our anchorage.

Within seconds I was in trouble. The combination of wind on the nose, the unruly waves, and my unique style of dyslexic steering caused the dinghy to wag alarmingly from side to side. Somehow I wasn't able to bring it back under control without accidentally executing a neat U-turn right in the path of an oncoming speedboat. It might have been obvious to everyone else that I should have been shifting my weight to the front of the dinghy to weigh it down, but it wasn't obvious to me.

I waved apologetically to the two guys on the speedboat as if I had merely changed my mind about where I needed to go. Gritting my teeth, I headed back into the wind. I was not going to let this dinghy get the better of me. But it was the first time I had ever driven it alone, much less in winds and waves like these. With no one in the bow to weigh it down, the front of the dinghy rose up as I increased speed, trying to plane, just as Herbert had instructed. It took no more than two seconds for a fierce gust of wind to swoop right in under the uplifted bow and throw it up vertically. In the next instant the dinghy flipped high into the air and I was thrown head over heels.

As the dinghy cartwheeled, I managed to leap out sideways so at least it didn't land on top of me. There I found myself, treading water awkwardly in long pants and a heavy sweatshirt. The bulging fanny pack containing all my important papers, money and credit cards, was threatening to slip down over my hips, and my left sandal was coming off my foot. The two fellows on the powerboat had enjoyed a front row seat for my acrobatic stunt and within a few seconds were by my side. "Would you like us to help flip her back over?" they asked, with nary a grin.

"Yes, please," I answered primly. I did this with great dignity and politeness, as if accepting their offer of a cup of tea.

After we flipped the boat over and threw all its floating contents back inside, it was my turn. Twice, I unsuccessfully attempted to drag my fully clothed and waterlogged body back into the dinghy. I just couldn't do it. In the end, I succeeded only with the help of a strong pair of hands that grabbed my clothes to hoist me over. I looked much like a disobedient kitten being carried by the scruff of its neck.

That night we had a family discussion about what to name the dinghy that had played a large part of my adventures for the previous two days. The four boys on board were actually fond of our inflatable, but I knew that there was some kind of malevolent anti-female spirit lurking inside that innocuous looking pile of red rubber. I wanted to name it *Male Chauvinist Pig*, or *MCP* for short. My idea, however, got vetoed, in favour of an absolutely ridiculous name the boys put forward and approved with great laughter and applause by a majority of four to one.

Flipper.

+

In Florida, with our departure from North America imminent, provisioning was a major preoccupation. It was my job to fill every possible free space with food before Herbert claimed it for tools. Each shopping trip would consume the better part of a day, as each item had to be carried aboard, removed of its packaging and labels (water makes paper labels fall off), identified by black marker and placed in some obscure little hole. By the time we were finished, *Northern Magic* was positively bulging; every drawer, locker, cupboard, bilge, and space beneath every floorboard was crammed full.

We had to think about many items we would need to stock for long-term travel: things like dental floss, deodorant, shampoo, insect repellent, and – oh yes – Hershey's Kisses. Somehow on the trip I'd fallen into the terrible habit of munching on these addictive chocolate morsels. My expanding belly was already beginning to emulate their shape.

Our waterline went down by several centimetres as we stashed away seventy litres of long-life milk, enough powdered milk for a few hundred litres more, eighteen huge tubs of peanut butter (four of which completed the circumnavigation with us and returned to our pantry in Ottawa), twelve large jugs of pancake syrup, twenty kilos of potatoes, ten kilos of Florida oranges, hundreds and hundreds of cans of fruits, vegetables and meat, many kilos of dried beans and grains, and quite a few kilos of hidden chocolate. Some people are said to wonder how many angels could dance on the head of a pin. I was much much more pragmatic; I spent my time calculating how many bags of Hershey's Kisses I could secretly stuff into my underwear drawer.

We spent our last day at Fort Lauderdale, in a frenzy of activity that was strongly reminiscent of our final day before leaving Ottawa. With supper dishes cleaned up, everything put away, and leecloths prepared on all the beds to keep people in place in case of a rocky passage, we eased out of our dock and past the twinkling lights of the city. Our route would take us on a course parallel to the coastline, down the Florida Keys and then across the Straits of Florida to Cuba.

Leaving the United States, we were all brimming with excitement. It felt as if our adventure had now truly begun.

3

The First Link in Our Chain

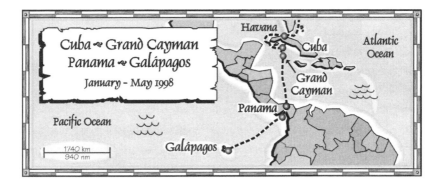

Cuba ⟿ Grand Cayman
Panama ⟿ Galápagos
January – May 1998

Havana
Cuba
Atlantic Ocean
Grand Cayman
Panama
Pacific Ocean
Galápagos

1740 km
940 nm

O ur two-day passage to Cuba began on a placid ocean unmarred by even the tiniest ripple. Soon the sun rose, and we found ourselves motoring along the south coast of Florida on a sweet and sunny morning, the tiny islands of the Florida Keys arrayed before us like a glistening string of pearls. Life was very good.

We didn't stop in the Keys, but continued on to the ninety-nautical-mile hop between Florida and Cuba, fearing a bit our entry into the often-rough Gulf Stream current, and the sometimes even rougher "Security Zone" that separated those sworn enemies of forty years, Cuba and the United States.

No U.S. coastguard officers boarded us, but the sheets of lightning that illuminated the sky for most of the night-time passage between Key West and Havana provided an eerie entertainment that had Michael waking up full of apprehension that the next bolt might be meant for us. No such catastrophe struck, however, and we entered Cuban waters in a buoyant mood, thanks to a welcoming committee of at least fifty small dolphins and two flying fish that frolicked around us as we made our bouncing way out of the Gulf Stream and into harbour at Marina Hemingway, west of Havana.

The process of clearing into Cuba was handled with incredible politeness and precision by a stream of officials who boarded our boat one after the other: a medical officer, two agriculture inspectors, two immigration officials, two customs officials, two coastguard officers, and two port officials bringing up the rear. Finally all the formalities were finished and we were free to explore before retiring to a good night's sleep.

Cuba can be a perplexing land, where the principles of Fidel Castro's socialist revolution butt and strain against the more powerful forces of the free marketplace. We soon discovered its citizens were gregarious and friendly, passionate Cuban music was played on every corner, and there was, we felt, no better spontaneous dancing to be found anywhere. But as cruisers we were, perhaps, more aware of the paradoxes of Cuba's distorted, dual economy than the regular tourist would be. Like ordinary Cubans, we had to invest hours each day hunting for everyday things that might or might not be available. The inconsistencies of the communist system and its unresponsiveness to the laws of supply and demand slapped us in the face everywhere we went.

This reality hit us on our first day in Havana. While we were there sightseeing, we decided to grab an ordinary loaf of bread for the next day's sandwiches. For miles we could see nothing that looked like a bread store, or indeed any store at all. Back at the marina, we spoke to some Dutch friends about our search. They, like us, had been on the hunt for bread, and told us that they had managed to find a small and sporadic supply in a nearby village. There was supposed to be some more available next morning at eight.

I dispatched Herbert at seven-thirty next morning, but he came back empty handed – all he could find were a few bottles of beans, sad wrinkled apples for a dollar each, some scrawny frozen chickens, and highly dubious-looking "Spam"-type luncheon meat.

The kids and I went for a bike ride to Jaimanitas, a small village near the marina. It was a shabby place that consisted of no industry that we could discern. The streets, mainly free of cars, as was most of Cuba, were lined with small ugly concrete bungalows with fenced front yards. At one corner we saw two large pigs dozing in the shade of a fenced-in lot. As the kids and I stopped to get a closer look, several friendly kids and a pretty young woman in her late twenties came over to get a closer look at us. We stood, smiling awkwardly at one another for a while before exchanging rudimentary phrases and compliments. The Cuban kids were friendly, but my three were pretty shy. Everyone made a big fuss over our blue eyes. I passed around cookies I had in our backpack, and before we knew it, Merita, the mother of two of the children, was escorting us to see the baby pigs in her backyard. Soon, various Cuban kids were riding our kids' bikes up and down the street with big smiles.

Merita was interested in the fact that we were staying at the marina. She had never seen it, even though it was almost around the corner. She either couldn't or wouldn't go there. It didn't take me long to understand why. I realized the only women, other than foreigners, I had seen at the marina appeared in the evening and slowly walked around in pairs: young, beautiful, and dressed in tight, revealing clothes and stiletto heels. Merita touched the ragged shirt her thin young son, Alejandro, was wearing. It was more hole than shirt. Better to be poor, she said quietly, than to be one of those women.

Our conversation was interrupted by a lovely young girl with long brown hair and almond eyes delivering half a dozen buns. This was Merita's daughter, Jadi. My eyes lit up at the sight of the buns. Did she know where I could buy some? Not today, Merita answered, but if I came back tomorrow she would take me there. So a date was made and a friendship was born.

I spent the next morning rummaging through Christopher's over-stuffed clothing locker. I was haunted by the thought of the rags little Alejandro had been wearing and the sad but proud look in his mother's eyes. Christopher had far too many changes of clothes, anyway, so I filled a plastic bag. The kids and I also selected a few small toys to give to their new friends.

Our next visit was a great success. We got a tour of the local bakery, although there was still no bread to be bought. However, after seeing the open vat of bubbling, fermenting yeast liberally sprinkled with the bodies of numerous large flies, some still alive and struggling in the sticky mess, and others dead, looking like plump dark raisins in a pot of porridge, I didn't much regret missing out. In fact, the experience was enough to cure me of trying to buy local bread ever again.

We returned to Merita's place, where we met many of her relatives. We chatted inside the front room as well as my limited Spanish would allow, and laughed to see chickens and dogs running freely around the sparsely furnished house. Merita was ecstatic about the clothing I had brought. I had included a dressy outfit I had purchased for myself in a thrift shop in Washington, and she held it in front of her as if it were Cinderella's gown. She beamed with excitement and put her arms around me, exclaiming, "Now we are really *amigas*!" She also cast a sly glance at Jonathan, who was a year older than her daughter, and made it clear she considered the two of them a good match.

Before I knew it, we had agreed to come back the next evening for a pork dinner. We all cringed a bit, wondering if the invitation would cost one of our piggy friends his life. We had a talk with the kids about it that night; I don't think the children had ever really considered the price to be paid for our nightly dinner of meat.

We had learned that in Cuba many people rarely get meat, eating one meal of stringy chicken perhaps once a month. Merita had, in fact, shown us an official booklet listing her family's monthly allotment of staples such as beans, flour, and cooking oil. Meat was not even on the list. They had been unable to get eggs for the past seven weeks, and neither of her children had ever tasted milk.

We accepted their invitation, and after much discussion decided to bring along an electric hand mixer we didn't need. The kids and I spent the afternoon baking the very best treat we could think of, Aunt Linda's Excellent Oatmeal Chocolate Chip Cookies. If this poor Cuban family could serve us meat, then we could certainly part with some of our precious supply of chocolate chips.

It was raining fiercely as we arrived. We were shown into the main room again, where many new family members awaited us, before Merita ushered us back outside. It was then that we realized we had been in her parents' house all along. At the side of the house, near the pigsty, was a little door, and we followed Merita through it into a single room just big enough for a small wooden table, a double bed, and two bunk beds.

Along a narrow corridor was a counter containing a sink and a single-burner propane camp stove. There was no fridge and no oven. This was Merita's home.

Merita's husband, Francisco, was at work preparing the meal on the narrow counter. He was a handsome man of about thirty with a neat moustache and a friendly face. He was busy deep-frying something that smelled delicious but paused from his cooking to offer effusive thanks for our gift of the clothing.

The two children – Jadi, the beautiful seven-year-old girl, and Alejandro, who was six – were finishing up eating with their fingers on the rickety little table, which seemed almost alive the way it squeaked and swayed from side to side. Both children were proudly wearing Christopher's old clothes: Jadi in Christopher's Batman pyjama top, her brother in another pair of Christopher's pyjamas underneath a yellow pullover I had always liked.

There were only three toys in the room: the small top, matchbox car, and prism we had given the children the day before. These three treasures were proudly displayed on a ledge next to the stove. Other than that, the room was absolutely bare. Both Herbert and I were taken aback. Our new friends were much, much poorer than we had thought.

Once the children finished eating, Francisco moved the table over so that some of us could squeeze onto the bed and eat off the table. One of the children found an extra chair, then hung back shyly, watching us eat. Francisco cooked while Merita presented us with each dish.

The first one turned out to be breaded, deep-fried plantains. It was delicious. It tasted something like French fries, and I said so.

"Do you like French fries?" Merita's husband asked, eagerly.

"Oh yes," I answered. Francisco said something rapid in Spanish I didn't understand and one of the children scooted out the door.

Next came the pork, beautifully prepared and very tasty. The family didn't own knives or forks, and we all had a little trouble sawing through the meat with the side of our spoons, but the dish tasted wonderful. The pork was accompanied by a huge plate full of rice and beans as well as a dish of interesting little brown cubes that Michael particularly liked. These turned out, upon close inspection, to be fried pork fat. Although I didn't mind the taste, I couldn't bring myself to nibble at more than one.

The food arrayed before me was far more than I could manage. I was already pondering how I could get out of eating it all without causing offence when I noticed our host appearing with some fresh potatoes in his hands. Suddenly I understood: I had said I liked French fries, and he planned to make me some! With much protestation, I finally convinced him we had plenty of food and there was no need to make more.

There was no room for our hosts to sit at the table; indeed, moving from one side of the room to the other with all of us sitting there required an athletic vault over the bed. So as soon as our kids finished, they moved over on the bed to make room for our hosts to devour their own plates of food.

We had a wonderful, warm, and happy evening. All our linguistic and cultural differences were somehow overcome. We were overwhelmed by this family's hospitality, especially considering how little they had to share with us. Before we left, I brought out our gift of the mixer, hoping it would please them as much as had the bag of clothes. I had, however, seriously miscalculated. Merita had no idea what this thing was for, or how she would use it. As we attempted to explain it to her, I realized my mistake. Merita did not have an oven. She had no way to bake. She didn't even own a mixing bowl. What good was a mixer to her?

It seemed the only thing to do would be to reciprocate by inviting them over to eat with us the next night. As we were to discover, following through on our good intentions would not be as simple as we had thought.

I didn't want to dip into our provisions more than necessary, so through the services of the marina, at inflated prices, I ended up finding the ingredients for a simple spaghetti. The meat I found for the sauce was supposed to be beef, but strangely enough it never lost its vivid pink colour no matter how long I cooked it. What it was exactly, I am afraid to know. Nonetheless, I had a mammoth concoction of magenta-coloured meat sauce bubbling on all four burners of my propane stove by seven the next night, our guests' anticipated arrival time.

Suddenly it occurred to us that we ought to notify the security guard at the front gate of the marina that we were expecting guests. I jumped on a bike and raced out into the howling night, the wind blasting and cold. There had been a terrible storm, a near hurricane, a few days before, and the weather was still miserable. After a long discussion with the guard at the gate, and another one with his boss at the guard hut, I finally got everything cleared away for their arrival. Or so I thought.

Seven o'clock came and went. By seven-forty-five we began to worry that there had been some misunderstanding.

Finally, at ten to eight, I hopped back on the bike to see if for some reason our guests were at the marina gate. I was sure they wouldn't have any problems getting in (*"No es un problema,"* the supervisor had assured me), but there I found Merita and Francisco, detained by this same, suddenly problematic, official. Merita was shivering violently, dressed only in the short-sleeved green velour dress I had given her two days before. She didn't own a jacket. She cast me a look of immense relief as I sped towards them, my long hair whipping in the wind.

It turned out that I needed the port captain's authority to receive Cuban visitors. Why I wasn't told this before, I have no idea. But luckily the port captain was in his office, so I pedalled off there at top speed.

The captain, a proud moustachioed specimen of Cuban machismo, unleashed a torrent of rapid Spanish on me as I arrived. Most of this I met with a blank gaze, although the essentials were clear enough. With a little patience I'm sure we would have made our way through it, but he looked annoyed and promptly towed me over to a nearby Cuban boat owner who could serve as our translator.

Cuba, despite its socialist ideals, remains a highly stratified society. Any Cuban wealthy enough to keep a motor yacht at chic Marina Hemingway was obviously very well connected and privileged. The imperious Cuban who emerged reluctantly from his sleek vessel to the impatient knocking of the port captain was certainly that.

The captain rapidly explained the situation to the boat owner. I understood the gist of it very well, but stood in quiet submission as the boat owner condescendingly reiterated it to me: "When you are in Cuba, you have to abide by the laws of Cuba. You can't just do whatever you want. You can't just invite anybody you want into the marina. We are very careful about who we admit here." *Yes, very careful indeed*, I thought, picturing the pairs of provocatively dressed young tarts strolling through the marina every night. I waited impatiently, thinking both of my freezing-cold guests and of my overcooked pots of pasta and pink meat sauce, trying not to interrupt his tirade. This boat owner was even more officious than the official.

Finally I had a chance to open my mouth. "Fine," I said. "I didn't know that this permission was required. If I had known, I would have certainly applied for it. But what do we have to do to get the permission?"

"Well, you have to start by talking to this man," he replied patronizingly, stating the obvious.

"That's exactly what I am here to do," I answered, trying to keep a sweet countenance. "How do I get the permission now? I've been working all day, and I spent a lot of money on the ingred– "

"This is not about money!" he interrupted indignantly. This has nothing to do with money! This is about acting according to the laws of the country!"

"I'm sorry, you have misunderstood me," I said with restraint. "I just meant to explain that we have invested a lot of time and money in preparing for our guests, and they are waiting right now for the meal which is burning on my stove. I don't need the permission tomorrow. What do I have to do to get it now?"

"Surely you knew such a permission was required." he retorted crossly. "It's the same everywhere."

"Well, I'm sorry," I answered, annoyed I was getting drawn into this ridiculous argument. "I'm from Canada, and in Canada I have never had to ask permission to invite friends into our home."

With quivering indignation, the boat owner drew himself up to his full height of 5'8". "Who do you think you are talking to?" he practically yelled at me. His moustache was vibrating. "I'm not some ignorant person. I have boats everywhere – Canada, the United States, Europe, and it is the same everywhere you go. In high-class compounds you *always* have to get permission."

"Well I'm sorry, I have never experienced this before," I conceded, still trying not to escalate the confrontation. "But what do I have to do to get the permission *now*?"

The two men exchanged a few words, and the port captain nodded.

"He's going to give you permission," the touchy skipper huffily informed me. "But you take responsibility for anything that happens in the marina tonight. If anything gets vandalized or stolen, you'll be responsible for it."

"Fine," I said.

The port captain hopped on a motorcycle. I pedalled hard behind him to the hut, where Merita and Francisco still waited. Many words were exchanged, and Francisco walked back to the front gate to get his father-in-law and children. I biked back to the boat to get shivering Merita a jacket. Then we waited, interminably, it seemed, as each of the guests had his or her papers inspected minutely by the port captain and his security officials. Then it was over, and we were on our way to the warm inviting glow of the supper and companionship that awaited us on *Northern Magic.*

Despite the lurching start, our dinner party was a great success. Merita and her family had never had spaghetti with meat sauce before – overcooked, pink, or otherwise. We offered them the leftovers to take home, and Francisco jumped at the opportunity. When we visited the next day, he was heating it up for lunch.

Our struggles with the overzealous Cuban bureaucracy were not yet over, however. We wanted to give away two of our bicycles to Merita's children. This doesn't sound like a big problem? Well in Cuba, it was.

Over the past months, we couldn't help but notice that rust was overtaking the bicycles we had brought along for the kids. We had hung on to them because we had the idea they would make a great gift for some poor Cuban family. Now we had found our family. When we entered Cuba, however, the Customs officials had made meticulous notes on all the items we carried on board. When it came to the bikes, we asked if it would be a problem if we left with a different number than we arrived with. Yes, it certainly would, they responded.

But we didn't give up, and as it came closer to our departure, we continued pressing for permission to give the bikes away. Herbert devoted hours to meeting with ever-higher echelons of officials without ever once being told why they should want to deprive their fellow citizens of our gift. If we did give them away without permission, we would face a stiff fine.

But we didn't want to let it go. Finally, Herbert made it to someone with the power to make the decision. If we gave the bikes to "the Cuban people," we could do it, she informed us. But if we wanted to give them to a specific Cuban family, we would have to pay duty.

"Well then how much would we have to pay?" he pressed. Clearly surprised at this question, the official followed him over to *Northern Magic*, where the small bikes awaited her scrutiny. Rusty and leprous with sea salt, they looked a million years old. She stood there for a long moment in silent reflection.

"All right," she said, abruptly, waving her hands and turning on her heel. "You can do it."

We have never had to work so hard just to make a simple gift, but it was worth it. We had already said our goodbyes to Merita and her family the day before, amid hugs and tears and promises to write and return in five years. As far as they knew, we were already gone.

Loading the two smaller bikes in our collapsible cart-trailer, Michael and I sped over to Jaimanitas, the subject of many curious stares from villagers. Merita's children were at school, so we didn't get to see the their reaction when they came home to find our gift, but we had already seen their faces, hungry for a chance to try them when we visited. It was like playing Santa Claus. All of us had many happy moments creating in our own minds the good feelings our old bikes would bring to these smiling children who had so little. To this day we continue to get regular letters from Merita, who has never stopped thanking us for the gift of those bikes, and who has never ceased reminding us of our promise to visit again.

✦

Leaving Havana, we continued hopping around Cuba, enduring storms at anchor, feeding giant iguanas, holding the tails of crocodiles, and even riding on the backs of huge hundred-year-old sea turtles. But our overwhelming focus continued to be hunting for basic food supplies, and dealing with attempts of overzealous officials to control our movements and our friendships.

At our last stop in Cuba, Cayo Largo, we met Octavio, who was a turtle keeper at a sea-turtle sanctuary. We found him patiently scrubbing the little turtles' shells clean with a toothbrush, since lack of a proper water supply caused excess algae growth on the young turtles' shells. He lent us some reading material for the kids' school projects on endangered turtles, but regretfully declined our invitation to come aboard. Cubans were not allowed on foreigners' yachts, he told us. By now we had begun to understand something about this, and didn't press further.

We suspected, in fact, that we had been marked for special attention because of our interest in befriending local folk. Many of the anchorages we had requested had been arbitrarily crossed off our cruising permit. We were denied permission to visit anywhere other than places with a military presence or harbourmaster to keep an eye on us. At Bahìa Honda, a policeman had even insisted on telling us where to anchor, at a spot where he could watch us, even though it was manifestly unsafe. He also required us to find him to get permission every time we wanted to leave the boat. No other yacht we knew of had been given similar constraints.

Perhaps we were being monitored extra carefully; perhaps our eagerness to make friends with ordinary Cubans was considered a threat. But it had been our hope to create a chain of friendships that circled the world, and despite it all, we had managed to forge that first link in Cuba.

$$+$$

After almost a month in Cuba, we made our first passage entirely under sail, bringing us twenty-seven hours later to the posh island of Grand Cayman. Immediately, we found ourselves in culture shock – or perhaps more accurately, supermarket shock. The contrast to impoverished Cuba couldn't have been much greater.

As a tax haven, Grand Cayman attracts the wealthiest of the wealthy, who establish their businesses and vacation homes there. We simply couldn't be restrained, on our first day in town, from heading straight to the supermarket. Forts, museums, and turtle farms could wait, but fresh milk, fresh fruit, and Hershey's Kisses could not. Three trips and five hundred dollars later we had calmed down a little, but our favourite part about Grand Cayman remained the grocery store. Even little Christopher shared our fascination. For homework one day, I asked him to make a collage of Grand Cayman's attractions out of a local tourist magazine. Eighty per cent of the pictures he cut out were supermarket advertisements.

By now, six months had passed since we had cast off from Ottawa. Since that rainy day in September, we had travelled 3,400 nautical miles and in the process begun to turn ourselves into something resembling a sailing crew. We were beginning to feel as if we knew what we were doing.

Herbert had lost about nine kilograms and was getting browner and more youthful with every passing day. The first part of the voyage had been particularly stressful for him, as we worked the kinks out of *Northern Magic* while travelling hard down the eastern seaboard. After hitting Cuba, however, we had begun living the life we had hoped this trip would bring us – exploring a new country together, sharing new experiences, making local friends, and being free to do whatever our moods dictated. The difference this brought to Herbert was remarkable. He was in his element.

Michael had been the most reluctant to join our adventure and yet somehow was the first of us to catch its spirit underway. He grew up enormously in the first six months of our trip. He faced and overcame the loss of friendships that were important to him and carried on cheerfully. He applied himself to his schoolwork, if not with total diligence, then at least with greater attentiveness than before and with a minimum of complaining. For the first time in his life, he discovered reading for pleasure.

He discovered a new love of history and would happily spend hours learning about things that were – museums, statues, and ancient society. He became our resident expert in Greek mythology. He had turned into the primary dinghy captain, and in an interesting reversal, thanks to my experiences in *Flipper*, *he* was now the one who drove *me* around. He was the one of us who would climb a coconut tree and send its bounty crashing down for the rest of us to gather. He would let his little brothers push him under large waves for hours on end with good humour. He had turned lean and brown and muscular and was thriving.

Jonathan, who was about to turn ten, had also overcome his rocky start to the trip. Although the keenest at the outset, he had fought me the most as his schoolteacher. Perhaps because he liked school the most, he found home schooling the biggest adjustment. Michael, on the other hand, much preferred the flexibility of lessons and assignments on *Northern Magic* to the structured classes of a regular school. To my great delight, Michael and Jonathan had by now almost completely set aside their rivalry and were becoming real friends, laughing and sharing inside jokes together. Jon also began showing me why his teachers used to so enjoy having him in their classes. All I needed to do was say, "It's time to do homework" or "set the table, please," and without further ado, Jon would be at work. In Grand Cayman he gained the distinction of being the first one to finish the entire year's math work. He wanted to be the first to earn summer holidays.

Although Jon missed his friends back at home, he made up for it by being outgoing and friendly to everyone we met, introducing himself with a hearty handshake and a broad smile. Women everywhere were quite taken by Jonathan, who lined up for a double serving when they were dishing out eyelashes. Merita's pregnant sister in Cuba told us if she had a boy baby, she intended to name him after Jonathan.

Jon was quick to pick up new languages and not shy to use them. He also became our resident expert on the natural world, referring to his library of reference books about the night sky, weather, fish, shells, birds, and dolphins. He could decipher detailed weather maps and make forecasts based on his own observations. He could devour a whole book in less than a day. He started using words like "sprawled" and "incorrigible." He took on the task of teaching his little brother, and took this job seriously, carefully marking and recording Christopher's progress. He was responsible, honest, and generous. Jonathan would, we could see, turn into an amazing young man. Our dream that this trip would help in that development seemed to be coming true.

And little Christopher: what a study in contradictions our last-born child was. Of the three, it was probably most difficult to know how this voyage was affecting him, because he was just at the beginning of his development. I often thought he was the luckiest of the three, because he was receiving this abundance of time with his parents at a younger age, although perhaps it made him more babyish.

"I want to be with you always, Mom," he would confide softly in my ear when we snuggled late at night. On the other hand, he had only just begun to know how to make friends as we left on the trip, and we weren't able to provide him with very many playmates his age. Although he didn't miss outside friendships the way his older brothers did, I would often find myself wishing we could have done better for him in that respect.

As we were walking past the beautiful shops of George Town, six-year-old Christopher, his active mind always turning, suddenly stopped to ask me, "What is capitalism, Mom?" He would spend hours poring over instruction manuals and rulebooks of complex strategic games. His favourite activity was filling his personal journal with pages and pages of charts, graphs, and maps of imaginary games of his own invention. He loved math, and did it in his free time, in his head, for fun.

Christopher was also the only child in the world who would forego Fruit Loops at the grocery store because they were not healthy. He was not by nature a risk taker, and it was a devil of a challenge trying to teach him how to swim. He was a strange combination of precocity, stubbornness, and babyishness, our little Christopher was. But he was above all our sunshine boy in those days, loving and affectionate, and I treasured each one of the endless days we shared together, living, learning, and growing.

As for me, six months into our voyage, I was feeling pretty good, although increasingly nervous about the large stretches of ocean that lay ahead. The time of our big sea trial was coming closer and closer. I still tried not to visualize that map of the Pacific.

Although I did like our new life, living on a boat had its own stresses. Taking care of the kids' schoolwork was an enormous challenge, probably the toughest thing we did on the boat. It required huge discipline of all of us, and especially of me. But even living on a boat took getting used to, getting accustomed to the cramped spaces and lack of storage space.

I hadn't for a moment regretted our decision to undertake this voyage, although from time to time, when we had days of uncomfortable conditions, I did wonder if we were totally crazy to want to do this. I never learned to enjoy passagemaking. But then we would get a spell like we had in Grand Cayman, playing daily on the beach, walking, taking life easy, and those other feelings would fall right away. Grand Cayman, after all those months of stress and hard travel, was a real vacation.

As we left Grand Cayman behind, with seven days at sea ahead of us, all my earlier worries about the nine-hundred-mile voyage to Panama evaporated in the warm sunshine. Thanks to calm seas, we were able to carry on a relatively normal daily routine, which included proper cooked meals, and, for the kids, homework. Herbert and I settled into a comfortable rhythm of standing watches, with one of us awake and on watch at all times. Even the children were mellow, playing together cooperatively day after day with no signs of strife.

Around ten at night on the fourth day, while I was trying to tear myself out of a good book in order to finish off the supper dishes, the sails suddenly started flapping. I jumped into the cockpit, thinking there had been an abrupt change in wind direction. The wind hadn't changed; it was our course that had. We were heading due north.

Herbert arrived from below in his underwear, looking tousled and sleepy. As I took over hand steering, he began rooting around to get at the autopilot, which seemed to be the cause of the problem. This involved about half an hour's worth of emptying lockers in Jonathan's cabin as he slept as well as in the cockpit.

As Herbert worked on the unit in the moonlight, we made an interesting sight. The cockpit was a jumble of six lifejackets, three safety harnesses, two paddles, a pressure sprayer with hoses, the emergency steering system, a TV antenna, power cords, various parts for replacement portlights, a gangplank, some ropes, and eight 2" × 2" pieces of ¾" marine plywood, all of which had been emptied from the locker that contained the autopilot. I was standing in the midst of this weird mélange, keeping our recalcitrant boat heading south, my bare legs sticking out of Jonathan's green, badge-studded Boy Scout blanket, which I was wearing as a poncho against the cool ocean breeze.

If you had been looking for Herbert in that unsightly cockpit, you would have found him harder to spot. The chief proof of his existence was his white underpants, which shone ethereally in the moonlight from his upended bottom. Less obvious were his legs, which looked as if they were growing upwards out of those eerily illuminated briefs like two fuzzy trees. His upper body was invisible, buried deep inside the emptied locker, out of which emanated periodic muffled groans, grunts, and exclamations of distress. Several times the captain issued me instructions, in the severest terms, that I was to stop the boat from rolling.

It was only a five-cent part that had broken, but we had no ready replacement. McGyver-like, Herbert ransacked the boat for something he could modify to replace the broken pin. Two additional lockers were emptied in the search. Finally, he rigged something together. By one o'clock the unit was working again and my weary body was given leave to go to bed.

I never did get to those dishes, but by the time I was woken at 7:00 a.m. for my next shift, they had all been washed and put away. In fact, all the emptied lockers had been cleaned up, and there was not a bit of evidence of our moonlight escapade.

But no sooner had Herbert returned to bed then he was forced to spring out again. Well, maybe "spring" is too energetic a word; it was more like a pathetic crawl. The pin he had fashioned had failed. *Northern Magic* was once again trying to follow the direction suggested by her name. As the kids made their way out of bed, I took the wheel while Herbert, who had worked ceaselessly since ten the night before, once more began emptying the lockers to begin all over again. I tried to convince him to grab some sleep before starting, but he wore "that look" and got right back to work, despite my suggestions.

He worked all day, assembling and disassembling the autopilot twice before admitting defeat. There was nothing he could do to hold it together. Finally, by late afternoon, I was forced to assume my role as chief medical officer and order the captain to bed on the grounds that lack of sleep had made him medically unfit to perform his duty. Herbert hates to admit defeat, but reluctantly he gave in.

He awoke at 11:00 p.m., still tired, but functional. Now I was beat after eighteen hours wrestling with the wheel. We were out of sync, each of us fighting accumulated fatigue from long hours standing in the cockpit. There was not a breath of wind as we motored, so our Aries mechanical self-steering wind vane was useless. For the next two days, our comfortable routine broke down as we each gripped the wheel for as many hours as we could before our bodies demanded sleep and forced us to wake our equally exhausted and depleted partner.

Because someone had to be standing at the wheel at all times, we of course both had to be awake for certain periods like meal preparation, plotting our position, and getting the kids to bed. The children took care of each other, as well as holding the wheel for short periods. In compensation they got off homework altogether. And so we blearily made our way across the Caribbean Sea.

✦

I spotted the lights of Panama around midnight at the beginning of our seventh day. Suddenly, the lights of many huge ships were around us and I was actually too excited to sleep after I passed the wheel over to Herbert. We entered Cristóbal Harbor as the sun was rising over the low green mountains of Panama. By 7:00 a.m. we had found the yacht anchorage and gratefully dropped anchor amidst dozens of other boats flying the flags of countries all over the world.

We had arrived.

Unfortunately, we had arrived at a dump. The port of Colón was the epitome of all that is bad about port towns around the globe. It was the ugliest place we saw on our entire trip. Filthy, unsafe, strewn with garbage, it had absolutely nothing to recommend it. At the bus stop, where big busses disgorged their streams of passengers, we saw the drivers simply dump out their large bins of collected garbage – plastic pop bottles, potato chip bags, scraps of food, cigarette packs – right onto a mound in the street, where they began blowing around in the wind and collecting in gutters already clogged with stinking refuse. Even the big grocery store was disgusting – the odour of putrefying meat seemed to follow me around, up and down the aisles, everywhere I went. Only after I got back to the boat did I discover the source of the disgusting smell: it was my own package of ground beef, reeking and turning green only an hour after I had purchased it.

Anxious to leave as quickly as we could, we set about preparing to transit the Panama Canal, forty-three miles from end to end. After having the boat measured to determine our fee, which amounted to just under five hundred dollars U.S., and making various trips to government offices to do all the necessary paperwork, our two priorities were to enlist sufficient crew and to prepare the boat for the transit.

The former task involved recruiting line handlers from other sailboats, to help us handle the ropes while going through the locks. The latter included scrounging up old car tires to protect our hull and assembling four heavy forty-metre ropes with which to secure us. As we, along with all the other boats, went through these rites of passage, it reminded me of the rituals young men in various cultures go through when preparing to become men. After a period of preparation, they are taken away from the rest of the tribe to go through a mysterious initiation, often a test of their bravery. None of the other boys knows exactly what is involved until he, in turn, is called away. Only then will he know what secrets the passage holds for him.

The most difficult task of our own rite of passage was finding the three additional handlers to hold the lines securing the boat to the sides of the locks. Herbert's adventures trying to round up helpers from other cruising boats ended up being unexpectedly stressful, including a swim across a crocodile-infested lake when our entire crew, including Herbert, got stuck in the middle of the canal on another boat. But by nine on the morning of our transit, the Panama Canal pilot and our three yawning, newly enlisted crew had arrived, and we were given permission to head for the first lock.

We entered the first giant, three-hundred-metre long chamber with four other vessels: a two-hundred-metre long freighter from China, a huge tugboat, and two other sailboats. Before entering the lock, we three sailboats were tied together side by side, forming a large, unwieldy raft. It was like being in a three-legged race.

As we ascended the twenty-six metres of the first three locks (there are six on the canal in all), the atmosphere aboard *Northern Magic* was festive. I ended up playing stewardess, running up and down the companionway ladder, serving an endless series of refreshments to our crew, who were dripping sweat in the fierce Panamanian sun. Meanwhile, at the salon table, our three boys happily painted Easter eggs, not finding it strange in the least to be doing this while progressing through one of the engineering marvels of the world.

That night, we anchored at jungle-rimmed Gatun Lake, in the interior of the narrow isthmus of Panama. We didn't see any of the indigenous crocodiles, but we did spot many black buzzards and a long-tailed howler monkey scavenging for food along the nearby shore, as well as thatched huts on stilts used by native tribes. Since the crocs weren't in evidence, we all jumped at the chance for a refreshing freshwater swim.

I will always remember that night as one of the finest of our trip. Once the kids were in bed, we adults talked by candlelight in the cool breezes of the cockpit until the early hours of the morning, the low words of our shared experiences and dreams blending in with the nearby sounds of the jungle. Sometime in the magical darkness of that night – it must have been after we adults finally went to sleep – *Northern Magic* received one more visitor. In fact, it might have been the first time ever this particular visitor was called upon to perform his duties in quite this way. But braving howler monkeys, crocodiles, and buzzards, the Easter Bunny actually managed to find us halfway through the Panama Canal. The next morning the boat was awash in Hershey's Kisses, and the boys hunted for them all over the boat.

Our descent down the three last locks went smoothly, in tandem again with another two sailboats and sharing space with a leviathan-sized ship or two. Finally, the last gate opened and revealed to us the majestic beauty of the Pacific Ocean, azure blue and dotted with lovely green cone-shaped islands. Then we bade a fond farewell to our new-found cruising friends, with promises to keep in touch as we all began to make our way into the South Pacific.

After exploring two wonderful islands in the Las Perlas group, and being surprised by large lizards that leapt down at us from the trees, we headed out into the Pacific Ocean. Herbert remarked nostalgically, as the hills of Panama receded in the distance, that this was the last mainland we would see for a very long time.

Imagine, now, a few days later: it is midnight, in the Pacific Ocean. We have put four hundred miles between us and the mysterious island of jungles and leaping lizards. *Northern Magic* is ploughing through the long, dark swells of the Pacific, half way to the Galápagos Islands, which straddle the equator. Inside the cabin, it is almost unbearably hot and humid, the holdover of another stifling day of tropical heat.

Outside, in the cockpit, the breeze is at last blessedly cool, actually fresh enough to raise goosebumps on skin that is still damp from the day's perspiration.

The night sky is dark. Clouds obscure almost all the stars except a few directly overhead. Earlier, the moon briefly grinned a slender smile at us, but now it, too, is gone, leaving the ocean unlit by its benevolent presence. It is impossible to see where the ocean ends and the sky begins. The night sky is an inky black cloak that wraps thickly around us.

As our boat slices through the water, the bow wave shines an eerie white against the dark sea. If you look closely in that wave, little bits of phosphorescent plankton twinkle, sending out tiny plankton alarms at having been disturbed by our passage. Some nights, these phosphorescent sparkles look like mirror images of the Milky Way, which arches across the sky in a magnificent array only visible far from the lights of civilization. But tonight there is no Milky Way, just a few stars bravely showing their faces from between the suffocating layers of cloud.

Hovering in the air there seem to be two spirits: white-winged shapes eerily flitting around our mast, swooping, fluttering, never clearly visible but casting shadows as they swing past our masthead navigation light and are briefly illuminated by it. They stay with us all night every night until we arrive at the Galápagos Islands, but we never see them in the day. We call these mysterious glowing figures our angel birds.

Watching out for any glimmer of light that may signal an approaching ship (a faint possibility, as it has been days since we have seen a sign that we are anything other than the only humans in the universe), we can easily mistake an occasional star peeking through low on the horizon for the running light of another sailboat. A few days ago we spotted such a light, a lone spark on the distant horizon. It must have been very far off, because it was hidden every few seconds behind the ocean swell. It was probably another sailboat, making, just as we were, for the fabled Galápagos Islands. But when daylight came it was gone.

We started the journey with nice twenty-knot winds and, with the aid of a southbound current, flew along at a speed of nine knots, sails crisply filled. On this night, we're still making a good six knots of speed, but now our sails lie useless, flaked against the boom. Our progress is only possible thanks to our good diesel engine and a thousand litres of fuel stored in our tanks. Our sails have been hanging slack for two days now. We sniff the breeze hopefully every few hours, hoping some wind has arisen, but so far no such luck.

For the first three days we wanted to do nothing but lie down, but today this lassitude has left us and we have been able to resume a more normal schedule. The children have now returned, although reluctantly, to their schoolwork, and the familiar routines of cooking and laundry have been re-established, modified only slightly by the constant rocking and swaying of the long Pacific Ocean swells.

After our work is done and Herbert has retired to bed to store up on sleep for his graveyard shift, the kids and I spend hours in the coolness of the cockpit reading *Charlotte's Web*. The children keep begging for yet one more chapter until it is long past dark and the smallest one's eyes begin shutting, the sweet half-smile of sleep on his lips.

I know the kids have gained their sea legs when they stop complaining that the waves make it too hard to brush their teeth. This night they go to bed without complaint. The purr of the motor and the rocking of the ocean make sleep come very easily to them. In just one more hour, when my watch is over, it will come easily to me as well.

$$\text{\Large +}$$

But the passage didn't continue as blissfully as that. First we began taking on water through the stuffing box on our propeller shaft. Then our headsail ripped. Finally, we found ourselves in mounting winds, our first gale at sea. Rain pelted down on us, forcing us to close all the windows and hatches and turning the inside of *Northern Magic* into a sauna. For the first time in our experience, waves began crashing right over our bow, forcing water all the way back into our cockpit.

The waves were close together and steep, and the unsettled weather caused them to come from several sides. As our powerful engine forced our bow through them, we were violently slapped around from many directions in a sharp bucking and rolling motion I found intolerable. Even our captain, whose innards were usually steel-lined, succumbed. After three days of seasickness and two days of peace, I felt badly betrayed by my body as the nausea and vomiting started up all over again.

It was a long night. Mercifully for me, my shift ended at 1:00 a.m. Herbert endured the worst of the gale on his watch. The winds reached forty knots during the night. I huddled in bed and tried to sleep despite the violent motion, but I felt surprisingly secure inside *Northern Magic*, with Herbert at the helm. Even after we motored out of the storm, the weather was grim and squally with almost constant rain. But our nightly angel birds never deserted us.

We didn't even get to mark properly our crossing of the equator, for which I had prepared certain frivolous and messy celebrations and set aside a bottle of champagne. We couldn't do the traditional crossing-the-equator-by-spraying-things-on-each-other celebration in the cockpit, because it was pouring rain. The best I could do, when Herbert announced we were at that very moment straddling the centre of the earth, was feebly lift my head from the bed and flash what I knew to be a pathetic imitation of a smile. No one had any appetite for nacho chips or champagne, so we simply let it be. Later in the day, I took an orange and drew a world map on it in felt pen to explain to Christopher exactly what the word "equator" meant. But that, sadly, was all we did to celebrate this milestone in our journey around the world.

On our seventh day at sea, we spotted San Cristóbal Island. The day was grey and sombre, as had been so many of the days before, and the island was shrouded in a strange mist that seemed to come and go. At one moment we could clearly see its sharp green volcanic outline, and the next moment it would almost disappear into a low-lying cloud.

The Spaniards used to call the Galápagos *Las Islas Encantadas*, "The Enchanted Islands." As we approached them, we could well understand why, as they took turns coming into view and then evaporating. Once, in a channel between two islands, the compass went crazy and the autopilot caused *Northern Magic* to turn in a 360-degree circle before resuming her route. We noticed on the chart the notation "magnetic anomalies," some kind of geological glitch that must have played this little trick on us. Once we had finally satisfied ourselves that we had gotten the boat moving in the right direction again, we looked up, and instead of the two islands we had been between the last time we looked, we were now back in the middle of the open ocean, with no land in sight. Both Herbert and I blinked, confused and disoriented. Then, as quickly as they had disappeared, the islands returned in their proper spots, the mist lifting and returning them to our grateful gaze once more.

4

Galápagos: Wonder
and Despair

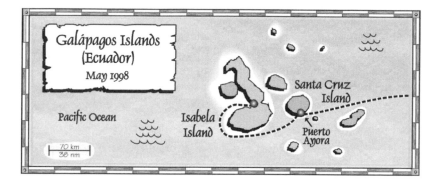

Galápagos Islands
(Ecuador)
May 1998

Pacific Ocean

Isabela
Island

Santa Cruz
Island

Puerto
Ayora

70 km
38 nm

We set anchor in Academy Bay at Puerto Ayora on Santa Cruz Island. As I had promised the kids, I did actually kiss solid land as we alighted from our dinghy.

The Galápagos Islands were everything we had hoped they would be. The small town of Puerto Ayora was clean and picturesque, its prices reasonable and its people friendly. But we had come for the animal life, and we were not disappointed.

Our favourites, by far, were the sea lions. As soon as we entered Academy Bay the first friendly, whiskered face peeped up at us from out of the waves. After that, we saw so many that their visits became hardly worthy of comment. Two of them in particular developed a fondness for us and spent most of their time around *Northern Magic*. The larger one we christened White Bum because of a patch of white on her flank. White Bum was gregarious and would be drawn to the sound of Jonathan doing cannonballs off the boat.

She announced her arrival with a series of huffy snorts. By following the noise of her exhalations you could spot her gently humping out of the water or swimming lazily on her side, flippers in the air. White Bum circled our boat for hours on end, and after taking ten or so good breaths, would perform a graceful backward dive deep into the water, often returning with a flapping silver fish in her mouth. Sometimes, she would make a special effort to show off her prize by swimming on her side so we could admire it before she gulped it down. She would let the children swim up quite close to her, even egging them on before disappearing under their feet, only to reappear a little farther off to start the game again.

Our second resident sea lion was a little smaller than White Bum, and took a liking to *Flipper*, our inflatable dinghy. Every night she hoisted her sleek, well-padded body over *Flipper*'s side and spent the rest of the dark hours lounging in it, her whiskered nose lolling over the edge. When she was in this pose we could get quite close and watch her from deck. Sometimes, returning our inspection, she looped her long neck over her back and gazed at us upside down in the most comical fashion, her large, liquid eyes dominating her face.

Although we looked forward to her nightly visits, we would have been more pleased if our sea lion friend had bothered to learn some basics of hygiene. Every morning, Herbert was faced with the unenviable task of cleaning up after her, for she used the dinghy not only for eating fish, but also for certain other bodily functions, all of which left a mighty strong impression on the nose. It took a good half hour of hosing down each morning before *Flipper* was fit for human use. Still, it was a good trade-off and we felt lucky she had chosen our dinghy for her temporary home.

We had never seen such a profusion of birds as we found in Galápagos – blue-footed boobies, pelicans, great circling frigatebirds. We spent days hiking through forests dripping with vegetation and marvelling at giant tortoises, thousands of lizards, and large black marine iguanas.

Our week of wonder in the Galápagos, however, was also one of despair. The mixture of these two contradictory emotions will forever colour our memories of these islands. Some weeks earlier, my grandmother had suffered a stroke. Each succeeding week brought with it ever grimmer reports about her condition. Our new satellite e-mail receiver (a gift from my father) had a little light that came on when mail arrived, and we had always been excited to see it light up, because it meant a message from home. In the Galápagos, however, that light seemed to shed a more ominous glow, and often I was scared to find out what news it signalled.

I couldn't help remembering how, for the year before we left, Nana had cried almost every time I talked to her about our plans to sail around the world. She had never stopped praying we would change our minds. Many times she told me she was sure she would die while we were gone. Now, as she hovered in a coma, ever nearer her own final passage, it seemed as if her morbid prediction might come true.

Years before, when I had written the biography of my grandfather, I had spent countless hours with my grandmother as she shared her life story with me. Somehow, I felt as though I had lived through the good times and the bad alongside her. Because of this, we had a special and close relationship. I was torn between the desire to remain in the Galápagos Islands, ready to fly home at short notice, and the knowledge that we were already eight days past our three-day visa limit and could stay only a few extra days before having to take to the ocean once more.

And then the e-mail light brought with it news of yet another calamity – my sister Linda's three-year-old daughter had fractured her leg at mid-thigh. Beautiful little Jenna, whom we had last seen dancing in a home video shipped to us in Panama, had been rushed into two hours of surgery and now was on heavy sedation to handle the pain. She was immobilized from the tip of her toes to her chest in a double leg and body cast, her legs secured together by an immovable bar. When my mind ventured into the realm of pain this must be causing to those I loved, my own tears flowed and the urge to rush home gathered even more force.

Yet life was not that simple. Apart from our expired visas, there was the forthcoming hurricane season in the South Pacific to be considered. Thanks to our extended stay in Grand Cayman, we were already more than a month behind schedule. We would pay for any further delays with an increased risk of hitting a tropical cyclone later on.

And so, as we prepared for the longest ocean passage we would ever undertake, we did so with a sinking feeling in the pits of our stomachs. In this context of grief and incipient disaster, the task awaiting us felt more awesome than ever before.

It was our last night in Puerto Ayora, our last chance to buy supplies before our big crossing. We had completed a full day of shopping, tramping up and down the length of the main street at least six times, searching out all the things we would need. Herbert and the two older boys headed back to the boat to unload while Christopher and I continued with a few final errands. As we wandered around town, my mind was a morass of fear and confusion as I wondered what awful news the next e-mail might bring.

Half an hour later, we were waiting under a storefront for Herbert's return. We waited more than an hour, taking shelter under the eaves during a torrential downpour of rain. There was no sign of Herbert. Finally, almost two hours late, as dusk was falling, the familiar figure of our captain came hurrying down the street. He was soaking wet, out of breath, and his face had a hard edge to it.

"We had a squall, out in the harbour. *Flipper* is ruined!"

Flipper had been tied to *Northern Magic* as the squall had hit, bringing with it sudden high winds and big waves. The swell in the harbour was already close to two metres high, but as the waves created by the storm piled on top of that, the effect on the anchored boats was dramatic. Suddenly, there was chaos as anchors began dragging and crews on every boat were jolted into high alert to avoid collisions.

Herbert had positioned himself at the wheel, his eyes scanning the chaos around him, formulating plans for every possibility. Then there was a sound, a dramatic explosion of escaping pressurized air. It took only a moment to realize what had happened. *Flipper* had popped! The protruding end of our steel wind vane had impaled her and split her wide open.

Herbert yelled for Michael. Quickly, the two of them began fishing *Flipper*'s contents out of the water. Michael, who was a strong swimmer, jumped into the big waves and swam after floating objects. But *Flipper* herself was foundering, her heavy outboard motor dragging her down.

Herbert quickly loosened the main boom and attached a belt and pulley to it to help raise the motor out of the water. With Michael back on board and positioning the boom over the side, it was Herbert's turn to dive into the water and sling the belt under the motor. Then the two of them hoisted the motor into the air, where it swung precariously from side to side with each wave, before raising it over the lifelines and drop-ping it safely on deck.

Now they were faced with the formidable task of wrestling *Flipper*'s remains on board. Her water-filled pontoons made her incredibly unwieldy. There was no way for the two of them to hoist her on deck. Crews from other boats had been watching sympathetically, but with their own boats to care for they had been unable to come to Herbert's assistance. Once the worst of the squall had passed, however, Greg from the Australian boat *Bimbimbi* hopped in his dinghy and helped Herbert heave *Flipper*'s heavy, water-filled corpse on deck.

Herbert, still concerned that our anchor might drag, had positioned Michael at the bow, ready to pull up anchor on command using the power winch. Michael stood there heroically, bracing his slender eleven-year-old frame against the driving rain and drenching waves that splashed up each time the bow crashed down.

Finally, the emergency over and everything secure, Herbert set about launching our second dinghy, *Northern Magic Junior*, so he could come and pick us up. Unfortunately, due to difficult conditions on the heaving deck, the forty-kilo fibreglass dinghy hit the water upside down and immediately filled with water. Somehow Herbert managed to manoeu-vre *Junior* into a more suitable position, and with Greg's help, bailed her out before setting off to his much-delayed rendezvous with Christopher and me.

It was fully dark and almost bedtime by the time everything was sorted out and we were all back on board. Supper was by now only a fan-ciful dream. We contented ourselves with a quick bowl of soup before collapsing into bed. The raging waves made sleep difficult, and *Junior*, carefully tied to our side to avoid being similarly trapped under our stern, was banging noisily against the hull as we bucked two metres up and down with each wave.

Herbert climbed out on deck during the night to reassure himself that everything was in order. But early next morning we were roused from bed by Jonathan, who was outside and shouting in alarm. When we emerged, bleary-eyed and tousled, we couldn't believe our eyes: *Junior*, so carefully tied up and rechecked during the night, had still somehow made her way to the scene of *Flipper*'s demise. Just like *Flipper*, *Junior* was now in the process of being demolished by the crashing wind vane on our stern.

She was already filled with water, her fibreglass hull almost smashed in two. The wind vane had knocked gaping holes all through her, and within a few minutes she would be completely gone, dragged down by our second outboard motor, which was already submerged. To lose not one, but two dinghies within twelve hours was not only a terrible blow, it was exquisitely embarrassing to boot. I thought Herbert would commit *hara-kiri* on the spot, using that lethal wind vane on himself.

The drama replayed itself – Herbert diving into the water, wrestling the remains of *Junior* away from the stern anchor line, dodging the wind vane, and slowly manoeuvring *Junior* over to the side. Hans, our friend from the German boat *Mahili*, now came to the rescue, and after some discussion he and Herbert towed *Junior* ashore, fearing that if we attempted to hoist her on deck she would break completely in two. Less than a metre of fibreglass was holding her together in the middle.

This was the morning we had been planning to leave, in company with *Mahili*. Clearly, now, we couldn't go without fixing at least one of our tenders. By the time Hans had finished helping us deal with the aftermath of our disasters, *Mahili*'s departure, too, had to be delayed until the next day.

Early the next morning, one more misfortune added to our feelings of fear and foreboding. Hans, a tall, distinguished, and superbly fit man of sixty-one, with finely chiselled Teutonic features, set about freeing his stern anchor in preparation for departure. Because the harbour was crowded and there was so much wave action, we all had two anchors out, one from the bow and another from the stern, to stop us from swinging into each other. Hans was following his stern anchor line, hand over hand, and discovered that it was set almost directly underneath *Bimbimbi*, beside us and slightly astern. As I watched, I saw him get closer and closer to *Bimbimbi*'s bucking bowsprit until he was bent over right underneath it, trying in vain to free his anchor. It was clearly a very dangerous situation for him to be facing alone.

I called over, asking him to dinghy over and get Herbert to help, but he reacted just as every German man I know would have done, by shaking his head and continuing his work unassisted. Undaunted, I shouted down to Herbert to swim over and help him before he got hurt.

My appeal came too late. Even as Herbert was donning his swimsuit, I watched in horror as a particularly large wave brought *Bimbimbi*'s heavy metal bowsprit crashing down on Hans's skull.

Herbert dived into the water to swim over to where Hans sat in his dinghy, cradling his head and still in terrible danger of being smashed a second time by that bucking bowsprit. His face was covered with blood. By the time Herbert got to him, Hans's entire upper body was crimson. Herbert just about suffered a heart attack when he emerged from the water to face that terrifying sight. He helped Hans back to *Mahili* and the ministrations of his wife, Renate, who had watched the accident in helpless horror.

With his wound bandaged, Hans stubbornly insisted he was fine and would leave as planned. Herbert and Renate tried to change his mind, but to no avail. I sympathized with Renate; I too am married to a German, and I know the type well.

Herbert and a bandaged Hans returned to free the anchor without further incident. Soon *Mahili* was sailing off into the ocean, to be joined by us at another island as soon as we could follow. We felt tremendous misgivings as we watched them disappear over the horizon.

✦

Two days later, with both dinghies nominally repaired, we followed *Mahili*, setting off for an uninhabited anchorage at Isabela Island, one of the westernmost islands in the Galápagos chain. By doing this, we knew there would be no chance now of flying home for my grandmother's funeral if she should die within the next month. We departed with *Futuna*, a German boat we would continue to sail with, on and off, all the way to Indonesia. We already had a good friend on *Futuna* in the person of Oliver, one of the last-minute line handlers who had helped us on our transit of the Panama Canal.

By early morning on May 18, we were passing beside the beautiful, volcano-studded, C-shaped island of Isabela. That afternoon we set out to explore, and Isabela Island paraded before us the most incredible display of living creatures we will ever see in this life.

First of all, there were the great frigatebirds, soaring and circling overhead like split-tailed pterodactyls from some prehistoric age. There were dozens and dozens of them, one after the other, gracefully swooping down and plucking fish from the surface of the water. As we got closer to shore in *Junior*, we entered the pelican zone – with literally hundreds of brown pelicans flying, swimming, sunning, and diving all around us. At times, there was barely room for our dinghy to progress with this seemingly impenetrable wall of pelicans in the water around us, oblivious to our presence until they were actually in danger of being run over by the slowly moving dinghy.

Next were the boobies, by the hundreds, proudly displaying their startling bright blue feet on the rocky shore or dive-bombing into the water all around us. And then we spotted what I had been hoping especially to see – a Galápagos penguin, the most northerly penguin in the world. There were dozens of them: swimming, head down, on the surface of the water, looking almost like miniature sea lions; paddling around in cheerful small groups; or standing in that pompous penguin stance among the ponderous pelicans and slightly silly-looking boobies on the shore.

Peering into the water, we noticed we couldn't see the bottom – we were looking into an absolutely solid mass of fish. Everywhere we looked, there were small silver baitfish, packed so closely they could have been sardines in a can, the backs and dorsal fins of the ones on top forced above the surface. The view resembled a million miniature shark fins cutting through the water. All a bird had to do was open its mouth and it was guaranteed a feed. Of everything we saw, this solid moving mass of fish was probably the most stunning. There were so many fish in the water, the birds didn't even bother to pick up the ones they dropped by accident from the air. The bushes around the water's edge were decorated with thousands of dead fish bodies, hanging down like sparkly Christmas ornaments.

We soon found ourselves in a small lagoon, right in the middle of hundreds – no, thousands – of creatures in an orgy of feeding: from above, frigatebirds swooping and boobies diving; from the surface of the water, penguins and pelicans coming up with a mouthful every time they ducked their heads; and from under the water, sea lions and large green marine turtles, lazily claiming their fair share. Baby sea lions would periodically take a break from their feeding to swim over to our dinghy and look at us curiously. You could imagine them saying, "Hey, Mom, look at the tiny humans!"

All around us, we heard nothing but the sounds of gluttony – splashing, snorting, flapping, and swallowing. It was a scene of wild and terrible beauty.

We stayed at mesmerizing Isabela Island for two days while making our final preparations for crossing the Pacific. Then *Futuna* was gone. The day after, *Mahili* and *Northern Magic* were to follow, into three thousand miles of empty ocean.

I awoke early on the morning of our departure. A familiar tightness gripped my throat, a strangling constriction that only happens when I am afraid. This was the day. There was no going back. Finally, I was so tired of dreading this passage I was actually feeling eager to get on with it.

Beside the computer, I noticed the little e-mail light was on. It had an ominous glow to it, so early in the morning. Suddenly all thoughts of the looming passage disappeared. "I know this is bad news," said Michael over my shoulder, voicing my own fears.

In a short but eloquent message from my father, we learned that my grandmother had passed away just two hours before.

There was no hope of returning home for the funeral. As much as my heart cried to return, I had known once we left Santa Cruz Island that there would be no way to make it back in time.

"Do you still want to leave today?" Herbert asked, softly, after a time.

"Yes," I nodded. There was no point in delaying the inevitable. So, as Herbert continued readying the boat for departure, quietly taking over my chores as well, I sat at the computer, with a mournful Michael trying his manly best to comfort me.

As we set sail for the Marquesas Islands, across an unimaginable expanse of water, I didn't stand on deck to catch a last glimpse of land receding in the distance. My place was inside, hunched over my computer. I said my goodbyes to Nana there, paying honour to her the only way I could – with my words of love and respect. My father had earlier asked if I would help write her obituary and eulogy. Now it was time to perform that last loving act. As I worked, my tears flowed freely.

5

Facing Fear and Grief in the Vast Pacific

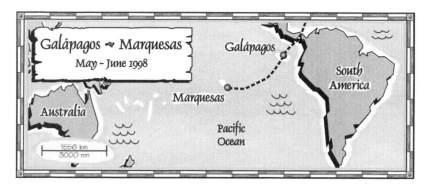

Our first week at sea was a low time for me. I had to deal with my usual lethargy at the beginning of a passage, my fear about facing the huge expanse of ocean, and my grief at the death of my grandmother. My thoughts, for the first few days, were focused on what my family was doing at any given hour – attending a memorial service, standing at graveside, gathering in the home I have associated with my grandparents since earliest childhood, a home I would never enter again. I felt my place was beside my family in Canada. Instead, I was heading out into three thousand miles of empty ocean.

On the seventh day, the funeral over and done with and my last tears shed, I awoke, bright and hopeful, to a sunny, perfect day.

Seized with a new energy, I decided to scrub down the galley. A boat is a terrific factory for the production of bad smells – a hot, close environment with lots of bodies, tremendous humidity, and not enough refrigeration for the amount of food that is packed into it.

So, armed with Lysol, I attacked every corner that might harbour mould, mildew, or any other unauthorized organism. Within an hour I had scrubbed the galley up and down so that it smelled like new. Now, truly hungry for the first time on the voyage, I decided to offer scrambled eggs and bacon to our crew. During a passage, when I was typically less than enthusiastic about cooking, they considered themselves lucky to get an empty bowl and a bag of corn flakes tossed at them. Herbert normally only managed to scrounge up one meal a day. My uncharacteristic offer therefore received a gratifying reception, and I set about retrieving some of the 150 eggs I had purchased in Galápagos for the voyage.

I had followed the instructions in my reference books as to how to preserve eggs without refrigeration. This involved either dipping them in boiling water for five seconds, or covering them with Vaseline. Jonathan and I had tried both methods. Now, almost two weeks after buying and carefully treating them, I would test the results of our efforts.

Cracking the eggs proved to be more of an adventure than the ocean passage itself. I discovered to my disgust and frustration that at least half of them were already questionable or worse. Soon, I was juggling eggs all over, trying to put all the good ones together in containers and isolate the baddies for disposal overboard. This was harder than it sounds, unless you consider that the rolling motion of the boat was constantly causing all my bowls of eggs to tip over and slide around. My original objective of making breakfast was soon put aside.

Then, for the first time in my pampered and sheltered life, I experienced the smell of a truly rotten egg. This evil thing simply exploded in my hand like a grenade, spraying its noxious contents all over me, the galley, and in particular the lid of the top-opening fridge. Before I could react, the egg-grenade's incredibly foul contents were dripping down right inside the refrigerator.

At the sound of this startling explosion, I issued a scream of my own. Everyone came running to see what had happened. Then, confronted with the stench of chemical warfare, my erstwhile rescuers, noses plugged, beat an equally hasty retreat.

By the time I had finally assembled the requisite number of eggs, had dealt with a second smelly egg explosion, and had cleaned up as best as

I could, my appetite had vanished. My pristine, fresh-smelling galley now smelled worse than the city dump. Rotten black egg goo had dripped and drooled its mucousy way everywhere.

Finally, I silently served the long-awaited plates of eggs, neglecting to set one down for myself. Everyone took exactly one bite and then, in unison, slapped their forks back down in disgust. "Yucck! These eggs taste funny!"

"They're not rotten," I said, defensively, my eyebrow raised scathingly. "I can assure you of that."

"No, they really do taste funny," said Herbert hesitantly, scarcely daring to meet my baleful glare, known in our family as a Hairy Eyeball. He was fully aware of the sacrifices I had made to prepare this meal. "They taste fishy."

They were right. The eggs really did taste like fish. So of the 150 eggs that I had so carefully bought, treated, and stored, there were approximately sixty left that had not gone bad. And still I couldn't serve scrambled eggs to my family. Instead I had a fridge that, even a week later, still smelled like something banned by the Geneva Convention. We didn't eat a single egg on the passage and eventually I dumped all the rest of them in the sea.

The opportunity for breakfast having long since passed, I now set about preparing lunch. I will confess that perhaps I was a little less cheerful than before. My stomach, which had started out the day feeling pretty robust, was now a quivering mess. Even the thought of an off smell made me want to retch.

Still, determined to carry on with the pretence of being the efficient, cheerful first mate, I gritted my teeth, braced my body against the inexorably rolling motion, and set about getting some potatoes out of the potato bin. If I couldn't get a decent breakfast together, at least I could offer a filling lunch.

But as I opened the bench where the potatoes were kept, my already overburdened olfactory sense went on high alert. Was I imagining it or could it be that my carefully stored Galápagos potatoes were already . . .

"Arrghhh!"

Having sailed south to the same latitude as our destination, we turned due west to take advantage of the trade winds blowing strongly and steadily at our back. *Northern Magic* had her jib and mainsail poled out on opposite sides, wing-and-wing, to catch as much of the easterly winds as possible. This gave her the appearance of a giant butterfly as she flew through the silvery waters of the South Pacific.

Unfortunately, this sail arrangement was much less comfortable than it had been when we were heading southwest. On that tack, we had been stabilized by the wind coming from one side and we assumed a calmer position, slightly heeled but relatively stable.

Now, everything aboard *Northern Magic*, which had been organized to stay put on a comfortable starboard tack, began flying from one side of the boat to the other, as three-metre waves rolled us mercilessly back and forth. Cooking, working, and even using the toilet took on new and sometimes exciting aspects.

As we each attempted to go about our tasks, you could hear in turn the same anguished cry coming from different throats as pantry contents tumbled out, scattering noodle shells and cream of wheat to create an almost beach-like display on the floor, carefully constructed Lego space-ships took off prematurely in disastrous flight across the salon, toilet lids came banging down on someone's bare back while they were occupied with important business, freshly washed cutlery took on new life as deadly projectiles in the galley, and glasses of juice and bowls of Honey Nut Cheerios upended themselves on people's laps.

This was simply daily life on a small boat in the open ocean.

Twelve days after leaving the Galápagos Islands, we celebrated our passing the halfway point of our passage. In the aftermath, this time it was the cockpit of *Northern Magic* that was a mess, covered with the remnants of our "Midpoint Party," in which we had sprayed each other with little cans of foam streamers and stuffed our faces with treasured morsels of marzipan saved for the occasion, all while balancing ourselves against the tremendous rolling forces of the large Pacific swell. That halfway-point party, 1,500 nautical miles from land, marked the end of the easy part of our passage.

The day after our festivities, little remnants of colourful foam stream-ers still festooning the cockpit, we were rollicking along with the trade winds at our back, making good speed. I was on watch and didn't hear anything remarkable, but suddenly I realized that the boat was rolling much more than before. I popped my head out the hatch to see why.

I couldn't have been more surprised. Our main boom, the huge wooden beam leading out from the mast, had snapped in two. It was loosely banging around the solar panels, held up only by the straining, flogging mainsail. It had been severed just at the point where a preventer had secured it from accidental swinging.

"Come out here quick," I yelled to Herbert, who had just gone to bed. "Our boom is broken!"

He looked up at me sceptically from the bed, clearly imagining that some minor fitting had given way. He didn't budge. He was off watch, and intended to stay that way.

"I mean it! The boom is completely broken!"

I could see in Herbert's disbelieving face, as he slowly and with exaggerated deliberation swung his legs over the side of the bed, that he was attributing some kind of feminine hysteria to my assessment of the situation. No doubt as soon as he spotted the problem, his demeanour said, it would be easy to fix. But to humour me, he got up anyway. His attitude changed as soon as he stuck his head out of the hatch.

While I began to prepare myself mentally for a much longer voyage under mizzen sail alone, Herbert was already making plans to patch the boom back together. By nightfall he had created an entirely functional plywood splint that enabled us to continue on our way only slightly the worse for wear with mainsail flying. Now, though, we had to watch the boom like hawks in case our band-aid solution did not hold. This became especially important as, throughout the next day, the winds became ever stronger and the waves ever higher. Soon, we found ourselves negotiating an endless series of ugly squalls in which the twenty-knot winds could suddenly double in intensity.

During these mini-storms, which typically lasted half an hour to an hour, we discovered that if a particularly strong blast of wind coincided with us being tipped over by a large wave, we would slew around broadside to the waves. The autopilot, tenuously held together by Herbert's penny parts from Panama, would be unable to correct it. We had to be on constant alert to prevent these dangerous accidental broaches. In this state of nervous watchfulness, we passed many sleepless days and nights.

With each day of strong winds, the ocean swell grew larger and larger. One morning I crept out of bed and found myself awestruck by the rolling masses of water that were approaching us from behind. Ominously, relentlessly, each watery wall would sweep up until it was right upon us, towering well over our heads as we stood in the cockpit, looking for all the world as if it would consume us whole. But then *Northern Magic* would always do as she was intended and rise buoyantly on top of each crest, letting the wave slide harmlessly under her keel.

On the third day after the breaking of the boom, we noticed that the repairs were beginning to give. The stress of these winds and waves was taking its toll, and the boom was slowly forming an inverted V, raised in the middle and down at the ends. To reduce the stress on it, we shortened sail even further and put ourselves back on a less rowdy starboard tack – a route that, while more comfortable, would require us to zig-zag back and forth and cost us time and mileage towards our goal. We had been used to many days of 150 miles of progress. Babying the boom in this way cost us severely, dropping our progress as low as a depressing eighty miles in twenty-four hours and adding days to what had earlier promised to be a quick passage.

Herbert and I had, by now, developed a system of watchkeeping in which we each took two periods of six hours on followed by six hours off. With six consecutive hours of rest rather than the more typical four that many other couples use, we found we were more refreshed. We were learning how to live on the constantly heaving surface of the world's largest ocean, seeing nothing but endless water from morning to night. We experienced what it's like to be totally alone in the universe, dependent upon no one but ourselves for our very survival. We spent hours watching the world around us – always the same, and yet ever changing.

We never had a day at sea where seabirds did not accompany us, even right out in the middle of the ocean. Many of them were surprisingly small, no bigger than a swallow. How they could survive thousands of kilometres from land is still a mystery to me.

The only signs of human life we observed were two large commercial fish factories. We could hear their chatter on the radio as they circled around, looking for their quarry, but they didn't respond to us. And once, in the middle of the Pacific, we saw a deep-sea weather buoy. After that first day at sea, we lost sight of *Mahili*, although we spoke to them at least once a day on the radio. We ended up losing radio contact with *Futuna*, although we kept calling out to them and talking to them at the appointed time, just in case they could hear us. Then we got a satellite e-mail from them, saying they could hear us and to keep on talking; their transmitter was broken but they liked hearing our voices every day. The three sailboats relied on each other to keep some kind of reassuring human contact going. Our brief radio chat with *Mahili* was usually the highlight of each day.

The other contact we had was by e-mail to home. Each night, to reassure my parents that all was well, I would compose an e-mail and send it by shortwave radio. One particular night not long after the middle of the passage, I had just finished composing my nightly message before going off watch at 1:00 a.m. I had been feeling proud that Herbert's creative repair of the autopilot was performing well, and mailed Dad to say I was very happy not to be standing in the cockpit hand steering, as it was stormy and the cockpit had already been flooded a number of times by particularly aggressive waves crashing into it.

Ten minutes after transmitting that message, the autopilot failed, and I found myself standing in the cockpit, my hands wrestling with the wheel, waves crashing down on me, while Herbert attempted yet another repair. For two hours I stood there, one hand bracing myself against the motion, the other hand gripping the wheel, one eye on a menacing black squall line advancing from behind, and the other on the unforgiving compass and its single, glowing eyeball. I could hear, from somewhere close by, the violent, flapping death throes of a fish pitched into the cockpit by a breaking wave. I was helpless to save it from its sad and useless death. Inside, I could hear unwashed dishes and a mixing bowl clattering around and spilling onto the galley floor, covering it with muffin batter. Those cursed words to my father echoed in my head as I became convinced that I had brought on this miserable fate. It is not without good reason that sailors are a superstitious lot.

In the days to come we were beset by new problems and challenges of every kind, as if to test the limits of our patience, resourcefulness, and sheer stubbornness. The autopilot got fixed, broken, and refixed twice more; the wind vane required repair; the topping lift for our spinnaker pole wrapped itself inextricably into our furling system; and, in the latest variation of Herbie's Law (which is what my father was now calling our personal law of boating: "if it can break, it will") three different inverters, including the one supplying power to our computer, sputtered and died. In order to send my dispatches to the *Citizen* or my nightly e-mails, I had to type without seeing the monitor; our last working inverter could power either the computer, or the monitor, but not both.

By the last day of our passage, twenty-two days after we had set out from Galápagos and eleven days after it had first broken, the jury-rigged boom began really giving way. We were forced to take down the mainsail entirely. Thirty of the forty large bolts Herbert had used to secure the plywood splint had either worked themselves loose or sheared right off from the strain.

Yet our long-feared voyage across the Pacific was coming to an end. Gradually, it started sinking in that we had actually accomplished this darkly anticipated feat. It was like getting a black belt in karate, or producing a baby after long months of uncomfortable pregnancy – you have to grit your teeth and endure a lot, but at the end of it you're left with a tremendous sense of accomplishment. As the distance to the Marquesas diminished to fewer than a hundred miles, we were vibrating with excitement. At the start of the trip we had organized a family betting pool on how many days the passage would take. Bets ranged from twenty-five days (Herbert and Christopher) to twenty-nine days (mine).

Herbert was the first to spot land. His exclamation brought four more eager bodies and straining sets of eyes on deck. Christopher wrestled in the cockpit with his dad for the grand prize of a red tube of Pringles potato chips. Barely visible in between the thunderheads that surrounded us were three misty mountainous green islands. There will never be anything to compare with that magnificent vista, the sight of land after twenty-three days at sea.

6

Hopping Across Friendly Islands

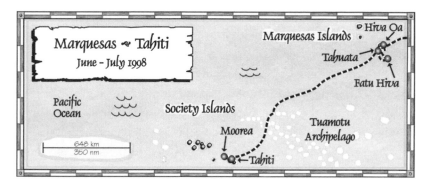

Marquesas ∿ Tahiti
June - July 1998

Pacific Ocean

Society Islands

648 km
350 nm

Marquesas Islands

Hiva Oa

Tahuata

Fatu Hiva

Moorea

Tahiti

Tuamotu Archipelago

Most sailors who have sailed across the Pacific and finally landed at the Marquesas describe it as the most beautiful landfall in the world. These remote and fascinating islands have captivated many sailors, writers, artists, and dreamers over the centuries. They are spectacular: towering green volcanic peaks with rounded tops, tumbling waterfalls, and a profusion of spectacular growth. The majestic Marquesas, cloaked in a beautiful green mantle, certainly fit our dream of a lush Polynesian paradise.

As we finally entered a tiny bay on the island of Tahuata, our greeting committee wasn't an outrigger canoe full of handsome Polynesians, but *Mahili*'s rubber dinghy, containing a broadly smiling Renate and Hans and a load of fresh grapefruit. We arrived at dusk, and couldn't go ashore until the next day. When we finally did, I was amazed at how dizzy and disoriented I felt – I could have sworn the whole island was swaying under my feet. All our legs were weak after more than three weeks on *Northern Magic*.

After one day of exploring the exquisite sandy beach and learning how to walk again without swaying from side to side, we headed for the larger island of Hiva Oa. We arrived on a Sunday, and were treated to a moving Christian procession through a series of beautiful flower-bedecked outdoor altars, with the entire congregation singing in harmony as they walked from shrine to beflowered shrine through the streets. The village of Atuona was a small, simple place, a hilly two-kilometre walk from the harbour. Some friendly villagers driving by stopped and offered us a lift back to the harbour when they saw us walking. We gratefully piled in the back of their pick-up truck and bounced happily along the road, making conversation with a beautiful but shy young Polynesian girl who shared the ride with us.

One day, we hiked up a mountain path to find ancient stone petroglyphs. The scenery was stunning as we walked through lush living tunnels of the most fantastic oversized vegetation. As we entered a grove of huge taro plants with leaves as big as an elephant's ear, Michael remarked that he felt we had been transported to the set of the movie *Honey I Shrunk the Kids*. At another spot on the island, a family of wild horses awaited us on a lovely dark brown sand beach flanked by two freshwater streams. The rounded mountains towering over us were covered with what looked like plush green carpeting. Bounding freely over the mountaintops, and sending their bleats down to welcome us, were wild goats whose ancestors once belonged to the inhabitants of this now deserted valley. We discovered a spring-fed waterfall bubbling right out of the mountainside into a little pool full of small crayfish. Around the pool, arranged artistically by Mother Nature herself, were huge hibiscus trees, coconut palms, banana trees, and other flowering bushes, creating a perfect scene of a tropical paradise. We explored an ancient overgrown alley lined with lava rock that led us to the remains of a village abandoned a thousand years ago. The kids held coconut shell races in the streams.

At Fatu Hiva, the southernmost of the Marquesas Islands, the scenery was unforgettable. The bay in which we anchored was surrounded by towering rounded pillars of rock. Early French sailors stopping at this bay called it Baie des Verges, or "Bay of Penises," due to the suggestive shapes of these remarkable rock formations. Later, missionaries found this name, however apt, to be unacceptable. They made a slight modification, from Baie des Verges to Baie des Vierges, thus transforming penises into virgins and protecting their Victorian sensibilities.

We alighted from our dinghy and walked past copra drying sheds, where giant trays of drying coconut were laid out in the sun. We passed a primary school just as school let out, and Jonathan, who happened to be carrying his Nintendo Game Boy, immediately became the most popular boy in town. Literally, the entire school, including teachers, crowded around to get a peek at this miniature computerized marvel. It took no time at all before we had made one or two special friends among the children, and we found ourselves being escorted from house to house to inspect the handicrafts made by virtually every inhabitant of the village.

The women, who were attractively plump in the Polynesian fashion, were typically dressed in wrap-around skirts and lacy black brassieres that made you feel you ought to avert your eyes. They made beautiful handmade paper, called *tapa*, with intricate paintings in Marquesan designs.

The men, who were adorned with the most interesting intricate tattoos on their upper bodies, carved statues of tikis, ceremonial knives, and masks out of local hardwoods. We had seen these crafts before, and they were, like everything else in French Polynesia, very expensive. But one of the reasons we had wanted to visit Fatu Hiva was a report that the people here were willing to trade their handicrafts for goods instead of money. And as *Northern Magic* was packed more with things than cash, we had come to Fatu Hiva ready to barter.

Herbert's collection of hand tools for trade made him a very popular man in Fatu Hiva. In exchange for a router, hacksaw blades, a sander, sandpaper, a Dremel tool, and a vise, we obtained a fabulous collection of exquisite Marquesan carvings in wood and bone worth about seven hundred dollars, and made friends in virtually every home in the village. By the end of our two days in Hanavave, in fact, Herbert had developed a reputation as Herb "The Tool Man" Stuemer. Men began flagging him down in the street, asking about his tools or seeking his help repairing some of their own, which he gladly did, creating more admirers in the process. We left Hanavave staggering under a load of gifts and bartered-for booty. We were laden not only with carved wooden bowls, masks, and tikis, but also with gifts of fruit and baking from the storekeeper whose power drill Herbert had fixed.

✦

After a second visit to Tahuata Island, we were sad to be taking to the sea once more, but it was time to leave. Herbert had by now make a more durable repair to our dismembered boom, and so we set off for the six-day passage to Tahiti.

From the moment we were underway, it felt very natural to be back on the ocean. For the first time, there was no period of adaptation, no lethargy or queasiness. We all felt alert and comfortable right from the start. Even when our autopilot had its customary failure, causing us to hand steer for considerable periods of time, I found myself enjoying the long hours in the cockpit. I spent my time just looking at the surface of the ocean, watching for flying fish and birds, and appreciating the shapes of the clouds and the colours of the sunset.

For the last two days to Tahiti, the winds gained in strength and blew from ahead. The idyllic conditions of before were soon nothing but a memory. Earlier, our Aries mechanical wind vane had been able to take over some of the steering, but we now found it was unable to hold our boat on course in these more difficult windward conditions.

Still, we had a great time. Herbert and I took turns at the helm in an exhilarating blur of wind and spray. There was no opportunity for boredom; the job required full concentration and a great deal of muscle power. It was a rich sensory experience – the roar of our bow wave, the billowing of the sails, the hiss of the breaking crests, the bucking of the boat as she slogged her way to windward, the splash of the spray, the wild, fragrant wind whipping into our faces, and the raucous calls of petrels and boobies as they circled hungrily over passing schools of fish.

This was really sailing. This was really living. This was great!

We spotted the high peaks of Tahiti almost a hundred miles away. It was incredibly exciting, even more so than our first sighting of the Marquesas. It was hard to believe that we were actually closing in on this fabled island of captains Cook and Bligh. As the sun went down and illu-minated the sky in shades of vermilion, those enticing twin peaks grew both taller and darker against the horizon. I turned to Herbert and said, "You know, 90 per cent of the world would love to trade places with us right now."

This thought echoed in my mind again, not twenty-four hours later, as we fell asleep, safely anchored in Papeete harbour surrounded by the sounds of Polynesian drums beating out their thrilling rhythms in the darkness of the cool Tahitian night.

One of the reasons we had looked forward to Tahiti was that we were expecting to receive a very special package there. There was nothing quite as fun as receiving a care package from home, complete with news, letters, videos, spare parts, gifts, and a few favourite food items. This package was especially important, though, for it would contain a new inverter as well as a spare laptop computer.

My father happened to know a Calgary businessman who owned a resort in French Polynesia and would carry a package and save a thousand dollars in courier charges. In the weeks before our arrival in Tahiti, I had compiled a list of special requests, things like the kids' favourite game of Magic Cards, Lego, brown sugar, Tuna Helper, Breton Crackers, and, yes, perhaps a few Hershey's Kisses. For the children, naturally.

On the morning of July 9, we turned out of the boat neatly dressed and freshly scrubbed. We were to meet our contact at the lobby of the Mandarin Hotel. We'd never seen him before, but we had his description: 5'11", grey hair, big smile. There was, however, only one person in the lobby, a woman reading a newspaper. I went to the desk clerk and told her we were there to meet a man.

"Let me check and see what room he is staying in," she offered helpfully.

"No, no, that's all right," I interjected, not knowing whether he was actually a guest in the hotel, "don't bother checking. I'm sure he'll be along."

"Perhaps you should go talk to that woman over there," she offered. This was, I thought, a dumb thing to say. Hadn't I just told her we were waiting for a man?

"No, thank you. We'll just wait for him over here."

"I really think you should talk to that woman there," she said, pointedly.

"No, thank you," I repeated even more firmly. *Wasn't she listening?* "There's no need. We'll just wait right here."

While I was busy standing my ground, trying to argue as best as I could in French, Michael began jabbing me urgently in the side. "Mom! There's an *Ottawa Citizen*! Someone over there has an *Ottawa Citizen*!"

I waved him away impatiently. I was busy with more important things, like fencing with an obtuse hotel desk clerk. Finally, the clerk gave up on her unwelcome efforts to be helpful and suggested, with a strange little smile, that I sit down while waiting for my friend. *Over by that woman.*

Relieved, I headed over to the chairs, kids and Herbert in tow. Michael, however, was still poking me and jabbering on about the newspaper he had seen.

He was right: there, straight ahead of us, was a woman sitting behind an opened copy of an *Ottawa Citizen*. I stopped for a moment, puzzled, trying to figure out what this meant. Then it came to me.

This was no 5'11" grey-haired smiling stranger. This was my own mother!

"I recognize those legs!" I shrieked, and out from behind the paper emerged my tearful and smiling mom. Then, from around a corner, where he had been secretly videotaping the whole scene, strode my grinning dad.

We all trooped to their room, and out of duffle bags and suitcases poured a whole cornucopia of goodies: all the treats we had ordered, including four whole bags of Hershey's Kisses, gifts and letters, our new inverter, and, best of all, a brand-new, state-of-the-art laptop computer with all the bells and whistles, a present from my parents. We were in a state of breathless shock for most of the day. We called our new computer Happy Lappy.

My parents had booked a hotel in Moorea, Tahiti's sister island about twenty kilometres away. Later that evening they took the ferry over, while we got *Northern Magic* ready to leave the next morning for the three-hour sail to what is surely is the most beautiful island in the world. We tied ourselves up to a small public dock in front of my parents' hotel, where for the next week we alternated between nights on the boat and days with my parents – exploring the island, visiting pineapple plantations, ancient archaeological sites, waterfalls, craggy peaks, and deep bays.

On the final day of my parents' visit we found our way to the three sacred waterfalls of Faarumai, back on Tahiti. The first of the sacred falls plunged hundreds of metres down the steep face of a mountainside into a clear, cold pool before bubbling its way down through the thick forest of Tahitian chestnut trees to the sea. On our way back from this awe-inspiring scene, a dozen young Tahitian men and women, dressed in matching suits and dresses, passed us. I stopped one of the men and asked if they were a wedding party. No, he answered, they were a singing group, there to have their picture taken.

So that is how we found ourselves, standing at the base of the sacred falls, the plunging water making a surreal white backdrop, thrilling to the clear harmonies of voices raised *a capella* in joyful Tahitian song. They invited us to stand among them as they sang. The leader of the group was a handsome young man named Ambrose. He became the next link in our chain of friendships.

On Monday night, Ambrose arrived at the boat with his wife, Mariella, his three-month-old baby son, Manahiva, and his sister, Natacha. They brought with them some guava pie and conserves made by Mariella's mother. At the end of the evening they invited us to spend a day with them touring the island. Two days later we set off with them in a four-wheel-drive pick-up truck with Michael and Jonathan bouncing around gloriously in the back, their hair streaming out in the wind.

Together, we circled the island and discovered more of the marvels of Tahiti: grottos carved in leafy mountainsides where trickling water created natural pools full of exotic water lilies; black sand beaches born only a year before, when the terrible forces of a cyclone had ripped out of the mountainside a brand new beach; a lofty mountaintop, where we stepped literally into the clouds and watched them swirl past at arm's length, and, best of all, a stream full of giant carnivorous eels, who snapped their toothy mouths at the fish that was offered, but let the children gingerly touch their backs.

Another of our highlights was our visit to a dance celebration. We were treated to an unforgettable spectacle when hundreds of elaborately costumed Tahitian girls wiggled and swivelled, while an equal number of muscular brown men thrilled us with ancient dances of lust and conquest. I was spellbound. The hairs on my arms rose up of their own accord to the sight and sound of dark-haired maidens and warriors undulating to the beat of wooden drums. Their rhythms seemed to reach inside and resonate within me. That night, through its music and its dance, the sensuous land of Tahiti wove its magic on us. To see the dancers of Tahiti is to remember life as it was thousands of years ago. To hear the drums is to resurrect ancient stirrings long since forgotten. The rhythms haunt me still.

7

We Were Kings on Palmerston Island

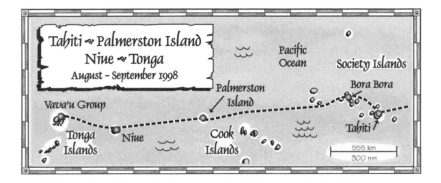

Tahiti ➤ Palmerston Island
Niue ➤ Tonga
August – September 1998

Pacific Ocean
Society Islands
Bora Bora
Palmerston Island
Vava'u Group
Tonga Islands
Niue
Cook Islands
Tahiti
555 km
300 nm

We continued from Tahiti to Bora Bora, and from there to Palmerston Island, which peeked over the horizon at us after six rolly days at sea. Part of the Cook Islands group, Palmerston Island was home to fifty-three people, all of whom were descendants or married to descendants of a single Englishman, William Marsters, who had three wives and twenty-one children. Today, his progeny are in their sixth generation, number in the many hundreds, and are scattered all over the Cook Islands and New Zealand.

Marsters, reverently called The Patriarch by his descendants, ruled his little empire with an iron will and established a male-dominated and hierarchical administrative structure that still survives on Palmerston – although not without dispute – a century after his death. Every family living on Palmerston, as well as every gravestone in the cemetery, shares the same last name. The island has no airstrip, and is visited by supply boats only three or four times a year. Its only visitors are yachties like us, whom they have the reputation of treating with unparalleled friendliness and hospitality.

When we arrived at the coral atoll – seven exquisite coral islands in a necklace seven miles wide and five miles long, enclosing a protected turquoise lagoon – a motorized skiff containing three smiling men and a boy waved us over and instructed us exactly where to plant our anchor. Two of the men had ample bellies showing through multiple holes in their well-worn T-shirts. One of them was Bob Marsters, our local host, whose full-time job was simply, in his words, to be friendly.

Palmerston Islanders compete for the privilege of being the first to escort an arriving yacht. During the sailing season, they scan the horizon with binoculars, and the first to see a new yacht claims it as his own. Then the family gets to host the yacht and its crew during its stay at the island. Only about fifty sailboats stopped at Palmerston each year, so competition for our attention was fierce.

Before we knew what was happening, Bob had whisked all of us ashore, introduced us to his wife and two daughters, was serving us refreshments, inviting us to dinner, and escorting us to the daily volley-ball game underway on a sandy court fringed with coconut palms.

Bob and his wife, Tupou, were friendly but reserved, but voluble little Taia, aged seven, was our instant friend and inseparable companion. Her smiling three-year-old sister, Monukoa, loved to be tickled and spoke shyly in the quietest of voices. I always cringed when I looked at her, because what remained of her teeth were only little brown stumps. Later, I learned that the children of the village were fed sweetened condensed milk from a bottle, and all the other young children's teeth looked just like Monukoa's.

On our first day, I joined in the volleyball game, grateful for some exercise after six days cooped up on the boat. The islanders loved volley-ball and played every afternoon, rain or shine, from 5:00 p.m. until dark. The most delightful thing was the way they giggled almost continuously throughout the game. They giggled when they made a mistake. They giggled when someone else made a mistake. They giggled when they scored, and they giggled when someone else scored. They giggled all the time. It was impossible not to join in.

One of the opposing players was an absolutely stunning young woman of about twenty. She was the picture of a Polynesian beauty, the kind you'd see on a calendar, with a willowy figure, long, shiny black hair, and a lovely face. When we were finally introduced, I couldn't help but blurt out, "You are the most beautiful woman I've ever seen."

Her eyes lit up in delight and surprise, as if no one had ever noticed her great beauty before. "I am?"

Later we were to learn why she had been so surprised: because of her slim, athletic frame, the other Polynesians considered her far too thin. Their ideal of feminine beauty was more Rubenesque, and they scornfully called this undiscovered pearl "the skinny one."

On our second day, Bob and Tupou invited us to lunch. Their house was a little three-room bungalow with concrete floors, unfinished wood-framed walls, and a corrugated tin roof. Although it had electricity – for ten hours each day – it had no running water. I saw no food on the shelves under the kitchen counter, no food of any kind other than what we ate. Bob's fishing boat had been out of commission for a year and a half, so his freezer was empty.

Nonetheless, Bob and Tupou put on an excellent feast for us: roast pork, papaya, rice, baked beans mixed with canned spaghetti, corned beef fried with onion, *toboi* (a kind of dumpling made from germinated coconut), and the rather astonishing blackened toothy head of a giant wahoo fish.

Over the next days, the one square mile of Palmerston Island became our personal playground. Every house was open to us, every doorway contained a friendly wave, and everyone we saw was our friend. In the company of the island's child population of ten, who, since they didn't attend school, were free to play all day, our kids ran all over collecting giant hermit crabs. Christopher hit it off well with our host family's two girls and another little girl named Pearl, and they ran around giggling with no interference from us.

We were befriended by a second village family, Bill Marsters and his companion, a lovely, plump young woman in her early twenties named Metua. Metua gathered us in her ample arms and made us her own, treating us to a nightly food extravaganza while refusing every offer of gifts in return. She threw together giant feasts consisting of chicken, crab, wahoo, parrotfish, rice, and doughnuts for about a dozen visitors and family members every night without apparent effort.

Not only did Metua invite us for supper every day, she also washed all our sheets and dirty clothes, she delivered freshly baked bread and doughnuts on a regular basis, and she even offered us the luxury of hot showers collected from rainwater and heated by the sun.

On the one evening when we declined her supper invitation, we were stunned when Metua prepared a take-out supper of breaded fillets of wahoo, fritters, and breadfruit and delivered it to us on *Northern Magic*. She categorically refused any attempt to give her gifts or repay her for all her hospitality. Finally, I managed to get her to accept a bottle of laundry detergent, but even that with difficulty. I also snuck her some Hershey bars, as well as some fabric I had intended for a tablecloth and napkins. Fortunately, Herbert was faring better than I at making a contribution and spent most of his days with the island's men, repairing a tractor, an ancient computer monitor, and various outboard motors.

Christopher and Metua hit it off famously, especially after he had a sleepover at her house. He spent almost every day at Metua's side, chatting inexhaustibly, as he always did, while they watched videos or she did our laundry. A few months later, Christopher confessed to me, "Mom, if you and Dad would ever die, I know where I would go. I'd go back to Palmerston. Metua would take care of me."

Our magical days on Palmerston Island raced by one after another – feasting, playing volleyball among the palm trees, combing the beach for giant clam shells, snorkeling, and observing all the other natural wonders of an unspoiled tropical island. We were, however, disturbed that the island's children did not go to school. We spent hours discussing these difficulties with Bill, who opened up the little schoolhouse for us and described the problems he had in attracting a Cook Islander to come to a backwater like Palmerston. It seemed to Herbert and me that many Canadian teachers would jump at the chance to spend a year or two in the idyllic surroundings of a South Pacific island. We promised Bill we'd do our best to find him a teacher for the kids.

The *Ottawa Citizen* agreed to publish an article I wrote about the situation, and for weeks afterwards, my sister Linda was flooded with e-mails from prospective teachers, some days receiving more than thirty requests. From our little boat far away in the Pacific, we communicated with these potential teachers by shortwave radio e-mail, answering their questions as best as we could. A few months later, a teacher from Ottawa was chosen to go to Palmerston to re-establish the little school there.

In the meantime, two other teachers from Ottawa visited the Cook Islands on a vacation and brought with them some school supplies. Their generosity was reported in the Cook Islands press. Much later, from Australia, I phoned the Palmerston representative in the Cook Islands government, who was delighted about the response and thought that some of the other applicants might be going to other outer islands that also needed teachers. All of this was very gratifying to us, the feeling that we had delivered on our promise and had done something to help the children of Palmerston. Although we heard later that the schoolhouse on Palmerston had burnt down, this didn't deter us from making a promise to ourselves to continue to offer help, and "pay forward" the hospitality others were so freely giving us. (The school is now being rebuilt.)

The men of Palmerston invited Herbert to participate in a ritual that takes place every year: bird picking. Bird *picking*? Yes. Every four weeks between June and September, the islanders head over to a nearby islet to collect nesting bosun birds for food. Bosun birds, large, handsome waterfowl with black and white spotted feathers, are protected everywhere else in the Cook Islands, but on Palmerston they remain an important food source. That year's young, fully grown but still flightless, are literally picked out of the trees, tossed in a pile on the beach, and put, screeching like cats, into sacks. The mothers also shriek in helpless rage, but there is no mercy for their offspring, who are noisy but stupid and make no effort to escape their captors.

The birds are brought in wheelbarrow-loads to a central location, where they sit quietly, awaiting their doom in a dignified fashion. Only if you approach too closely do they emit their unearthly feline scream. The birds are then divided up among all the families, an equal number for each person on the island. In this case, there were one and a half birds for each of sixty-two people, including the five in our family and four other visiting yachties.

We were concerned that, despite the birds' status as a threatened species, the islanders were culling all the young before they could reproduce. Several times, Herbert and I asked how the bosun birds were going to survive as a species if the islanders kept on taking all the unfledged birds every month. "It's not a problem," was the constant answer, delivered in wise and reassuring tones. "You see, we don't take the mother birds."

Our plan had been to stay until Sunday morning, go to church, partake of the farewell bosun bird feast to be held in our honour, and then leave for the three-day trip to the island of Niue. But we never got to taste the bosun birds that had been lovingly prepared for us. During the night before the feast, the wind began shifting in a dangerous direction. Not only was it now threatening to push us onto the reef, but as it swung us around, our anchor chain snagged on a coral head. With each wave, our chain jerked and grated against the coral, and we began to fear it might break.

After staying awake all night, we called the island by radio and informed them that we had no choice but to leave at first light. The only thing holding us back from leaving immediately was that we had loaned out all our videotapes to different families. Someone agreed to canvass the homes, collect the tapes, and bring them to our boat as soon as possible.

When a boatload of islanders finally appeared, they brought with them not only our videotapes but also a parting gift of two still-warm loaves of bread. As we handed over our own bag of gifts, my throat choked up unexpectedly, stopping me from speaking. These people, all of them, had been so kind, and so generous with sharing what little they had, that I didn't know what I could possibly say. Finally, I simply blew them a kiss while Herbert shook their hands. We motored away, out of danger but very sad to be leaving our many new friends, who waved as we left.

+

After Palmerston, we continued hopping our way across the Pacific, in passages of several days or a week each. In Niue (pronounced Nee-you-ay), where we spent six days, we discovered that Palmerston Islanders did not own the monopoly on South Pacific friendliness. Then we departed for Tonga, in company with three other boats. We formed a beautiful and stately caravan as we made our way back out into the ocean, sails billowing and spirits high.

They say that the definition of a race is any two sails on the horizon, and this was true now, even though no formal declaration was ever made. But as we four sailboats kept in touch with twice-daily radio sessions, you could just about hear the gnashing of teeth as we each reported our position and made our calculations as to who was ahead of whom. We were no match for the two speedy fibreglass boats, but the race of the steel boats was more of a match.

"Where are you?" Dee from *Axe Calibre* asked hopefully as we rounded the island of Vava'u after two days at sea. "We're only twenty-five miles away."

"Well, we're just circling around the north part of the island now," I answered, trying to keep any trace of a smirk out of my voice. "You're about four hours behind us." Later, I learned that when Tom on *Axe Calibre* heard this, he broke his pencil and spewed forth some choice seafaring words. We, on the other hand, tried to confine our jubilation to some quiet, dignified dancing and screaming.

Tonga was a cruisers' paradise. For several weeks we travelled from anchorage to anchorage, from island to island, encountering new mysteries and discoveries at each idyllic spot: giggling children, hospitable local people, feasts baked in underground ovens, a solemn Tongan wedding at which others sat on the grass so that we, as guests of honour, could sit at the head table. We also enjoyed watching baby octopuses, exploring underwater caves, investigating mysterious blowholes, and the companionship of other cruisers who, like us, were reliant on each other for friendship far away from home.

One night we went walking on the coral reef, lit only by a crackling, hissing torch, to hunt for clams. As we walked in the ankle-deep water, our footsteps activated the tiny, phosphorescent plankton that lived on the coral. Throwing down the torch with a big hiss, we saw in the perfect darkness that our feet were surrounded with brilliant twinkles of light. These sparkling underwater constellations echoed the real stars and planets blazing in the dark night sky above us, the Milky Way clearly visible as a shining arc reaching across the sky.

It was a magical sight, a magical night in Tonga. Only one of many.

8

Forced to Drink Muddy Sawdust Water

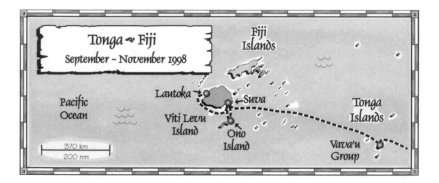

Tonga ~ Fiji
September - November 1998

Pacific Ocean

Fiji Islands

Lautoka

Suva

Viti Levu Island

Ono Island

Tonga Islands

Vava'u Group

370 km
200 nm

We set off from Tonga for Fiji on a windy, wavy day. Four hundred and fifty miles of ocean lay ahead. With the mainsail boomed out to starboard and the jib poled out to port, there was nothing to moderate the rolling motion that pushed us relentlessly from side to side. It was difficult to cook, eat, walk, or sleep. All we could do was hang on tight.

The rolling lasted the entire four days of our voyage, making all of us queasy and miserable. But at least we made a fast passage, and had we been an hour or two faster we would actually have reached the safety of Suva Harbour on the evening of our third day at sea. In late afternoon, however, it became clear we wouldn't make it before darkness fell, so we began to reduce speed. Our destination, the island of Viti Levu, was surrounded by a reef that, in places, extends a mile or two out, making it a dangerous place to approach. Just the week before, a sailboat had run badly aground on this same reef after having attempted to enter in darkness. We had no intention of sharing that fate, so, as much as we wanted a respite from the motion, we reduced sail to be sure of arriving in daylight.

We dropped both the main and the mizzen sails and furled in the jib until only a tiny handkerchief was left flying. Even still, we were making progress towards the reef at four knots and more. Without the big sails up, we had even more motion, rocking wildly back and forth so much we had to put leecloths on the beds to keep bodies from flying out. It was a long, long night.

Herbert decided during his watch to reel in a line he had been trolling, using a lure Jonathan had bought him for his birthday in Tahiti. As he pulled in the line, he felt some resistance. Judging from the pull, he surmised he had caught a medium-sized fish. He was surprised, there-fore, to meet the angry gaze of a large dorado at the end of his line. In that proud he-man voice of the successful hunter, Herbert called me on deck to help pull in his prize, but my help was not necessary; the dorado gave so little resistance we realized it must have been dragging behind us for many hours.

Although it was three in the morning, we roused Michael and Jonathan, and we all watched as Herbert pulled the rainbow-coloured fish on board, using a flashlight for illumination. We had to hang on for dear life as the boat rolled and the fish struggled. As tall as Christopher, the dorado was a magnificent specimen.

I have to confess that I do have considerable empathy for any fish caught on a line, even a big brutish dorado with sharp teeth and a Neanderthal brow. Secretly, I always root for the fish. I'm the first one to grab onto any excuse to return it to the water. For years, I've been the butt of many a family joke for my unwillingness to kill even a spider. All this to say that I didn't stay around to see how Herbert put the poor keel-hauled thing out of its misery.

Finally, daylight broke, and the island of Viti Levu was in sight. Although the kids were fresh as usual in spite of the dorado episode, Herbert and I were bone-weary.

Herbert was hand steering and having trouble planting his feet, because the carcass of that huge fish filled most of the cockpit. Its large glassy eye stared up reproachfully at its murderer. Its increasingly powerful odour filled the cockpit and wafted down into the cabin as we made our approach into Suva Harbour, adding its own pungent note to the haze of our fatigue. At last, we made it in through the reef. We were happy we had waited until daylight to do so, as the approach was riddled with shoals and wrecks. By the time we dropped anchor and finished our formalities, we smelled more like a fishing trawler than a cruising yacht. Later that day, our fridge broke and we ended up giving most of that dorado away.

To our delight, we discovered that Fijians are among the friendliest people we had met – and that is really saying something after our five months of cruising in the friendly South Pacific.

We found Bobby Kumar, a Fijian of Indian descent, tending his fresh fruit stand at the bustling Suva marketplace. A nice-looking man in his late thirties with a friendly, open face, he struck up a conversation with me as I rested in front of his stall. Half of Fiji's population is made up of people of Indian ancestry, descendants of indentured labourers who came over to work in the sugarcane fields a century ago. Fijian Indians have clung to their Indian culture and now run most of the small businesses in Fiji, despite being legally discriminated against in their own country.

Bobby and his beautiful wife, Niru, were successful and proud of it. "The Fijians don't work as hard as we do," he explained. "They want to have Saturday and Sunday off. We work seven days a week. Why should we waste a day resting?"

As a reward for their industry, the Kumars and their three children lived in a comfortable three-bedroom home. The Kumars seemed full of pity for us, living in such confined conditions on the boat. Niru confided to me that her thirteen-year-old daughter, Norris, had felt sorry to see us walking through the market, carrying a load of bags just like ordinary people.

"You'll see when they come over," Niru had explained to her daughter, "that they *are* just like ordinary people."

"But they must have such a fine house in Canada," Norris had persisted. "They must be very rich."

Our standard of living in Canada was in fact the object of intense curiosity. Did we have a washing machine? A dishwasher? How big was our house? We spent many hours comparing our life with theirs. They pored over our photos and books about Canada.

As if to give us a complete picture of both sides of Fijian society, we were also befriended by a native Fijian family. We met Kasa, a handsome woman in her thirties, while the kids were horsing around on a rope swing on a nearby hillside. Just as we were leaving, Kasa came running out of her house with a papaya from her tree, shouting for us to stop.

She breathlessly handed me her gift and asked if we would come by again another day. Her husband, she said, would really want to meet us. Without setting a time, we agreed to return on Sunday for a visit. That Sunday, the Kumars were going to meet us at 1:00 p.m. to go to the beach, so at 10:00 a.m. the kids and I ran up the hill to spend the morning with Kasa. Herbert had stayed behind to work on the fridge.

When we arrived, Kasa was busy preparing a traditional Fijian feast for us. The underground oven was already smoking, and Kasa said everything would be ready for one o'clock. I was horrified. They were going to all this trouble and we had no way of cancelling our other invitation for the same time. Kasa was gracious when I explained the situation. She simply said, "That's okay. You don't need to stay to eat it. I'll pack the food all up, and you can take it to the beach with you."

There was no way we were going to do that. The only choice was to return for Herbert and eat as quickly as we could, even if it meant keeping the Kumars waiting.

I sat with Kasa on a woven straw mat as she deftly prepared a mixture of tomato, onions, canned corned beef, and coconut juice, all wrapped up in large taro leaves and aluminium foil to bake in the underground *lovo* oven. Sheets of newspaper protected the mat from food drippings. She prepared a fish the same way, stuffing it with mashed garlic and fresh ginger root.

Her husband, Joe, appeared, a large, handsome man with feet fully twice the length and width of my own, muscularly built like the rugby player he was. Together, they buried the meal on hot coals under a blanket of banana leaves and covered it with earth. As we waited for it to bake, the kids and I returned to the boat and granted our long-suffering captain a temporary reprieve, time off for good behaviour.

The meal, unearthed at 12:45 p.m., was delicious. Everything was eaten Fiji-style, sitting on the floor and without cutlery, something we were by now adept at doing.

The living room of Kasa and Joe's simple but clean three-room home was unadorned by furniture. The small concrete house was provided to Joe as one of the perks of his job as a prison guard. Kasa worked as a receptionist in a government ministry. As we sat, cross-legged, on straw mats rimmed with colourful wool fringes, using our fingers to scoop up fish baked in taro leaves, I realized that Kasa and Joe were probably a pretty typical middle-class civil servant family. Coming from a government town like Ottawa, it made for an interesting comparison.

＋

Before leaving Suva for Ono Island, our next stop in Fiji, we went to the fresh market and invested thirteen dollars in a tangled bunch of dirty old roots wrapped in newspaper. We chose those roots carefully, paying a little extra to be sure of getting the best. This was kava, the root of the pepper plant. According to ancient custom, it must be presented by visitors to the village chief in a ceremony known as *sevusevu*.

Kava is common to the people of Tonga, Fiji, and Samoa, where the precious root is pounded and mixed with water to make a non-alcoholic, tranquilizing drink. When we arrived at Ono Island, armed with our special kava offering, we waited for someone from the village to invite us ashore. Our host ended up being a middle-aged man named Kimi, who brought us into his home and explained the rules of Fijian village etiquette.

In Polynesia I had already, long before, given up shorts for a more modest long skirt. I always felt I'd blend in better and make friends more easily if I dressed as closely as possible to the local customs. Other cruisers had told me the long skirt wasn't necessary, but Kimi looked approvingly at my attire and said, "That is beautiful. This is the proper way of dressing in a village. You will have no problems here."

Later that day, we gathered in the house of the chief for our *sevusevu* ceremony. Like every other house we saw in the village, this one was adorned with many large pictures of Princess Diana. My own name, being so similar to hers, made me very popular all over the South Pacific.

We sat in a circle with the village elders and handed Kimi our offering of kava root. He accepted it almost reverently and placed it carefully on the mat in front of him. He made a lengthy speech in Fijian, in which he explained to the others why we were there and requested our acceptance into the village. Then, clapping his hands three times, he handed the roots over to the other men in the circle. Each of the village elders handled our offering of roots in turn, making a short acceptance speech and clapping his hands as he handed them to the next. When all had signalled their acceptance, hands were clapped in unison once more. Everyone turned to us with smiles and welcomed us into their village. We were now one of them.

We moved over to the home of Rachel and her husband, a friendly giant of a man named Romeo. Romeo retrieved a large, heavy pot called a *tambili*, placed our kava in it, and, heaving a long, iron rod like a huge pestle, began pulverizing it. Watching him at this job, I understood why Fijian men were so muscular. The peeling skin on Romeo's dark brown legs looked white and ashy, symptoms of an excessive fondness for kava. I asked him about it, and he nodded and grinned.

After half an hour of hard work, Romeo had reduced the gnarled and twisted roots into a fine brown powder. If I hadn't known better, I might have called it sawdust. Now, Herbert followed the men into a bamboo shelter in the centre of the village. I stayed behind with Rachel while the boys played with their Fijian counterparts.

The powdered kava, Herbert later reported, was placed in a small bag and immersed in room-temperature water in a large, elegantly carved wooden drinking bowl, the *tanoa*. It made a muddy-looking tea. After Romeo judged the mixture to be perfect (and complimented Herbert on the excellent quality of the root), he made a loud speech in Fijian to the half dozen other men who had joined in. Romeo ran his hands around the rim of the *tanoa* and clapped three times. This was followed by more ceremonial clapping and statements of approval. Then Romeo filled half a coconut shell with the mixture and handed it ceremoniously to Herbert, the guest of honour, to drink.

We'd read that the polite way to drink kava is to guzzle it down in one slurp. Herbert did that manfully. As he finished his cup, the men all made three loud claps and joyfully shouted "*Matha!*," "Empty!" Then the cup was refilled and passed around the circle.

Herbert had meant to take one cup politely and then decline further offers. But his drinking companions absolutely refused to drink unless the guest of honour started each round. So Herbert continued unhappily chug-a-lugging the muddy sawdust water while I, who could hear all the enthusiastic clapping and *matha!*-ing from my spot outside on the grass, began speculating how long he would hold out.

It took half an hour. Herbert quietly exited the shelter and tip-toed up behind me. "I need you to rescue me," he whispered in my ear. "They won't let me stop drinking, and if I have any more, I'm going to throw up."

I excused myself from Rachel and respectfully entered the male enclave to see what was going on. Jonathan joined me. He was worn out from playing tag with a dozen village children, who, in their excitement, had made it rather tough on him; whenever Jon was "it," he remained "it" no matter who else he tagged. Even if he was not "it," the entire gang chased only him.

Under the bamboo shelter, we found our poor captain being forced to guzzle yet another cup of kava. He threw me a look of intense gratitude. Jon and I sat down in the circle, the ceremony began again, and I was treated to my first taste of the drink. Yup, if it looks like sawdust, and smells like sawdust, it tastes like sawdust, too. The men offered Jonathan a cup, and Jon, to my everlasting admiration, took a hearty gulp. After swallowing, he smiled and said, enthusiastically, that it tasted good. That brave boy actually took a second big swallow before handing me his cup to finish.

After only my second cup, my tongue and lips began to feel numb. My mouth tasted like I'd been licking a sawmill floor. I could hardly believe Herbert had managed to hold down what was now seven coconut shells full of the detestable brew. Finally, we were able to woozily beg off and leave the rest of the grog to people who actually appreciated it. The woody aftertaste the kava left in our mouths was noticeable even the next day. I did, however, make the important discovery that Mars Bars are an excellent antidote.

Thankfully, we managed to spend several more days at our village of sixty people without running into any more kava. Instead, we went on long mountainous hikes, collected enormous quantities of shells, went scuba diving in a "blue hole" forty metres deep inside the coral reef and full of a wonderland of coral. We wanted to climb the mountaintop for a view of the village below, but this, our host Kimi sternly admonished us, was not permitted.

"One village woman climbed up there," he stated gravely, "and when she came back down, her leg was ruined and she could no longer walk. It is *tabu* to go there. That is a holy place, where the spirits of our ancestors live." If we went up there he could not be held responsible for the consequences.

The men of the village had gotten wind of the fact that they were in the presence of Herb "The Tool Man" Stuemer. Herbert ended up carrying out a roving two-day radio-repair marathon. His most interesting project was a malfunctioning tape deck that, upon opening, proved to house twenty three-centimetre long, very perturbed cockroaches. As they scuttled madly around looking for a new home, I leapt madly around, too, trying to make sure that none of them made that new home inside my backpack.

The children made dozens of friends, each in his own way. Christopher's tried and true chase-and-tickle method was a success as always; Jonathan persevered in his brave attempts to play tag; and Michael engaged the older kids with his rubber-faced Jim Carrey imitations, which, even if not understood, were certainly appreciated. We made more friends, too, when many of the village's men unexpectedly came swimming over to *Northern Magic*, hoping for a tour. After they were finished, most of the village ladies arrived in small boats and got to satisfy their curiosity as well. Finally, we managed to leave Ono Island, and after a few more stops in other parts of Fiji, we were ready to continue our long journey across the Pacific.

9

Life and Death in a Force Ten Storm

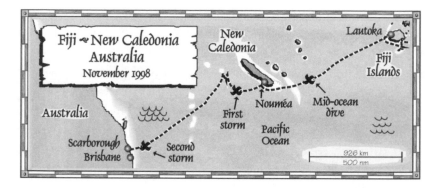

We'd spent a month in Fiji, making many friends and having wonderful new experiences on one hand, and racking our brains trying to fix an ever-lengthening list of mechanical problems on the other: our alternator had given up and the spare didn't have the same capacity; the watermaker broke down, necessitating strict rationing; and, of course, the refrigerator had packed it in. But every day spent in Fiji brought us one day closer to hurricane season, and our route west was taking us directly along the path of those destructive super-storms. We needed to get going.

We began the week-long journey to the island of New Caledonia, about half way between Fiji and Australia, on the first of November, a month in which early hurricanes are known to form. For the first few days, our chief problem was not too much wind, but, rather, a lack of it. *Northern Magic* ambled along at a leisurely pace of about three knots, heedless of our urgent desire to get out of harm's way. Since our autopilot was still on the casualty list, Herbert and I, spelled occasionally by the kids, were forced to spend twenty-four hours a day standing at the wheel. We spent many stimulating hours staring at the sea and then the compass. Sometimes, for variety, we stared at the compass and then at the sea.

Herbert attempted to jury-rig the autopilot – soldering, gluing, and wiring together the broken motor parts – but none of his inventive solutions lasted more than a few hours. Since the wind showed no signs of picking up, we became resigned to spending an exhausting passage this way.

After three days, our prayers were answered. The wind increased, the wind vane (which hadn't been useful with so little wind) kicked in again, and we were liberated. For one delightful day we were able to make ourselves comfortable inside the cabin again rather than standing out exposed to the elements.

It was on my shift late the next night that the wind started really blowing. I had a nervous, edgy feeling, and the grim line of dark clouds ahead on the horizon didn't alleviate my anxiety. I remembered how, the day before, I had pointed out thin cirrus clouds in the sky, called mares' tails, to the kids. I had explained that they were often harbingers of a storm.

It was one in the morning. I had just finished brushing my teeth and was ready to wake Herbert for his shift when I heard the sails banging around. I put my head outside and discovered that the wind had died completely. We were wallowing in a dead calm. That ominous dark line of cloud was now very near, obscuring the full moon. Our mainsail had backwinded. We were going nowhere. As I woke Herbert, I giggled nervously and said that I was turning things over to him in a bit of a mess.

We went outside together to try to sort things out. No sooner had we jumped into the cockpit than the calm was shattered. The wind, which had been northerly, suddenly returned with a blast from the southwest. Although Herbert began reorganizing the sails into their proper positions, the wind grew rapidly stronger until, within a few minutes, it was clear we would have to drop them entirely. Ironically, after all our days of painfully slow progress, all we could think about now was slowing ourselves down.

It was 3:30 a.m. by the time I finally got to bed, but now there was no blessed sleep to embrace me. The motion of the boat was violent. The shift of wind direction, combined with the sudden gale, produced steep five-metre waves that were close together and battered us mercilessly from all angles. We staggered from one brutal slap to another, heading almost directly against the wind. *Northern Magic*'s decks were completely awash. Her bow was buried as it beat into wave after wave.

From my bunk in the forward portion of the boat, all I could do was brace myself against the wall. Each time we reached the peak of a particularly steep wave, we would fall off it with a sickening drop. I passed the rest of the night without sleeping for more than a few minutes at a time.

At 7:00 a.m., the children began waking up. Christopher and I staggered to Michael's narrow, vacant bunk in the navigation station and lay there together, hugging. I instructed the older two boys not to leave their bunks. Water dripped onto our mattress and our lower bodies from the hatch above. Every few minutes, I had to stick my head out of it to make sure there weren't any ships in the vicinity, although this was largely useless since the pelting rain had reduced the visibility to almost zero.

By the middle of the morning, the gale had abated. The kids were now able to sit up and play computer games, and I was able to make Kraft Dinner for lunch. In fact, by the time Herbert woke up from his much-needed nap, the wind had reduced substantially and we were able to raise the mainsail again, helping to reduce the motion. We all sat around, smiling and congratulating ourselves. We had been through several violent squalls before, but they had never lasted long enough to kick up ugly waves like these.

One of Herbert's private miseries during the gale had been an excruciating toothache. When the pain had become unbearable, he had actually fashioned and installed his own tooth filling using some temporary filling material we had in our ship's medicine chest. His repair worked, completely eliminating the pain. It even held together for the next five months. The dentist he eventually visited in Australia was amazed at it, commenting that he'd never seen a homemade filling before, much less one fashioned in the middle of the ocean, on a boat bucking wildly in a gale.

Using the radar had almost completely drained our batteries, so Herbert prepared to turn on the engine and motor for a few hours. As soon as the motor went into gear, however, there was a strange shuddering. Some equally alarming utterances began emanating from the cockpit. I rushed outside to discover that we now faced a new problem. Unnoticed by us, a jib sheet (the rope that controls the jib, or headsail), had washed overboard. When Herbert had engaged the propeller, the thick rope had been sucked right into it. It was now hopelessly tangled. Unless he could somehow work it free, we would have to complete this trip without a motor.

Herbert tried all the obvious things to get it loose, but to no avail. Wearily, we put our heads together to decide what was to be done. I thought we should continue sailing and find ourselves a little island behind which to anchor and free the prop in safety. But Herbert believed there was no choice but to free it right where we were. Ahead of us was a nasty maze of coral reefs complicated by a tricky set of unpredictable currents. This was exactly the wrong kind of place to be without a motor. The wind turning against us at the wrong time could spell the end. No, he would have to dive under the boat and untangle the rope right here. The boys and I were queasy about our captain diving under a moving boat in the middle of the ocean, but Herbert could not be deterred.

I wanted him to do it with a scuba tank, but he vetoed that idea, too, not wanting to be hampered by bulky gear while getting in and out of the pitching boat. We hove to, by backwinding the jib and jamming the steering wheel in such a way that the boat would stand still. By now the waves were only a metre and a half high, but still big enough to bang an unprotected human against a steel hull pretty badly. Or slice him neatly open on a sharp propeller. Even hove to, the boat was still making leeway at a couple of knots, so we tied a rope around Herbert's middle and cleated it up to make sure we wouldn't lose him. Before diving, he climbed into the water, and Michael and I practised hauling him up to the side of the boat to make sure we could do it.

Then he was gone, and only the drag on the line in my hands confirmed that he was still there, suspended over a kilometre of dark water. Who knows what kind of evil creatures were down there looking up? The boys and I scanned the horizon nervously for signs of a menacing fin. Herbert was dangling from that rope just like a large, juicy piece of bait.

Up and down he came and went, gasping for air for a few seconds before returning to his work. After his third try, he clambered back on board, breathing hard. His shoulder was scraped open. At first it looked like his whole arm was covered in blood, but it turned out to be mainly red anti-fouling paint. The jib sheet wasn't fully freed, but he had managed to unwind it five times. Back on deck, shivering as much with nervousness as cold, Herbert wound the line around the winch and, with superhuman effort, finally managed to unsnarl the rest. The end of the rope was frayed and much the worse for the wear. So was our captain. But the dirty deed was done, our motor was back in service, and all we had to do now was haul our weary bodies over this unfriendly ocean for four more days.

+

After sailing tantalizingly close by the southernmost island of Vanuatu, we finally spotted the main island of New Caledonia. It is the fourth largest island in the South Pacific, an incredibly beautiful land whose abundance of minerals gives it a stunning reddish hue. Its rosy hills are dotted with bright green stiletto-shaped pine trees, making it quite unlike any of the other South Pacific islands we visited.

Our destination was the capital, Nouméa, a surprisingly cosmopolitan and very French city. There, we found ourselves not in Melanesia, but in the French Riviera. In the streets of Nouméa, most of the faces were white, the French spoken was Parisian, and the thin, carefully made up and well-coiffed women wore tiny, body-conscious mini-skirts and high heels. Elegant fashion boutiques and restaurants lined the streets. The long, tree-lined parks with fountains would have looked quite at home in Paris. Even the outdoor fruit market was classy.

We couldn't afford to buy anything in New Caledonia other than pineapples and baguettes. Even still, it felt like a vacation, with its clean streets, well-stocked stores, and a cultured veneer. We attended a sculpture festival that featured native artwork, and laughed to see the local children dance in traditional Polynesian style, not to the powerful beat of native drums, but to rock music. I'll never forget the little beflowered girls, looking, just like the native girls of Tonga or Tahiti with their long dark hair and grass skirts, gyrating their hips to the rhythm of "Come on baby, do the locomotion!" Somehow, though, this seemed perfectly in sync with the reality of New Caledonia.

All of us needed the chance to recuperate and prepare ourselves for our coming journey to Australia, but none more than Herbert. Already exhausted by having to spend his whole precious month in Fiji buried in repairs, Herbert was going through a real down period in which he agonized over all the other malfunctions that seemed to be cropping up faster than he could fix them. The storm on the last passage, and his mid-ocean dive to free the propeller, had really got to him, already weighed down as he was by the coming hurricane season and by an ever-lengthening list of repairs. Autopilot, alternator, watermaker, bilge pump, toilet, a complete exterior paint job, boom, exhaust system, ripped sails, and now even a failed video camera were only the beginning of his list, which, like Jacob Marley's chain, was getting heavier and heavier with each day.

All this prevented Herbert from really relaxing and enjoying our stay in New Caledonia. If it wasn't repairs, he was contemplating storms and hurricanes, studying weather charts carefully each day and trying to pick a good weather window in which to make our final sprint to Australia. The weather situation did look pretty messy, with nasty fronts marching their way regularly and inexorably across our intended path. After our last encounter with bad weather, we didn't want to go through that again too soon. One mistake in judgement, one important piece of equipment failure, or a simple misreading of a weather chart, could cost us our lives.

✦

On November 16, our weather window appeared. Today was the day. Nine hundred nautical miles separated us from Australia, where we would be safe from the cyclone season that was about to start.

As we set out, we felt a little nervous, but relieved to finally be getting this passage over with. We sailed with almost no wind for the first day, and all night the lights of New Caledonia remained in sight. By morning we had made only twenty or thirty miles, and our new position on that big Pacific Ocean chart was not even worth noting.

On the third day something ominous began to show up on the weather charts and in e-mail messages from my dad, who, as usual, was serving as our personal weather forecaster. Some mild lows floating around south of us had done something we hadn't predicted, coalescing into one massive low-pressure system. The barometer began falling. The weather forecast began talking about a "significant depression." Soon, we had not too little wind, but too much. It was coming directly from the west, where we had to go.

At this point, about two hundred miles west of New Caledonia, we had a choice to make. It was impossible to head into the westerly gale that was building, so we were forced to abandon our route and run either south or north. Normally, we would have gone south, since Brisbane lay to the southwest. Instead we chose north. Even if it meant taking longer to reach Australia, going north, we figured, would take us away from the centre of the system. The next days would show whether we had made the right choice.

By nightfall the winds had grown even stronger. As the system to our south turned from a gale into a full-fledged storm, the winds around us strengthened to forty-five knots, creating steep, high waves and an increasing swell. The violence of our beating into these waves brought on the worst attack of seasickness I had ever experienced. Even Herbert succumbed, being laid flat for the first time ever. Only the kids, tucked safely into their beds, were immune. How they ever slept I don't know.

After a long, miserable day of battling the storm, I plotted our position and was shocked to discover how far north we had been pushed. Because of the way New Caledonia tilts to the west, as we headed north we found ourselves drawing closer and closer to its northern tip. At the same time, we were considerably farther away from Brisbane than we had been two days before. By now the depression was spewing off storm force winds within five hundred miles of its revolving centre. At the beginning, we had been only two hundred miles away from the vortex, but since it was moving southeast at the same time as we ran northwest, we were now on the outer edge of its fury. We received a disturbing message that another sailboat just two hundred miles to the southwest had been dismasted and abandoned. We didn't know it then, but two people had died on that boat when it had rolled 360 degrees and been torn apart.

So, our northerly route was taking us out of immediate danger. It was, however, putting us on a collision course with a set of mid-ocean reefs. We simply couldn't continue on this path. Just before it got dark, we braved the howling winds and tacked the boat around, heading south and back towards the centre of the storm. Several times it crossed our minds to simply turn around and head back to Nouméa. But somehow we couldn't bring ourselves to admit that we had gone through all this for nothing.

Although the winds had calmed down now to only about thirty-five knots, the waves were still sickeningly steep. And we had something new to contend with. All around us, dark thunderheads roamed, sometimes directly overhead, sometimes to one side or another. We tried to dodge these squalls as best as we could, but when one hit, the winds would suddenly pick up by ten knots or more and we would be viciously pelted by rain.

To complicate things further, our engine had begun overheating. Herbert, who was prostrate with vomiting, dizzy, and weaker than he had ever been before, was faced with the prospect of working head down in the stinking engine room while the boat slammed and rolled in the waves. That was a sure-fire recipe for nausea at the best of times, and in these conditions almost unthinkable. So we waited for two days, fighting the storm, our batteries draining and our fridge slowly warming, until things had quieted down enough to attempt a repair.

Squalls and evil dark clouds with black horizontal lines were still all around us as Herbert finally summoned up the resolve to face the broken engine. We were down to a bare minimum of battery power, unable to use even our lights at night. He opened up a hatch in the floor of our salon to expose the engine room and got to work. I hovered around, ready to hand him tools.

Finally, his face flushed and sweaty, he asked me to turn on the motor from the cockpit and rev it up a bit to see if it was cooling. As I clambered into the cockpit, I was shocked to see a particularly fast moving black border low in the sky just ahead. As I watched, I saw it was a racing line of wind and rain. In the next instant it hit.

The wind from this squall line was like nothing I had ever felt before. It came upon us like a line of charging stallions. Instantly, we were blown right over at an obscene angle. We had both our jib and our reefed mainsail up, and with the wind vane still trying to hold our course, our mast was pressed right down, close to the seething, roiling surface of the ocean. Water roared up over our gunwales and to my horror continued rushing up until it was actually on top of our lower cabin roof. All the portholes on the starboard side of the boat were under half a metre of water. If any of them had been open, the ocean would now be flowing freely into the boat.

My red-hot priority was the wide-open hatch through which I had just come. The tumult of water was boiling and licking right at its lip. One more degree of tilt, and hundreds upon hundreds of litres of water would rush unimpeded into that gaping mouth. In that instant, for the first time on this trip, a sudden vision of us being forced to take to our life raft leapt unbidden into my mind.

Banishing the thought, I yelled at the top of my lungs to Herbert, not sure if he could hear me over the louder screaming of the wind. I didn't know it, but the sudden lurch to starboard had slammed the heavy engine compartment hatch down on his back as he was standing under it. He certainly knew, even without my screaming, that something was very wrong.

Tearing my eyes away from the gaping maw of the open hatch, I quickly disengaged the wind vane to take manual control of the steering. My first thought was to steer the boat so the wind was behind us. That would stop us from heeling over and also reduce the wind's apparent speed, since we would be going with it instead of against it. But no matter how hard I pulled on the steering wheel, I was not strong enough to counteract the force of the wind. Twenty tons of steel boat wanted to point upwind. I tried for five or ten seconds until there was nothing to do but head into the blow instead.

By now Herbert had clambered into the cockpit. Michael was peering wide-eyed out of the lower hatch. We yelled for him to close both hatches and make sure all the inside windows were shut. There was a look of pure terror on his face as he saw the water boiling up on the deck right under his nose. He slammed the hatch shut and ran to check each of the crazily-tilted starboard side portholes. Of the children, he alone appreciated the nature of the crisis upon us. This was the first time I knew for sure on this trip that he was afraid. As soon as he was done checking windows, he lay, quaking, in his bed. He said nothing to his brothers about the fact that all he had seen through all our starboard-side windows was water.

At the same time as I began trying to steer us into the wind, Herbert released the jib sheet. These two actions had the effect of both turning and righting us immediately. The danger of flooding was over as quickly as it had come. Our jib began flogging violently, however, slamming around and bashing into the stays. Only a few minutes of this and it would be shredded to bits. Herbert manned the winch and struggled to furl in the jib, all the while praying it would hold together until he was done.

That accomplished, he had somehow to drop the mainsail. This was a much more precarious manoeuvre, since it meant leaving the relative safety of the cockpit. Herbert snapped on a safety harness and, attaching himself to a steel line that went around the bow of the boat, began making his way to the sail. But the harness attachment on the starboard side somehow disengaged itself as he scrambled forward, and he was forced to return to the cockpit. Re-attaching himself to the port side jackline, he managed to lurch his way along. But from the port side he wasn't as well positioned to take down the mainsail and found it impossible to wrestle it completely down.

While he was at work, my job was to try to hold the boat on a steady course into the wind, but not so much that the boat would tack and send the main boom slamming over into Herbert. It took all my power to hold her on course.

The squall was still blasting us at full intensity, the rain pelting down, shooting into our bodies like steel needles, sharp and cold. We were both dressed only in T-shirts and shorts, and in seconds we were drenched and freezing. Between the cold, the exertion, and the adrenalin coursing through my body, my arms and legs began to tremble until they were shaking so badly I could hardly hold the wheel. My right leg, which took most of the force of bracing my body against the downward side of the cockpit, was tapping so furiously I had trouble supporting myself on it.

How much time passed in that cockpit that way? Five minutes? Fifteen? Somehow it was all just a blur. All I know is that at some point Herbert managed to get the sail down and we found ourselves braced there in the cold, penetrating rain, shaking and huddling together in the cockpit in a mixture of terror and relief. Somehow we realized that with this squall and the storm of the previous two days we were passing perhaps our first real test as sailors.

Within minutes after returning inside, however, there was a new problem to cope with. Unbeknownst to us, the alternator was malfunctioning. We had no idea anything was wrong until Herbert opened the engine compartment for the routine turning off of a valve and happened to notice a very bright light inside. The light he was seeing was created by red-hot alternator wires. They could have burst into an engine fire at any moment.

Once again Herbert was forced into the engine room, as sick and as exhausted as he was, to replace the alternator. It was our spare that had given out, so he re-installed the higher capacity alternator that he had just finished fixing. Throughout the rest of that troubled passage, we had problems with that large alternator, chewing through fan belts and making a screaming sound every time we used a lot of power. It seemed our troubles, our endless hours of fear and misery, just wouldn't end.

✦

By the end of Day Five, the storm was still not willing to relinquish its grip. We were again heading north and once more nearing those same reefs. We turned the boat south a scant twenty miles west of where we had tacked back the day before. It was sickening to think of how difficult the past twenty-four hours had been, and yet all we had gained for our suffering was a pathetic twenty miles.

Through the early hours of Day Six, we virtually retraced our path of the day before. But the cause of all our troubles was now moving well to the southeast of us. By the middle of the day, the winds finally dropped below gale force, and soon we were able to resume a southwest track. We had been at sea six days, three of them in a storm. We were closer to New Caledonia than we had been before the storm started.

By Day Eight, about the time we had originally expected to be making a joyous landfall in Australia, we were instead carefully creeping through a set of banks and reefs only halfway to our destination. As we threaded our way through, nervous about the danger of running into the half-hidden mid-ocean Kelso Reef, we both felt full of unaccountable tension.

We had hardly eaten or slept since the storm had begun five days before.

Many a time we wished we could just let our little ship drift so we could get some rest. But that was impossible. We still had many days to go before we were safe, with the probability of encountering another storm increasing with each passing day. Herbert remarked, as we puddled our slow way through, that he felt just like the unfortunate bosun birds of Palmerston Island, sitting helplessly on the ground until they were picked up, thrown into bags, and carried off to their doom. All they could do was scream.

Days passed. We were tired, dog-tired, unable to recover from the trauma of the storm, because we were stuck in the cockpit hand steering day and night. There wasn't enough wind to sail, so our wind vane was useless. We were still two days away from Australia, on Day Ten of our final, stormy passage of the South Pacific, when we received our first inkling that more trouble lay ahead.

Word that another storm awaited us first came in the form of an Australian small-craft warning passed on to us by my father. Dad e-mailed us that we could expect to get a "wet and rolly ride." Then a few hours later, thinking he had better not let us be deceived by the flippant tone of that message, he sent a more strongly worded warning. It was perhaps just as well that we didn't know exactly what was coming.

There was a depression just a hundred miles west of us, directly on our path. This time there was no escape; we would have to force our way right through the centre of the storm. We felt fragile and nervous, physically and mentally tired and desperately anxious for our ordeal to end. Still two hundred miles, and now another trial, separated us from safety.

We calculated that we were likely to approach the Australian coast during darkness the following night. We had never approached a strange harbour at night, and doing so during a storm was totally out of the question. We therefore made the painful but necessary decision to heave to, or stop the boat, so that we could time our arrival for early morning two days later. Although we wanted nothing more than to arrive as soon as possible, instead we bobbed in place like a sitting duck, waiting, not knowing what sort of misery the next day might bring.

It was a calm night, a beautiful night. Hard to believe bad weather was on its way. While the boys and I admired the beautiful orange sunset in the cockpit, we picked up Australian newscasts on our radio. They spoke of a huge storm, of the cancellation of professional sports events, of warnings for people to stay home, of chaos. Herbert and I grabbed snatches of sleep.

Next morning those spectacular orange heavens had been replaced by a sky that was ugly, ominous, and grey. In order to cook some fried eggs for Christopher's breakfast, I turned the wheel over to Michael. I could see that I didn't have much time, for there was an all-too-familiar black line hanging low on the horizon. That line looked like grim, pursed black lips.

It wasn't ten minutes after I returned to the cockpit that the first squall hit. Our jib and small mizzen sail were both raised and hauled in tight. It was important that we not be knocked over by a blast of wind as we had been before. As soon as I could feel the wind jump in force, I turned *Northern Magic* north so that we were propelled along with the squall. Although conditions in the cockpit were miserable, with the pelting rain and whipping wind, the strategy was successful, and we were able to weather that first squall safely.

The sky all around us had now turned into a witches' cauldron. "Bubble, bubble, toil and trouble" popped into my head. Shakespeare himself never imagined a more sinister sky, nor evoked a sense of foreboding greater than mine as I looked helplessly at the maelstrom surrounding our small floating home, all alone in a dark and violent sea.

Even if our weather reports hadn't said that the storm was spawning directly over us, we would have known it from the furious activity overhead. Low dark clouds with black borders swept from south to north; solid grey sheets of rain reached down to the water; huge thunderheads sprouted, blossomed, and towered ominously, like mushroom clouds from a nuclear bomb. Black cloud formations rose and reached out over us like giant hands ready to crush us. Even the sun hid, as if in fear of these evil storm lords clashing in their battleground. Standing exposed in the open cockpit of a tiny boat, this clash of titans was an awesome and fearful sight. We looked and felt very small.

Squall after squall came racing across the water. The wind had picked up to thirty-five knots, and each time a squall rampaged by, it increased to forty-five knots, a shrieking hard blast. I continued steering around and through the squalls as best as I could, minimizing the strain on the boat and the sails. The squalls would come fiercely and last half an hour or so, during which time we would be pelted with slanting rain. The waves rose from three or four metres to five metres high or more. Once I really got in the rhythm of steering with them, I actually felt a sense of power and exhilaration, a keen awareness of being alive. Everything depended upon my concentration on my duties. Often, it took all my physical power to keep the boat on course, leaning my entire body onto the wheel. In this way we withstood perhaps ten squalls.

Then, as we sailed through the dark curtain of the final squall, to my amazement the sky behind it was blue. The rain stopped. The wind calmed down. I was able to take my hands off the wheel for the first time in five hours. My right shoulder ached, and I had no sensation at all in my right thumb, which had been gripping the wheel for hours – for days, for weeks – with all its might. I stepped into the navigation station down below, where Herbert was resting on Michael's bunk. Although exhausted, I felt proud and happy. I had brought us through the worst, and Australia was only sixty miles away.

Herbert, who again, for only the second time in his life, had been laid flat by seasickness, sat up looking feverish. His head was hot, yet his limbs were shivering under a thick blanket. For half an hour I rested beside him.

Then I felt a strange change in the rhythm of the waves. I stuck my head out of the hatch and couldn't believe what I saw.

Outside, that pleasant blue sky had been swallowed by a hideous black and grey tumult of clouds, a maelstrom of unbelievable propor-tions. Before my eyes, a solid white wall materialized and began gallop-ing across the frothing surface of the water. It was heading directly towards us: a squall line of an intensity unequalled by any we had met before. As I turned the boat to run with it, the squall slammed into us. Rain smashed horizontally onto my body. Foam from the wave tops blew sideways as quickly as it formed and covered the water with a white froth. My wrap-around sunglasses were blown right off my face from under the snug hood of my foul weather suit.

Those long-ago nightmares of storms at sea, encountered in the safety and warmth of my bed at home, did not do justice to the reality of the fury that now enveloped us. Everything we had gone through before had been just a trial run. Now the real storm started.

Scudding along at eight knots with the wind, our wind indicator registered close to fifty knots, which meant we were experiencing about fifty-eight knots, or sustained wind of 105 kilometres per hour. During gusts, it went even higher. This was almost hurricane strength, a Force Ten storm, perhaps even Force Eleven. The kind of storm sailors talk about for a lifetime. The kind that is termed a "survival storm" in the definitive book on heavy weather sailing. Within minutes, the waves rose to seven metres, more than twenty feet high. Huge whitecaps roared on the tops of the waves, breaking and often crashing down all around us, onto our decks and into the cockpit.

I steered with a steely gaze on the compass and forced myself not to look at the chaos around me. I asked God for strength. Sometimes, out of the corner of my eye, I could see broad sheets of electrical flash, lightning hidden behind the clouds or beyond the horizon.

At first I hoped this was simply another squall. But when it showed no signs of abating – if anything, it was becoming worse – I yelled for Herbert to come into the cockpit and take down our sails. I knew I really should have done this much sooner, but foolishly I had been trying to protect him from having to leave his sickbed.

Herbert furled in most of the jib and put a deep reef in the mizzen. Later, he took down the mizzen sail altogether, and we ran under bare poles. Attached to the boat by our harnesses, Herbert and I sat there together in the cockpit, taking turns steering. Hour after hour it went on, the dark day slowly giving way to an even darker night. But still the storm continued, and the waves grew even steeper.

Down below, the children had been left to their own devices. They had naturally put themselves into the safety of their bunks. As darkness enveloped us, I staggered inside to make sure their leecloths were all in place.

Soon we were speeding along in total darkness, being tossed by nightmarish waves that had grown at least ten metres, more than thirty feet high. The waves towered over us, more than halfway up our mast, as high as our spreaders. Now that it was dark, everything looked even more ominous. We could see very little in the black night other than the painfully bright fluorescence of the breaking crests of the waves and periodic sheets of lightning.

As we sailed through the deep trough between two waves, a frothing mass of foam loomed high up over the boat, advancing threateningly, looking as if it would surely crash down right on top of us. Just as it looked as if we were going to be engulfed, the wave would begin to lift us up until the foam was no longer above us, but beside us, washing onto our decks or roaring into the cockpit. It was as if the wave was a muscular Titan, a Goliath of the sea, lifting us onto his huge shoulders, intent upon our destruction. For a moment, we would perch there, swept up in the giant's tangled, shining hair while *Northern Magic* rose bravely up, decks awash with foam. Then the giant would rush on past us, letting us slide down his back, his wild white mane streaming out behind him as he continued on his malevolent path.

A few seconds later, the next wave would arrive. Up we would be hoisted again. These monstrous Titans never tired of rushing at us, toying with us, and then throwing us down again with a deafening roar. I found I couldn't even bear to look at them. I kept my eye fixed on the compass so I wouldn't be distracted from my work. It kept me from thinking about my fear. Herbert stood beside me, watching the waves rush at us from behind, directing me how to steer so we would slide diagonally down their sides, warning me about particularly big ones. If we went directly sideways to the waves, there was a danger of us rolling over and capsizing under a breaking crest. If we went straight down, we might trip on our bow and pitchpole, flipping end over end. A hundred times as we ran with the storm under bare poles at a speed of four and a half knots, I was grateful for our strong, slow, stable steel boat. *Northern Magic* seemed to know what to do.

By now it was near midnight, and we were only thirty-five miles away from the coast. We'd been hand steering through the storm for fifteen hours. We decided to try lying ahull, which means to close up, lock the wheel, and simply let the boat take care of itself. Since we'd never done this before, we tried it cautiously, ready to take control again in case it made us less stable. We sat back, our hearts in our mouths, wondering what would happen next.

Nothing happened next. Even without our guidance, *Northern Magic* continued on her former path, meeting each wave at an angle on her stern, rising and falling just as before. We sat there for half an hour, reassuring ourselves that we were safe in her hands before we finally went below in relief.

Inside, it was actually quite comfortable. In the warm homey cabin, free from assault by the wind and rain or being forced to watch those terrible marching waves, everything felt much less dramatic. To some extent, we managed to rest. We had a strong sense that *Northern Magic* was taking care of us, doing what she was meant to do.

We each rested in turn while the other kept watch, sticking a head out every few minutes to make sure we weren't being run over by another vessel. In fact, our radar showed there were three large ocean liners within a few miles of us, all of us retaining our positions relative to each other. The storm was so bad even the big ships had given up trying to fight it and were riding it out the way we were. There was little we could do except keep a good watch and hope it would end soon.

We were nervous the storm would prevent us from entering the harbour in the morning. With winds and seas this high, we simply could not afford to try to enter the narrow channel. Losing control of our boat and being driven onto rocks would be the most dangerous kind of disaster. If the storm continued, we would have to head back out to sea or continue north to the next harbour, about two hundred miles away. Either way, it would mean several more days at sea. The very thought of this filled us with despair.

Around midnight, the Inmarsat alarm went off. I jumped to it, hoping for news. I could have kissed the machine when I read that the storm was moving away from us and the winds would begin dropping within six hours. The knowledge that an end was in sight made the small hours of that dreadful morning immeasurably easier to bear. It looked like our nightmare passage would soon be over.

I tried to rest while Herbert took over his watch, but sleep was impossible. The best I could manage was a fitful doze. Around 3:00 a.m., I was jerked out of bed by the Inmarsat again; now only three hours remained before our deliverance. How I loved those faithful Australian forecasters, working late at night to send us those much-needed words of hope.

By five in the morning the wind and waves were distinctly calmer, dipping below forty knots for the first time in almost twenty-four hours. We were now fewer than twenty miles from land.

At six-thirty we raised Brisbane on VHF radio and asked what the conditions were for entering the harbour.

"No worries," answered the harbourmaster in his Queensland drawl. "It's a great day here. We've got fifteen knots of wind, and you'll have no problem at all."

Herbert and I were almost numb with exhaustion as Michael woke up from his makeshift bed in the salon and said brightly, "Well, that wasn't so bad!"

All we could do was look at him in stunned silence, then head back up to the cockpit to raise our sails and at last turn our battered boat for shore.

10

Mechanical Mutinies
Down Under

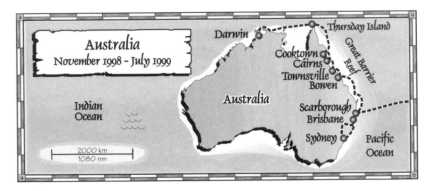

Australia
November 1998 – July 1999

Darwin
Thursday Island
Cooktown
Cairns
Townsville
Bowen
Scarborough
Brisbane
Sydney

Australia

Great Barrier Reef

Indian
Ocean

Pacific
Ocean

2000 km
1080 nm

O
ur planned seven-day passage from New Caledonia had taken twelve days. Herbert and I had not eaten or slept in the previous thirty-six hours. Practically every muscle from my thighs to my shoulders was stiff and sore. My right arm, which had taken the brunt of the steering during the storms and for months before, felt numb to the wrist. My right thumb was so useless I couldn't even hold a pen. That arm continued to be numb for another whole month.

Although I hadn't been seasick during the worst of the storm – protected by adrenalin, perhaps – that morning I found myself racked with nausea and bent over the toilet repeatedly with the dry heaves. It took us until seven-thirty that night to make our way around the reefs and into the safety of the harbour.

We jumped to the dock to stretch our legs and look for a suitable spot to kiss the ground. A sandy-haired man with a big moustache sauntered over and spoke to us through a fence. "Welcome to Australia," he said with a broad smile and that unmistakable Aussie accent. "You've made it."

"We are very happy to be here," we answered, shaking our heads with a rueful smile. "You have no idea what we have been through."

"Oh yes I do," he answered, his grin suddenly replaced by a grave expression that chilled my heart. "You've been through some real bad storms. You can congratulate yourselves that you made it. Lots of boats didn't. There have been four boats lost, and at least four people are dead."

Those words hit us like a shot. Until that moment, the enormity of our escape hadn't really penetrated our fog of fatigue. I staggered back as questions crowded into my mind. Who had died? Did we know them? What happened to their boats? Had we really been that close to ultimate disaster? *Northern Magic*, our tough and sturdy little ship, had brought our family through unscathed. Although safe at last in Australia, Herbert and I found ourselves reeling.

The winds had blown *Northern Magic* to Scarborough, just north of Brisbane, a lovely little town on Queensland's west coast. It was now our second day Down Under, and we were still suffering from fatigue, shock, and disorientation from our difficult passage, especially once we learned that one of the boats lost in the storm belonged to friends. They had been rescued by helicopter as they stood knee-deep in water inside their sinking boat.

At *Northern Magic*, there was a knock on the boat, and a pleasant-looking gentleman named Brian Shoobert introduced himself. He was a representative of the local Rotary Club, and he was at our service. (My father is a Rotarian in Calgary, and he had sent an e-mail about our arrival to his counterparts in Australia.) Over the next few days, Brian really did put himself at our disposal, doing all manner of favours for us.

But the best thing Brian did was to introduce us to Steven and Melissa Griffith. A few days after our first meeting, Brian tracked us down on one of our early morning jogs along the waterfront. Hailing us from his car, he introduced us to a smiling couple in their thirties. From the adoring looks they gave each other, they were clearly head over heels in love. It turned out they had been married only a few weeks. On that day, loading us down with apple pie and chocolate milk, Steve and Melissa gathered us under their wings and adopted us.

Steve was a studious-looking chiropractor, understated but with a sly sense of humour. Melissa was a gorgeous buxom blonde who oozed warmth and generosity, sprinkling her speech with words like "darling" and "divine." They invited us to their "love shack," a charming two-bedroom bungalow, for dinner. Then they gave us the keys to their house so that we could go there the next day while they were at work and finish off the leftovers. At first, we were a little shy about intruding into their home when they weren't there, but Melissa insisted that their house was ours and that she'd take offence if she found I was hand washing on the boat instead of using her machine and backyard clothesline.

I must say how much fun I had with Melissa's electric washing machine after a year of washing by hand. In fact, many of the things we took for granted at home rated as major pleasures in Australia: grapes, fresh milk, non-soggy crackers, frozen waffles, and the biggest and best of these, the long, hot shower. Cruising had certainly given us real appreciation for the luxuries that seemed like necessities back at home.

A few days before Christmas, on a hot, humid, Queensland summer day, there was another knock on our boat. I emerged through the companionway, and there was a young woman with a big smile on her face.

"You must be Laura," I said, climbing out of the cabin. I had been told to expect a visit from a friend of my sister.

"Yes, I'm Laura," she said, "but I'm not your sister's friend. I'm Laura Robin, from the *Ottawa Citizen*, and I'm here to deliver your mail." In her hand was a gigantic plastic bag filled with hundreds of letters, all tied up with a huge velvet bow.

"Yeah, right," I said with a cynical smile. I, the worldly-wise traveller, was not going to be taken in that easily.

"No really, I work for the *Ottawa Citizen*," she insisted.

"I don't believe you," I answered. Yet some tendrils of doubt were now beginning to sprout.

"Do you want to see some ID?" she said, laughingly. "It's true! The *Citizen* actually sent me here to deliver these Christmas cards. All these people have written to you."

I looked more carefully at the bulging sack of letters, and it occurred to me that she might actually be telling the truth. The camera-bearing photographer standing behind Laura's shoulder also tended to lend credibility to her claim. But it was the letters that clinched it. It was true;

hundreds of people, readers of my weekly reports back home, had actually sent us Christmas greetings. I was stunned. There were six hundred letters.

As Herbert and I, helped by the two older children, began opening the letters, tears began rolling down our cheeks. We started reading through our tears and couldn't stop until we had read every last one. Many of them contained small gifts. I don't have the words to express how much each and every one of these letters meant to us. It was the first time we understood the degree to which people back at home had been caught up in our adventures, hoping and praying for us as the months went by. The impact on us was enormous, and the downcast spirits we'd been struggling with since the storm seemed to wash right away.

+

We spent four months at our home base near Brisbane, fixing up *Northern Magic* in a major binge of painting and repair work, and waiting out the cyclone season. During that time we did an extensive overland camping trip, had a visit from my parents, encountered kangaroos, emus, possums, and koalas, and sent the kids to an Australian school. Our life was busy and full of adventure and new friends.

Gradually, the sweltering hot summer days began melting away, until there was a refreshing cool tang to the humid evening air. Autumn was coming to Australia, and it was the signal for sailboats to loose their dock lines and begin dispersing on the winds. The cooler temperatures were quenching cyclonic activity in the warmer waters north near the equator, making it safe at last to continue on our track. We celebrated Easter on our last day in Scarborough before commencing our long trek north.

Just before leaving, we received a wonderful gift from my father, a $15,000 piece of equipment known as the Windhunter. It was a state-of-the-art autopilot and wind-operated self-steering device that was even supposed to generate energy, truly the answer to our dreams after endless hours of hand steering across the Pacific.

We left Scarborough with high hopes for our fresh start at sea, but the Windhunter didn't work. No matter what we tried, it would neither steer us nor produce energy. And the British manufacturer proved unwilling to help. This, coupled with a seemingly endless series of other mechanical problems, most of them involving brand-new equipment Herbert had installed in Scarborough, made the next two months one of the most painful and frustrating periods of our circumnavigation.

We pushed our way shakily up the east coast of Australia, dogged by mechanical and steering problems, seasick and heartsick, all the way. Eventually we made it behind the southernmost end of the Great Barrier Reef. Now we had the world's largest coral reef to shield us from the big Pacific swell, which is generated by distant winds and continues sloshing right along for thousands of kilometres until interrupted by land.

Protected by the reef, we discovered a magnificent Pacific Ocean that was, for the first time, truly pacific. With almost no wind, we found ourselves motoring alongside leaping dolphins in a huge, glassy pond. This was quite an unaccustomed feeling, because in the open ocean, even without wind, that long restless swell is always present. But here it was supremely calm, with only the dull roar of the motor to detract from a feeling of total peace. Christopher actually woke up one morning saying sleepily that he had dreamed we had been on a passage overnight.

"We *were* on a passage, sweetie," I said with a smile, "and we still are."

We had a very exciting time at the small town of Bowen, when we witnessed a horrific harbour fire. It had begun on a catamaran and, whipped by high winds, spread rapidly to six fishing trawlers. Herbert noticed it when the blaze was in its very early stages, being drawn on deck after hearing a sound like a gunshot. Boat after boat went ablaze, burned through its mooring lines, and drifted into the next boat or launched exploding propane tanks like giant rocket-propelled grenades into other vessels. Fortunately, our boat was safe, since we were in another part of the harbour, but my video of the fire and its huge propane explosions was played for days on all the national Australian TV networks. Eventually, my video made it onto NBC's *World's Most Amazing Videos* and was shown all over North America.

Having filmed the conflagration and been interviewed on TV, we became instant celebrities. Even a policeman made an appearance at our boat on a jet ski and asked if he could get a copy of the tape. The fire department wanted one to study as a training video. The local paper wrote a little story about us entitled, "Baptism of Fire for Canadian Visitors." I have to confess I was strutting pretty proudly around town, especially after I was stopped by a lady at the library who said – and I kid you not – "Hey! You're that famous TV personality!"

We continued up the coast, from Bowen to Townsville, and Cairns. Like a festering boil, our problems with our new self-steering system came to a head. When the Windhunter wasn't sending us in 360-degree circles, it was making us waddle from side to side like a drunken duck. Our relationship with the manufacturer became very strained when they refused to answer our questions or help us troubleshoot the problem. They tried to stop us from e-mailing them – our only practical means of communication – and insisted we send faxes instead. Passage after passage we tried different things to make the system work. Our daily – and hourly – struggles with it, and our guilt that Dad's generous present was giving us more anguish than it had saved, were constant companions during our problem-fraught weeks of sailing up Australia's windy east coast. Finally, we had no choice but to admit defeat.

In Cairns we removed the failed Windhunter from the boat and replaced it with a new unit, costing a third as much, also paid for by my father. The autopilot we chose, the TMQ, was an Australian-made hydraulic self-steering system that had been recommended by a number of other cruisers. The gleaming TMQ was to be our knight in shining armour, whose job it was to free us at last from the tyranny of the wheel, and of the Windhunter. In a fit of optimism, the boys decided its initials stood for The Magnificent Q, suggesting that it was superior to our original old electric autopilot, Q (named after the omnipotent but capricious Star Trek character).

As for the Windhunter (now re-named Windblunder), we packaged it up and returned it to England, demanding a full refund on the grounds that after two months of daily trials and two thousand kilometres of sailing, it continued to turn us in circles and was manifestly unsafe. My father started digging around on the Internet, and found more than a dozen other cases of people – including engineers and, literally, a rocket scientist – who'd had similar experiences. In fact, other customers had picketed the company and even involved the police in England. I was beside myself with anger over the way the company had treated us. My days became filled with impotent rage at how my father's generous gift had gone so wrong.

Eventually, Windhunter agreed to refund the price of the unit. They refurbished our autopilot and resold it, but contrary to what they'd promised, they only refunded three-quarters of what Dad had paid. They suggested they would refund the rest only if I retracted what I had said about the unit in the *Citizen*. This, of course, I could not do. Soon after, my father assembled a group of more than a dozen equally angry former Windhunter owners and began organizing a class action lawsuit. Windhunter declared bankruptcy. They now continue in business, although under a new name. My father ended up losing more than five thousand dollars.

We left Cairns for an overnight sail to Cooktown on a sunny, breezy day. Our mood was as upbeat as the weather. It was our first chance to try the confidently named Magnificent Q and free ourselves at last from endless hours at the wheel. So hopeful were we, we couldn't wait one minute longer than necessary and actually called it into action inside the narrow channel leading out of the Cairns harbour. We put ourselves right in the middle of that long avenue of red and green markers and engaged our new autopilot for the first time.

Northern Magic responded by shooting joyfully down that course like an arrow, straight and true. A flood of relief and joy broke over us, and all five of us sat in the cockpit, whooping and hollering in delight. As the wild green mountains of Cairns receded behind us, we broke out soft drinks and peanuts and had an impromptu party.

From that first moment on, The Magnificent Q performed flawlessly. For the next three years, it steered us all the way back to Canada without so much as a hiccup. Even in the North Atlantic, where we were battered and slewed around mercilessly by violent waves, The Magnificent Q performed heroically. How we loved it! Never again did we have to worry about self-steering. Soon, our terrible memories of anguish and struggle with the benighted Windblunder receded into the past. We began to shake off our mechanical problems and learned to enjoy life again.

After Cairns, the Great Barrier Reef presses closer and closer towards the mainland, making navigation increasingly difficult. The famous navigator James Cook explored here during his world-changing voyage on *Endeavour* in 1770. He was unaware the reef even existed and had no idea he was heading into the world's most dangerous waters. *Endeavour* sailed the same path we were now following 229 years later almost to the day. On a calm and moonlit night, just like the one we were now enjoying, *Endeavour* smashed into a coral reef, holing her hull and almost putting an end to that historic voyage. Unlike Captain Cook, we had charts, lights, and GPS to guide us, and as we carefully picked our way through the labyrinth of reefs, we couldn't help marvel at Cook's amazing feat of navigation. At one point, there was just a small channel through the large patches of coral blocking our way. Just as Herbert was gingerly piloting us through in the darkness, carefully plotting our position on the chart every few minutes, the lights of two large ocean liners and a flock of fishing boats converged on us alarmingly, all jostling for sea room.

During the night, we safely sailed past the reef that had just about ended the voyage of *Endeavour* and continued passing landmarks named by Cook as he limped along with only a sail covering a gaping hole in his ship's hull. Mount Sorrow, Cape Tribulation, and Weary Bay were all named by a desolate Cook as he searched for a port in which to repair his gravely damaged ship. Then Cook discovered the Endeavour River, and on June 17, 1770, landed at the present site of Cooktown. When he and his men spent the next forty-eight days there restoring *Endeavour*, they established the first European settlement in Australia. We, too, anchored in the mouth of the Endeavour River, its northern bank looking just as it had in Cook's day.

I was particularly curious about Cooktown, once a booming gold rush town but now a remote backwater connected to the rest of civilization by dirt road. Until recently, only four-wheel-drive vehicles had been able to make the journey to Cooktown, and then only in good weather. I was first to set foot ashore, but the intended graceful effect of my elegant leap off *Northern Magic Junior* was ruined when I landed knee deep in the soft gooey mud of the riverbank. By the time we had disembarked and carried *Junior* past the high tide mark, we all looked as if we were wearing thick brown knee socks. Now I knew why Captain Cook's men had carried him ashore.

As we stood, laughing at ourselves and squeezing sticky mud through our toes, we were met by none other than John F. Kennedy, who turned out to be the harbourmaster. He had a few words of caution for us: only the month before, a 4.2 metre saltwater crocodile had made its home on this very stretch of shore, and the muddy waters into which I had just jumped were also populated by poisonous stonefish.

"You be careful, mates," said Mr. Kennedy to our junior crew. "A fellow here two months ago lost a great big dog, bigger than you, to a crocodile. Them crocs would snap you up for a snack, just like that!" Behind him stood a large sign: "WARNING: This river is home to estuarine crocodiles." We nimbly took our sticky brown feet up to Cooktown's main street, out of the reach, we hoped, of any reptilian predators.

The next day was the start of a two-day celebration of the landing of Captain Cook's Endeavour, and the town of 1,500 really went to a lot of effort to put on a good show. It was a boozy Aussie version of a country fair. There was scarcely an arm to be seen, male or female, that was not amply decorated with tattoos and connected to a can of beer. People even strolled around pulling coolers (which the Australians call eskies) on wheeled carts, enabling them to bring their personal supply of beer wherever they went. We saw one particularly innovative fellow towing a little train of two rolling eskies hitched together. Cooktown's sizable Aboriginal contingent was there as well, but standing apart from the rest, always hovering in quiet groups on the sidelines like a dark shadow.

The crew of Northern Magic, with fresh haircuts administered on the dock at Cairns a few days before, felt quite out of place among the rough and rowdy citizens of Cooktown. My favourite part of our visit was a conversation I overheard between two muscular, tattooed, beer-drinking young men waiting for the wet T-shirt competition to start (it was delayed because the organizers forgot to organize the water). To me, this exchange summarized the entire atmosphere of Cooktown.

Beer drinker number one: "G'dye, mite! What'r you doin' in this
    neck o' the woods?"

Beer drinker number two: "Oi've come to see some tits!"
Beer drinker number one (with a serious and understanding nod of his head): "Fair enough!"

Early next morning, we set sail, following the tracks of Captain Cook ever deeper into the no-man's-land of Australia's far north. Many people had warned us about the winds in far north Queensland. The fierce, unceasing winds, howling day and night, are said to have driven desperate souls to suicide. In Cooktown, John F. Kennedy had told us that when the forecast predicted winds of fifteen to twenty knots, we should just add the two figures together, thirty-five knots. He was right. For weeks, we never had winds of less than thirty knots.

Blown by these endless rushing currents of air, we speedily sailed up to the tip of Australia. Between the strong winds and the claustrophobic proximity of the many menacing reefs and islands, I was becoming more and more uneasy about the idea of sailing at night. Everywhere we went, there were reminders of the many vessels that had been lost before us; the Great Barrier Reef is a veritable graveyard of ships. Although Herbert felt confident and even exuberant about our fast sailing times, in the darkness I found myself haunted by history, battling an unshakable sense that we were rushing headlong into disaster, bearing down at high speed on some unseen, razor-sharp reef or an uncharted rock. Even my off-watch sleep was restless and disturbed, filled with unpleasant dreams and premonitions of catastrophe. I knew I was only being spooked by the darkness and the relentless wind – with good charts and GPS it was really no less safe than sailing during the day – but still I could not shake my feeling of impending doom.

As we continued our trek north up the wild Cape York Peninsula, our selection of comfortable anchorages became more and more restricted. Morris Island, our intended shelter for one night, showed up as just a tiny dot on our chart. After another boisterous day's sail, making a speedy seven and eight knots under jib alone, we came upon the little speck of sandy earth that would serve as our shelter for the night. On it, a solitary palm tree stood in lonely vigil, bent to the shrieking winds that pummelled it day and night. It felt as if we really had arrived at the ends of the earth.

Yet even in that desolate, windblown place, a sense of history pervaded. The single surviving coconut palm had been one of many planted a century before to provide sustenance for any shipwrecked sailor unfortunate enough to be washed up on this God-forsaken shore. It was for them, as it was now for us, a tiny port of refuge in a hostile, reef-strewn sea.

After several long debates and gnashing of teeth (mine), we agreed to make one long last sprint from Morris Island up to the top of Cape York without stopping to rest. This way, we could compress many days of travel into one or two and not have to endure any more long nights in uncomfortable anchorages.

It was another grim, overcast day. The wind continued to blow like blazes, between twenty-five and thirty-five knots. *Northern Magic* was once again flying over the water. Hazards were around us on every side, and constant vigilance was required. In particularly narrow channels, we calculated our position every ten minutes.

I had been lying down most of the day, trying to convince my uneasy stomach not to rebel against the motion of the steep, choppy waves. Finally, I had fallen asleep. In the middle of another bizarre and disjointed dream, I heard Herbert yell, "Oh, no!" And then, "Michael! Switch off the autopilot! Quickly!"

I staggered to the main hatch. My first thought was that my nightmares were coming true: our autopilot had failed and we were about to crash on a reef.

I stuck my head up as Herbert took over the wheel. He had been down below, plotting our position. Outside, my blinking eyes took in the scene: the grim, tousled ocean was grey, the hazy sky was grey, the scudding clouds were grey, and the huge container ship that was bearing down on us was grey. We had less than a minute before being ploughed right under its charging bow.

"Do you want me to radio him?" I croaked, as Herbert attempted to steer us out of the ship's path.

"Yes!" he shouted over the screaming wind. The giant ship was heading directly for us, at perhaps twice our speed. Its brutish, gun-metal bow was parting the ocean like a knife, a large white wave curling out on either side.

I had no time to find out where we were, so I scurried inside, abandoned good radio etiquette, and simply called, "Southbound ship, southbound ship, this is northbound sailing vessel. Do you read me?"

There was no response, and I waited only a few seconds before trying again, in a voice which sounded to me frantic and high pitched. Finally a man answered, in a calm and professional British accent.

"This is *APL Emerald* responding to the sailing vessel. Did you say you are heading northbound?"

"Yes, we are! We're right in front of you! What are your intentions?"

There was a pause, during which it was clear the captain was trying to locate us. He obviously had no idea we were right in his path. His ship was large enough that even if he ran over us, he wouldn't have felt a thing.

Quickly, he was back on the radio and in a rather more clipped and urgent voice than before, said, "I'm altering course to port. I'll pass on your starboard side."

A few dozen seconds later, the ship passed just a stone's throw away. The air was filled with the throb and drone of huge engines and we rocked in the wave created by this man-made leviathan. In some eerie echo of Captain Cook, this, too, was our closest brush with disaster, the nearest we'd ever come to a collision. What if Herbert had taken just one more minute to make his plot on the chart?

There was no more sleeping for me, and so I curled up in the cockpit, my body swaying in tune to the waves, and realized it was going to be a long, long night.

✦

A few days later, we rounded Cape York, the northernmost tip of mainland Australia. We'd promised ourselves a treat of some chocolate-covered marzipan at this milestone, and the kids wasted no time pillaging my chocolate supply. Australia's a huge country, and with thousands of miles of harsh, bushy, uninhabited wilderness seemingly always ahead of us, we had often despaired that we'd make it around so much land. But now we had done it. As we sailed over the top and turned *Northern*

Magic west once again, we left the vast Pacific Ocean and sailed into the waters of the Indian Ocean. What a glowing surge of accomplishment we felt, and on my fortieth birthday!

Once again we were in the wake of Captain Cook, who, having used up all the names he could think of in his marathon of discovery, had now resorted to the days of the week to name the islands in the narrow Torres Strait between Australia and New Guinea. Thus we passed Tuesday Island and Wednesday Island before finally reaching Thursday Island, with Friday Island almost in sight. Unlike Captain Cook, though, we arrived on a Wednesday.

Over the previous days, Herbert had again been developing a terrible toothache, and now it reached an intolerable level. In spite of the most powerful pain relievers we had on board, his throbbing tooth had kept him awake all the night before. We just prayed there was a dentist on tiny Thursday Island, which covered three square kilometres and had a population of only a few thousand people.

The people of the Torres Straight are of Melanesian stock and the laid-back island settlement looked more like Fiji than Australia. As in the other friendly islands of Melanesia, men sitting under the trees at the beach nodded and smiled their welcome to us. Within an hour, a local dentist discovered that the root of one of Herbert's molars had died and developed gangrene. This was the same tooth that had given Herbert trouble on our stormy passage to Fiji. Now, the root of this troublesome tooth was extracted and the infection drained, giving Herbert virtually instant relief. Appallingly, he could smell the gangrene as the tooth was opened. It still makes me shudder to imagine gangrene festering in his mouth, of all places, especially since we had been out of reach of medical assistance for the previous few weeks and the next large town was Darwin, a whole week away by sea.

At the front desk of the clinic, I stopped to study a curious sign that said, "If youpela have an appointment, youpela should go to the reception desk and mepela will help you as quickly as possible." I'd heard about Pidgin English, but this was the first time I'd seen it written.

From Thursday Island, we continued on through the Gulf of Carpentaria, where the combination of strong winds, shallow water, and the meeting of two oceans often results in abnormally steep waves. We got the wet and uncomfortable ride we had expected, with a gale thrown in for good measure.

Every now and then an especially large rogue wave would rear up, capped with a miniature surfer's curl that would break over us and cover our decks with white water. The water would race up and down the walkways and, unable to find its way back out through the scuppers quickly enough, rush into the cockpit instead. Twice, the teak floor grating of the cockpit floated up almost to the level of the cockpit seats.

Keeping watch under these conditions involved an interesting game of cat and mouse in which these freakish waves would leap up over the side of the boat and attempt to catch us unawares with a saltwater shower. Every time we opened up the hatch to peek nervously outside, we had to be quick in case one was about to pounce. Only if the coast was clear could we actually stick our heads right out, and, even still, we got wet a significant proportion of the time. The boys had great fun keeping score of which of their parents got the most satisfactory dousing.

By 3:00 a.m. the winds were screaming by at between forty and forty-five knots. *Northern Magic* shuddered as she was battered by the ugly waves that continually reared up over her. From our bed near the bow it sounded as if we were on a fast-moving locomotive. It felt like we were screaming through a winding, high-speed obstacle course around giants who were taking swings at us with tree trunks wielded like baseball bats. I just lay there, my body braced against the inevitable shuddering blows. Every half hour or so I jumped up and went to see Herbert, who was similarly braced in Michael's bunk. There, both the motion and the noise were less alarming, but every time I staggered back to our bed I found myself becoming more and more awake.

Finally I decided to try lying down next to Michael on the narrow salon settee. I curled into a ball and wedged myself under his feet, bending his legs up to make enough room for me to crunch my body in a ball below his. It was far from comfortable, but the motion and sound were less perturbing in the centre of the boat. After fifteen or twenty minutes, interrupted only by occasional skirmishes with Michael's folded legs, I could feel my tired body relaxing and sleep approaching once again.

(I asked Michael later whether he knew that he had shared his slim bench with me the night before. "I was wondering about that!" he exclaimed. "I thought something had been pushing my legs in the night, but in the morning there was no one there and I thought it was just a dream.")

Once out of the Gulf of Carpentaria we found some additional relief, so our third day of sailing passed more comfortably. The next night, we were sailing along quite contentedly in twenty-five knots of wind. The kids had just gone to bed, Herbert was asleep, and I was curled up happily with a book when suddenly the motion of the boat increased sharply. In the next instant, the shrill off-course alarm of the autopilot began beeping, and I raced to wake Herbert up. Something was very wrong.

Together, we jumped into the cockpit and discovered that we had no steering. *Northern Magic* had turned into the wind, sails straining and bucking wildly into the waves. Her steering wheel was loose and flying freely. The great bronze steering arm that connected the shaft of our wheel to the rudder had, for the second time on our voyage, sheared right through.

Herbert quickly came up with a mess of ropes and a steel emergency steering arm, which he fitted to the floor of the cockpit and led around, in a spider's web of criss-crossing ropes, back to the wheel. Until our steering arm could be attended to in Darwin, there would be no more help from TMQ. We had no option but to hand steer once again for the remaining days of the passage.

You might imagine we were upset by this, only the latest in a series of steering disasters that had dogged us since the beginning of our long struggle up Australia's endless coast. In fact, the reverse was true. For some reason both of us were in a great mood, feeling somehow triumphant that we had known exactly what to do and had done it quickly and efficiently in difficult conditions.

Herbert offered to steer, but I sent him back to bed after asking him to put on some music for me. Soon a full moon had risen, and mingling with the rush of the wind and the crash of the waves was the sound of my voice, singing as sailors have sung on small boats in vast oceans since time immemorial. My feet were spread wide to brace against the motion, my hands gripped the wheel tightly, my arms wrestled with the waves for control of *Northern Magic*, and my face became crusty with salt. Occasionally, I was forced to duck as an especially large wave landed on me, finding sneaky ways in through my foul weather suit. Often, water swirled around my ankles. My bare toes began wrinkling up like prunes.

I stayed at the helm until 1:00 a.m., waking Herbert every hour to take a plot of our position as we navigated close by small islands about twenty miles off the northern coast of Australia's wild and mostly unpopulated Northern Territory. At six in the morning, I took over again and had the pleasure of watching the sun rise over my shoulder, casting a glorious golden sheen over the boat and the low islands of Arnhem Land barely visible on the horizon.

Soon, a little face popped out of the lower hatch. It was Christopher, my sunshine boy, wearing that wonderful smile that lit him up – still lights him up – each and every morning. My pet name for him was particularly apt today, as his rounded little boy's face caught the golden glow of that spectacular sunrise. I couldn't help but pause to drink in the beauty of the scene, trying to engrave the image on my memory so I could feast upon it in years to come.

A few minutes later, Jon appeared through the same hatch, excitedly informing me of the progress he had made on the logic puzzle we had been working on the day before. We had spent many happy hours wedged together in Jon's narrow bunk with his puzzle book, trying to figure out a series of increasingly difficult problems. To my amazement, he was every bit as good as I was at figuring them out.

After Jon returned to his puzzling, Michael made his appearance. As usual he was the last to rise and the first to say he was hungry. This was a problem: how to get some food into the kids without leaving the wheel or waking up Herbert? Most of the easily accessible foods had already been gobbled up. Then I remembered a special treat I had bought back in Scarborough and squirrelled away for just such a day as this: a precious box of Fruit Loops, the perfect thing to keep the kids happily munching until I could come down and prepare something better.

Michael didn't need to be invited twice and disappeared instantly to find the sweetened cereal in the secret spot I described. From the cockpit, I could hear excited exclamations as the kids discovered their windfall. It made me realize that a handful or two of Fruit Loops would go over very well with me, too; it had been four days since we had eaten a full meal. On the couple of occasions I had tried to prepare something hot, the ordeal of holding down various bowls and cutlery to prevent them from flying around the cabin while trying to shovel the contents into our mouths between jolts made the whole effort more trouble than it was worth.

Then Michael reappeared, carrying a bowl of Fruit Loops for me. For the millionth time I was reminded of how blessed I was to have such wonderful kids; how many twelve-year-old boys would be thoughtful enough to think of their wet, hungry mom, standing alone in the cockpit, and share their treat with her?

After lapping up the Fruit Loops with my tongue, I continued standing at the wheel, water swirling around my feet. I felt very strong, very happy, and very, very alive. What more can you ask from life than to find yourself sailing along the top of Australia with your family on an awesomely beautiful, wild and windy day such as this?

We eventually made it to Darwin, tired but jubilant, and there we had a new steering arm constructed. While Herbert fussed around with the steering, de-rusting, and paint touch-ups, ascending the mast, checking all the rigging, and generally getting *Northern Magic* shipshape, I slipped once again into my provisioning mode, stocking the boat to the gunwales with as many groceries – including even kangaroo meat – as she could handle without sinking.

Then it was time to go. Eight months after arriving in that great island continent, *Northern Magic* cast off from Australian shores for the last time and headed off into the Indian Ocean. It was an exciting, even joyous moment. As Darwin receded in the distance, our pangs of regret about leaving the familiar comforts of Australia began to disappear. Soon we were focused only on the seven-day sea voyage ahead, and the adventures that lay in store for us in the mysterious and fascinating continent of Asia.

The Land of
Dragons and Smiles

We had first met Yves Matson, a witty twenty-six-year-old Canadian, back in Fiji. He had left Canada around the same time we had, with the objective of circling the world without ever using an airplane. He had crewed on two boats before ours, compiling a hilarious collection of stories that kept us in stitches. The kids in particular adored him, and when they found out he was looking for a boat to Indonesia, they begged us to take him along on the ride from Darwin to Bali.

Having an extra crewmember made this a very easy passage. Another person on night watch meant each of us could get at least eight hours of consecutive sleep. I was really pampered by having to stand only one four-hour watch each day in compensation for my duties as cook.

But the best thing of all about having Yves was that he made us laugh. His jokes and true stories kept us rolling around on the floor. There was the "Bear Story," which the boys would beg to hear over and over. There was the "Bare Butts in the Crowded Bar" story, which ended with Yves's parents having to call him in a panic after receiving (cleverly doctored) photographic proof that their travelling son was working as a nude dancer in a gay bar in New Zealand.

Our favourite, however, was the story of "The Defiled Oreo." This story got me in big trouble later on in the trip, as I was attempting to retell it to friends on a longboat at midnight moored in the jungles of Borneo. I was recalling how Yves, in his initial telling, had baulked at explaining exactly how that legendary Oreo had, unbeknownst to him, been "defiled" by a high school-buddy. His reluctance to explain the nature of this defilement had forced me to coerce the information out of him. Now, at the very moment in Borneo when I blurted out Yves's reply, there had, quite by accident, been a lull in conversation on the boat that was tied up beside us. My unexpected, incriminating, and disgusting punchline rang out like a church bell in the dark and silent jungle air. Fifteen pairs of shocked eyes, including those belonging to a rather proper older British couple, immediately turned accusingly my way. My reputation was as defiled as that long-ago Oreo. But the rest of the story – of how Yves got his ultimate revenge on the evil defiler – still makes us roar with laughter. All I can tell you is that it had something to do with an opened can of coke that had languished in a locker for six months and had grown an extravagant fur of thick green slime.

I needed Yves's good spirits to revive mine on the third day of our passage to Indonesia, when I found myself staggering for the bathroom and bowing in supplication before that smooth white altar, a penitent pose I was forced to repeat numerous times over the next two days. Now I realize I was being punished for having confidently boasted to Yves, who normally suffered from *mal-de-mer*, that I had regained my sealegs and was once again immune to seasickness. Yves had made no such boast and was therefore spared my undignified fate. He was gentlemanly enough not to gloat about it.

Our captain succumbed as well, but understandably so, after having being forced to hang head-down in the engine room repairing, in turn, a broken fan belt, a baulky watermaker, and finally the alternator. He had been forcing himself to remain in good humour throughout his seemingly endless travails, and was even stoic when our mainsail began to rip along a seam, rigging up a line to take the pressure off the tear so we wouldn't have to fix it underway.

The biggest blow, however, came on our fifth day at sea when our refrigeration once again stopped working. With both fridge and freezer brimming with two months' worth of meat and half a year's worth of bacon and cheese, this was a significant disaster. It sparked a debate about whether we should stop at Komodo as planned, where we would have no prospect of solving the problem, or head directly for Bali, where we certainly would. After some discussion, we decided to stick with our original plan, even if it meant throwing all our precious supplies into the sea.

Catching our first glimpse of Asia quickly turned our minds away from our rapidly defrosting cache of beef and chicken. The volcanic peaks of Flores Island, piercing the clouds at acute angles with their sharp, serrated edges, were stunning. The scene was unmistakably exotic, and an involuntary shiver of excitement passed through me as I realized how very far away from home we had come.

When I got up the next morning, we were sailing along the south shore of Rinca Island, whose ragged volcanic peaks plunged right down into the ocean beside us. The island was clearly outlined in the misty grey pre-dawn light. As the sun began rising behind it, I realized it was actually shaped just like a sleeping dragon, with its head resting on the ocean surface and a long tail that curved elegantly alongside its body. It was almost as if this mighty beast was guarding the entrance to the island, home of the real Komodo dragon, and anyone foolish enough to intrude might find themselves snapped up in its hungry jaws.

My imagination feasted on this primeval scene as the sun began to stretch its first golden rays over the back of the sleeping dragon and we began tiptoeing our way in through the strait. The narrow channel between Komodo and Rinca islands is notorious for its unpredictable currents, whirlpools, and riptides. Sure enough, waves suddenly reared up to bash us, and the current pushed us violently away, as if they, too, were sentries whose job it was to discourage unwanted visitors. But at last, around noon, we made our entrance into the shelter of Komodo Island.

As much as we wanted to see the dragons for which this island is famous, our first priority was to locate ice for the freezer. Ashore, several men and a handful of young boys were standing by some small souvenir stalls, hoping for tourists, of which we were the only ones around. One of them helpfully sent his brother to fetch us some ice from the nearby village. In the meanwhile, perhaps we might be interested in inspecting his wares?

After some protracted and dramatic haggling, we did end up buying one of his beautiful carved dragons. But the messenger returned empty-handed, explaining that the generator in the village was broken. Our faces fell. Then another fellow stepped forward, saying he knew of someone else who would be able to help us . . . and, in the meantime, perhaps we'd like to look at his selection of shells?

We were beginning to think that we'd have a better chance of finding a real fire-breathing dragon than of getting our hands on a cold block of ice. But desperate measures require desperate actions, so we invested three dollars in a shell and persuaded our newly enriched guide, a small smiling man named Ardi, to escort us on our quest to find some of this precious ice. We motored over to the tiny village on *Northern Magic*, our new friend standing proudly at the bow. The little wooden houses of Komodo Village were virtually identical. Built on stilts, they were packed neatly in a row along the water's edge, with a fleet of slim wooden fishing boats lined up in front.

Throngs of curious ragged children materialized on the beach. Every time one of us pulled out a camera, they all shrieked with laughter and fought for a spot in front of the lens. I really created pandemonium when I began filming with the video camera, which had a swivelling viewfinder that allowed people to see themselves as you were filming them. The minute I did this, twenty or thirty children began screaming and jostling for position. I had to stop after only a few seconds.

We made our way to a little food shop at the far end of the village. Ardi helped translate our wishes to the proprietress, who displayed a small plastic bag filled with water that she proposed to freeze for us by the next morning. We ordered fifteen of these, not even bothering to haggle over price. We were just praying that there really was a working generator connected to a working fridge and this was not just another ploy to keep us, and our wallets, in the village a little bit longer.

We then strolled through the village, where friendly faces appeared in just about every window and our entourage increased by the minute.

We passed two tiny silver-domed mosques, one of which looked as if it had been made from tin foil, before reaching the home of our guide. On the way, we saw a group of men constructing a wooden fishing boat without benefit of glue or nails, using long wooden pegs instead. Outside another little shop, some colourfully dressed women, slender like almost all Asian women, were grinding coffee using a giant wooden mortar and pestle.

At Ardi's home, on stilts like the rest, we removed our sandals and climbed up a ladder to get inside. There we sat on woven mats in his living room and met his shy, giggling wife, his baby daughter, and two of his brothers, none of whom spoke English. The room was furnished with only a small cabinet and a bed. The walls were made of woven panels, and plenty of sky was visible through the thatched roof, even right above the bed. Yet the two-room home did not give the impression of poverty, but rather that of a quietly prosperous small shopkeeper. There were glass cups in the teak cabinet, and Ardi's wife soon appeared with dark, sweet coffee and tasty creme-filled cookies.

I passed around some candies I had brought. The minute I produced these, the door and windows came alive with the outstretched arms of dozens of children standing outside. They were just as quickly swatted away by Ardi's brother. As Ardi unwrapped our sweets, he pushed the plastic wrappers through the gaps in the floor to fall into the open space below his raised house, joining a collection of refuse there through which chickens and goats happily rummaged. After our refreshments, the fatigue of our long day began to settle over us, and we decided it was time to make our way back to the boat. The minute we emerged from Ardi's house, the horde of children reappeared. Soon, to their delight, Christopher initiated the tickle-and-chase game at which he had excelled in similar villages in Tonga and Fiji.

At some point we lost track of Michael, who had wandered ahead. Suddenly, from somewhere far away down the beach came a strange sound, almost like the war cry of an army, running to engage the enemy. Except it was children's voices, and they were screaming not in anger but in delight. As the noise came closer, around a bend in the beach appeared Michael, loping along in his easy athletic stride, a great big grin on his face. The clamour grew and in just a few more seconds we could see the source, a throng of children following in Michael's wake, screaming and laughing as they ran. Our Pied Piper must have had fifty children streaming behind him, and they joined an almost equal number that were already dancing around us, waving and shouting as we returned to *Northern Magic* for the night.

Even the King of Siam couldn't have outdone the welcome we received from this roaring, running river of children, the grand finale to our first day in Asia.

By six the next morning, Herbert was in our dinghy, heading for the little village on stilts. He returned triumphantly with fifteen bags of slushy ice, buying us a little more time at least.

Before leaving, we had a more important mission to accomplish. We had to seek out an encounter with the legendary Komodo dragon, the real-life giant lizard that was probably the basis for the ubiquitous dragon of Far East legend.

In years past, it was the practice for tourists coming to Komodo to bring a live goat along with them. The poor doomed creature would be left, bleating, tethered to a tree as the people stood back and watched the monstrous lizards tear it apart. People no longer bring goats, but the dragons, which reach three metres in length and live fifty years or more, haven't forgotten, and still gather at the former feeding spot, hoping for a snack. Park officials have stocked the island with deer, and it is now up to the dragons, of which there are only a few thousand left, to hunt for their own food. A Komodo dragon is an adept hunter, capable of bringing down a fully-grown water buffalo.

We headed into the forest with a young guide. He was heavily armed to protect us from these carnivorous dragons – with a long forked stick. Our guide had a real nose for the dragons, and kept peeling off the path into the underbrush after suddenly pricking up his ears, like a German Shepherd, at some sound or smell we were not able to perceive.

As the seven of us walked down a narrow path deep into the orchid-filled forest, we began to make jokes about which of us was most liable to be snapped up by a hungry dragon. It's not unknown for them to eat humans, especially small ones. A few years before, a Swiss man had been separated from his tour group, and only his glasses and camera were ever found. I joked that as long as you weren't the last in line you were safe.

This sparked a game like musical chairs in which whoever was bringing up the rear would try to sneak into a safer spot in the middle.

Finally, we reached the dragon-feeding spot. And there, indeed, a Komodo dragon lay in wait, his two-metre length spread out languorously in a sunny spot on the forest floor. He was sleeping, or resting at least, storing up the sun's energy like a living solar panel.

We got within a few metres of the great black leathery beast, watched over by our guide and also by large unblinking black lizard eyes. Michael was a little too nonchalant for my taste, and I had to keep reminding him not to get too close. As I was filming the dragon close up with the video camera he sneezed, making me jump. The dust raised by his sneeze looked just like a puff of real dragon smoke.

+

We saw several other dragons on Komodo before setting off. We planned to sail up the narrow strait between Komodo and Rinca islands and continue overnight along the north coast of the large island of Sumbawa.

Our problem was figuring out how to get through the tricky strait. Our book of sailing directions said ominously that the channel was "little or never used because of strong, little known currents." With the help of a local fisherman we established that the best time to transit the strait would be around high tide, at five that afternoon. So off we set, hoping to get through the narrowest part of the strait by sunset.

It was a perfectly calm day, and the sea was flat, but as we reached the end of the bay in which we had anchored, the waters began to churn. Soon giant whirlpools began forming all around us. There was a perfectly calm pond of unruffled water in the middle of each whirlpool, perhaps five metres across, but outside that glassy eye the waters swirled madly. It was enough to make us wonder whether we were in danger of being flushed right down the drain, as if in a giant toilet.

Then came the tidal rips. We would see a distinct raised line of water slashing across at an oblique angle, like the drawing of a giant curtain. The minute we reached that line, we would sheer away along with it. Between the eerie whirlpools and the raging rips, our captain's hands were full keeping *Northern Magic* on course.

We had been motoring at a speed of six knots, but the instant we turned north into the strait we found ourselves virtually at a standstill. Herbert revved up the engine, and although our knotmeter registered a speed of seven and a half knots, our GPS told a different story; over land we were only progressing at a little more than a knot, or about two kilometres an hour.

We stood there, virtually in place, for the next two hours, swimming hard but really only treading water. That same little bit of scenery along which we were frantically motoring simply refused to budge. But what scenery it was! Between those swirling whirlpools, the silvery schools of leaping tuna, the craggy volcanic peaks, and the living dinosaurs we knew roamed those distant hills, we felt as if we were in some surreal scene out of The Odyssey. We wouldn't have been in the least surprised if a Cyclops had popped his head out from behind one of the mountains and reached out to grab us . . . come to think of it, maybe bringing a goat along wouldn't have been a bad idea after all.

As the sun disappeared, we began to debate whether we should just turn tail and run. Despite two hours of hard motoring, we had still barely left the harbour and could be safely back at anchor within half an hour. On the other hand, if we gave up now, who could say whether we'd do any better next time? Luckily, it was a clear night and there was a full moon, so even though there were many small rocks and islands in the narrow channel ahead, we decided to struggle on.

But there was definitely witchery in the air that night. That same capricious god who had sent the whirlpools and the current decided to have still more fun by sending a lunar eclipse our way. Eventually, a third of the moon was obscured, enough to darken the sky and make us laugh nervously about what further tricks lay in store.

Indeed, the bag of tricks was not yet empty. In the darkness, many little fishing boats began to appear out of nowhere. Some of them were lit, others were not, and soon our radar showed many alarming specks that could be uncharted rocks, unlit fishing boats, or something else altogether. Whatever these blips were, we didn't want to hit them. We began zigzagging erratically through the water, dodging invisible and perhaps even imaginary obstacles.

Yves and the boys had already gone to bed, and Herbert joined them while I piloted the boat around the last of the invisible fishing boats and safely out to sea. It had taken us seven hours to cover twelve miles, but at last we were free of the treacherous Komodo Strait.

✦

After arriving in Bali, we transferred our soggy, semi-frozen meat to the freezer of friends on an American boat. That taken care of, we left *Northern Magic* behind for a week's vacation in paradise. My sister, Linda, and her eight-year-old daughter, Katie, had arrived. They were loaded with gifts from home, hugs, and big plans for their visit, and they had booked a hotel for us in Ubud, an inland village famous for its crafts-people and cultural events.

Along the road to Ubud, the beautiful terraced rice fields for which Bali is famous were dotted with tranquil people in coolie hats planting, weeding, and winnowing. Beautiful women dressed in colourful sarongs walked slowly beside the road balancing enormous loads on their heads. Grandfathers too old for the rice fields held babies on their hips. The very old women often worked topless, their tired old breasts swaying as they washed clothes, dishes, and themselves in the running water of a roadside ditch.

The next morning we walked from our hotel to the nearby village of Keliki, whose artisans are skilled woodcarvers. As we walked, passing row upon row of home-based factories with their finished products spread out by the thousands, we were greeted with friendly smiles and waves. The voices of small children rang out musically, singing "Hello! Hello!" everywhere we turned. After being mobbed by school children out on recess, we were invited into the home of Jengki, whose family, like virtually every other in this village, supported itself by carving wooden flowers.

Jengki's daughter, a Balinese beauty in her late teens, showed us how she used a lathe to fashion the basic flower shape out of a block of wood. We watched as a basket of unpainted blossoms slowly grew. Each finished flower earned the family less than two cents; a skilled carver might be able to turn out a hundred or two a day.

Sheepishly, I realized entire villages of smiling, gentle people like these were toiling all day in the heat for no more reward than the amount I might unthinkingly throw away on an ice cream. If there was anything our children learned from sailing around the world, it was how fortunate they were to have been born in Canada. In Bali, Herbert and I began an endless series of discussions about whether it was better to buy these crafts for a song, thus providing hardworking people with at least some financial reward for their efforts, or whether this was just exploitation. It was an argument we continued for most of the rest of our trip, and to this day. As time went on, however, we found ourselves bargaining down the price of our souvenirs less and less, and looking for excuses to buy things from hardworking craftspeople, even if we didn't really need them.

The island of Bali is predominantly Hindu, while most of the rest of this diverse country is Muslim. Later that day we prepared ourselves to visit a Hindu temple ceremony. In order to do this, you had to be properly attired, which in the case of both sexes meant a sarong with a sash around the waist. Men also wore a headband, tied in front with a flourish. Our hotel provided these for us and helped to make us presentable, Balinese style. Our boys weren't exactly keen on the skirt part of the costume, although I thought they looked quite fetching.

As we approached the temple, we saw dozens of women, beautifully dressed with golden sashes and transparent lacy blouses, walking with huge pyramids of fruit balanced on their heads. This was the time of day for women to make their offerings, and after depositing these towers of food on a table, they fell to their knees and prayed.

But where were the men? They were gathered on the other side of the street in tight circles placing bets on cockfights. We left the temple and watched with increasingly horrified fascination as the bloody spectacle unfolded. Linda, Katie, and I were the only females in a crowd of a hundred or so eager, jostling men.

As the cockfight began, the men who formed the human fighting ring stood up to cheer, obscuring our view. It was just as well; after having watched them lash small knives to the cocks' legs – not "spurs," as our guidebook said, but truly lethal miniature daggers several centimetres long – I wasn't sure we'd have the stomach to watch the birds slice each other apart.

The actual contest lasted only a minute or two. At the end, the two cocks, too exhausted and wounded to want to fight further, were forced together inside a small woven cage. There they had no choice but to fight until one of them could no longer stand. The losing bird, bloody and barely breathing, had its neck wrung by its owner, whose considerable investment in this prized animal was now lost and whose family would therefore be eating chicken that night. Men who had earlier collected bets moved through the crowd dispensing cash to the winners while the next two combatants were prepared for battle. The winning cock, white feathers now stained with red, was placed in another cage to nurse his wounds. He would probably live to fight another day. Next to him, a dozen other birds waited unknowingly for their turn at glory – or death.

I couldn't help but compare the bloodthirsty scene with the beautiful women still forming their stately procession in the background, bearing their offerings to the holy temple. There was something incongruous about this picture, and I left the cockfights feeling troubled, and liking the otherwise very likeable Balinese just a little less.

Another day we went to a monkey forest, where we found ourselves walking around with living monkey-tail hats on our heads. Christopher giggled non-stop. We had been watching a handful of monkeys swimming and wrestling in an ornamental pool when Michael discovered one of them trying to kill a large black scorpion. The monkey had grabbed a leaf, and, using it gingerly to cover the scorpion and thus protect itself from a poisonous sting, was hammering on it with his fist. Scientists had been excited to discover tool use among chimpanzees and orangutans, but here we were, witnessing it among a lower-order monkey. The ten-centimetre long scorpion fought back, jumping out from under the leaf with its evil tail arched. As soon as the scorpion got too close, the monkey would leap in the air and swat it away. Once it batted the scorpion just a scant metre away from our feet, so we jumped away right smartly too.

The macaque bashed that scorpion for five full minutes before it finally succeeded in tearing it in two. Both parts of the dismembered creature were still moving when the monkey scooped them up and, without further ado, stuffed them into its mouth. We watched the victor crunch away in noisy satisfaction until the last bit of still-twitching scorpion tail was slurped into his mouth like spaghetti.

After making friends with a local artist and engaging in one last mad shopping spree in the bargain-filled shops of Ubud, we were ready to head out and explore the rest of Bali. We hired a van and driver to take us around the island for two days. Our first objective was to climb Ganung Batur, Bali's second highest mountain and an active volcano. It is actually a kind of double-decker, tiered like a wedding cake – a huge ancient volcano containing a beautiful turquoise lake and a smaller, higher volcanic peak which had thrust up more recently from inside the old caldera.

We stopped at a park gate in order to pay a small entrance fee, whereupon we were inundated by half a dozen aggressive young men on motorcycles who insisted on being our guides. We knew from our guidebook, and from friends, that no guide was necessary, so we waved them away and continued driving towards the inner crater. We didn't notice that four of them had jumped on their motorcycles and begun tailing us.

At one point we stopped to study a possible route up the volcano. Suddenly the four young men surrounded our van. One, wearing a black leather jacket and clearly the ringleader, began speaking. His voice was not friendly.

"You have to have a guide," he said. "This is our holy mountain, and you cannot go up without a guide."

"Thank you," we answered. "But we don't need your services."

"Yes, you do!" he answered angrily, his eyes flashing. "You are our responsibility. If you die up there – which just happened to someone last week – we will have to bring down your bodies. You are under our protection, this is our land, and you may not climb the mountain except with one of us!"

"We're sorry, but we aren't going to use a guide."

"Well then, you must go! We will not permit you to climb our mountain! We will stop you from climbing! Go away!"

"Even if we needed a guide, we wouldn't use you," retorted Linda calmly. "You're too angry. We don't deal with angry men!"

We instructed our driver to carry on, but as he rolled up his window, the ringleader made a threatening gesture and shouted, "We'll follow you! We won't let you climb the mountain!"

What had we gotten ourselves into? While we continued over the bumpy roads, at least two motorcycles followed us through bend and turn. We wanted neither to associate ourselves with the local Mafia, nor to fight our way through them to climb the mountain. What would happen once we stopped the car again? I pulled out my little canister of pepper spray and Herbert attached it to his belt, just in case.

By the time we made our way around to the far side of the mountain and found the path we wanted to use, there was only one motorcycle still on our tail. We decided that I would emerge from the car with a notepad, introduce myself as a journalist, and take down the name and identification of this last remaining thug while Herbert videotaped the exchange as if for TV.

Luckily, the fellow standing before me as I got out of the car was not the angry ringleader. He looked almost apologetic. I pulled out our business card, which showed a picture of *Northern Magic*, and began: "We have come half way around the world on this boat without a guide. We certainly don't need a guide to climb this mountain."

He took one look at the card, jumped back on his motorcycle, and tore off down the bumpy road without another word of protest. Another vehicle containing four tourists had just passed, and he must have decided they would be easier targets than a bunch of stubborn, self-reliant sailors.

We began walking through a small village on our way up the mountain. Several people ran out, trying to attach themselves to us as guides, but we waved them away. One or two shouted angrily at us. It was a good example of how too much tourism can ruin a place, especially where the disparity of wealth is so high.

One boy in his teens simply fell in cheerfully beside us.

"We don't want a guide," we cautioned him.

"Oh no, I'm not a guide," he answered cheerfully. "I'm bringing drinks to sell at the top."

And so we joined up with Wayan, which in Balinese means "Number One Child" and is therefore a very common name, and began the long, hot climb. The flanks of the mountain were covered with small, loose volcanic rocks that were hard to walk on, and as we got higher up the path, we could see we were walking on a recent lava flow: in places, the smooth dried lava was a bright red colour. The mountain had exploded several times in the previous sixty years, twice wiping out nearby villages.

It took us almost three hours to reach the summit, during which our own Number Three Son, called Nyoman in Balinese, held hands with our likeable drink seller. Christopher even got a brief ride on Wayan's shoulders. Three-quarters of the way up we bought some drinks, even though we were carrying our own, cheerfully paying rather more for the privilege than usual. There were four or five other young men already at the top of the mountain, but no other people to be seen. Obviously, the other car of tourists had either given up on their attempt or were still in a stand-off with the local Mafia man we had fobbed off on them.

By now we had a good rapport with Wayan and his friends and began needling them over the high price we had paid for the Cokes. "Oh, but it's such hard work carrying them up," Wayan answered with a twinkle in his eye. "And I'm very tired." We handed out little candies to everyone on the mountaintop, and as the local boys popped them into their mouths, we jokingly suggested that they now owed us 10,000 rupiah each, since we were also very tired, having carried the candies all the way up. They laughed and helpfully suggested 20,000 rupiah instead. We departed good friends.

The view from the top of the volcano was spectacular. Although we couldn't see any lava spewing, there was smoke rising from inside the crater. We picked our way around the rim of the caldera and then began our descent down the opposite side. It took us a couple of hours, scrambling down volcanic scree and then through a teak forest, past temples and finally a small village. We didn't yet realize that we had ended up just a stone's throw away from the site of our original confrontation.

Our driver wasn't there, because we had not ended up where we had agreed to meet him. Linda ended up hitching a ride with some Swedish tourists in a jeep and then on the back of a motorcycle with an Indonesian teenager before she was able to find where our driver and his van were waiting to pick us up. While waiting for Linda to return, a motorcycle man appeared, asking who our guide was. Without thinking, I answered that we hadn't used one. He gave me a distinctly hostile scowl and roared off. When the next biker appeared, again asking which guide we had used, I simply answered "Wayan," which, in Bali, I knew, wouldn't narrow it down too much.

"How much did you pay him?" he asked greedily. "A hundred dollars U.S.?"

A hundred dollars U.S.?! That was double what the average Balinese earned in a *month* of hard labour. This guiding business was really nothing less than an extortion racket. We were doubly pleased that we hadn't added to the profits of these young punks by succumbing to their bullying tactics.

We drove several hours to the north coast of Bali before finding ourselves a lovely beachfront cottage for twelve dollars a night, which included access to a natural spring-fed swimming pool. After a refreshing swim to wash off the volcanic dust that still coated our bodies, we ate in a small restaurant, where we got to know a sweet young man named Ketut, who was our waiter.

We had a long conversation with Ketut about his life. The contrast with the angry motorcycle gang at the mountain couldn't have been greater. This gentle young man slaved away a whole *year* in that restaurant for about the same amount that those ruffians had tried to extort for an afternoon's work. The waiter's wage was fifty cents a day.

Ketut questioned us carefully about Canada. Although he came from a very poor family, the boy was intelligent and ambitious and was clearly trying to figure out how to improve his situation. We considered how to answer him, wondering what we would do if we were in his place. In our country, a young man like him would have every opportunity. Here in Indonesia, though, he had very few options. The knowledge of his dilemma hit us in the face.

As we left, we shook hands and wished Ketut good luck. Somehow as we parted, five dollars discretely made its way from Herbert's hand into his. The fact that we had no good answer to give this young Balinese waiter as to how he might break out of his cycle of poverty continued to trouble us.

Our family vacation in paradise was coming to a bittersweet end. Back on *Northern Magic*, our crewmember, Yves, was about to leave us to make his own overland journey. We were sad to see him go after all the fun we'd had together.

Weeks before, a day or two after Yves arrived, he had asked me innocently whether I'd seen a certain grey plastic bag containing some photos. At the time, we had his stuff stashed in little dribs and drabs all over the boat for lack of any one place to put it. I hadn't seen the bag but said it was sure to turn up.

Over the next weeks, he would ask from time to time about the missing bag. I didn't understand why he was so preoccupied with it and kept answering that it would surely turn up. Finally, that last day, while the rest of us were off the boat and he was alone with Herbert, he found the bag. Herbert asked him what was in it.

"Pictures of my girlfriend," Yves answered.

We'd heard quite a lot about this beautiful girlfriend, and Herbert, quite naturally, asked to see what she looked like. Yves shuffled through the photos and then confessed, blushing a bit, that he couldn't show any of them. His meaning was clear enough.

When I came back, Herbert whispered to me, with a wicked grin, about the supposed contents of the long-sought-after plastic bag. Yves was sitting up at the entrance to the cockpit, and could see me, but not Herbert.

"Hey, Yves," I called up, "I hear you found the photos where I stashed them."

Yves looked down at me with great big eyes. There was a moment of silence. "Did you look at them?" he finally asked, gulping.

"Of course! That's why I had to hide them! I wouldn't want the kids to find them. You didn't really think I had no idea where they were all this time, did you?" Beside me, Herbert was convulsed in silent laughter.

There was another long pause, as Yves digested this information. A flush of colour appeared on his cheeks.

Finally, he said, "I imagine you had a good time looking at them."

I grinned back wickedly. "Oh, I'm afraid imagination wasn't necessary."

Yves's face, already turning pink, flushed a crimson red. There was another long wait before he could bring himself to speak further. Meanwhile, Linda was chattering happily to him in the cockpit, unaware of his discomfort. Herbert was strangling with laughter beside me. I kept a bright grin on my face. Then Herbert remembered something Yves had said about his girlfriend taking some pictures, too.

"I especially liked the ones with you in them," I said, with a sly and knowing smile.

Yves's worst fears were now confirmed. I really had seen them. He sank down, practically transforming into a puddle of red ectoplasm on the hot teak deck.

I milked this for several minutes. I revelled in his agony. This was my payback for all his fart jokes. Then finally, I smilingly said, in a very low voice, so he could hardly hear it, "*Hook, line, and sinker.*"

⟡

Northern Magic wasn't quite the same without Yves. Yet he somehow managed to leave us a lasting gift, and that was the gift of laughter. After our month with him, we had all learned to laugh a lot more, and we continue it to this day. After leaving us, Yves continued around the world overland and by sea, and had many fantastic adventures of his own. He continues to be our close friend, and regularly exchanges e-mails with us and with Jonathan. When we were about to cross the North Atlantic, Yves e-mailed us that he would wear his lucky underwear on our behalf. I mailed back that it wouldn't work unless he sent a photo. He never did.

Linda's trip to Bali was now also at an end, and we began preparing *Northern Magic* for our own departure. Over the previous days, Herbert had twice taken time away from our hotel in Ubud to attend to our failure-prone fridge, and it was once again humming nicely. We sailed to the islands of Lombok and Bawean, meeting more new friends and seeing other aspects of that fascinating collection of diverse islands that is Indonesia. At every stop we made, seven-year-old Christopher, being the smallest, found himself the centre of attention. Curious fingers reached out to touch him, caressing his cheek, his arms, or his fair hair. Many ladies were so delighted with him that they repeatedly pointed to him and then to themselves, indicating their desire to take him home. It always seemed to be the most wrinkled old crones, with ragged stumps of red teeth, rotted from years of chewing betel nuts, who most wanted to hug and press their faces against that of our youngest child. Christopher shrugged off this unwelcome attention, eying large crowds warily and sometimes hiding behind my skirts when necessary.

We continued into the Java Sea, and leaving the beaten tourist path produced in us a new and unwelcome sense of insecurity. Southeast Asia was at that time the world's hotspot for piracy, and our worries were reinforced by warnings and just about daily descriptions of pirate attacks we kept receiving on our Inmarsat satellite system. There had been a recent plague of incidents against ships on both the north coast of Java and the east coast of Borneo, so this troubling thought rested uneasily on our minds as we travelled between those two very spots.

In the daytime everything felt fine, but at night our fears ran rampant. Every light, rather than representing a friendly beacon or a sign of humanity, signalled the presence of a potential murderer or thief. In fact, just four days after our departure from Bawean, pirates attacked a boat in the very harbour in which we had been anchored. There was much fishing activity near the north coast of Java, and we were never out of sight of at least two or three lights. At three in the morning Herbert roused me from my sleep, saying one of those lights appeared to be following us. He had already been watching it for an hour as it had approached from ahead, circled completely around us, and then began following in our wake. It was now less than half a mile away, close enough that we could clearly hear its throbbing engine. We were drifting along placidly at around four knots under a spinnaker, and our pursuer – if indeed we were being pursued – was certainly speedier than we were.

Chances were it was only a curious fishing boat, but given that it seemed to be following us, what should we do if it attempted to come alongside? Should we try to outrace it? Take out our flare gun? Shine a bright light in the pirates' faces to blind them? Use our pepper spray? Ram their wooden boat with our steel one? Do nothing at all?

We had the VHF radio on, and although there was no talking, people were definitely communicating with each other – a series of whistles went back and forth, perhaps in some kind of secret code. We had heard these whistles often enough before, but the division between realism and paranoia is blurry at three in the morning when you are alone in the dark Java Sea and being followed by a mysterious vessel with unknown intentions.

While Herbert continued to keep his eye on the boat, I went below and turned on our satellite e-mail. It felt ridiculous to be doing this, and as I typed the following, I partly wanted to sit back and laugh at this unreal situation. This is what I typed: "At 3:06 a.m. we are at position 6 degrees 23 minutes S and 113 degrees 38 minutes E. Being followed by another vessel, possibly pirates. If no communication in next hour we are in trouble."

I didn't transmit the message; I just left it there, glowing on the screen, ready to send with a single keystroke if necessary.

We were a hundred miles from the nearest sailboat, but there was nothing stopping me from pretending we had a buddy boat just out of sight. Often, if the second boat is farther away, you can hear only one side of a conversation. I took the radio and spoke huskily into it, "*Futuna, Futuna*, this is *Northern Magic*. Situation 68. Situation 68 . . . Roger." It sounded pretty corny, but at the time my puny, sleep-deprived brain just couldn't think of anything better to say. Even as I spoke, that other part of me had a good laugh at my ridiculous and rather transparent charade.

After a while, Herbert decided it was as good a time as any to turn on the motor, charge the batteries and run the fridge – not to mention adding a few extra knots to our speed. The boat continued following us for a long time without making any threatening moves, only whistling occasionally on the VHF. Eventually, we left whoever it was behind us, and our alarming computer message was never sent. Morning's light left us feeling rather silly about the whole episode.

It took several more days to traverse the Java Sea. The morning of our last day, the VHF radio crackled into life just as the sun was about to rise on Herbert's watch. It was the early morning call to prayer, a loud singing chant you would normally hear broadcast from the minarets of a mosque. This was the first time we'd ever heard it at sea. Herbert looked outside and watched half a dozen small fishing boats respond to the call by simultaneously turning their bows to face west, the direction of Mecca, as their devout Muslim crews performed their morning prayers.

The wild and mysterious island of Borneo lay just over the horizon.

12

Standing on the Front Line

We didn't even see the large, low, jungle-covered island of Borneo until we were almost upon it. As we entered the mouth of the heavily wooded Kumai River, an enormous variety of vessels passed us, from modern passenger ferries to wobbly dugout canoes. We passed large wooden cargo vessels that looked as if they ought to be centuries-old Portuguese trading ships laden with silks and spices. In fact, they were carrying huge logs cut from the rainforests of Kalimantan, the Indonesian province that constitutes the largest part of the island of Borneo. We dodged the surprisingly fast arklike ships and, by late morning, were anchored across from the rough and bustling logging town of Kumai.

Kumai had the look of a lawless frontier outpost, with a chocolate-coloured river and a weird assortment of boats lined up along the water's edge. Large floating islands of jungle vegetation often made their way down the river, getting tangled up on our anchor chains and requiring fending off with poles.

The people of Kumai, looking rougher and wilder than their more cultured Balinese counterparts, were nonetheless just as friendly. "*Hello, Meester!*" rang out from every corner, and dark faces invariably lit up with broad smiles as we passed by. We began calling "Hello Meester!" back to the flocks of children, causing them to break into uncontrollable fits of giggles.

Garbage was strewn everywhere. An open sewer ran beside the crowded outdoor market, adding its own pungent note to the riot of smells that rose up from the dirty stalls selling overripe bananas, withered carrots, raw seafood, whole chickens, with heads and outstretched legs still attached, and large smelly bins of dried fish that looked like strips of shoe leather. Walking through the market was an experience that involved all the senses.

The market offered many surprises. We spotted a child thoughtlessly dragging around a small brown ape on a chain. The young black-handed gibbon was terrified, clinging to anything it could reach with its long delicate arms in order to stop being dragged through the milling crowds of people. The boy was oblivious to the gibbon's terror and continued yanking on the chain looped tightly around the animal's slim hips, dragging it through the dust behind him. The skin under the chain had been rubbed clean of fur.

We immediately arranged a trip into the jungle by longboat, along with friends on three other sailboats: our old friends on *Futuna*, with its young German crew, *Nanamuk*, another Canadian family, and *Blue Ibis*, a retired couple from England. We were heading into Tanjung Puting National Park, one of the world's greatest natural treasures and home to a critically endangered species, the orangutan.

From the moment we had heard that we could actually see the great orange apes, nothing could stop us from going. Many months before, we had stood on a dock in Australia, holding in our hands cruising notes and updates on the situation in Indonesia, pondering whether to come to the archipelago at all. There were so many potential problems: ethnic warfare in Kalimantan; possible all-out war in East Timor; political instability; an economic crisis; and pirate attacks. Many cruisers were steering clear altogether.

Strangely, all the things we had feared before going actually happened while we were in Indonesia. There was armed conflict, right in Kumai, between Madurese and Dayaks. East Timor, a province that wanted to re-gain its independence against the wishes of the Indonesian army, did explode into full-scale war. Indonesia's government was toppling, and new political leaders were trying to establish themselves. Piracy was rampant throughout the archipelago. The Indonesian economy was imploding. A state of chaos ruled. Yet despite all this, Indonesia, with all its variety and mystery, held us in thrall.

For our group from four sailboats, we hired four small riverboats, called *kelotoks*, four captains, a cook, a cook's helper, two English-speaking guides, and half a dozen other miscellaneous boatmen. We also engaged four young men to sleep in the cockpits of our sailboats and chase away any would-be thieves while we were gone.

We bought our provisions on the morning of our departure, with the help of our hired cook, a young man of twenty-five with the unlikely name of No. Over the next three days I was to become particularly fond of our hardworking and talented cook, who, outfitted in a feather head-dress and tomahawk, would have looked every inch the archetypal handsome North American Indian brave. He had shoulder-length shiny black hair, high, slanted cheekbones, and flashing dark eyes. Indeed, my initial assessment that No looked like a warrior proved accurate, as later in our trip we were transfixed by his stories of local wars between the men of Kumai and those from the island of Madura.

In between endless hours of peeling vegetables for our large contingent, the quiet young man told us about the most recent battles. The Kumai men had been victorious, he explained, because the local witch doctor had used black magic to give them extra courage and valour in battle. A few months earlier, they had avenged themselves on the Madura men, unwelcome transplants from an island near Java. One of the Madurese had wounded a Kumai man with a machete. In return, the Kumai men murdered several of them. Only the arrival of the army had prevented a full-scale war.

The four women in our group met No at seven in the morning on the day of our departure to buy food for all of us and our hired crew, thirty-five people in total. We Western ladies, clad in our usual attire of modest long skirts but still looking very large and conspicuous, followed No as he wound expertly through the market, carefully selecting bundles of fresh ingredients. Many of them, we couldn't even identify. Watching what No bought, and in what quantities, and comparing this with the delicious dishes he concocted over the next three days, ended up being one of the more interesting parts of the adventure. He bought, for example, more garlic than he did onions, three different types of fresh ginger, many packets of tofu, and small neon-coloured shrimp chips which, when deep fried, expanded like popcorn. After watching the stall-owner's children play in the open sacks of rice with their dirty bare feet, we ladies unanimously voted to buy a complete unopened twenty-five kilogram sack of rice, even if it ended up being too much.

It took us five hours to complete our purchases. Then, with watch-men installed on our sailboats, we were soon gliding smoothly in our blue wooden *kelotoks* up the Sekonyer River. The river itself was slug-gish, narrow, and the colour of milk chocolate. Exuberant plant life crowded in from either side. It was just like the Jungle River Cruise ride at Disney World, with monkeys in the trees and colourful birds overhead, with one big exception: this was real. I had to keep pinching myself to make sure I was awake.

A couple of hours' travel through a narrowing river, surrounded con-tinually by dense greenery, brought us to Tanjung Harapan, the first of three stations inside the nature reserve. We were greeted by the gregari-ous character who was, in the end, to define our magical experience in Kalimantan.

Michael Junior stood up to about my knee, although if he stretched up his long, hairy brown arms they would have reached well over double that height. As he walked, which he did in a comical side-to-side bobbing gait, his elongated hands had to bend sharply inwards to avoid dragging on the ground. His face was brown, furry, and utterly adorable, with an oval-shaped white fringe around his eyes. The eyes themselves were large, perfectly round pools of liquid brown. Michael Junior was a gibbon, a black-handed agile gibbon to be exact, and the friendliest, funniest, most endearing creature you could imagine. He looked like the ideal monkey of everyone's childhood fantasies. He wasn't a monkey, though; he was an ape, a higher order of primate that includes the orang-utan, the chimpanzee, and the gorilla. Apes, we learned, are offended if you call them monkeys.

"Agile" certainly was an apt description of Michael Junior's physical prowess. He looped nimbly around, swinging off the limbs of trees and humans alike as adeptly as any circus acrobat. He wanted to play, and whoever was prepared to indulge him got to swing him around, let him do flips between their arms, and throw him into the air, with Michael Junior fearlessly holding on with various combinations of his four hands. He loved people and saw them simply as a friendly extension of his jungle playground. At two years old, he was a teenager, rescued from captivity six months before as a desperately ill and mistreated creature. Animal-loving volunteers in the park had helped transform him from that pathetic creature into the fearless, mischievous, delightful clown he now was.

Michael Junior's only simian companion was Nyo, a grey female long-tailed macaque similar to the ones we had fed in the monkey forests of Bali and Lombok. Nyo had also been rescued from captivity and, like Michael Junior, chose to make her home around Tanjung Harapan. Macaques have rather fierce and aggressive-looking faces. They have pointed Vulcan ears and expressive protruding eyebrows that bob up and down, communicating curiosity, mischievousness, and, sometimes, anger.

Christopher learned about the mercurial nature of macaques the hard way. As soon as our boats arrived, both Nyo and Michael Junior had hopped on board. Nyo, to everyone's great delight, had immediately nestled into Christopher's lap for a snuggle. Seven-year-old Christopher wasn't wearing a shirt, and Nyo was immediately attracted by his right nipple, plucking at it curiously with her dexterous fingers. Then she did something unexpected. As if suddenly understanding the purpose of that little pink bud, she made an exploratory nip at it with her teeth, and then, satisfied with the results of her investigation, began to suckle!

Christopher, understandably, didn't like this. He pushed Nyo's hungry little mouth away. Nyo didn't like that. As I helped separate the monkey from the object of her interest, she bared her teeth, revealing alarming canine-like fangs and emitted a combination growl-hiss. The one thing Nyo couldn't stand was rejection. Eventually, we had to chase her right off our *kelotok*, but that made her really mad. A few minutes later, she darted in without warning and gave poor Christopher a nasty bite on his ankle that he truly didn't deserve. Christopher wasn't badly hurt, but naturally enough he didn't want to have anything further to do with Nyo, or with any other of the many macaques we met during the rest of our travels.

For her part, Nyo was slow to forgive as well. She continued to snarl at Christopher from various treetops. Evidently hell hath no fury like a female macaque scorned. For the rest of our time there, Christopher hung close by my side, jumping onto my hip whenever Nyo came near. In order to make my proprietary relationship perfectly clear, I began to pick conspicuously through Christopher's hair, as if searching for lice, just as a mother monkey might do. I hoped that this would make it obvious to Nyo that if she made any further advances on my baby, she would have to fight me first. My attempt at monkey language worked, and Nyo made no further hostile advances. All the boys thereafter made very sure they were wearing T-shirts at all times.

We had timed our arrival at the next stop, Pondok Tanggui, to coincide with dusk, because that is when proboscis monkeys came to the river to feed. And sure enough, the jungle was alive with large brown monkeys whose weight bent the branches of the trees as they moved.

Proboscis monkeys are so named because of their elongated noses, which grow almost as long as Pinocchio's, but which, being made of flesh instead of wood, hang down somewhat more limply. The males, especially, have huge noses, hanging ridiculously from their faces like droopy sausages. We saw hundreds of the endangered monkeys congregating alongside the river, and counted as many as seventeen in a single tree.

At night the boatmen unrolled our futons and hung up mosquito netting. Michael and Jon chose to sleep in the shoulder-high space below decks, while Christopher, Herbert, and I lay down in the airier but more exposed position on top, covered by an awning. From there, we fell asleep to the quiet buzzing of the night jungle.

Next morning, as soon as dawn broke, we received our first visitor of the day. It was Jekky, a young male orangutan about five years old. He ambled around in slow and deliberate orangutan fashion on his knuckles, hoping to snag some of the bananas he was sure we were hiding. In wonder and delight, we softly came towards him and made our offerings, and soon we had a good relationship going with the young orangutan. His main interest was breakfast, but he was also content to be swung around by his arms or legs. There were many of us willing to oblige on both counts.

Soon we were also joined by Rosemary, a fully-grown female orang-utan, and her two children. When we learned Rosemary's story, we fell in love. About two years before, Rosemary had become interested in an orphaned orangutan baby being raised by veterinarians at the station. Full of maternal concern, Rosemary had broken in and kidnapped the infant so that she could raise it herself in the wild. When Rosemary's own infant was later born, she continued to care for her adopted son as if it were her own. She appeared with her two babies, the adopted one about twice the size of her little one, which was now a year old and clinging to its mother's body for all it was worth. It was hard for Rosemary to walk or climb with the two heavy bodies attached to her, so she often brushed off the older one, making him climb on his own whenever he could. But he never left her side, nor let go of her long orange fur.

We approached Rosemary and her babies with awe and fed them bananas, which Rosemary chewed first before giving to her infant. She did not object when we stroked the fur of her little ones. A sleek black cat had appeared, a pet of one of the park rangers, and it positioned itself comfortably on a wooden bench nearby. Rosemary spotted the cat and, with her smallest baby positioned like a backpack and her adopted son clinging to one side, slowly ambled over to where the cat was curled up on the bench. The cat watched her approach, apparently unconcerned. The great orange ape stood directly in front of the little puss and inspected it closely for a minute. Then she extended her muscular, hairy arm and gently, so gently, began patting the cat on the back. The older of her two babies got very excited about this and began waving his own arm in the air in a jerky patting motion as if he wanted to do the same.

Then Rosemary gently took the cat's short black tail and half-lifted the cat into the air, as if to check whether it was male or female. Unbelievably, the cat submitted patiently, although with glaring eyes, to this uncomfortable inspection. When one of our guides made a threatening noise, Rosemary guiltily dropped the cat and backed away, looking just as I do when I'm caught sneaking Hershey's Kisses in the middle of the night. Later we learned that Rosemary had quite a reputation for fighting with other grown orangutans, but she clearly had a soft spot in her heart for tiny helpless creatures.

Rosemary and her babies left, after being convinced that they had depleted our supply of bananas. This enabled little Jekky, who had been warily hanging in the background, to return to the water's edge. Jekky had shown a particular fondness for Herbert, and now he grabbed his hand, leading Herbert down the boardwalk towards the feeding station a kilometre or two away. But Jekky had not the slightest intention of walking that whole distance. Instead, he boldly shinnied up and settled himself happily on Herbert's hip, draping his long hairy arms casually around Herbert's neck.

Before long, our captain, while flattered at the attention, began remarking on the weight of his solidly built buddy, who was a good thirty kilos. But if he made any motion to put Jekky down, the orang-utan clung on with his powerful arms in such a way that it became clear he was not going to be put off very easily. Christopher used to do the very same to me when I was trying to throw him into the water: he called it "barnacling." Herbert was forced to continue walking through the jungle with his giant hairy barnacle, and the look on his face suggested he wasn't altogether unhappy with the arrangement.

Halfway down the path, Jekky jumped down and went over to take Christopher's hand. We soon discovered the new game Jekky had in mind. As soon as he had one of Christopher's hands firmly in his, the orangutan grabbed Christopher's other wrist and then swiftly clamped on to both of Christopher's ankles with his feet. In a flash, Christopher found himself bound, hand and foot, to this orangutan, which was about the same size he was. Rolling over onto his back, Jekky pulled Christopher over right on top of him. He wanted to play!

Christopher, giggling nervously, was a little taken aback by this overture. He didn't know quite what he was supposed to do. Jekky released Christopher's hands while keeping his ankles in handcuffs and lay on his back, his long arms outstretched over his head. He seemed to be inviting a tickle, so Christopher obliged. Then the wrestling began in earnest, with Jekky's incredibly powerful arms pulling Christopher over on top of him until they were rolling around together on the spongy jungle floor. Christopher, to his credit, entered into the spirit of the thing and didn't panic at being manhandled by a wild ape many times his strength.

The orangutan clearly understood that the smaller humans were children like he was, and saw them as potential playmates, albeit spindly and weak ones.

After Christopher found himself spilled on the jungle floor once too often, he decided he'd had enough. Herbert and I gently disentangled the two wrestling partners. Unlike the mercurial Nyo, Jekky accepted the end of the match with good grace. There can't be many seven-year-olds in the history of the world who have wrestled with a wild orangutan. Christopher took it all in stride, as if this kind of thing happened to him every day.

We had become separated from our guide and the rest of the group. We hadn't gone too much farther before Jekky signalled to us that we were going the wrong way. Just like a little boy at the candy counter, he began tugging insistently on Herbert's hand, leading us on the correct path towards the orangutan feeding station. Having set us straight, Jekky dropped Herbert's hand and quietly evaporated into the jungle, leaving us alone among the wild orchids, carnivorous pitcher plants, and vines on the tree-shrouded path.

Then we noticed another visitor knuckling down the track. This was Toyo, a baby orangutan a little smaller than Christopher. No doubt he and Jekky had compared notes, because Toyo also wanted to play with these special small-sized human visitors, a pretty rare event in these parts. Toyo headed straight for our boys and a brand new and equally unforgettable match of orangutan wrestling began.

Soon the park rangers arrived, carrying bananas and sweetened milk, and our attention became focused on the orangutans of all shapes and sizes that began emerging out of the trees in response to the rangers' bellowing calls.

From far away you could see the treetops ominously sway and bend as large apes weighing fifty to a hundred kilos swung over to the elevated feeding platform. Using hanging vines and bending branches, they catapulted themselves expertly through the forest canopy. A dozen true "Georges of the Jungle" quickly congregated on the raised platform, gorging themselves on bananas and using their hands as cups to drink fortified milk from a bucket.

We capped off the day with a delicious cool swim in the tea-coloured water, while our boatmen watched out for crocodiles, before falling asleep again to the hum of the jungle.

Our next day's objective was a visit to a notorious illegal gold mine. Many of our boatmen had been nervous about taking us there. One of our guides was absolutely against it, but our favourite guide, Andi, assured us that the miners would be welcoming provided we brought gifts of cigarettes, sugar, coffee, and candy. We headed up the river in our narrow wooden boats to visit the mine, which government officials and international environmental groups like Greenpeace had been unsuccessful in closing down. On the way, we stopped at a rickety wooden store on stilts, built to service the nearby loggers' camp, and bought our peace offerings.

The mine was located at the very end of the navigable part of the Sekonyer River, which became increasingly choked by vegetation the farther up we penetrated. Often, branches and fronds of plants brushed against the walls of our little boats and their leaves fell inside the big square lower-deck windows, where the five children played cards while watching the passing scenery, with frequent stops for monkey-spotting.

The mine itself was a giant scar on the land, a moonscape completely denuded of trees. The men, women, and children who lived there, in dust, dirt, and squalor on the perimeter of the national park, placed their very lives on the line each day in order to scrabble out a few dollars worth of gold dust from the scorching earth. Under their depredations, the rainforest was turning into an arid wasteland. Once the trees were cut down, the topsoil had quickly been washed away, leaving an ugly, sterile sandpit that might take hundreds of years to grow over again. It was the exact opposite of an oasis, a splotch of desert in the middle of the rainforest.

Using a giant hose, the miners blasted water at the soil, creating a pool of sandy sludge that was slurped up by a pump then run over a piece of ordinary carpet and down a sluice, where it collected in a pond that eventually drained back into the river. As the men blasted the water into the hillside, the sandy pit in which they were standing sank deeper and deeper. The lower it got, the greater the risk of the wall above them collapsing. When this happened, as it did regularly, anyone unlucky enough to be standing beneath it would be killed instantly. In this mine and a handful of others in the immediate area, on average one person died in such a landslide every month. This means that twelve people out of a workforce of three hundred died *each year*. And that doesn't include the unknown number of people who were killed by long-term exposure to the toxic mercury that is used to extract the gold from the mud.

This particular mine was almost at the end of its life, producing only seven grams of gold a day, for a total income of seventy dollars. Almost half of this amount was remitted to a boss in Kumai, who laid out the capital for hoses, pump, and diesel generator. The thirty-five dollars that remained supported about forty men, women, and children. Of course, the children had no prospect of going to school; they began working in the mine at the age of eight or ten and would continue doing so until they died.

After bathing the rugs to remove the gold trapped in their fibres, the miners dumped the sandy residue into a water-filled bucket, to which they added half a vial of pure mercury. By running the liquid mercury through their fingers, the miners helped it to bond with the almost invisible grains of gold. The miner we watched seemed to have no idea that by handling the mercury with his bare hands, he was slowly but surely poisoning himself.

When a small, quivering, silvery blob of gold-mercury remained in the miner's hand, he dumped the rest of the bucket's mixture of sand, water, and mercury into the pond, where it ran directly into the river and through the national park. Before this operation opened a few years before, the river had run clear. Now, thanks to run-off from the mine, it had turned an opaque brown, and the aquatic life the river supported was dead or dying. The volunteers at the first station in the park were forced to use this mercury-laden water for bathing and sometimes even for drinking. No one knows what it may be doing to the orangutans and other animals that have no other source of drinking water.

We watched as the gold was smelted. This was the most hazardous phase of all. Using a foot bellows and a blowtorch, a young woman, who looked to be about six months pregnant, burned off the mercury until there was nothing left but a molten blob of liquid gold. One moment she held a red-hot blob of liquid in her spoon; the next she immersed the spoon in a bowl of water and the blob was magically transformed into a gleaming seven-gram nugget of pure gold. She probably had no idea that the mercury she was burning off was entering the air she breathed, poisoning her and her developing baby. Beside her were her two little children, even more vulnerable than their mother to the effects of the mercury. At another illegal goldmine, a young worker gave birth to a baby badly deformed by mercury poisoning, with its intestines formed outside its body. It died shortly after. God only knew if the same fate awaited this young woman's unborn child.

We each reverently held the still-warm nugget, surprisingly heavy for its small size. This alluring little dot of gold, with its new quality of menace, contained an unmistakable symbolism.

✦

As we left the gold mine and descended back downstream in our blue and white longboat, we passed many other fresh wounds upon the Kalimantan jungle. The scars on the otherwise beautiful face of the rain-forest were not like the ugly exposed pits of the gold mine; these were logging tracks, chains of newly cut trees reaching out in pairs of parallel lines into the jungle, joined together by a series of smaller logs like oversized train tracks. The tracks were to allow huge logs to be slid down to the river from deep within the jungle, where sixty- and eighty-year-old hardwood trees were being felled. We passed a great many log booms, rafts almost half a kilometre long of huge rainforest logs tied together for their trip to the voracious sawmills of Kumai. Each night, while we slept on the river, we would be awakened by more of these log booms passing by, the narrow way lit by powerful torchlights. The long rafts, illegally taken from the jungle, were being secretly brought to market under cover of darkness.

The loggers were not only destroying valuable rainforest, they were actually pushing right inside the national park, a protected area and the jewel of Indonesia's park system. This destruction of one of the world's most precious parks was happening right before our eyes.

The logging was also directly contributing to the death of the orang-utan in one of its last refuges in the world. Once, hundreds of thousands of orangutans ranged throughout southeast Asia. But human kind, one of the orangutan's closest relatives, is also its most vicious enemy. As people claimed ownership over the vast forests, logging and clearing them for cultivation, the orangutan's few remaining places of refuge dwindled away. Some scientists predict that the species will be extinct in the wild in only ten years more. The orangutan is in critical danger, and logging is its principal enemy.

Our guide, Andi, was a Dayak tribesman who had grown up deep in the jungle, a six-hour walk from the nearest village. Over the previous three days, we had found Andi to be not only an intelligent, deep thinking, even intellectual, man, but also remarkably well informed. Over his working life (Andi was in his late thirties), he had been a fisherman, gold miner, logger, bricklayer, and now tourist guide. While he had the heart of a conservationist and was actively involved in working for the protection of animals, which endeared him to us, Andi also had strong ties to people on the other side of the fence. This made him the perfect guide, since he had inexhaustible knowledge of just about everything we could think to ask him.

It was Andi who agreed, against the objections of the other boatmen, to take us to the gold mine, and now it was Andi who asked whether we were interested in visiting the illegal loggers in one of their camps.

We stopped at a ramshackle collection of houses tottering on tall stilts at the river's edge. This was a logging camp, where a team of half a dozen loggers and their families lived while exploiting the timber in the immediate area. The houses were just outside the park, across the narrow river, but each day the men crossed the river to steal logs from inside the park. These particular homes had been there for two years. Young children wearing fake designer watches smiled at us from rickety boards that joined the crudely built houses. Small dugout canoes served to link the miserable collection of raised huts, and to transport the men across the river.

We sat outside one of these homes and passed around candies while Andi translated our questions to the loggers and their families. They refused Andi's request that we go to where the loggers were actually felling trees inside the park, but they were friendly enough and willing to talk.

Later, we visited a second group of loggers, and with the gift of sugar, coffee, and cigarettes, we convinced them to let us go with them into the park. We watched as they hauled a gigantic illegally felled tree all the way to the river. As we watched, a powerful boat filled with armed policemen, whose job it was to prevent just this activity, sped by. Our loggers were not dismayed, however. The police, we were told, had come not to arrest anyone, but to collect their bribes.

Gradually, our eyes began opening with horror to what we had been seeing over the past week. Before, we had admired the hustle and bustle of the Kumai riverfront, where dozens of muscular wooden barges fifteen metres wide and three times as long were being loaded with huge red logs. But now it slowly dawned on us that everything we had seen was based on the theft of trees from the national park. And it was being done right in the open, under the very noses of authorities whose job it was to protect the park.

We asked Andi what proportion of the logs we had seen in Kumai came from the illegal logging within the park. Andi looked at me quizzically, as if I had asked a stupid question.

"They are all illegal," he replied.

"You mean to say that *everything* we see in Kumai is illegal logs coming from inside the park?"

"All the legal trees outside the park have already been cut. At least 95 per cent of the logs you see come from inside the park," he answered.

When we'd heard enough, we climbed back into our longboats, waved goodbye to the loggers, and continued down the river. My head was spinning. On our right, on the non-park side of the river, we could see old logging tracks, no longer in use because all the valuable timber had long since been removed. On our left, fresh logging tracks led right into the park, and we could see long rafts of illegal logs waiting to be pulled down the river to Kumai, where sawmills and log barges eagerly awaited them.

A cluster of fresh logging tracks soon told us we were getting near to Natai Lengkuas. Here, just a few weeks before, a huge group of loggers armed with machetes had confronted American researchers and chased them away so that they would be free to log wherever they pleased. Our journey had brought us to the front lines of a world-wide struggle, and signs of the most recent battle were still fresh. Now we were going to see what remained of the abandoned research camp. As far as I know, we were the first outsiders to visit the scene. The other boatmen were afraid to come here, we learned later, because the loggers had warned them to keep tourists away.

We tied up at a wooden boardwalk similar to those at the three earlier stations. At this one, however, no friendly apes greeted us; instead, all we found was the broken glass of a notice board whose contents lay on the ground, the announcements it once contained crumbling into the moist earth. There were no humans or animals in sight.

We entered a small wood-frame house. Outside was a whiteboard with the duty roster for the day still marked on it in felt pen. There was a large hole in the screen of the front window, and the doorframe had been hammered in and was toppled over inside. Papers were scattered all over the floor. An empty egg carton and other food debris gave clues that there had been an abrupt departure, and a torn photograph showing a young Indonesian man hung forlornly on the wall near Sierra Club wildlife posters.

Our boys picked up some notebooks they had found on the floor and brought them over to me. A lump rose in my throat as I realized that these were field notebooks filled with data. The children collected all the notebooks they could find, and we placed them all in a cardboard box for safekeeping.

Next we found a building with a sign on it that read "William Mason Center for the Natural Sciences." We entered it through a smashed window. Everything of value to the loggers had long since been stripped away, but medical supplies, the remains of lab equipment, and reams of papers remained scattered all over the floor. I picked up a wooden machete case that lay abandoned on the ground.

When the loggers had attacked, on July 8, 1999, sixteen people, mostly volunteers, had been working here. Most of them were an expedition of conservationists who had arrived just days earlier on a volunteer work experience program. I picked up one of the prospectuses the Earthwatch volunteers had brought with them, describing their role in saving Borneo's rainforests. I also picked up the business cards of Dr. Yeager and her husband, Trevor Blondal, which I found among the litter on the floor. I put the two dusty cards in my pocket.

Then we entered the most heartbreaking room of all. It was knee-deep in rubbish. The floor was covered with envelopes, all containing seed samples that had been carefully catalogued and labelled. Thousands of envelopes had been torn down from where they had been carefully stored in shelves on the wall. Samples going back a decade had been trampled on the rough wooden floor. This was someone's life work, reduced to a messy pile of refuse. I felt like crying.

We continued to make our way through the various vandalized buildings at the camp, feeling more and more depressed at the wanton destruction. The smiling loggers with whom we had shared our candies just an hour earlier had been among the very men who had laid siege to this camp.

I asked Andi if Dr. Yeager was planning to return, and what would happen to her if she did.

"Oh, I don't think there would be a problem," he answered. "By the time she comes back, the loggers will have finished here."

Before we left to continue down the river and home to *Northern Magic*, we paused to listen to the sounds of the jungle. And there it was: a high-pitched drone, the faint but unmistakable sound of a chainsaw.

13

Magic and Heartache in the Jungles of Borneo

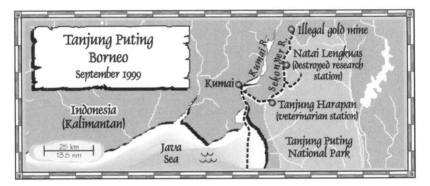

O n our way back from our expedition, we came to a family decision that we wanted to give something back to the rainforests of Borneo, a place that had opened our eyes and stolen our hearts. Herbert and I had been having long talks with Andi, who worked as a park volunteer, about what we could contribute. Andi did have a suggestion.

We had learned that the people who were caring for Michael Junior were hoping to find another gibbon to be Michael's mate. They wanted Michael to establish his own family and thus discourage him from further human dependence. And so, after meeting with the park veterinarian and the Forestry Department to make sure that they supported the idea ("*Itu bagus*," nodded the park ranger, "That is good"), we decided to buy an ape.

I have to say now, after having learned so much more about the conservation of endangered species, that purchasing the gibbon was wrong. While it's true that we had official approval, and it seemed this was, in

Indonesia, the way things were done, by buying the animal, even if from private people, we helped establish a market value for the gibbon that would only encourage more to be captured from the wild. We would have been horrified to learn that for every live gibbon that survives to be sold or held as a pet, nine others have been slaughtered. Most baby gibbons die when their mothers are shot out of the trees. Others die in the traumatic first days and weeks after capture.

But at the time we didn't know much about the issue. We hoped and believed we were doing some good. Certainly, we offered this one young gibbon a chance at a better life.

Late one afternoon, we followed Andi down the main street of Kumai, handed over eight dollars for the use of two motorcycles, and went off in search of a gibbon. Andi drove on one bike with a friend, Mr. Ambon, and Herbert and I doubled up on another.

After a fifteen-minute drive on our rented motorbikes, we drove up to a large fenced property containing a prosperous-looking white house with a red tiled roof. Three young children, two boys and a girl, played in the barren front yard. In the middle of the dirt driveway was a wooden post. Chained to that post was one forlorn little gibbon.

The ape was only about a year old, not fully grown, and perhaps the size of a large, but very thin, cat. She had the same long, long arms, dainty black fingers, and endearing round face that we so loved in Michael Junior. It was a sweet, curious face with huge round eyes that you couldn't look at without breaking into a smile. Except there was no smiling at the pathetic little creature we found cringing in the dust at our feet. This animal's resemblance to Michael was purely physical; in total contrast to that other confident, gregarious, hilarious character, it was clear that this gibbon, in its short life, had known nothing but fear.

It turned out that this was the same gibbon we had earlier seen in the Kumai market – terrified, dirty, and yanked along at the end of a chain by a young boy oblivious to its anguish as it clung fearfully to everything in sight. The same young boy now regarded us inscrutably. We saw that even the gibbon's owners couldn't come near without the little animal baring her teeth and backing away to the limit of her short chain. Her owners told us some friends had found her abandoned in the jungle six months before. We knew, however, that the only way she would have been separated from her mother was to have been pried off her dead body.

Magic screamed in terror as her chain was cut away, as if she were about to be killed. Once freed of her odious chain, the gibbon just crouched there, with long arms wrapped around her knees, looking for all the world like a scared little girl. Her large round eyes darted nervously back and forth at the menacing people who towered around her. She was too frightened even to try to move away, and just cowered there passively as if waiting for the executioner's axe to fall.

The gibbon's owner produced a cardboard box, and I wondered how we were going to get her into it. But she was happy to take refuge inside and climbed in on her own, although her furry black-and-white gibbon face once popped out through the flaps as we closed them. Later, as we were tying the flaps down with string, five long elegant fingers with manicured black fingernails snuck out and tried to pry them open.

We had left the kids playing with their friends on *Nanamuk* without being sure we really were going to buy the animal that day, and not considering at all that we might actually be bringing it back to *Northern Magic*. But here we were, with one black-handed agile gibbon in a cardboard box marked *Mi Goreng Ayam* – chicken fried noodles.

Our three kids, plus the two on *Nanamuk*, shrieked with excitement to discover we had actually brought the gibbon, soon to be named Magic, back to the boat. We opened the box and tied the end of Magic's rope near the cockpit. Immediately, she jumped up onto the stainless steel rigging of the mizzenmast and climbed as high as the rope would allow her. Dangling by one hand and one foot above our heads, she looked quite comfortable as she surveyed her new surroundings nervously but with obvious interest. She wanted nothing to do with any of us, but was happy to go looping around on her long arms from one wire to another, as if she had spent all her days growing up on a sailboat.

Soon, Magic no longer looked like a terrified little girl with large round eyes, but like a real ape. Jonathan sat himself on the boom nearby, patiently watching her, offering her bananas, and resisting my attempts to get him inside for dinner. Eventually, Magic started to approach him, and by bedtime was actually sitting in his lap, letting him pick through her fur as we had so often seen monkeys do in the wild. Magic still didn't like big people, but gradually Jonathan, and eventually the other children, too, gained her trust.

We had made a little shelter for Magic to sleep in, but she made her own nest on top of the mizzen sail, right where the boom meets the mast. Although it was soft, it didn't offer any protection from cold or rain. As we went to bed, it tugged at my heartstrings to see Magic huddling beside the mast, her arms around her knees in that same sad pose that had brought tears to my eyes before. As I tucked Jon into his nice cosy bunk down below, I could see my eleven-year-old was also troubled.

"I don't like where Magic has to sleep, Mom," he said sadly. "It's not a good bed at all. She's going to be cold and lonely out there on the boom."

"I don't think that's the way Magic feels about it, Jon," I answered, groping for a way to make my kind-hearted son – and myself, too – feel better. "Where do you think gibbons sleep in the wild? In trees, of course. But where Magic lived, they didn't even give her a tree to climb in – only an awful wooden box on top of a post.

"But now, for the first time since she was a baby, Magic has found a kind of tree – our mast. And she has a nice cosy branch to sleep on – our boom. And as we rock in the water, the boom moves a little, just like the branches of a tree would in the wind. So right now her instincts tell her she has found the perfect place to sleep."

The next morning, with our little gibbon friend swinging in the rigging, *Northern Magic* left the Kumai waterfront and headed up the river into the Borneo jungle, tracing the same route we had taken in our wooden longboats days before. Behind us motored Grace and Rob Dodge on *Nanamuk*, from British Columbia. Our guide, Andi, was with us also, as well as a park volunteer. As far as we know, we and *Nanamuk* were only the second and third sailboats to have ever gone up this narrow, uncharted river. And we were definitely the first to do so with a black-handed agile gibbon dangling from the mast.

For one glorious day we had our very own little ape. It warmed our hearts to watch her transformation from the frightened creature of the day before to the curious little personality who watched the jungle scenery go by from her favourite vantage point, hanging under the cockpit awning. Although she still didn't like to be approached by adults, she was now quite tolerant of the children. It was thrilling to be bringing her back into the jungle, and to know that she had a chance to be happy again after her traumatic start in life. Magic's wild primate cousins, the proboscis monkeys, looked down at us from the treetops as we made our way up the narrow, chocolate-coloured river, dodging floating islands of dislodged jungle vegetation as we went.

After three hours, we tied up at the wooden dock of the first station, Tanjung Harapan. The staff were expecting us, and it didn't take two minutes before Michael Junior had swung onto our boat to check out his new playmate. We'd spent hours speculating on exactly what would happen when our two prospective love birds met for the first time. Michael Junior didn't disappoint us. He was so excited to see Magic he practically did flips in the air, racing over to see her as she sat uncertainly under the cockpit table, and tapping her lightly on the shoulder in a gibbonish game of tag.

Magic tapped him back, but the contact wasn't exactly friendly, and each time Michael Junior approached, Magic swatted him away. They continued their game in the rigging, where Michael Junior had a big advantage because he wasn't tied up. Finally, he tried a different tactic and sat quietly beside Magic, showing her his back in a primate gesture of friendship. Magic was supposed to respond by giving him a friendly grooming, but she didn't get the hint and continued spurning his overtures. It wasn't exactly the joyful first meeting we had dreamed of, but it was, we hoped, a start.

When it came time to bring Magic ashore to her new home, she really didn't want to leave. With the abundance of things on our boat for her four hands to cling on to, we had a hard time getting her to let go. Finally, her best friend, Jonathan, coaxed her away. Once disentangled from the rigging, she grabbed her rope as though holding someone's hand, wobbling beside Jon in her side-to-side gibbon gait. They were a funny looking, mismatched pair as they trotted down the jungle path together, with Magic standing only a little taller than Jonathan's knee.

After a little rest in a tree, it was time for Magic to get her check-up from Dr. Gede Suarsadana, a slender young veterinarian from Bali whose name sounds like "g'day." Gede's was the first adult hand able to comfort and calm poor Magic, who was once again cowering in fear. Gede was helped by Andi, whose sturdy Dayak body seemed equally adapted to soothing a frightened little monkey as it was to hunting wild boars in the jungle with a blowgun – which he also did, on occasion. The two men worked patiently for a long time to soothe Magic's jangled nerves. She needed some anti-worm medicine and a shot. Both men worked together with infinite patience, talking to Magic gently, patting her, and getting her calmed down before Gede, in a practised motion so swift as to be almost invisible, pinned her down on the examination table and quickly gave her the injection she needed.

This time, Magic did not scream or make a sound. In a minute it was over, and she was free to return to the outdoors, where Andi carefully tried out several possible spots before finally tying her to a chair near the edge of the clearing. For an ex-logger and jungle man whose people have traditionally eaten orangutan as part of their diet, Andi had an amazing empathy for Magic. I loved him for it.

Magic took to the trees and crouched there in the branches, looking down on the rest of us with her big round eyes. The plan was to keep her on her rope for a few days so that she would realize food was available to her if she wanted it, and then to let her go free. Over the next days, Michael Junior got more and more frenetic in his efforts to impress Magic. The more hyperactive he became, the more Magic withdrew. Surprisingly, it was Nyo, the macaque, who had earlier attacked Christopher, who became Magic's first primate friend. We knew this for sure when the sun rose one morning on the sight of Nyo and Magic grooming each other companionably.

The hoped-for friendship between Michael Junior and Magic just didn't develop. Magic wanted nothing to do with him. Finally, she was forced to seek refuge from Michael Junior's over-eager advances by hiding inside the rangers' cabin. The rest of us tried to release some of Michael Junior's unspent energies by tossing him up and down and spinning him in the air until he became dizzy and staggered around the clearing like a little drunken sailor. It was only the next day that we discovered why Magic and Michael Junior weren't hitting it off. Rather sheepishly, Dr. Gede released a bombshell. Our little Magic wasn't a girl at all: she was a he!

In that instant our whole delicious, elaborate fantasy of being god-parents to a bunch of adorable baby gibbons collapsed around us like shattering glass. Magic, a boy? But, but, but – we had checked! They told us she was a girl!

Soon, we were laughing in disbelief. What bozos! Instead of a mate for Michael Junior, we had brought him a rival! No wonder Magic felt so uncomfortable!

Eventually, Magic would be pronounced fit, healthy, and possessed of sufficient wild instincts to be able to make a go of it on his own. For many months, there was no news of him, and we began to fear that he had not survived. But a year later, a young male gibbon the veterinarian felt was almost certainly Magic, briefly returned to the station. So we feel comforted that for one animal at least we made a small difference.

We were so impressed by the tender care given to Magic that Herbert and I approached Dr. Gede and asked him how we could help in his work. We learned that Gede's practice was funded by a small non-profit organization named Friends of the National Parks. The group operated on a shoestring budget of less than four hundred dollars per month from donations made by passing tourists and by a few conservation-minded travel agencies. We began questioning Gede about his needs. I had imag-ined he would say he required medicines or special equipment, but his wish list was much more simple than that.

"We need food," he answered immediately. "Not for the animals, but for us. We need to eat. We have nothing for ourselves but rice, and not enough of that."

We were shocked to discover that Gede, a highly trained veterinar-ian, was living and working in the park seven days a week, in a simple communal wooden house, for not much more than a plate of rice at the end of the day. That his most urgent need was something as basic as food for himself and the other volunteers boggled our minds.

In our time at Tanjung Harapan, we came to know Gede quite well, as well as Wanto, another volunteer in his early twenties. Unlike the mild, clean-cut Gede, Wanto looked a little threatening at first glance, with a great shock of long wavy black hair that he often left loose around his shoulders, and a small carved bone tusk around his neck. We kept on teasing Wanto that he was the original Wild Man of Borneo, until we discovered that he was, in fact, a university graduate in economics from Java. He had left the corporate world behind to fulfil his ambition to work in the park.

In the evenings Gede and Wanto joined the crew of *Nanamuk* and us in the cockpits of our sailboats. We grew to like them both enormously. With all the turmoil in Indonesia, Herbert and I considered the personal and economic sacrifice that these young men were making, purely out of their love for these animals, as something infinitely precious. After seeing the gold miners and the loggers and all the filth and floating garbage in Kumai, such dedicated and forward-thinking young Indonesians, who were willing to make personal sacrifices to help preserve their environment – *our* environment – felt like nothing short of a miracle. It seemed vital to us that such people be supported and nurtured if the natural world was to have any chance of surviving an onslaught of too many humans thinking only about short-term profit or day-to-day survival. That day, we made a promise to them that we would do our best to find a way for people outside Borneo to make contributions to their work and help provide the extra funding they so desperately needed. It's a promise we carried through on, and we continue to raise funds for them to this day.

During the days we stayed at Tanjung Harapan, Michael Junior and Nyo began making themselves at home on our boat, darting inside to make raids on our fruit hammock, swinging boldly around the rigging, and generally turning *Northern Magic* into a primate playground. All five kids were in our salon, engrossed in the board game Risk when Nyo made one of her surprise attacks. Swiping up a handful of plastic Risk army pieces, she stuffed them into her cheeks the way a squirrel does, then leapt off the boat and scampered up a tree. There she sat, cracking the plastic artillery, cavalry, and infantry in her teeth as if they were nuts. Her bushy eyebrows bobbed up and down all the while, giving her an expression that looked alternately shocked and intent. Every few minutes, she would eject a few pieces of mangled plastic from her mouth, and they would tumble as colourful red, blue, and green crumbs into the water below her perch. Nyo did this with tremendous satisfaction and much eyebrow waggling all evening long – and even the next morning still had a few unchomped pieces in her mouth.

Michael Junior's naughty tendencies weren't as destructive and tended more towards the stealing of food and the receiving of attention. He succeeded admirably at both. By the time we left, Michael had turned every last one of us into gibbon fans for life. As we sat in our cockpits in the evening with Robert and Grace from *Nanamuk*, and Gede and Wanto from the station, little Michael would curl up in someone's lap and happily fall asleep. They were golden moments, and they bound our hearts even more firmly to this place.

14

Water Spouts and Lightning Strikes

Borneo ~ Singapore
Malaysia
September – November 1999

Malaysia
Johor Bahru
Singapore
Batam
water spout
Malaysia
Borneo
Indonesia
(Kalimantan)
Indian
Ocean
Indonesia
(Sumatra)
Serutu
Kumai
300 km
162 nm

W e departed Borneo for a two-day sail, enlivened by the discovery of jumping maggots in our Kumai cucumbers and a violent rainfall and thunderstorm. In company with our Canadian friends on *Nanamuk*, we paused at the island of Serutu, almost half way to Singapore. Although there was a village nearby, the bay we chose was uninhabited and beautiful. The pristine waters were crystal clear and full of transparent, undulating jellyfish and masses of small squid. Parrots and monkeys roamed the trees of the jungle that crowded up against the sandy beach. In a freshwater stream perfect for swimming, we soaked off weeks' worth of Borneo grime in the most refreshing cold bath imaginable. There were no people around. This undisturbed piece of paradise was exactly what we needed.

As we bathed, tiny tropical fish such as you might find in a home aquarium darted around us. Those strange air-breathing fish we called mud skippers frolicked on the rocks at the water's edge, squiggling and jumping around as we came near. By following the stream upriver, we discovered a small waterfall under which we could take an actual shower. Sitting half-submerged in the pool under the waterfall was like being in a cool Jacuzzi, with tiny bubbles from the waterfall making us tingle all over. We wanted to stay forever.

Herbert and I brought all the dirty laundry from the boat and washed it in the stream, rinsing the clothes luxuriously and lavishly. On the boat, we were normally forced to use and re-use washing water until it was a dark and murky grey. Immersing our sweaty bodies in the water as we washed was almost nice enough to make me wish for even more dirty laundry to appear. Never have I enjoyed the washing of laundry as much as I did on that steaming hot day near the equator.

The next day we bade farewell to our little paradise for a three-day sail to Batam Island, our last stop in Indonesia and just around the corner from the great city-state of Singapore. The winds were again light and the seas calm, and *Northern Magic* was chugging along peacefully under a spinnaker when we crossed the equator and entered the Northern Hemisphere again for the first time in eighteen months. At virtually the same time, we achieved another milestone, for we were now exactly halfway around the world. From now on, every mile we covered would be bringing us nearer to home.

We were heading now through a particularly bad area for piracy, where a boat in our group of friends had actually been attacked. We had banded together with *Nanamuk* for safety against pirates, but we had never imagined that Robert and Grace's alertness would save us from a very different kind of danger.

It was mid-morning, my watch, the day after crossing the equator. I was very tired from a poor and sweaty sleep the night before and had asked the boys to keep watch in the cockpit while I grabbed an hour's rest. Increasingly, as Michael and Jonathan got older, we had been asking them to take short periods of watch. I was thus happily snoozing down below in the navigation station when the VHF radio crackled to life beside my ear. It was Grace on *Nanamuk*, sailing a quarter mile away off our port side. She curtly instructed me to get outside, quickly.

The kids were still in the cockpit, playing cards on that hot and windless day, and dutifully keeping an eye out for oncoming ships. But what they had not noticed was something emerging from inside a dark, low cloud to our starboard side. It was a waterspout, a large and ominous-looking one, and it was less than a mile away.

We'd seen a waterspout once before, a rapidly spinning air mass that sucked water up into the sky, but it had been a thin and ephemeral thing, more of a curiosity than a threat. This one was different. It truly was a tornado, swirling up the ocean in a thick grey column that reached all the way into the cloud above. What really gave us an idea of its tremendous force was not only the diameter of the main spout, but the secondary circular wall of water being churned up around its base, spun hard by the tremendous centrifugal force at the centre. The base of the spout looked to be perhaps half as big as our boat. It was heading across our stern, in the direction of *Nanamuk*.

I gave more juice to the engine, hoping to increase the distance between us and the spout. With some luck, we would be able to outrace it. For a short time, it looked as if we might. But no sooner did we tuck in our tail and begin to scoot away, than the spout appeared to notice us for the first time. It abruptly changed direction and veered directly towards us. All of a sudden we realized the danger we were in. We practically threw the three boys into the cabin, followed in quick succession by two bags of sails and our cockpit seats.

We had no time to do anything more before scrambling inside ourselves. If the spout passed directly over us, there was no doubt we would lose our sails, which were flaked loose on the boom, and quite possibly much more. For all we knew, it might rip away our dinghy and life raft, and everything in the cockpit lockers besides. If it was powerful enough, it might even suck open the main hatches and strip the inside of the boat, too. We had no idea what kind of chaos might soon envelop us. Waterspouts can sometimes severely damage or even sink big ships.

The safest thing we could think of for the children was to have Jonathan and Christopher huddle together in Jonathan's well-enclosed bunk, with the leecloth tied up to protect them from flying objects or, God forbid, from being sucked up themselves. Because Michael was now as strong and almost as big as I was, he stayed in the salon with Herbert and me to help.

We closed the two open hatches into the cockpit. Then we pulled the curtains aside and watched with horror as the waterspout continued to move towards us. It was now only a few hundred metres away. In the few minutes that had passed, it had grown much bigger. The sight of that churning wall of water being spun out from the centre of the spout still had me transfixed. My heart was thumping painfully in my chest.

Suddenly we realized that although we had shut the hatches, we hadn't done anything about the open windows. The three of us rushed around anew, making sure all the ports were tightly closed. When we had done all that we could do, we returned to the big salon window, where for a few seconds I tried to videotape. My legs were shaking hard as I tried to film the advancing spout. I could hardly hold the camera still. The sight of that thundering, churning wall of water around the spout's base is what continued to scare me the most. It, more than that column of water reaching into the clouds, gave the sense of the power of this awesome, awful thing.

All we could do was wait. Even during our storms, I had had the sense that we were in some kind of control, that we had the ability to manage our boat and thereby influence the outcome. But now, in these few brief minutes, we were truly helpless.

The spout was directly beside us, less than a hundred metres away. Its base was broader than ever. Suddenly, it seemed as if the force of the tornado couldn't support its enlarged base. Right before our eyes, the waterspout lifted from the sea. Then it evaporated, with the middle collapsing first, then the top and bottom. In seconds, the spout was nowhere to be seen.

For an instant we couldn't believe our eyes. We wondered if it had somehow jumped over us. We rushed over and tore open the curtains on the other side of the boat to see. But it was gone. Miraculously, it had dissipated just a stone's throw away.

We had barely enough time to catch our breath when the weather disturbance that had created the spout hit us with a fury. The sky turned dark and we were slammed with a deluge so heavy that we were completely blinded. All the water that the spout had sucked up was now being returned to the sea. We were being drowned in it. The radar was useless.

At first we just sat there as if stupefied, trying to get our nerves back after the close call of moments before. Then we made contact with

Nanamuk on the radio and got their position, allowing us to compare it with ours and make sure we didn't run blindly into each other.

In fifteen minutes the deluge passed. Eventually our hearts, too, returned to their normal rhythms. Even now, I still periodically have a horrifying picture run through my mind, the scenario of what might have happened if the spout had really hit, and if *Nanamuk* had not been there to alert us. The thought of our three boys being sucked up by the spout freezes my blood every time. The worst of it was that it was my watch, when it was my duty to be alert. For me, waiting for that waterspout to hit was the single most terrifying moment of our voyage.

+

The next day, recovered from the excitement of the waterspout, we arrived at our last stop in Indonesia, Batam Island, at a lovely, empty, marina and resort. Apart from a handful of yachties and a few dozen staff, it was completely deserted. The Asian economic recession of 1997 and 1998 had left this resort high and dry. It was almost eerie to swim in the glorious swimming pool at night when it was beautifully lit only for us, with dutiful staff in their white uniforms standing nearby in the glaringly empty restaurant, hoping against hope that some actual people might arrive for them to serve. We never enjoyed staying at a marina more than we did at this sadly expectant island resort all dressed up but no place to go.

Then we crossed the Singapore Strait for Malaysia, which is a modern, sophisticated country with every possible service, product, and convenience. The kids were particularly fascinated by modern shopping malls completely filled with little stores selling pirated computer software and the latest movies. You could find any computer program or movie you wanted for a flat price of two dollars a disk.

Although predominantly Muslim like Indonesia, Malaysia also has a large Chinese population. This meant we were able to buy pork again for the first time since Australia. But when we brought our pork chops to the checkout counter of one large supermarket, it posed a major dilemma for the cashier, a demure young woman wearing a traditional Muslim head covering. She was obviously new to the job and had never come face to face with a pork chop before.

Her distress at our arrival was clear. As we unloaded our purchases at her counter, she began making frantic motions as if to send us to a different cashier. In our ignorance of both her customs and her language, we didn't understand at first what the problem was. We stayed there, in some confusion as to what was going on. It took us a few minutes before realizing that it was our little plastic wrapped package of pork chops that was causing all the fuss. To Muslims, pork is an unclean food. This young girl couldn't bring herself to touch even the plastic covering of our meat, nor the two cans of cooked pork we had innocently laid before her. Finally, she called over her supervisor, who showed her how to take a double layer of plastic bags to cover her hands. Only in this way, safely protected from any contact with the unclean meat, was our poor cashier able quickly and distastefully to spirit the offending pork into our bags and out of sight. Her disgust at our dinner left us feeling rather sullied as well.

On the other hand, Malaysians love some foods that we found repulsive. One of these is the durian, a large, green, spiky fruit whose smell can only be compared to that of raw sewage and whose taste isn't much better. But despite durian being prohibited from many public places, due to its smell, it is eaten in large quantities and in many unusual forms.

My vote for the most creative use of a noxious fruit was the durian mousse cake I spotted at a fancy bakery. In the disgusting snack food category, however, I would definitely vote for that ubiquitous Malaysian favourite, dried jellyfish on a stick.

It rained almost every day in Malaysia, and during most of these storms there was a terrific show of thunder and lightning. Many boats had come to grief in these waters on account of lightning, which usually results in extensive damage to the boat's electrical systems. We know of people who were forced to delay their trips the better part of a year and spend $70,000 or more repairing lightning damage. While some boats carry insurance for just such an eventuality, we did not. In fact, like a significant proportion of long-distance cruisers, we carried no insurance of any kind; it's very expensive and, in our case, because of our lack of experience we had found ourselves to be uninsurable.

Herbert and I had left the kids playing on board with Alan, the thirteen-year-old boy from *Nanamuk*, one muggy afternoon while we went to pick up a few groceries. While we were gone, there was a brief but violent electrical storm. A mile away, Herbert and I were loading wet groceries into a taxi when we saw the lightning and simultaneously heard a tremendous crash.

"That one's not that far away," remarked Herbert.

Grace, on *Nanamuk*, anchored about thirty metres away from *Northern Magic*, at first thought *Nanamuk* had been hit. Later she told me she had actually felt the electricity surge through her body, standing all her hairs on end. But nothing seemed to be wrong, so she heaved a sigh of relief.

Then a loud siren started blaring. It was the intruder alarm on *Northern Magic*, signalling to all the world that something was wrong. *Northern Magic* had been hit.

Someone on another boat witnessed the bolt of lightning as it hit our main mast. The lightning had actually changed direction in mid-air, doubling back from its original oblique course away from our boat to strike us. I got shivers up and down my spine as I heard the story; it sounded all too similar to the way that waterspout had changed its course to intercept us just weeks before.

The four boys later couldn't recall if it was the enormous bang or some surge of electricity that made them all jump together, but jump they did. Then they heard a clattering sound: the wind indicator mounted at the top of the mast had crashed to the deck. Jonathan ran out and picked it up, still hot. Now they knew for sure lightning had hit. But before they could do much more, the alarm started shrieking, and somehow they had to find a way of turning it off. Although Michael found the key to disable the alarm, it didn't work; no matter what he did, the siren continued blaring.

After Jon went outside to yell over to *Nanamuk* to turn on their radio, Alan called his parents on VHF to tell everyone was fine. Amazingly, even though its antenna had been blasted off the masthead, the VHF radio still worked. It was up to the boys to figure out how to silence the alarm. Michael and Alan traced the alarm wire all the way to the fuse box and, using a screwdriver, managed to disconnect it. At last, after ten minutes of screaming, the alarm was silent.

A few minutes later, Herbert and I arrived, totally unaware of the drama that had taken place in our absence. As soon as we pulled up to *Northern Magic*, four boys began excitedly jumping around the cockpit, brandishing the poor blackened wind instrument and proudly relating how they had handled the crisis.

Herbert immediately swung into action. "Have you tested anything?" he asked. "Is anything broken?" This was his worst nightmare, and he ran all over the boat, looking for signs of damage.

But just as someone had been watching out for us that day of the waterspout, our guardian angel must have been looking over us during the lightning strike too. Although it turned out to be an expensive event, the vast majority of our electronics were undamaged. Possibly because *Northern Magic* was a steel boat, well grounded to the water, most of the current went around the outside of the hull rather than through crucial electrical systems. In any event, here is what happened when a couple of hundred thousand volts of electricity went through *Northern Magic*.

Our radar was totally destroyed, the VHF antenna was blown to smithereens, but through a miracle, none of our radios was damaged. Herbert was able to repair the mechanical wind indicator that had been blasted onto the deck. It was soon reinstalled, although slightly shorter, and a little the worse for wear. Our electronic wind indicator, on the other hand, no longer worked, although the rest of our wind instrumentation was fine. Our little TV lost both sound and colour, at least for several months, after which it fully recovered. And our steel anchor chain was covered with a layer of messy soot.

One of the more dramatic personal changes that had taken place on this voyage was how Herbert had learned to handle unexpected setbacks, though I must confess, he'd had a lot of practice. Bearing in mind that handling frustration had never been one of his strong points, consider the following, an exact quote to show how my newly mellowed husband reacted to the knowledge that lightning had destroyed our expensive radar: "Well, that's one more thing to order."

That was all.

Because, in fact, it could have been so much worse. Our guardian angel really was looking after us that day.

Long Neck Ladies
and Singing Apes

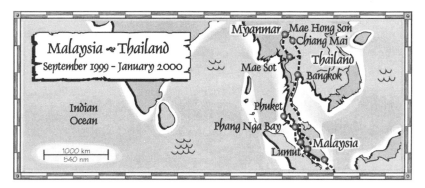

Malaysia ⋄ Thailand
September 1999 – January 2000

Myanmar   Mae Hong Son
                Chiang Mai
Mae Sot   Thailand
                Bangkok
Indian
Ocean   Phuket
        Phang Nga Bay
1000 km   Malaysia
540 nm   Lumut

S oon we found ourselves making our way up the Strait of Malacca
between the island of Sumatra and the Malaysian peninsula. Our
first challenge was negotiating the Singapore shipping lanes, a
four-lane superhighway of the sea. Like any freeway, it had on- and off-
ramps, secondary roads leading to it, parking areas, and a lot of high-
speed traffic carrying raw and manufactured goods to and from the
busiest port on earth.

Mixing and mingling with these bustling leviathans and tip-toeing
our way through felt something like crawling across a busy freeway on
hands and knees. These fast-moving ships could crush small, slow, vulnerable *Northern Magic* without even realizing they had done so. It was
up to us to make sure we didn't get in their way.

On our circle tour around the island of Singapore, we passed huge
warehouses, oil and gas depots, giant shipyards, oil rigs being recom-
missioned, and countless ships, both anchored and under way. But by
nightfall we had made it out of the shipping lanes and could happily sail

during the hours of darkness without too much worry about being ploughed under by a three-hundred-metre supertanker.

After three days, our windward journey ended up a tree-choked river, at a small marina in Lumut, about 150 kilometres north of Kuala Lumpur.

On a sultry Malaysian morning a few days later, the five of us donned backpacks and set off on an overland trip into Thailand. Each of us was slightly bowed by our burdens, selected to match each person by size. In fact, we resembled a family of ducks waddling in single file, with heavily loaded Papa Duck in front (carrying Happy Lappy and various cameras), three little ducklings marching behind in descending order of size (carrying Magic Cards and Game Boys), and Mama Duck bringing up the rear (carrying Oreos, Mars Bars, and Honey Nut Corn Flakes).

After a bus ride and twenty-two hours in a train, we arrived in the large, chaotic, unquestionably Asian city of Bangkok. We were in another world, a world where few people spoke our language, where the signs were written in an incomprehensible swirling script, and where no one seemed to smile.

We found Bangkok surly and conniving. We'd been spoiled in friendly Indonesia, where smiling seemed to come as naturally as breathing. But in Bangkok we had to constantly guard against unscrupulous taxi drivers and touts. The architecture of Bangkok, however, was as magnificent as its people were sullen. We rapidly overdosed on glorious Buddhist temples and palaces, glittering golden, mirrored, and sequined marvels more elaborate and ornamented than a department store Christmas tree.

Leaving the kids in a hotel, Herbert and I went to see the red-light district for which Bangkok is famous. The streets were crowded with tourists, street stalls, hookers, and sex shows. Curious, we went inside to see one show. The beautiful Thai girls were so sad-looking, however, that we ended up feeling depressed. One prostitute attached herself to us, trying desperately to interest one or both of us in any of her services, and did it so mournfully we felt like crying. It didn't seem to us that any of those girls had truly chosen to be there.

We couldn't arrange adjacent sleepers for the train ride to Chiang Mai, the next leg of our overland journey, so Michael ended up sleeping in one air-conditioned car, Jonathan and Herbert were at different ends of another, and Christopher and I bunked together in a lower class, fan-cooled car far away from the rest. The two older boys enjoyed travelling alone and made some interesting friends. Jon ended up with a group of four young, friendly, orange-robed Buddhist monks. Two of them spoke English and were kind enough to explain their religion to Jon. He even got some expert instruction in meditation, which he claims to find useful even to this day.

Michael also did well, befriending a group of nice Thai grannies. Herbert made friends with a tour guide. As for Christopher and me, we got along just fine with the many cockroaches sharing our less desirable neighbourhood.

Waiting at the Chiang Mai train station for us was a breed of taxi we hadn't met before, the *songtao*, a small pick-up truck with two rows of benches in the back. Our attitude towards Thai taxi drivers had become hardened after several bad experiences in Bangkok, and so we approached the waiting *songtaos* with faces grim and elbows up. We were wrong, however, and although we eventually used many *tuk-tuks* and *songtaos* during our stay in Chiang Mai, we never once had the kind of problem that had been the rule in greedy, grasping Bangkok. Gradually, we relaxed our guard and began to enjoy our experiences in Thailand, finding that people outside of the capital were gracious and smiling, just as we had come to expect.

After visiting an elephant camp and participating in the annual Loy Kratong festival, in which we, like hundreds of others, lit giant rice-paper lanterns and sent them up blazing into the sky, we boarded a bus for a winding six-hour ride to the small town of Mae Hong Son, near the border with Myanmar, formerly known as Burma.

We had come to Mae Hong Son because it was near to one of the few remaining villages of the so-called Long Neck people, actually a branch of the Karen tribe. The tribe is famous for its practice of women wearing coiled brass rings around their necks. Over time, the pressure of these rings stretches their necks longer and longer, giving them a giraffe-like appearance. In fact, x-ray analysis has shown that their necks don't stretch at all; the weight of all that metal actually pushes down their shoulder blades and compresses their ribs, giving the impression of a long neck when it is actually their chests that are progressively deformed.

We had plenty of reservations about visiting this tribe. The last thing we wanted was to gawk at some human freak show, yet our curiosity about this practice, and how the women felt about it, was compelling. Surely, the pressures of modern civilization would soon put an end to it, and how could we pass up the opportunity of witnessing something that in a generation may have vanished? So we swallowed our misgivings, rented a Suzuki four-wheel drive (which, like all the other rental cars we found, was uninsured) and set off into the hills.

Lack of insurance was the least of this car's problems: of more pressing concern was the gas pedal's unfortunate tendency to get stuck at full throttle. That, and the fact that the brakes were in critical condition as well. Thankfully, we experienced no major catastrophes and made it to the village we sought, just a kilometre away from the Burmese border. The last few miles were painfully slow, on narrow, pitted dirt roads overgrown with foliage and crossed by small streams.

After paying our entry fee of ten dollars per adult (our guidebook said access to the village is controlled by Kareni rebels who use the money to finance their illegal activities across the border in Myanmar), we hesitantly proceeded into a typical rural hill tribe village. It was a small collection of simple thatched huts with dirt floors and a communal pond for bathing. We were eager to snatch our first glance at these unusual women and yet at the same time somehow embarrassed to look.

Soon, we came upon a woman in early middle age with a small baby at her breast. She had a welcoming smile and stood behind a stall selling souvenirs – long-necked dolls, postcards, jewellery, decorative daggers. Around her neck was a long coil of polished brass, starting right under her chin and ending on the top of her chest. It was, in fact, two sets of coils, the main section enclosing her elongated neck, and a second flaring out over her collarbone. The rings forced her into an erect, slightly forward-leaning posture, and prevented her from seeing her baby, who was greedily suckling in the manner of infants everywhere. Her shoulders were markedly narrow and downward sloping.

If we worried that it might be a freak show, or that these women were somehow miserable and abused, how different it was in reality. The woman was gracious and dignified, and only too happy to answer our many questions. (She actually removed her lower neck coils to show us, rather proudly, the bruising on her collarbone that comes from the weight of carrying her many brass rings.) As we walked around the village and chatted with many different women, we realized that, rather than looking strange or weird, they were truly beautiful in a way we had never expected. The effect of their long necks and erect posture was striking and elegant, even aristocratic.

We saw shy young girls of about five with only a few coils, as well as wrinkled grandmothers in their fifties with the longest necks of all, every one of them beautifully attired with flowered headdresses and adorned with kilograms of well-polished brass on their necks, arms, and legs. On some of the young girls I grimaced to see that the brass leggings had created marked indentations in the flesh of their calves. The grown women typically wore five kilograms of brass, although some carried as much as ten kilos of weight on their necks and shoulders. The women polish the rings daily and never take them off, even for sleeping, except to replace them with a longer set every five years. We hefted a coil of medium size, and I couldn't imagine wearing that heavy a burden around my neck for even an hour.

Of course, the neck rings prevent them from bending their necks or even properly looking down. If a small boy needs attention, his mother has to bend at the waist in order even to see him. Yet none of the women we spoke to gave us any indication that they felt anything but proud of the rings and the tremendous price they were paying by wearing them. One can, of course, never know for sure.

The highlight of our visit was meeting a beautiful young girl of fourteen, Ma Chok, who spoke English and invited us to sit down with her in the shade of the booth she was tending with her mother. Her rings were not as shiny as most, and she confessed, gigglingly, that she had been stupid – no, no, she meant lazy – and had not bothered to polish them that morning. Ma Chok had an endearing habit of covering her mouth delicately with her hand whenever she laughed, which was often. She questioned us about Bangkok, and we asked if she had ever been there, before realizing the obvious fact that even a trip within Thailand was virtually impossible for her. She giggled again and said, "No, but maybe tomorrow I go!"

Of course, none of these women could travel anywhere – not only are they a stateless people, but their self-induced deformity would subject them to unwelcome attention and stares wherever they went, even assuming they could afford to leave their protected little enclave. Their world is a very tiny one.

Ma Chok was intelligent and full of questions. We pulled out our photo album and showed her pictures of home. She went through it delightedly. In the end, she said she would very much like to visit our country. We all joked that maybe tomorrow she could go there, too.

We left the village feeling touched by both the inner and outer beauty of its inhabitants. We've done a lot of soul-searching about whether paying to see them was a good thing or bad. Clearly, the tourist revenue allows them to live better than they ever have before and helps maintain their culture. On the other hand, it prolongs a practice that deforms the women's bodies and inhibits them in countless ways.

Yet, this is their culture, developed over centuries, and is it really so different from Canadian women getting bunions from years of wobbling around in pointy high-heeled shoes? I do know that the brief time we spent in this remote and time-warped village left us feeling both uplifted and privileged.

Our guidebook enticingly called the next phase of our travels "one of the most adventurous journeys in Thailand." It involved using little-travelled roads from Mae Hong Son south to the town of Mae Sot, where we planned to visit a private gibbon sanctuary nestled in the hills along the Burmese border. The first day, we travelled in an air-conditioned bus, but the hilly, winding roads took their toll. I spent half the trip with my head down on my knees and a barf bag at the ready, a condition shared by at least half my fellow passengers.

The next day, we embarked on a six-hour ride to Mae Sot. After the previous day's ordeal in air-conditioned comfort, we were a little apprehensive about this part of our journey. Our mode of transport was no longer on padded seats, but on the hard benches of an open *songtao*. At first we were the only passengers, but the *songtao* stopped frequently, picking up and discharging many interesting people. None of them travelled for more than an hour or so, and some for only a few kilometres, from one little thatched village to another, often lugging large bags of vegetables or rice. The best were the colourfully dressed hill tribe people, wearing costumes in neon colours of orange and lime green. Although clearly interested in us, they were uncomfortable coming too close to such strange-looking foreigners, preferring to hang off the end of the truck rather than sit in the vacant spots right beside us.

We realized we really were in a different world when we began noticing huge brown deposits of the cow-pie variety in the middle of the road. Soon we passed the source – a real, working elephant, plodding along the road with a driver on its back. This beast had been hauling logs in the rainforest just as elephants have done in these parts for centuries.

By the time we arrived at Mae Sot, we were windblown and covered with a layer of fine brown grit. An elegant Thai woman, Pharanee Deters, was waiting for us at the bus station with her air-conditioned car to take us onwards to the gibbon sanctuary she ran with her American husband, Bill. We wound for almost fifty kilometres through the picturesque hills that separate Myanmar from Thailand, passing prosperous farms and beautiful homes owned by a pantheon of wealthy Thai generals and staffed by illegal Burmese workers earning less than two dollars a day. Finally, we came to Highland Farm, perched prettily on top of a hill, looking down over orchards, rose gardens, and a small forest.

We stayed for three days, in a beautiful little guesthouse of our own. Every morning, before the sun rose, we woke to the sound of the gibbons, and learned for ourselves why they are called "the singing ape." The cool pre-dawn air was vibrant with a chorus of primate voices chanting "*whoop-whoop-whoop, wuccka-wuccka-wuccka,*" gibbon songs that made us laugh with delight and at the same time grieve for the jungle homes that were lost to them forever. Christopher formed a special bond with a gibbon he nicknamed Denny, who sat and held hands with him every evening and only reluctantly let go.

The next day we headed off to explore the Burmese border area. Myanmar was once one of Asia's richest countries, but now, after decades of misguided and dictatorial rule, was its poorest. Our guidebook described it as an example of how not to run a country. The result of this gross mismanagement was that virtually all low-paying jobs in Thai border areas were filled by illicit Burmese workers earning a dollar or two a day, which was a dollar or two more than they could earn at home. There had been a crackdown in the previous weeks in Thailand against these illegal workers, and we were told that this had virtually shut down all the farms in the area.

The poor and desperate Burmese were willing to do menial tasks, earn next to nothing, and live in appalling conditions shunned by the more prosperous Thai workers. At Highland Farm, Bill Deters had shown Herbert the quarters where his Burmese workers were housed. There was one hut for the male farm hands and another for the two shy and pretty girls, fifteen and sixteen years old, who worked as maids. Both staff houses were depressing little cells made entirely of unpainted cinder block, with a woven mat for a door, no windows, no furniture, a hanging lightbulb, a concrete floor, and just enough room for the occupants to roll out their sleeping mats at night. Yet Bill was proud of these pitiful accommodations. He told us he treated his workers better than average. Indeed, he fed them three times a day, which, according to him, was more than most Burmese received. But he also told us that his two newly hired maids were unhappy and had wanted to return to their families. This was unacceptable, he told us, because we had been due to arrive; he needed the girls to cook and clean for us.

Without a hint of embarrassment, Bill explained that he had convinced the girls to stay by threatening to report their families to the authorities. Thereafter, knowing that we were indirectly responsible for what amounted to the girls' indentured servitude, we felt guilty every time we saw them. At the end of our stay – to expiate our guilt, perhaps – we left them a small gift. For some reason, we tried not to let Bill see us doing it. (In May 2002, we were shocked to learn that Bill Deters had been murdered by a former employee, along with four of his staff. Pharanee survived.)

We jumped in a *songtao* and rumbled off to see the bridge to Myanmar, just five kilometres away. Everyone else in the truck seemed to be Burmese, and most of them were carrying packages. A long, graceful bridge spanned the Moi River, and crossing over into Myanmar was a steady stream of Burmese, carrying their precious burdens of Thai goods, purchased from their meagre earnings. There was no vehicle traffic at all, just this slow, single file of Burmese. There was something very sad about these stooped walkers, looking like refugees as they slowly plodded against the setting sun back to their troubled homeland. In Thailand, they were virtually slaves; back at home they were the wealthy deliverers of much-needed goods. The economy of Myanmar had so completely collapsed that not a single item produced in official government factories was actually available on the open market. As much of 80 per cent of the national economy was black market. (Burma's richest industry is, in fact, the production of opium, and vast poppy fields in the northern part of the country are responsible for fully 50 per cent of the world's heroin supply.)

We walked under the bridge to the banks of the river, where there was a thriving market in Burmese goods. Beautiful hand-painted lacquerware, teak carvings, ornately carved wooden furniture, and amazing antiques speaking of a long-lost age of former glory were all for sale at bargain prices. The antique shops had a poignancy about them, the sad feel of a country selling its birthright for a handful of rice.

✦

After utterly foreign Thailand, returning to developed, industrious Malaysia gave us a distinct sense of coming home. It felt as if we were back in the Canada of Asia – prosperous, moderate, comfortable, businesslike. Soon, we sailed to a beautiful marina resort on tiny Rebak Island, a satellite of the duty-free resort of Langkawi.

It was December 31, 1999. We had found an ideal spot to welcome in the new millennium. Tiny lights sparkled in a tropical garden, gentle waves lapped up on a beach, in the distance small islands rose up out of the ocean, and the lights of a town beckoned on a far shore. It was a place of perfect beauty. We realized how blessed we were to be there, to be celebrating this milestone together as a family, to be on this great adventure. That night a wonderful fireworks display launched us into the new millennium. Two days later, *Northern Magic* continued on her odyssey.

We sailed for Phuket, in Thailand, our last stop in Asia before setting off across the Indian Ocean. There were many small islands along the way, and so we day-hopped between them. On Ko Rok Nok, a tiny, uninhabited island, we could see there was some kind of shrine on the beach, for there were conspicuous pieces of colourful material tied around an old tree. As we clambered over the rocks to visit this holy place, the boys leading the way, Michael abruptly turned back and said, with an expression of pure disgust on his face, "Oh, man, this is gross!"

Jon chimed in, "This is a shrine for mating!"

Indeed, we found ourselves in front of what was clearly a phallic shrine, decorated appropriately with dozens of large wooden carvings of an unmistakable shape. Visiting fishermen, who used this island as a daytime stopover, had obviously been worshipping here for many years. Many of the carvings were ancient and weathered, while others were brand new and brightly varnished. Some of the carvings were made from logs more than a metre long, others even longer, and painted in all kinds of gaudy colours. While a few were standing upright, most of the giant penises were stacked in a big pile like firewood. Our kids found the whole display totally disgusting, and couldn't get away from it quickly enough: "How can you stand there and look at this, Mom?"

After the boys beat their hasty retreat, a group of about ten Thai fishermen arrived. I tried to wipe the bemused grin off my face and display what was, I hoped, an attitude of appropriate respect and admiration. One of the young fishermen invited me to videotape him as he stood reverently in front of the shrine, placing his hands together in a praying gesture and closing his eyes for a few moments before finishing his prayer with a little bow.

One of his buddies, who wore a carved bone phallus around his waist, lifted up a few of the larger specimens and demonstrated his manliness to me by hefting them onto his shoulder. I nodded and smiled approvingly, which I assumed was an appropriate response to this lavish display of masculinity. None of the young fishermen spoke English, so I never got to ask them whether they were praying for fertility, potency, or perhaps that they might become endowed with proportions equally majestic. Nor did I find out whether their hopeful prayers, whatever they were, were ever granted.

Our island-hopping finally brought us to the large island of Phuket. We had assembled a long list of chores to get done there, our last stop before crossing the Indian Ocean, but we did take a couple of days off to tour around the island. First, we headed to Patong Beach, Phuket's

veland · New London

TAWA · CITIZ

ESTABLISHED IN 1845

Christopher and Michael on the first
day of a four-year voyage

a odyssey, 2001: Family to circle globe

Leaving Manhattan, heading into the Atlantic

Cape Hatteras

Charleston

Cape Romain

Beaufort

The crew of Northern Magic in South Carolina

Merita Infante Zuñiga (top left), of Jaimanitas, Cuba, and her children, Alejandro (bottom left) and Jadi (behind her brother)

Jon concentrating at the wheel

Michael riding a sea turtle in Cuba

A Galápagos sea lion making herself at home in our dinghy, Flipper

Galápagos tortoise

Broken boom in the Pacific, 1,500 miles from land

Herbert wrestling Christopher for a can of Pringles,
a prize after 23 days at sea

Island of Moorea, French Polynesia

Jonathan swarmed by school kids at Fatu Hiva,
Marquesas, eager to see his Game Boy

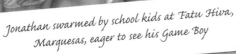

Christopher and Jonathan in T

Michael, arriving in Tahiti
thinking about Tahitian babes.

Jonathan on Northern Magic with his new Marquesan frien
Eddy Barsinas, playing ... guess what?

Macho Mike with his brothers and friends in Moorea

Herbert and the cockroach radio repa
Ono Island, Fiji

Diane in the galley

Herbert reefing the mainsail

Taia Marsters, Palmerston Island

Images of Niue

Tongan wedding procession led by bride and groom

In Australia:
Herbert installing
the Windhunter;
barnacle-encrusted
propeller;
Northern Magic
hauled for painting

Jonathan nose-to-nose with a kangaroo

Diane giving Chris a haircut

Sailing up through the Great Barrier Reef

Chris doing homework on deck

Michael, Jonathan, and their cousin Katie, at Bali watergarden

Michael at the Sacred Monkey Forest, Bali

Temple, Bali

Jonathan and Yves playing in the cockpit on the passage to Komodo

Balinese women carrying offerings to a temple

Our kelotok; illegal loggers; and illegal logging camp, Sekonyer River, Borneo

Rosemary and her two babies

Magic the gibbon, swinging from the rigging

Nyo, the evil macaque

Wanto, park volunteer, with an orphaned orangutan baby

Young illegal goldminers, Borneo

Borneo orangutan wrestling, starring Chris, Michael, Jonathan, Jekky, and Toyo

Pharanee Deters introducing Christopher to Denny at Highland Farm Gibbon Sanctuary, Mae Sot, Thailand

Jon and elephants in Thailand

Karen Tribe member with baby

Phang Nga Bay, Thailand

With Ma Chok and her little sister, members of the Karen (Long Neck) Tribe near Mae Hong Son, Thailand

Kodah Chotung, fisherman, Phang Nga Bay, Thailand

Police Chief Anam (right), who arrested us in the Nicobar Islands

Christopher highlighting reefs and shallows in Maldives on our photocopied nautical chart

Ekka's tuk-tuk

Australian yachtie baking bread over a campfire in Chagos

Ekka and his family, Galle, Sri Lanka

Jon's Sri Lankan mask – a birthday surprise

Snake charmer, Sri Lanka

Octopus and fish on offer in the Zanzibar market

Zanzibar

Michael eagerly trying to spot Africa

Maasai boy trying on Jon's glasses

Jonathan and Michael on Northern Magic, showing Boniface how to use a computer for the first time

Hamisi, making shark-tooth jewellery

Hamisi (in white cap), Andrew (standing, hand in pocket), Mark (between Andrew and Jonathan), Boniface (front row, holding baby)

Buying Magic, the cow, for Hamisi

Hamisi's older brother, a medicine man, holding a soon-to-be-sacrificed chicken on top of praying woman's head

Northern Magic in Shimoni, Kenya

A Maasai grandmother (and, above, warming Christopher in her robe)

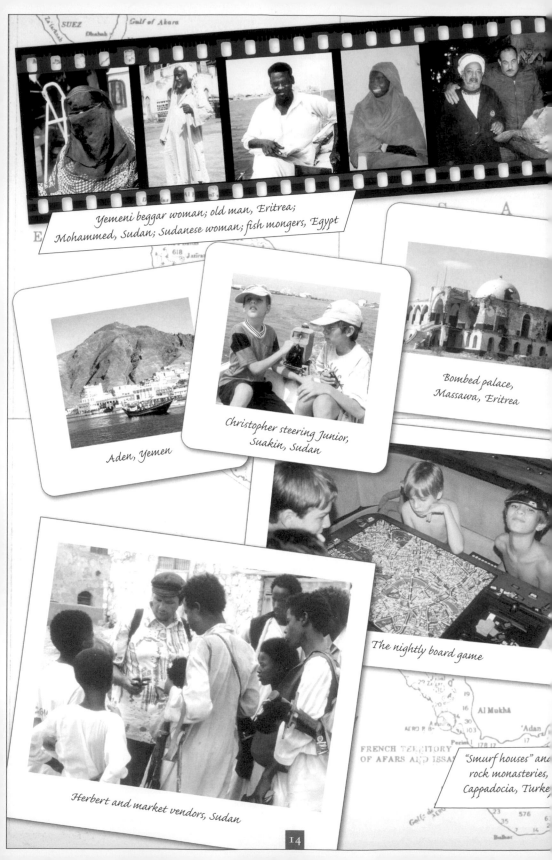

Yemeni beggar woman; old man, Eritrea; Mohammed, Sudan; Sudanese woman; fish mongers, Egypt

Aden, Yemen

Christopher steering Junior, Suakin, Sudan

Bombed palace, Massawa, Eritrea

The nightly board game

Herbert and market vendors, Sudan

"Smurf houses" and rock monasteries, Cappadocia, Turkey

14

Chris hugging Gramps on a
surprise visit in Israel

Captain George, Greece

Peppino Falabella, Sicily

Herbert working in engine room

Northern Magic under full sail

Camel ride, Aswan, Egypt

Christopher keeping watch on a
flat North Atlantic

15

Sao Miguel Island, Azores

Michael jumping ship

Northern Magic

Arrival in Nova Scotia after 12 days at sea

Tiger roars back
Woods wins a duel with Jim Furyk to break his long losing streak. C1

Partying offline
Internet chat fans leave computers behind to meet in Montreal. B1

The end of the odyssey

Thousands cheer as Stuemers return

Trip around globe ends with heroes' welcome

At last, they understand what they mean to Ottawa

Diane reunited with her mom, Jeanette, her father, Frank, and sister, Linda

Welcome home, August 26, 2001

tourist and nightlife centre. It was a pretty classy place, featuring fine establishments like the ever-popular "Rock-Hard-a-Go-Go."

We carried on into astonishing Phang Nga Bay, whose myriad small islands burst dramatically out of the ocean in gravity-defying formations. We passed unmistakably Asian-looking islands with vertical walls and rounded tops, mushroom-shaped islands dripping with external stalactites, and huge rocky pillars thrusting from the sea. Surely, this must be one of the most exotic places on earth.

One of the stops we made was at Ko Hong, near a collection of three small islands. Michael and Jonathan wasted no time in assembling our inflatable kayak, which Michael had named *Goblin War Buggy*. The boys begged to be permitted to go off and explore on their own, and a few minutes later, paddled off on a voyage of discovery. When they returned an hour later and submitted their report, the rest of us wasted no time in following.

Taking *Northern Magic Junior* with *Goblin War Buggy* tied up behind, the boys led us back into the lagoon they had found. It was a miniature version of Phang Nga Bay itself, with tiny islets jutting up here and there and stalactites hanging menacingly, like daggers, from the walls of the larger islands that enclosed it. We tied up *Junior* on a stalactite and proceeded in *War Buggy* into a narrow cavern that was only a little wider and higher than the kayak itself.

Inside the dripping cave, our paddles were useless, so we pushed our way through with our hands. At one point we slid tightly through a portion that forced us to lie back inside the kayak with damp stalactites practically scraping our noses. I wondered what had possessed the boys to explore this far into such a claustrophobic and unpromising cavern.

But once through that bottleneck, we emerged into a brand new world. We had entered a *hong*, which in Thai means "room." It was the interior of a massive cave, except that its roof had long since tumbled down, leaving it open to the sky above. The walls of the *hong* were covered with greenery. It was beautiful.

The boys knew exactly where to go from here, and they excitedly paddled to another rocky opening. After pushing our way through, we found ourselves in yet another hidden *hong*, this one even more spectacular than the one before. Its vertical walls were covered with plants whose roots had somehow managed to find a foothold. Foliage – trees, vines, bushes, and wildflowers – was everywhere. The brilliant blue sky overhead capped what looked like a solid wall of rock and greenery around us.

A single crow circled overhead and landed at the water's edge not giving us a second glance. Other than its occasional *"caw, caw,"* we were entirely alone. We stopped paddling and just sat there in awe, taking in the breathtaking scene and not wanting to disturb its verdant beauty. Although it was a windy day, inside the *hong* it was perfectly calm.

"All we need now are about a million little fish, some pelicans, frigate birds, and a few sea lions," Michael remarked after a time, remembering a similarly intense experience at the Galápagos Islands in another wild and beautiful lagoon. Michael's words echoed as they bounced their way up the rock wall to the open sky above.

"Row, row, row your boat," he began, tentatively, and satisfied with the acoustic qualities of the chamber, Michael launched into his own special variation on that old song, a more exciting version involving crocodiles and screaming. Jon and I joined in lustily, singing in rounds, and after we finished and listened to the last refrain echoing up into the sky – *"All except your underwear, floating down the stream . . ."* – we wondered what our music must have sounded like from the very top of the *hong*. But there was no one to laugh at this performance but ourselves – and one large black bird, who, thankfully, kept his thoughts to himself.

✦

The next morning we were about to set off on another island exploration when a fishing boat approached us. Several of these had already stopped by to offer us fresh prawns or fish, but we weren't keen on seafood and had reluctantly waved the friendly fishermen on. The difference this time was that unlike the others, this fisherman spoke English. His name was Kodah Chotung, and he proudly displayed a wallet full of the names of other yachties he had befriended over the years. His face was open and friendly, and soon he invited us to visit his home on a nearby island.

This was too good an offer to refuse. Herbert decided to stay behind, as we had heard reports of robbery in the bay, but the boys and I jumped into Kodah's wooden longtail boat, joining his two partners, one of whom was crippled, as if from polio. This poor man could hardly walk and had to be dragged on and off the boat on the shoulders of the other man. Also sharing the boat with us was the day's catch, about twenty bright blue crabs as well as a handful of small stingrays with their tails cut off. The crabs scuttled pathetically around our feet with their claws bound tight with bits of string. The baby stingrays, not much larger than dessert plates, were, mercifully, already dead, and they sloshed around in a few inches of water at our feet.

First, we stopped at a large tour boat. After a brief negotiation, our cargo of crabs was unloaded in exchange for a small handful of bills. Then we sped noisily around various ever-more beautiful islands towards the shallow edge of the bay and entered the mouth of a small muddy river, passing many fish traps and small fish farms. As the river began to peter out, we tied up at a crowded dock at an island village of 250 fishermen and their families, all of whom owned long, slender, brightly painted wooden boats virtually identical to the one on which we had arrived.

This was a Muslim village, something of a surprise because Thailand is predominantly Buddhist. Just as before, we were greeted with smiling faces as we walked through the village, helping to forever banish our earlier misconception of Thais as being unfriendly. Kodah brought us to his sparsely furnished small home, where his dignified wife was caring for their year-old son. The baby was asleep, hanging from the corrugated steel ceiling in a small hammock made from a sarong; their other two children were at school. As we entered the house, several other people from the village gathered and watched us with unabashed interest.

I had brought a little bag of small gifts, and it was tremendous fun to see the women inspect the things I had brought: small soaps, lipstick, some treats, a colouring book and crayons. They examined the preserved guava from Malaysia and the little Indonesian jello cups carefully before accepting them, making sure they were *halal*, or suitable for Muslims to eat. When they discovered a tiny bottle of perfume, Kodah scrutinized it carefully, and then asked me a question in his simple English that sounded something like "Any a ko hon?"

"Pardon me?" I asked.

"Any a ko hon?" he repeated. "Any a ko hon?"

Finally I figured it out: he was asking if it contained alcohol, something strict Muslims refrain from using.

"Oh, that's not for drinking," I clarified. "It's for smelling!" I helped him open it up and demonstrated how it was to be dabbed on the wrists, an action he copied, sceptically. I was impressed at the family's commitment to their religion and remembered how the same was true in another village we had visited a few days before, where our host had taken pains to make it clear that alcoholic drinks would not be welcome there. Perhaps being a minority made these villagers especially devout and protective of their faith.

When Kodah dropped us off at *Northern Magic*, we shook hands warmly and thanked him for his hospitality, paying him for his time and fuel. I felt very warm towards this man, who worked hard all day in an open wooden boat to support his family and yet had offered his friendship to us so unstintingly. I was proud when Jonathan gave the youngest of the fishermen his own baseball cap, as this young man's cap was so tattered and full of holes it was about to fall apart.

As they were about to leave, Kodah held up a piece of frayed rope, and asked whether we had any line to spare.

"Actually, I do have some," said Herbert, and began rummaging around in a cockpit locker. He emerged with a large spool of strong yellow nylon rope, and I held it in the air, asking Kodah how much he needed.

"Give him all of it," Herbert said quietly in my ear. "I really don't need it."

Watching Kodah's face light up in surprise and delight as I handed over the entire roll of brand new line was by far the best event of the entire day. He could have been a child on Christmas morning, and if I had that moment on videotape, I'd play it over and over whenever I needed a lift. After thanking us profusely, Kodah putted off in his rough wooden boat, waving as he receded behind the sheer rock walls of Ko Hong. This was his lucky day, and ours as well.

16

Staring Down the Wrong End of a Gun

Thailand ↝ Nicobars
January – February 2000

India

Sri Lanka

Indian Ocean

555 km
300 nm

Andaman Islands

(India)

Nicobar Islands

Great Nicobar Island →

Ruined jib

Thailand

Sumatra Indonesia

I t had been a long time since we had made major ocean passage, and I, for one, felt a little apprehensive. But after one last big stock-up with fruit, vegetables, sixteen litres of precious fresh milk, and a few miraculous and rare packages of Hershey's Kisses, we set off from Thailand on a thousand-mile passage halfway across the Indian Ocean, to the island of Sri Lanka, just under the bottom tip of India.

Only after we were well underway did I remember how liberating it was to be far from land and all the menacing obstacles close to shore. Soon, we began to fall back into that familiar rhythm of life at sea. With a light breeze blowing from astern, we hoisted our spinnaker, which cheerily inflated like a colourful hot air balloon and pulled us gently across the water. Despite our slow pace, the sea was kind, and life was fine.

Michael loved to stay up late on my watch, and on the pleasant early days of this passage, he sat with me at night on deck, long after everyone else was asleep, watching the stars and the phosphorescent sparkles in our bow wave, talking about life, love, and geosynchronous satellites.

When people have romantic ideas of what it is like to be sailing, they are probably imagining starry nights just like this, with God's entire creation arrayed overhead as if for us alone. When we imagined taking the trip and growing closer as a family, it was a scene just like this that played in our minds. And our dream had come true.

During our second night at sea, the wind began to shift subtly to the north. The spinnaker, which we had rigged to float loosely off the bow, adjusted automatically and positioned itself on the port side of the boat. Seduced by our gentle movement across the water, Herbert and I, alternating in six-hour shifts, were lulled into complacency. In the darkness, neither of us noticed that the line holding the bottom of the spinnaker was now rubbing against the jib, which was neatly rolled up on the forestay beneath.

I was awoken by Herbert at seven the next morning. He flopped into bed beside me with a pained look on his face that told me something was wrong.

"I've got some bad news," he said. "Our jib is ruined."

Ten or twelve hours of that rope sawing back and forth on the rolled up foresail had chafed it right through, not only the outer cover, but through the underlying layers of sailcloth as well like twine rubbing through a roll of toilet paper. Our jib, probably the most important sail we had, was shredded, and we had only ourselves to blame.

Herbert collapsed into bed as I trudged up to the cockpit to assess the damage for myself. Yes, indeed, the jib was hanging in tatters. How long it would take to repair was anybody's guess.

There was as yet no urgency, for we could continue to fly the spinnaker for the time being. But the minute the winds picked up or changed direction, we would need that jib, and we still had more than eight hundred miles to go before reaching Sri Lanka. Fixing it while underway would at best be a nasty job, with no guarantee that the winds would cooperate in the meantime.

I did next what any prudent mariner would do under the circumstances: I whipped up a big batch of Aunt Linda's Excellent Oatmeal Chocolate Chip Cookies. I was actually sitting on deck, stirring the dough, meditatively tasting it every few strokes and pondering how to go about fixing that sail, when my reverie was interrupted by a crash. In an instant the spinnaker, the cause of our problems, disappeared into the ocean. It was as if, in penance for its misbehaviour the night before, it had honourably decided to commit suicide.

Herbert was in the cockpit like a shot, roused from his sleep by that cracking noise. Soon he and I were madly hauling sodden lengths of nylon out of the sea while *Northern Magic* began rolling drunkenly back and forth, robbed of the stability the spinnaker had been providing.

"What happened?" he asked in puzzlement. I didn't have a clue. As far as I had seen, the spinnaker had simply fallen down into the water. In fact the block, or pulley, at the very top of the mast had snapped in two.

So now we not only had major sail repairs on our agenda for the passage, but a trip to the top of the mast to install a new block as well. We looked at each other and agreed that it was time to find a place to stop.

Our route was taking us across the Andaman Sea, near the northern tip of the Indonesian island of Sumatra, and past the Nicobar Islands, which belong to India. We could anchor at either of these places. Great Nicobar Island was directly on our path, we had a good chart of its waters, and it was the obvious choice. However, our cruising guide advised us that yachts were not permitted to stop there; in 1997 one boat had been detained before being asked to leave. On the other hand, a magazine article I had read a few days before had suggested that the Nicobars were beginning to open up.

Sumatra involved a detour, and not only did we not have any good charts of those waters, we wondered whether it was even safe to go there. Most of the piracy in Indonesian waters happened off Sumatra, so this alone, we felt, made it a poor choice.

We therefore decided to stop at Great Nicobar Island, taking advantage of a maritime tradition that permits vessels to seek refuge for reasons of safety or distress. We were certain that once we explained our circumstances, we would, in fact, be welcomed.

We arrived at the island very early the next morning. We waited just offshore for almost two hours until we judged it was a reasonable time to make radio contact and ask permission to anchor. The last thing we wanted to do was sneak in, but after a further hour and a half of fruitless attempts to contact anyone by radio, we proceeded into the nearest anchorage. This turned out to be an apparently uninhabited bay. There we began to assess the damage.

The sail was in even worse shape than we had thought. The first two layers had disintegrated in numerous spots and were hanging like limp rags. All together, the sail had chafed though in eight places. I got to work right away, making patches for each of the rips, starting from the innermost tear, with each one getting larger and more difficult to repair as I worked towards the outside of the sail.

Our sewing machine wasn't up to the task of penetrating the tough sailcloth, so I applied sail repair tape and patches of new Dacron and had to sew them on slowly by hand. It was difficult and painstaking work, and much more time consuming than I had expected. By the end of the day, Herbert had successfully ascended the mast and replaced the broken block, but I had fixed only three of the eight rips.

I got back to work early the next morning, enjoying the lovely scenery of the island as I sewed. Apart from three people walking on the beach, we hadn't seen or heard anybody during our time in the bay. It seemed to belong only to the many birds whose joyous calls filled the clear morning air. By the middle of the afternoon, I still had the three largest tears to fix. As I worked in the cockpit, I could again see people on the beach, and soon thereafter I heard shouting and whistling.

Herbert came out and through the binoculars saw people waving branches and pieces of cloth in unmistakable gestures of invitation. We hadn't intended to go ashore, but the people were so insistent we finally decided to hoist the dinghy and see what they wanted. In every island we had visited, without exception, the people had been friendly. We had no reason to assume it would be otherwise here.

Leaving the kids on board, Herbert and I took the dinghy ashore, where three dark-skinned men stood waiting for us. Even before we disembarked, however, we realized intuitively that something was wrong. As we got out of the dinghy, we went to each of the men with our arms extended to shake their hands. They, however, took our hands only reluctantly, and did not return our greetings or our smiles.

The minute we had finished dragging *Junior* onto the beach, a fourth man, older than the other three, suddenly stepped out of the bushes and stood before us, grim-faced and glaring.

Then, three more men emerged from the foliage where they, too, had been hiding, the green khaki of their military uniforms providing perfect camouflage. Each of the soldiers held a rifle in his hands, a long, greedy-looking weapon that gleamed darkly in the sunlight. With stony faces and hard eyes, the men silently stepped beside their leader and stood with legs slightly spread, creating a human wall in front of us.

The man whom we presumed to be the leader began to speak.

"What are you doing here?" he demanded. His English was good, spoken with an Indian accent.

We explained our situation and handed over our business card, on which the names of all five of us were printed. The man, dark, lean, middle-aged, and with a thin moustache that would have been fashionable in the 1930s, studied it carefully.

"You must bring your boat to Campbell's Bay," he finally announced. "You may not remain here. And you," he continued, motioning to Herbert, "will stay here with my men. We will take you by Jeep."

"Oh no," said Herbert, "if we are going to move the boat, I have to do it. My wife can't do it alone."

"What about your crew?"

"But they are just children!"

At the news that the three other names on the card belonged to children, the leader turned to his men for a rapid discussion in Hindi. It was decided that he and two soldiers would come to *Northern Magic* and escort us to our destination. The reason for this was not explained. It was clear enough that we had no choice in the matter. As they got into the dinghy, tip-toeing so as not to get their army boots wet, the men clicked on the safeties of their rifles.

The kids were inside the boat and didn't realize we had returned with visitors, never mind uniformed visitors with guns. They didn't seem too fazed when I told them about our sudden change of plan. Each of the boys came into the cockpit and introduced himself, and there was a definite lightening of the mood when the soldiers saw we really were a young family and not a band of spies, drug runners, or whatever else they had imagined. Our cockpit was full of sail and sewing materials, and I showed them all the work I had completed so far, and the rags of torn sail I still had to finish. They did look impressed.

As we settled into the cockpit, I asked the leader for his name.

"Mohammed . . . Mohammed Anam," he said, after a moment's hesitation. "I'm Muslim, you know," he added irrelevantly.

"And what is your position?" I inquired.

He hesitated again. "Let's just say I'm a police officer."

During the two and a half hours it took us to get to Campbell's Bay, Mr. Anam asked us many questions but answered very few himself. Some of his questions were very personal, detailed questions about our finances, our religious beliefs, and our views on child rearing. These were topics that might have been more comfortable if we hadn't been sitting at the wrong end of a loaded gun. Neither of the soldiers, who were well-trimmed, good-looking young Indian men, said a word. They just stood on deck protecting their weapons from the splashing. Each of the men, in turn, went inside the cabin and looked around.

Herbert and I tried to pretend they were our guests, and we were taking them on a pleasure cruise. In fact, we were very much on edge. We had no idea why our boat had been commandeered, why we were being brought to the bay, the purpose of this strange and insistent questioning, and what would happen when we got there. I developed a splitting headache.

Mr. Anam instructed us to write a letter to the chief of police describing our situation. When I asked him the chief's name, he said just to write "To: Chief of Police." When I came to the point in my narrative where I described meeting him and the other men on the beach, I asked for the spelling of his name.

"Uh, just put, 'I met you and your men,'" he said, with some discomfiture. Obviously, he, himself, was the chief of police. For some reason he hadn't wanted us to know that.

By the time we arrived in the bay, Herbert and I, struggling to maintain polite conversation as though we were guests at a dinner party instead of prisoners, were feeling queasy – and it wasn't seasickness, although I must confess I was secretly wishing that very fate upon our unwelcome guests. The chief had been regaling us with tales of other yachts whose crews he had sent to prison and whose vessels he had confiscated. He proudly pointed out fifteen or twenty wooden fishing boats that littered the shore, evidence of his extraordinary diligence to his duty of keeping unwanted visitors away. All of them had been seized from unfortunate souls who, like us, had entered Nicobari waters without permission.

We asked him why visitors were not allowed. He explained that there were some tribes of native peoples still living naked in the jungle in the island's interior. He seemed preoccupied with the tribes' lack of clothing, mentioning this fact at least half a dozen times. It was to protect these primitive, naked jungle people from gawking foreigners, he explained, that boats were not allowed to visit.

He told us to anchor next to a yellow fishing boat that had come all the way from Sri Lanka. "Actually, our coastguard found that boat drifting; its motor had failed and it ended up in our waters," he said. "We confiscated it, and its crew has been in jail for the past month. They will be up for trial in the next few weeks. They will be convicted, of course."

"What will their sentence be?" I asked.

"Oh, they'll go to jail for at least six months."

The chief took our passports and left, saying he would submit a report to his superiors and wait for their instructions. It was now too late to do any more work on the sail, so we ate supper and went to bed. It was a nerve-racking night.

Next morning I began sewing as soon as it was light. When I climbed into the cockpit, I was surprised to see two armed soldiers standing alertly on board the Sri Lankan boat beside us. Obviously, the police chief intended to make sure we didn't escape in the darkness. We really were under house arrest.

My final sail repairs took almost all day. All in all, I had spent more than twenty hours fixing the damage. During the afternoon, we were surprised to hear another sailboat calling in on VHF radio, asking for permission to stop to repair their steering system. Although their initial request was refused, they continued to make their request until the port control official did not respond further. We assumed he was calling the chief of police on the phone.

In the meantime, Herbert got on the radio, painfully conscious that everything he said to the other yacht could be overheard. He quickly told them about our situation, hoping to warn them away if their repair was not absolutely crucial. "We've been brought here . . . uh . . . not under our own will," he explained delicately. "I strongly advise you not to stop without permission."

Later that afternoon, having gained the reluctant approval of the port control, the fifty-foot yacht *Marco Polo*, with crew from Italy and New Zealand, anchored near us and was immediately visited by Chief Anam and five armed guards. The passports of the four crew members were taken away, just as ours had been. By nightfall, they shared our predicament. Their repairs were by now also finished, but, like us, they had inexplicably been denied permission to leave.

We accepted the situation stoically, but Romano, the volatile captain of *Marco Polo*, did not. Both we and the four people on *Marco Polo* spent the next day under guard on our boats, cooling our heels – or, in the case of Romano, steaming with livid anger. We had no idea when, or even if, we would be released.

That night, we received a visit from the police chief. He was rowed over to our boat by a native islander of the Nicobari tribe (clad in shorts, thank goodness, or else I might have been forced to stare, and that would have gotten me into even more trouble). We had earlier seen him climbing to the top of a tall coconut palm as nimbly as a monkey. Police Chief Anam had brought some ripe bananas and a bunch of drinking coconuts, which the tribesman hacked open with a machete and passed around.

"Do you have any alcohol?" the chief asked, "Beer, or whisky?"

We explained that although we had a few beers, they weren't cold. That was fine, said the chief, and he and his two companions settled happily down in our cockpit with their warm beers, throwing the empty cans overboard as they were emptied. The tribesman stayed in the rowboat.

"Don't you have any whisky?" the chief asked again, when the beers were gone.

"I think we might have one very old bottle, half empty," I answered truthfully. "Do you want me to look for it?"

He paused to consider. "No," he finally said, "I'll take more beers."

We had a spare set of binoculars on board, and Herbert and I had earlier decided that we might offer them to the chief as a token of our esteem.

"As a gift?" the police chief clarified, as Herbert handed them over.

No, as a bribe, you freeloader! I thought vengefully, but instead I smiled. "Yes, as a gift from us to you, to thank you for your hospitality." I said this sweetly, without choking even once on my words. "Perhaps you can use it to spot more illegal yachts."

When our meagre store of beers was sufficiently depleted, the tribesman rowed the chief and his cronies over to *Marco Polo*. Herbert and I went to bed wondering how the crew of that boat would feel about the Happy Hour that was about to be imposed upon them.

Next morning we asked how *Marco Polo*'s late night visit had gone. Steve, the amiable Kiwi skipper, smiled and pantomimed with his hands the opening of many liquor cabinets. The chief had obviously had better luck aboard *Marco Polo* than he did on *Northern Magic*.

"I'm surprised he wanted so much alcohol," I commented. "He's Muslim, you know."

"Hmmm, that's strange," answered Steve. "He told us he is Hindu."

The next day we were given permission – on account of the children needing exercise – to go ashore. At a predetermined time, we landed the dinghy and set foot on the southernmost point in India, looking curiously around at the many people, who looked curiously back at us. There were beautiful women in colourful saris, walking with large flat baskets on their heads, dark-skinned men in white undershirts with dots of colour on their foreheads, shy young children in crisp, white school uniforms, and countless cows, chickens, and ducks. Almost all of the cattle had large open sores on their necks surrounded by hordes of flies. One was lying on the ground while a rooster pecked daintily away at the bloody wound. On the beach, washed up among the other refuse, was an Anker beer can from Indonesia we had served to the chief the night before.

As the children occupied themselves on a tire swing, Herbert and I spent the rest of the morning in the police station, inexplicably watching the police chief fill out paperwork. We were meant, I think, to be impressed with the stylish way he stamped and signed the papers on his desk. Romano, also forced to watch this display of bureaucratic machismo, was fit to be tied. Finally, Herbert cleared his throat and asked me, "Don't the kids have to do some homework?"

"Oh yes," I remembered brightly. "I think we'd better be getting back to the boat. It's important for the kids to keep up on their work, you know."

Romano watched with narrowed eyes as we were granted permission to leave. He was obviously wondering what excuse he could give to be able to return to his boat as well.

About half an hour later, Romano came knocking. "We've got to do something!" he said frantically. "We just can't sit here like this. How long is he going to hold us? We've got to develop a plan! We need a strategy! If my government heard about this, I'd be out of here in a day! This is intolerable!"

While we were talking about the necessity of diplomatic intervention, the police rowboat arrived. Chief Anam had asked us several times if we needed any fruits or vegetables. Figuring he was wanting to make a little money selling us supplies, we had obliged him by placing an order. Now his soldiers had arrived with two small plastic bags of groceries.

Romano, frustrated with our passive, cordial approach, grabbed the opportunity to speak to the men. "I would like to talk to your captain," he said, in his delicious, exaggerated Italian accent, most of his words ending in superfluous vowels. "Not about boats, and problems, you understand," he continued, "but about life." He pronounced these last two words "about-a life-a."

The soldiers looked back at him in total bewilderment. Behind Romano's back, Herbert and I made motions to indicate that this weird guy was not with us.

"Go and talk to your chief," ordered Romano imperiously. "If he has time to see me, wave to me from shore and I will come. Tell him I want to talk about life."

Half an hour later, Romano got his summons. As he set off to talk about life, Herbert and I debated whether setting him loose was really a very wise strategy. We wondered how the angry, opinionated captain and the police chief with the Napoleon complex would get along.

Several hours later there was a knock on our boat. Romano was back. He had no progress to report and was depressed and troubled by the chief's continued evasiveness. Then, he went despondently to face his angry crew, who were on the point of mutiny. Later, we learned that all of them had voted against coming to the Nicobars, and it was only at Romano's insistence that they had stopped at all. In fact, they hadn't really needed to repair anything. Romano had wanted to buy some lobster.

Herbert and I were getting ready for bed when there was yet another knock. This time, it was the enigmatic police chief himself with, as always, a retinue.

"I have your passports, and you are free to go," he announced. "The captain of *Marco Polo* was in my office all afternoon crying about his crew members missing their flights, so I made a special effort and called up my superiors to explain the situation. I didn't need to do this, you understand," he added meaningfully.

"They were talking about laying charges," he continued, "but I assured them that both of you had truly stopped in distress, and I managed to convince them that no charges needed to be laid." There was a dramatic pause, enabling us to properly reflect upon the great lengths to which he had gone on our behalf.

"So you may leave. I will be back in the morning."

We were stunned. Romano's little tête-à-tête had worked. Or perhaps the chief, after a couple of hours' exposure to the stubborn Italian, realized it was in his interest to get rid of him as quickly as possible – otherwise he'd have to spend every afternoon listening to Romano's long-winded monologues. In any event, we were free, and in the morning we broke the good news to the kids. Jonathan was the winner of the "Release from Arrest in the Nicobars" betting pool we had set up the afternoon before.

At nine the next morning our good friend police chief Anam arrived at *Northern Magic* for the last time. He was in a jovial mood and full dress uniform. He looked magnificent. His lean frame was topped with a tall officer's hat, he had decorations on his breast, and he even carried a natty little black and brass swagger stick. With a monocle in his eye and an Aryan face, he could have passed for a general in the Third Reich.

Herbert and I had been wrestling with the question of whether the chief was a rogue, toying with us while raiding our liquor cabinets – and, presumably, at some point, our wallets – or just a decent and basically powerless guy doing his job and trying to be friendly. Depending on the day, the hour, or the minute, either seemed to be true. Now he presented us with a beautiful shell, and the scale definitely began tipping towards "decent."

For some reason, I had felt compelled to put together some tiny gifts for the chief and his wife, in return for his "hospitality." I was gamely continuing our little charade that we were his guests, not his prisoners, to the last. Herbert had looked at me strangely when I showed him the bag, and just shrugged, "Well, you do whatever you want."

Feeling a little like Patti Hearst, I gave the chief his goodie bag. A few minutes earlier, he had refused to have his photo taken, but during the burst of goodwill that followed my presentation of the bag and my telling him how wonderful he looked in his uniform, he posed for a picture and even signed our guest book.

Now came the final transaction. "So, for the groceries," I began, "how much do we owe you?" I had a twenty dollar U.S. bill in my pocket, which was probably double or triple the value of the food we had received.

"Oh, whatever you wish," he answered grandly. "I only did it as a favour. You are, after all, my guests."

"Well, at home the food wouldn't cost more than this," I said, bringing out the bill. "Will this be sufficient?"

The police chief's face, which had, up until that point, been beaming in the glow of our mutual friendship and admiration, crumpled and fell. This was very clearly *not* sufficient. His disappointment hit like a slap in the face.

"You have to understand," he said quietly, leaning forward, his eyes glittering, "that my men and I, we have expenses. I think fifty dollars would be more appropriate."

Ten minutes later, fifty dollars poorer, we turned *Northern Magic*'s bow into the Bay of Bengal, heading for Sri Lanka at last.

17

Rorschach Test

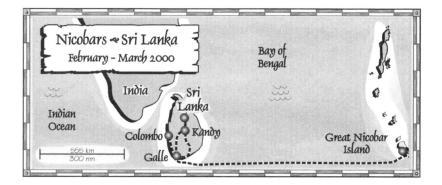

On this passage, for the first time, we gave the two older boys regular shifts on watch. They had often helped out for an hour or two when one of us was especially tired, but only when conditions were good and we were far from land. This was the perfect passage for something more regular, with mild seas and little traffic, so Jonathan began proudly taking a daily shift from 6 p.m. to 8 p.m., while Michael took his own two-hour shift in the morning. The result of this was that both Herbert and I got an extra hour of sleep at the beginning and end of our night-time shifts, giving us a full and luxurious seven hours in bed. Suddenly, we both felt much more rested and comfortable, freeing up more time to be all together as a family during the day rather than blearily passing each other in a fog of fatigue like ships in the night.

During the days, the kids occupied themselves with computer games and an orgy of book reading, with both Michael and Jon polishing off a novel each day. I instituted a game that all three boys took up with gusto, promising a chocolate bar to anyone who could find ten English words that I couldn't define. Suddenly dictionaries were in great demand, and the boys spent hours poring through pages and excitedly coming up with words they thought would stump me.

By the end of the passage, Christopher was in the lead with six, besting me with words like "bast," "barm," and "zucchetto." Michael and Jon were tied at four, counting "rosaceous," "sigil," and "foxing" among their triumphs. Christopher would spend hours beside me on watch, intently studying the Oxford dictionary in hopes of claiming his prize. I was forced to end the game abruptly in Sri Lanka, when another cruiser lent the boys a dictionary dedicated to impossible and preposterous words.

The Sri Lankan navy tied up alongside to board us even before we had finished setting our anchor in the harbour at Galle. This was a country racked with civil war, and security was stringent, with special passes and military inspections required every time we went ashore. At night, ropes were stretched across the inner harbour to prevent large vessels from entering. Small boats were put under a bright searchlight. A gunboat bristling with weapons was waiting at the pier, and men with automatic rifles and binoculars kept careful watch at several points around the harbour. Unlit boats, looking like fishing boats but for the radar, patrolled around the anchorage at night.

Most disturbing of all were the nightly underwater explosions, detonated to deter Tamil Tiger suicide bombers equipped with scuba gear from entering the harbour. The war between the majority Sinhalese and minority Tamils, who were mostly concentrated in the north, had brought terrorist attacks from Tamil Tigers, including many suicide bombings and assassinations in recent years. Because the capital city of Colombo was no longer safe, much of the sensitive ammunition stores had been moved to Galle, where we were anchored. These security measures had been put in place to protect them – and us.

Galle itself was an interesting town with relics of centuries of occupation by colonial powers – first the Portuguese, then the Dutch, and finally the British, who had left the island nation with enough of an English-speaking tradition that we had no trouble communicating with the friendly, dark-skinned people who watched and hovered curiously around us everywhere we went. Cows roamed freely everywhere, grazing incongruously beside busy streets and blocking traffic as they walked across lanes of traffic already complicated by cars, trucks, three-wheeled *tuk-tuks*, bicycles, pedestrians, goats, dogs, and the occasional ox-cart.

We went on an overland expedition to central Sri Lanka, but during the trip something was weighing on my mind: I had discovered a lump in my breast. Since my melanoma, I had become acutely conscious of every change in my body, every lump, twinge, or pain that might signify the return of my cancer. I needed to have this checked out. If I didn't put this worry to rest here, it would be ten months before I'd find a better place.

Luckily, we had made a friend in Sri Lanka, a twenty-seven-year-old *tuk-tuk* driver named Ekka. We liked him enormously. He had been helping us in many ways, driving us everywhere we needed to go, saving us money on our shopping, and actually refusing payment if we offered him extra money. Ekka drove Herbert and me to a very basic little hospital. The two women who sat at the reception desk didn't appear to understand my request and seemed afraid to even look me in the eye. We decided to try another place.

At the second clinic, strangely deserted like the first, the routine was the same. Everyone seemed to want to avoid helping me. I felt as though I was a creature from another planet, or had a huge gob of spinach in my teeth. Ekka tried talking to them on my behalf, but with no better results.

Frustrated, we tried a third hospital, but still without success. The receptionist behind the thick glass partition kept repeating a single sentence, something that sounded like "Doctor on loo," by which, I assumed, she did not mean that all the surgeons were suffering from constipation. Finally, we ascertained that there were no doctors there. We gave up and returned to the boat without having accomplished a thing. Our first impression of the Sri Lankan medical system was not good.

The next morning we returned to hospital number two, determined to find a doctor somehow. Since it still appeared to be doctorless, we trudged back to the first hospital, where at last I managed to find the house doctor sitting behind a desk in a small cluttered office. He listened to my request and without saying much scribbled the name of a surgeon on a little piece of paper and sent me back to reception, where I was told to return at 5:00 p.m. I paid 250 rupees, the equivalent of five dollars, and got a little receipt showing that I was number 19.

We returned at five. The hospital, which had been deserted on both of my earlier visits, was now packed. There were about fifty people jostling about in the tiny waiting area outside examination room number 30. I felt overpowered by the stifling heat, the lack of air, and the pungent smell of hot human bodies.

It was clear that I was in for a long wait. I managed to push myself into a spot leaning against the wall at the top of the open stairway; a young woman wedged herself against me, practically sitting on my lap. For an hour and a half, I observed the people who came and went. Despite the discomfort, almost everyone looked amazingly cheerful. Each family group coming out of the examination room had broad smiles on their faces.

Finally, at ten to seven, it was my turn. I pushed my way to the front of the throng, which was as large now as it had been two hours earlier. The doctor spoke excellent English and helped dispel some of my growing uneasiness about the whole situation. He agreed the lump was worth investigating and recommended a needle biopsy, which could be done in Galle, as well as a mammogram, which would have to take place in Colombo. Although I had certain misgivings, I agreed this did seem like the most sensible course. I don't think, though, that there was a broad smile on my face as I left.

That evening we ate dinner at Ekka's house. We were served like royalty by the women, who fussed and bustled around with food prepared in the backyard kitchen. They presented us with half a dozen delicious dishes, including dhall, curried chicken, and buffalo curd with honey. Ekka was the only one who sat to eat with us; the women hung back shyly and ate in another room with their fingers, as all Sri Lankans do.

The next day, I set off for the biopsy, which turned out to be back at hospital number three. The doctor had told me to present myself at 4:00 p.m. Although Herbert wanted to accompany me, I suggested he stay on the boat and get supper fixed so that it was ready when I returned, when-ever that might be. So I set off alone on the fifteen-minute dinghy ride through the rolly swell in the harbour, followed by a dusty walk dodging trucks and cattle through the harbour zone, followed by the security check by half a dozen soldiers with machine guns, then around a few sand-bagged barricades and I was at the spot where Ekka was faithfully waiting, as always, in his battered green trishaw. By the time I reached him, it had begun to rain, the usual Galle afternoon downpour. About a block from the hospital Ekka's vehicle stalled. I ran the rest of the way on foot.

Dripping, I presented the note from my doctor to the girls at reception. They looked at it scornfully and thrust it back. "Doctor on loo today. Come back tomorrow." That was all. When I asked whether I could make an appointment, they simply shook their heads. If I'd had a pack of laxatives in my pocket, I would have thrown it at them.

I slumped out of the hospital. Luckily, Ekka was still there, wrestling with his *tuk-tuk*. He, too, was having a bad day. It took about twenty minutes before he finally got his little cart going and we putted off to the market, a pretty glum pair.

At the bakery, I decided to make both of us feel better by buying a cake for Ekka to take home. When I asked him which he wanted, he modestly picked the plainest and most inexpensive one. I bought the fanciest chocolate confection in the store and my investment of a few dollars was repaid with one of Ekka's million-rupee smiles, my best transaction of the day.

Back at the harbour, I had trouble getting *Junior* to start. It took about ten minutes and thirty or forty hard pulls on the starter cable before I could get underway. While drifting farther and farther away from the dock as I struggled, I was conscious of the entire crew of an Indonesian cargo ship tittering at my efforts. By now the skies had really opened and the rain was falling in solid sheets.

I began bailing as I drove, but the skies poured in water more quickly than *Donovan Bailer*, which is what we had named our speedy plastic bailing device, could toss it out. Soon the potatoes and carrots I had bought at the market had spilled out of their bags and were sloshing around in four inches of water at my feet. As I slowly drew closer to *Northern Magic*, I noticed a small fishing boat with two men in it, holding on to our mooring buoy and waiting out the deluge under a tiny blue tarp.

Just as I stood up, grabbing a steel rail on *Northern Magic* to steady myself against the swell from the Indian Ocean, there was a blinding light and terrific thunderclap in the sky directly overhead. I realized that I was holding on to the metal rail and released it, much too late, of course. But nothing had been hit. I was still alive.

I looked over to the nearby fishermen, who stared back at me with a look of glazed amazement before lifting their hands together to the heavens in the universal gesture of prayer. I did the same, and we grinned at each other, feeling we had all narrowly escaped the wrath of God. At last, I dragged myself and my poor drowned vegetables aboard *Northern Magic*. I was as wet as if I'd gone swimming in my clothes.

While all this was going on, I hadn't said a word to anyone at home about why we weren't leaving. Dad kept faithfully e-mailing weather information, and we kept inexplicably missing weather windows in which we might have departed. I was hoping to handle the situation without telling them anything about it, on the assumption that this was all a false alarm. I didn't want my mom to suffer any more than necessary.

The next afternoon, I steeled myself and set off again. Luckily, the daily thunderstorm began only after I was already inside Ekka's *tuk-tuk*. I turned down his offer to wait for me. Marching up to the desk, I presented my chit once again. The women I had come to hate looked at my paper briefly. "Doctor on loo until Friday," one of them said. Friday was two days away.

"No, this is not right!" I argued frantically. "You said yesterday, the doctor would be here today!"

But the doctor was not there, and there was not a thing I could do about it. The women shoved my little paper back at me and turned away.

To my embarrassment, tears welled up in my eyes and began rolling down my cheeks. I rushed back to the entrance of the hospital, but Ekka was already gone. I stood there for a while, leaning on a concrete pillar, sniffling and snuffling and ineffectually wiping my face, conscious that there were at least twenty people watching my distress. After so many fruitless visits to doctorless hospitals, I was beginning to feel as if I was stuck in some kind of time warp, my own weird version of the movie *Groundhog Day*.

I climbed into another *tuk-tuk*. It was pelting now. My thoughts were a reflection of the ugly bloated clouds overhead. On slippery, potholed streets on the way back to the harbour, a cyclist unexpectedly cut right in front of our path. My driver had to veer sharply onto someone's property in order to avoid running him down. As we came to a screeching stop just a few feet away from a building, I found I was looking directly into the eyes of a very thin, very old man.

He was lying on his side in the mud, squeezed under a low overhang, taking what shelter he could from the rain. For those two or three seconds that we careened towards him, the beggar's stoic dark eyes were strangely fixed on my weepy blue ones. Suddenly, I realized how ridiculous my demonstration of self-pity really was. No matter what the tests might show, no matter how many more times I was fated to take that wet boat ride to some dingy hospital to be rudely turned away from seeing a non-existent doctor, I still wouldn't want to trade places with him.

In a moment, we were back on the road and continuing on our way. But thanks to a wordless gift from a ragged old man, now my eyes were dry.

There was no longer any choice but to explain to Mom and Dad the reasons for our delayed departure. My e-mail to Dad unleashed a wave of concerned action back in Canada. Dad had a friend whose brother's brother-in-law was a prominent lawyer in Colombo. The lawyer would arrange an appointment with Colombo's top cancer surgeon for me, and I would stay at his home while I underwent treatment.

I insisted, against Herbert's wishes, on going to Colombo alone. This lawyer would be my ally. There was no point in dragging the kids all that way to what was likely to be an unpleasant and dangerous city. Plus, neither of us felt comfortable inflicting the entire family on our unknown benefactor. In two days, I was on a train to the capital.

The train deposited me in downtown Colombo before noon, so I had a lot of time to kill. My appointment at the hospital was at four in the afternoon. I spent hours wandering through a huge outdoor market, pretending the large duffle bag on my shoulder weighed significantly less than it did, shooing off the touts who tried to attach themselves to me. The market was a chaotic blur of competing vendors, selling everything from baskets of smelly dried fish smaller than discarded pencil stubs to cheap electronics.

In mid-afternoon, I found a taxi and went to the lawyer's house, a large, two-storey building within a walled compound, with expensive cars in the driveway and many servants. I followed the lawyer to his courtyard garden, where he asked me nothing about myself, but instead entertained me for half an hour with stories of his losing nine hundred dollars a night in poker games. He was in his seventies, spoke flawless English, and boasted about his prestige and status as a Queen's Counsel. Then he called for a taxi, and off I went to the hospital.

The hospital was quite a bit larger and less congested than the ones in Galle. My new doctor – a cultured-looking woman in her forties wearing an elegant *sari* – boosted my confidence. Although she believed the lump was unlikely to be cancerous, considering my history she recommended I undergo a lumpectomy, which would leave me with nothing to worry about during the rest of our voyage. Although I had come only for a biopsy and mammogram, I agreed to the surgery, which would take place in two days.

I returned to the lawyer's house. I felt uneasy, because he hadn't exactly been welcoming, nor had he made mention of the fact that I would be staying with him. Once again I was led to his little garden and listened to him talk some more. Inside, a servant was setting a large table for dinner, but there was no sign that I was invited.

He didn't introduce me to his daughter, a woman about my age, or to his wife as she passed through a nearby room. I just listened as they made small talk. Finally, the daughter asked where I was staying. "I don't know," I answered.

The lawyer opened up a phone book and pointed out a five-star hotel. There was no way I was going to spend that kind of money, but nonetheless I accepted when he asked if I wanted one of his servants to drive me there. By now, I just wanted to get out of that house.

The driver left me at the hotel, which was not only expensive but also full. The sun was dipping below the horizon as I stood outside on the street after he had gone and hailed myself a *tuk-tuk*. I directed the driver to a part of town my *Lonely Planet* travel guide said had a lot of budget tourist guesthouses. All I wanted was a safe place to sleep.

After two unsuccessful tries, I found myself a small guesthouse. It was only after I paid my money and collapsed on the bed that I noticed the marks on the walls all around me. There were vivid dark handprints, many of them clearly showing five spread-out fingers. More surprisingly, the wall was covered with distinct black footprints as well, some of them half way up. The overall effect was reminiscent of a homicide scene.

The hotel provided no top sheets. I yanked off the bottom sheet from the spare bed, revealing a panoply of dark splotches on the mattress. These, along with the wall prints, formed a kind of Rorschach test of my sanity as I awaited surgery in a dingy hotel in a big city in a foreign country convulsed in civil war. And in Colombo, the signs of that conflict were obvious: military police were posted every block or two, patrolling around with automatic weapons, stopping passing cars for inspections. Every day, while using a taxi, I was pulled over to be inspected at least once.

The next morning, I set off in search of breakfast and an Internet café, but found neither of these within easy reach. The sign at the hotel promising a restaurant on the premises was a lie. So I settled for a small pack of arrowroot biscuits and a box of UHT milk, and continued tramping down one of Colombo's main roads. I was surprised to see a group of eight small goats milling around in front of a restaurant, waiting their turn to cross the busy street.

I walked past street vendors and beggars, churches and temples, putting miles on my battered old sandals. I spent most of the next two days walking. There were many places advertising Internet access, but I walked miles and tried no fewer than five before I found one that actually worked. Several of them said "Not working!" but frustratingly, two of them had personnel who didn't know their own computer password to connect to the system. "Don't you know it?" one of them asked me beseechingly.

Because I never found a restaurant during my stay that sold anything in the morning other than curried chicken or fish, I never ate breakfast – or supper either, as it turned out, eating oranges and arrowroot cookies in my room on that awful stained mattress rather than wandering around alone after dark. I spoke to almost no one. At night, as I lay, hungry, in bed underneath a mosquito net, staring at those footprints, I missed my four men enormously. I had no way to communicate with Herbert other than by Internet, which always involved a day's delay. Back at the boat, he was angry at himself for having let me set off alone. This wasn't the way either of us had planned it to be.

My surgery took place at six in the evening. I hadn't expected the full-scale surgical set-up – a real operating theatre, complete with sterile fields, several nurses, and two surgeons. I quailed a bit at the overpowering sense that I was having a real operation, not just some snip-snip in an examination room. The surgeon poked around for a long time and eventually fished out not one, but two tumours.

After changing back out of my hospital gown into my own clothes, I returned to the room where I had waited before in a wooden school chair. An old lady in a hospital gown and her hair up in a silly paper cap was still there, clutching her papers, just as she had been earlier. She was wearing the same extremely silly plastic flip-flop sandals with garish multicoloured plastic flowers on top that I had worn as part of my hospital ensemble. We were in a kind of all-purpose room, with nurses bustling back and forth, three desks cluttered with paperwork, and a doctor, face concealed by a mask, making an occasional appearance. We two patients looked and felt like intruders in this busy scene, sitting awkwardly in those two chairs squeezed in next to a desk covered with piles of papers.

On that desk was a plastic jar containing someone's excised body parts, large kidney-coloured nodules floating in a solution of formaldehyde. As I waited, my breast starting to throb as the anaesthetic wore off, I couldn't keep my eyes off that jar, wondering whose nodules these were and why they were sitting there, unattended, in the middle of that mess.

Then a nurse plopped down another jar. The papers she put beside it were mine. Suddenly, I realized that the second jar contained my very own body parts, two little fuzzy whitish nubs the size of marbles. Each was pierced painfully with a length of black thread. I stared at them in morbid fascination.

I paid $150 for the surgery, and the nurse handed me my files as well as the jar and instructed me to take them to the lab. For the next fifteen minutes, I found myself wandering around the hospital, up and down stairs, through a maze of hallways, unsuccessfully trying to find the right place to deposit them. When I finally did find the lab, they waved me back to the cashier, one floor down, where I had to pay for the lab tests first. Then I climbed the stairs to the lab again to submit the specimen and my proof of payment.

As I was wandering around all these dingy back hallways, with my own little globules jiggling merrily in their jar, I considered that I know quite a few squeamish people who would have keeled right over when faced with their own disembodied parts – and, even worse, been asked to traipse all over the hospital with them. Some corner of my mind found this funny. I began imagining other scenarios, such as amputees hopping around with their severed leg balanced on one shoulder, looking, as I was, for the lab, but somehow never finding it.

The laboratory itself was packed with people – a few patients, like me, but mainly lab personnel, the administrative clerks sharing desk space with the lab technicians themselves. There were about twice as many bodies as there were chairs or desk spaces. There was no horizontal surface visible anywhere that was not covered with papers and implements and files and specimens of human tissue in various stages of analysis. I wanted to scream and run out of there. But I simply handed over my jar and set off to the pharmacy to fulfil my prescription for a painkiller.

There were a few people ahead of me at the pharmacy counter, behind which the harried looking staff bustled around. As new people came into the room, they jostled ahead and elbowed me out of the way, succeeding in getting their own prescriptions filled while I was shoved to the background. Perhaps in other circumstances I would have held my own ground better, but, tired and hurting, I had no stomach for this. Eventually, I thrust the prescription back into my pocket and left without filling it. Instead, I went outside and looked for a *tuk-tuk* to take me back to the security of my own hotel room, however stained and footprinted it might be.

On the ride back to the hotel, my injured right breast reacted angrily to every pothole and swerve. After dark, Colombo looked different and, to my eyes, ominous. The driver took me back a different way than I had gone before, through small and creepy-looking residential streets. I felt vulnerable and very much alone. I fished around in my pouch and clipped my little can of pepper spray to an outside pocket.

At the hotel I fled to my room and slept heavily until the first filtered glimmerings of dawn began to light the sky, and the travelling fish salesmen began their cheery morning singsong, "*All-lo! All-lo!*" in the street below. I had planned to take the train back to Galle that morning, but the surgeons had left in place a little plastic tube to drain away internal bleeding. I was forced to stay one more day. I felt guilty knowing that Herbert would be condemned to worry as the day dragged on and I didn't arrive as planned. Eventually, I knew, he would take the long dinghy ride and head into town to check for an e-mail from me, but there would be a lot of fretting first.

I had been completely oriented to leaving that day, and this time I really resented my long trudge to the Internet café, several miles away. I wanted a breakfast of bacon, eggs, and hash browns, but settled for some dry arrowroot biscuits instead. They make great cookies in Sri Lanka, but I was by now getting a little tired of them. From all my walking and my one-meal-a-day regimen, I was noticeably thinner than I had been four days before.

I made my last trip to the hospital that night to have the shunt removed and my dressing changed. I walked in and then out of the pharmacy again without filling my new prescription, waited in two or three line-ups, visited the cashier twice more, and then left, a free woman at last. Early the next morning, I was on a bus for the bumpy, three-hour trip back to Galle. This time, the narrow streets, the cows placidly crossing in front of traffic, the row of shoemakers sitting under umbrellas near the old fort, the pineapple seller with his mountain of fruit, even the soldiers at the harbour checkpoint, all looked familiar and welcome.

There was no use in delaying our departure while awaiting the results of the laboratory tests, which could take a week or more. Of course, if the diagnosis was bad it could mean the end of our trip. We arranged to get the results by e-mail, so after my return we immediately began our last major provisioning of the boat until Africa.

We took a day off to accept an invitation from Ekka to visit his in-laws' home in the country. Ekka and his wife had been growing dearer to us with each passing day, a badly needed beacon of light in what had been a rather dark and miserable time for all of us. I couldn't help but compare Ekka, the trishaw driver, in his warm and loving little shack, to that vain and self-absorbed lawyer in his cold mansion. Later, from someone else, we learned that once a month Ekka and his wife visited a local orphanage to donate supplies to the children. I found this much more impressive than losing nine hundred dollars at poker. When it finally came time to say goodbye, Ekka cried, and of course, I did too.

18

We Place Last at the Chagos Fish Olympics

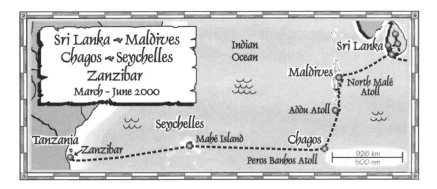

Sri Lanka ～ Maldives
Chagos ～ Seychelles
Zanzibar
March – June 2000

Indian
Ocean

Sri Lanka

Maldives

North Malé
Atoll

Addu Atoll

Tanzania
Zanzibar

Seychelles

Mahé Island

Chagos

Peros Banhos Atoll

926 km
500 nm

O n our passage to the Maldives, Christopher asked to join his older brothers in taking his turn at watch, so he was given the eight to nine morning shift, with supervision. Promoted to a position of such responsibility, our eight-year-old puffed up his chest with pride and vigilantly kept watch for the first time.

After three days at sea, we caught sight of the atolls of the Maldives. They first appeared as smoky smudges on the horizon, tricking us into thinking we were looking at distant ships. What we were seeing were palm trees, as the islands themselves were only a metre or two above sea level and hidden until we were almost upon them. Mariners of the past often discovered this too late, and the spectacular azure waters of the Maldives are studded with the wrecks of unwary ships. If the sea level rises because of global warming, the Maldives will disappear.

We had been expecting something rather primitive and were therefore surprised to see the tall buildings of Malé, a town of 65,000, rising up on the horizon. Many of the buildings were four and five storeys, brand new, and painted in the vibrant colours of the coral on which these islands are built – rose, aquamarine, white, yellow. The gleaming golden dome of a mosque glinted brightly in the afternoon light.

Malé is a pretty little town, a labyrinth of seemingly identical narrow streets paved in interlocking stones right up to the edge of its coral-rock buildings. Between the colourful architecture and the signage throughout the town featuring the distinctive swirling script of the Dhivehi language, which is unique to this place, it made a very pleasing and exotic effect. We began our exploration of Malé around noon and were charmed by the call to prayer that echoed through the narrow streets, the musical chant evoking mental images of far-away Arabia. We then watched with surprise as shop shutters rolled down, store doors were locked, and little signs, saying, *Closed For Prayer*, sprouted everywhere. Men swarmed the streets and made their way to the mosque, where they removed their shoes, washed their feet carefully in pools and fountains provided for this purpose, put on head coverings, and knelt on the floor of the beautiful and airy interior.

Every afternoon, we had to plan our shopping around these prayer times so as not to find ourselves being shooed out of a store because its owner needed to pray. Since almost everything closed for half-hour periods around noon and three-thirty, there was nothing to do during these interludes but stand around and wait for the men to stream back and reopen their shops. However annoying this was for us, there was something very touching about the Maldivians' devotion to their faith.

"I think Muslim people are a lot more involved in their religion than Christian people are," Michael observed.

The Maldives provided us with a break, and it was one we badly needed. Sri Lanka and its frustrations had not been good for us. We were crabby and homesick, tired of the extreme heat and the constant rolling. We had not enjoyed a calm anchorage or a good night's sleep for almost three months. Deadlines for my lab results had twice come and gone without any word. But the morning after we arrived in Maldives we received the e-mail message we had been awaiting. The tests were clear; no cancer had been found.

+

Sometimes you don't realize how dark the day has been until the clouds disappear and the sun begins to shine through. Certainly, it was a glorious day now, as we raised our anchor and headed off to where a tiny island beckoned in the distance, our own little quiet corner of paradise.

We decided to take our time meandering through the Maldives. Our plan was to sail twenty or thirty miles each day, stopping by mid-afternoon for a swim, supper, and a good night's sleep. It would take us ten or fifteen days to make it to the southernmost atoll this way, but the Maldives were so beautiful, and we weren't in a rush, so we adopted this unambitious plan enthusiastically. We had by now all developed our special routines for negotiating our way around the reefs. Christopher had appointed himself to the job of colouring in our black-and-white photocopied charts to highlight reefs and shallows, a painstaking and important task at which he excelled. Michael climbed the mast and shouted instructions from the spreaders, Jonathan either stood at the bow or stationed himself at the GPS, reading out our position to the captain, who stayed at the helm, while I perched myself on the foredeck transmitting instructions from one crew member to another. At most anchorages we snorkeled as often as we could, marvelling at the amazing undersea world around us.

At Mulaku Atoll, we anchored in front of a tidy little village. It seemed to be a merry place, for the shoreline was peppered with playing children, the air full of their laughing voices. We were quite used to being the object of friendly curiosity wherever we went, but we still weren't quite prepared for the enthusiastic reception we received in a village that rarely saw a white face. Every head turned curiously in our direction, and a glance from us was more than enough to provoke a beaming smile in return.

It was in the faces of the children that the most surprising reaction took place, for they skittered and laughed and made way for us exactly as if we were furry creatures from space: funny and cute, but different enough to be just a little scary. The schoolboys laughed openly, while the girls giggled with their hands hiding their mouths, looking away shyly and peeking over their shoulders when they thought you weren't looking, then collapsing in convulsions of self-conscious laughter when they saw that you were. Younger children ducked behind houses when you looked their way, and then, when your back was safely turned, came bravely rushing up behind you. All it took was a quick swivel of your head to make them run away, shaking with laughter. Eventually we began playing a game in which we would duck around a corner and spring out with a roar, making them scatter to the wind in gales of giggles.

Our final hop took us to Addu, the last atoll in the chain. As everywhere in the Maldives, it was all impeccably neat, its inhabitants smiling, as if still ready and waiting for the inspection by Her Majesty that never came. We had two major items on our agenda for Addu.

The first was our final provisioning before heading for Chagos, an uninhabited archipelago about five hundred kilometres to the south. We planned to spend several weeks there, waiting for the monsoon season to set in and the southeast trade winds to establish themselves for our onward journey to Africa.

At the best of times there was not a lot of fresh food to be had in the Maldives; about the only things that grew were bananas and papayas. We'd tried our best while in Malé, the capital, to stock up, but by the time we hit Addu we were hungry for fruit. Everyone grew what they needed, so the way to get fruit was by going from house to house and buying whatever you saw growing in someone's yard. It took a little longer than going to the supermarket, but it definitely was more social.

Our second order of business was celebrating Jonathan's twelfth birthday. For weeks, we'd been pulling Jon's leg, telling him that we hadn't bought him any presents that year. This wasn't as outlandish a tale as it sounds, as it had been months since we had been anywhere with any kind of reasonable store. In fact, on our overland trip in Sri Lanka, we had each bought Jon a special souvenir: Herbert and I had found him a brass ceremonial dagger, Michael a carved mask, and Christopher a painted drum. By the time his birthday rolled around, we had got him so well primed for disappointment that he had actually agreed to be content with one small, four-dollar pack of Magic Cards.

The night before the big day, we went to bed at our normal times, and thus were all fast asleep at 12:20 a.m., our consciences giving us no qualms whatsoever about the trick we were playing on a hopeful, innocent boy. Soon, all would be set right.

The next thing I knew, something was wrenching me out of a deep sleep. It was dark. It was the middle of the night, and there was some kind of ruckus outside. I could hear men's voices.

Shaking Herbert awake as I clambered over him, I staggered to the main hatch. Alarmingly, there were men standing right there, in our cockpit, and they weren't other yachties. A dark face with a black moustache was peering into the cabin, holding a bright flashlight. Behind him I could make out the shapes of four more large, dark strangers. I couldn't understand the muttered words they were exchanging with each other.

The men backed up a bit as they saw me climbing the companionway ladder. As I emerged, I could see that the man with the flashlight was holding something long and tubular in his other hand. Another man was holding something flat and round that glistened strangely. The men were tall, muscular, and Maldivian. They were wearing T-shirts and jeans. I recognized none of them.

"What's going on?" I asked in a croaky, sleep-clogged voice.

"Surprise!" they shouted. "It's a happy birthday surprise!"

I shook my head as Herbert popped up behind me, and then comprehension slowly began to dawn. What the men were holding were presents. Their faces were wreathed in broad smiles.

"We knew today is your son's birthday," the man with the flashlight explained. "We're from the coastguard, and one of us saw it on his passport when you arrived. We baked him a cake!"

Herbert and I started laughing. This sure was a surprise! Only in the Maldives would a bunch of strangers break into someone's home in the middle of the night to wish him happy birthday! While Herbert entertained our guests in the darkened cockpit, I went below and shook the birthday boy awake.

"Wake up, Jon!" I said, laughing. "There is a bunch of visitors here for you. It's your birthday, and they've come to give you a surprise party!"

Jonathan emerged from his bed, sweaty and tousled, barely comprehending the fact that five grown men had come by boat in the middle of the night to wish him happy birthday. I was by now wide awake, and still having trouble believing this myself. For a while, Jon could hardly talk; he just sat there in a daze, as the five men, all but one Maldivian coastguard officers, gleefully presented their gifts – a pink birthday cake they had baked themselves on their ship, moored nearby, and a bottle of fruit drink, both done up in fancy metallic wrapping paper.

The whole gang squeezed into our salon, where we ate pink cake and drank fruit cocktail. Every few minutes, I found myself bursting into laughter at the absurdity of the situation. We had never laid eyes on any of the men before, except the nice young immigration officer who had been on our boat the day we had arrived, and who was the one who made note of Jon's approaching birthday.

"But why did you come in the middle of the night?" I asked Captain Hassan.

"Because we really wanted it to be a surprise!" he answered with a grin.

"Oh, it was a surprise, all right," I nodded, wondering if he realized that there are plenty of places, and plenty of boats, where this kind of surprise might have been greeted with the wrong end of a loaded gun. Yet what wonderful things it said about the peaceful and generous Maldivians, who had probably never even contemplated this possibility.

Jon awoke with a grin on his face the next morning and could hardly wait to tell his brothers about the midnight surprise. It still seemed a little hard to believe, like a strange but pleasant dream. From time to time during the day, I found myself giggling aloud as I recalled it. That evening, after the traditional birthday cheesecake, I told the birthday boy, "Well, it's a good thing that the coastguard brought you those presents last night, because, as we told you, we weren't able to find you anything this year."

"Why don't you check, Mom?" Herbert interjected. "I thought there was that one little thing."

"Oh yes, the Magic Cards," I said and hurried away, returning with one tiny pack of fifteen collectible playing cards – a really old set, not a particularly useful one. Jon gamely opened it and did a creditable job of expressing delight at his one and only present, as chintzy as it was. He gave each of us a big hug, saying with genuine gratitude that this was better than nothing at all. He is quite a special boy, our Jonathan.

"Oh, yes," I said finally. "I forgot. Maybe there was one more thing . . ."

Much later, after all the unwrapping was finished, I asked a beaming Jon if he really had believed that we had forgotten to buy him presents.

"I wasn't sure," he said, "but the more you talked, the more I believed you. Anyway, I couldn't see how or where you could have bought them. But now I realize why you kept on dragging me away in Sri Lanka every time I saw something I liked."

In the end, however, it was the five midnight strangers who so thoughtfully remembered a young boy celebrating his special day far from home who had brought the best gift of all.

✦

A few days later we left for Chagos, but we had a rough time getting there, battling adverse winds and currents. We arrived on our fourth day at sea, battered and weary, the floor of the cabin covered with books, toys, and kitchen implements that had launched themselves in various new and innovative ways from their particular storage spots.

We anchored in impossibly blue water at a place that was nothing but an apostrophe in the middle of the Indian Ocean, a tiny speck that doesn't even show up on most world maps. As soon as we arrived, we realized that we were now in company with a different bunch of sailors altogether. Here, we discovered a whole new breed of overgrown hippies who had specifically come to Chagos for the chance to live cheaply off the land. They spent decades sailing back and forth between Malaysia and Africa, staying at this place, devoid of other humans, for three, five, seven months at a time, existing mainly off coconut, breadfruit, and, of course, fish.

They lived their entire adult lives on board, stopping from time to time to work at anything they could find to earn a few dollars, then continuing to cruise another year or two. They had leathery skin and long beards (the men, at least), ate homemade muesli for breakfast, and guzzled home-brewed beer and wine in the afternoon. Those with children gave them names like Ocean and Forest. On board, they often went without clothing.

There were two older American men there with young female partners, one from the San Blas Islands in Panama, and the other from Thailand. These long-haired, dark-skinned beauties were widely admired for their uniquely tropical talents. During the days, we would see them at semi-permanent camps they had ingeniously erected ashore, with tables made from split bamboo and hand-woven mats, a hammock hanging from the trees, and a few opened drinking coconuts scattered around. At one party on the beach, they actually showed up wearing hats made of palm fronds that they had woven themselves.

Then there were the two British couples who had cut all their ties to home. One had three older boys who had long hair, spent most of their time surfing, and did not worry about schooling. The other was a younger couple, a nice-looking woman in her late thirties and a husband with very bad teeth. They explained to me that they still had a property back in England, but the tenants had moved out a year earlier and they hadn't bothered to re-rent it. By now, the house had probably been repossessed; they didn't know and they didn't care. The previous year, they had arrived in Tanzania with a broken motor and only twenty dollars to their name. I don't know if they were joking, but they claimed to be living on a thousand dollars a year. That just about matched my annual budget for chocolate.

The family with the children pooh-poohed their uptight relatives back at home, who were worried about things like savings and pensions. "I think pensions are a load of rubbish," the husband said vehemently. "Of course, when we're old, we'll probably be living on the streets!" said the wife with a giggle.

Our closest friends were an American couple we had met in Sri Lanka, whose twelve-year-old son, Falcon, had never lived anywhere but on a boat. Falcon and Jon spent a lot of time palling around together, swimming, and building secret forts in the trees. Falcon was a fanatical fisherman. His mother told me he had eaten five entire dried tuna over the previous two days – in addition to his regular meals, which consisted mainly of fish and rice.

The most interesting boat was a little twenty-six-footer on which an Australian couple had lived for eight years. The boat was so small the husband couldn't stand upright inside it and was now suffering from back problems. They didn't have an oven or even a toilet on board ("We just bucket and chuck it!") and spent almost all their energies gathering food and cooking it at a campfire ashore, since their single-burner alcohol stove was almost out of fuel.

Among this eclectic group, the crew of *Northern Magic*, feeling boringly conventional and middle class, was forced to make a heretical and shameful admission that caused us to fall under quite a cloud of suspicion among the rest. We didn't like fish.

This had never struck us as a crucial issue before. In Chagos, however, our spurning of fish made us somehow suspect – freakish, even. We were constantly forced to run a gauntlet of questions about why we weren't fishing, why we didn't eat fish, and what was wrong with us that we were not in on all the fun? Why, the whole *point* of being in Chagos was fish!

"We just love fishing," Falcon's bearded father told us, looking supremely content as he relaxed in a ragged T-shirt under a palm tree. He was explaining that he didn't know how he would eat all the multitudes of fish he had caught that morning. "I don't know what we like more, the eating or the killing!"

When somebody had a particularly good haul, as our bloodthirsty friend did that day, the proud fisherman called for a communal barbecue on the beach to show off his catch. I'm sure there was some kind of point system in which they competed to be the one to announce the barbecue. In fact, the whole thing was some kind of Chagos Olympics, where the team to talk about, catch, cook, and eat the most fish wins.

When all the athletes were assembled on the beach at the appointed hour, the men launched the Olympics by engaging in the manly exercises of chest-puffing and muscle-flexing, an event required of all successful hunters since time immemorial. "I caught five tuna today!" our American friend announced proudly. "I caught three rock cod!" another said, preening. And of course a third piped in with the obligatory, "My grouper was a full fifteen pounds!"

Herbert did very poorly in this event, with nothing to contribute but "I fixed my bilge pump today."

Next was the Cavalcade of Fish, in which the women paraded around, handing out samples of their creations. Your score was based not only on the taste and creativity of your own dish, but also on the extent to which you raved over others'. Herbert opted out of this event entirely, but I did my best, gamely nibbling on fish with tomato sauce, fish with lime, fried fish, grilled fish, dried fish, raw fish. Well, maybe not the raw fish. I'm competitive by nature, but one could only take this thing so far.

"Isn't that great?" the rest of them said with enthusiasm, reaching for another drippy piece. You could just see the scores tallying up. "Have you tried Jen's sushi? It's to die for!"

I nodded enthusiastically and pretended to agree, but the judges weren't fooled. It didn't look good for the *Northern Magic* team. We were only hanging in there because of Christopher, who was holding his own by gobbling down piece after piece of fish marinated in coconut milk.

But I hadn't given up yet. Lack of suitably fishy raw material forced me to greater heights. I had shamelessly been searching my cookbooks for something that would really make a splash – figuratively, I mean. Now I proudly produced my contribution, a two-tier banana cake, with real sliced bananas between the layers (thereby also cleverly using up some of our last remaining bunch of bruised brownish-black Addu bananas, all seventy of which had ripened at the same time). I heard "oohs" and "ahhs" from the crowd. A murmur ran through them. Fresh fruit! The judges looked impressed. The cake disappeared quickly; everyone else had run out of bananas a month before.

My banana gambit was a bold move indeed, but, alas, the clear winner was the Panamanian girl, whose entry contained a most alarming collection of purple tentacles and was accompanied by a real heart-of-palm salad, from a palm tree she had selected and chopped down herself.

✦

Two weeks after we arrived in Chagos, a front went through. When it left, all the boats had swung on their hooks and were now facing southwest. The trade winds had arrived!

We set off on our thousand-mile passage to the Seychelles after one last visit to a deserted village to fill our water jugs in an abandoned well and take one last delicious cold bucket shower. We were as ready as could be: cinnamon buns baked, three advance meals waiting in the freezer, spare pizza slices in the fridge, boat scrubbed and painted.

We were really looking forward to getting to a place with a grocery store. Our forty kilos of Addu potatoes had exploded, oozed, and stink-bombed their way to oblivion weeks before, most of them consigned to the bottom of the sea. We had used up all our flour, and had been reduced to some rather clumpy and smelly Kenyan flour we had scrounged from the Australians. Tomatoes, apples, oranges, bananas, were, of course, gone. We were down to the last of the slightly rancid butter, cheese, and oatmeal. As we had dug deeper into our long-term stores, we discovered many of the things we had counted on were no longer in prime condition – tinned fruit from Australia that tasted sour, packaged noodles with an unpleasant aftertaste, containers of UHT milk that, when opened, were only full of curds and whey. Our last precious tacos, saved for a special occasion, turned out to be black with mould.

About the only fresh food we still had was our beloved stash of carrots, which we had managed to track down in Addu. We still had about a kilo, only slightly slimy and starting to sprout.

Halfway through the passage, we were making good progress under our spinnaker. It was pulling us nicely, and not only were we making about four knots of speed, but, under its moderating influence, hardly rolling at all. Then a rain cloud approached, and the wind began to rise. Although it was Jonathan's watch, both Herbert and I were on deck, nervously watching as the wind surpassed ten knots. This would be nothing for our regular Dacron sails, but for the light nylon spinnaker pulling on twenty tons of boat, it was quite a bit. *Northern Magic* picked up speed, making more than five knots through the water.

Herbert and I began nervously chewing on our bottom lips. This was probably too much wind for the spinnaker, yet, on the other hand, in ten minutes or so it was sure to return to its usual five to eight knots. By the time we pulled the spinnaker in, we would have to put it right back out again. So we chose the lazy route and left it flying, praying it could handle the extra strain. That's the problem with playing chicken: how does one ever know what is too much, until it is too late?

It was too late. With a loud bang, the spinnaker exploded, its fabric ripping from top to bottom on each side, like two long zippers parting in an instant. Suddenly, all we had left of a few thousand dollars worth of sail were large shreds of red and purple fabric billowing in the wind. We had gambled and lost.

Without much comment, we ruefully hauled in the remains of our spinnaker and raised our jib and mainsail, which, of course, began slatting back and forth as soon as the wind resumed its normal lazy pace a few minutes later. Every few seconds as we rolled, the jib would collapse against the spreaders, and the mainsail, its boom secured to stop it from flying across the boat, would bang as the wind filled it first from one side, then the other.

"At least you have other sails," my dad responded optimistically by e-mail when we told him of the demise of our spinnaker.

It was this fate-provoking sentence that we blamed, the very next day, when our mainsail suffered a similar disaster. It parted, not from top to bottom, but from side to side along a seam about three quarters of the way up. Suddenly, it, too, was dangling, fluttering loosely in two pieces held together only by the ropes along its edge.

"Well, you could use pyjamas," suggested ever-resourceful Dad in his next e-mail. "Just make a new sail out of Michael's, Jonathan's, and Christopher's pyjamas. But don't use Herbert's; we don't want him running around naked all over the boat in the middle of the night."

I e-mailed Dad back that since I was the only one on board who used pyjamas, I was vetoing that plan.

Instead, Herbert rummaged around in our sail locker and came out with an ancient mainsail we carried around as a spare. Once up, the thirty-year-old sail rewarded us with an extra knot of speed. It was made of a much lighter material than the sail that had split, and so it was actually better suited to the conditions. It filled better, and when it became backwinded on a roll, its bang was not as violent.

Over the next days, the wind remained steady out of the southeast and gradually picked up, until our sails remained bellied out full and stopped slamming around from side to side as we rolled. We began to heel over under the wind's firm pressure, returning more respectable speeds of four and five knots. Eventually, the winds grew even stronger, and in the end we actually had to take down the mainsail to save it from too much strain.

It was, however, a difficult passage, both psychologically and physically. Towards the end, most of us began complaining of shaky, weak legs. Upper bodies on a sailboat tend to be exercised automatically – not just in turning winches or pulling on ropes, but in bracing yourself or hanging on to grab bars as you move around. Probably the best source of arm exercise we had was pumping the toilet, an energetic but not entirely pleasant activity that Christopher couldn't always manage on his own, and which, therefore, fell disproportionately on Herbert and me.

Our lower bodies, on the other hand, got next to no use, and soon my legs were feeling like flibberty gibbets (and my mid-section like flibberty giblets). On my late-night watch, I began forcing my reluctant body to do deep knee bends, sit-ups, or calf exercises whenever I got up to check the horizon, both to help in the de-flibbertization of my underused muscles and to help me stay awake. This doesn't sound like a big achievement, but on a rocking, heaving boat it takes a lot of self-control and careful bracing to complete even simple physical movements. Depending on the attitude of the boat at that particular instant, my feeble efforts at sit-ups would either be very easy – if we were pointing downhill – or impossible, and I'd frequently find myself straining but stuck in mid-sit-up until the boat began to tip the other way.

Our bones were also aching from too much lying. When rolling it's tiring to sit, since you slide around on your seat and have to use both arms to brace yourself. Even lying on your side is impossible, as you tip over from side to side like an unsteady log. So we were forced to spend much of each day lying flat on our backs, either sleeping, trying to sleep, or reading.

Our minds as well as our bodies began rebelling. This passage just seemed to go on forever, and we began having talks about the things we missed most from home.

"I'd love a Caramilk bar," Michael was musing dreamily.

"I'd like a chocolate truffle mousse cake," I contributed with a wistful sigh.

"I'd like a flush toilet," our captain muttered darkly.

✦

When Michael traded shifts with me on our ninth morning at sea, I was greeted with a thrilling sight. Mahé Island jutted proudly out of the ocean surrounded by several smaller islands of the Seychelles, its soaring green mountaintops wreathed in a halo of mist. Unlike the flat coral atolls of the Maldives and Chagos, this was a tall granite island, with sheer black and brown cliffs exposed on its flanks. Looking at this majestic panorama, I was seized with a frisson of excitement. *Land ho!*

We arrived at an unexpectedly prosperous place that reminded us of some posh French island in the Caribbean. Shining white houses with bright red roofs gleamed on the hillsides. Fountains and statues and a wonderfully ornate silver clock tower dominated the bustling town core. People hurried around with cell phones and drove nice cars. At the supermarket, we stocked up on baguettes, garlic sausage, and cheese. Our soggy, sea-weakened legs already needing a rest, we sat ourselves down on a park bench for a feast, surrounded by the cacophony of the busy open market. The triumphant feeling of having finally arrived was as magnificent as it had ever been – only Herbert's restraining look prevented me from kissing the blessed ground beneath our feet.

The Seychelles were formerly a colony of both England and France, and remain today a colourful polyglot mixture of African, Asian, and European cultures. There was an unmistakably French quality in the fashions, with svelte young women showing off in high heels and tight, revealing outfits, alongside hefty African women in broad-brimmed straw hats and flowery colonial-style dresses. A rasta beat pulsed in the air, and many of the street vendors, offering shells, carvings made out of coconuts, or new and unfamiliar fruits, wore their bulky masses of dreadlocks stuffed inside large colourful knitted tams. The language on the streets was Creole, a fascinating mixture of African languages and French, but Seychelles is a truly trilingual society where just about every person we met could converse easily in French and English as well. Every day, the kids and I spent at least half the day visiting museums and markets in Victoria and doing our daily schoolwork at the beautiful new library.

Herbert was not as lucky; to him, as always, fell the task of keeping *Northern Magic* afloat. It seemed as if the long passage had tried the boat's mechanical and electronic systems just as it had our bodies. Our poor captain ripped out his hair dealing with a seemingly endless series of minor problems: a propane leak, several small leaks in our freshwater supply, a faulty water pump switch, a malfunctioning freezer, two failed computer CD-ROM drives, and two failed hard drives. Poor Herbert worked for the better part of a week getting everything working again, alternating frantically between flaky computers and leaky fittings.

When both the computer joystick and the mouse packed it in as well, the kids knew enough not to mention it to their wild-eyed dad and instead whispered the news quietly in my ear.

After all these problems, we felt jittery and nervous about heading back to sea, as if the other shoe was about to drop. But the passage had to be accomplished, whether we felt ready for it or not, and so we set out.

The first day was lovely, with moderate winds and seas, and my body accustomed itself to the motion quickly. I didn't experience the terrible lethargy that I usually felt at the beginning of an ocean passage.

"If the whole trip is like this," I remarked brightly the next morning, "then we had no reason to dread it at all. This is just fine!"

Near the end of the second day, however, the wind began to pick up. At our shift change, Herbert and I debated what to do about it. To my surprise, Herbert took in two reefs on the mainsail. I thought this might be overly conservative, but in the next hours, he was proven right.

The wind began howling. Twenty, twenty-five, thirty knots and even more, until we found ourselves battling a gale. Now, instead of trying to speed *Northern Magic* up, our job was to stop her from running too fast. Inside, she sounded like a charging freight train.

As the wind rose, so did the waves. And they were ugly, malicious, mean-looking waves. It took my breath away to watch them sweeping down on us, their white tops shining brightly in the feeble light of a waxing moon. They were steep and close together, coming at us broadside and forcing us to lurch over abruptly at a sharp angle as they passed. Every minute or so, two waves would come together from different angles. Together, they would form an especially tall wave that would break as it slammed into the boat, making a tremendous bang and pounding a deluge of water onto our decks.

We stayed inside, because water was regularly sweeping our decks and even cabin tops. Every few minutes, we had to open up a hatch and check the horizon for ships and the sky for any indication of change in the weather. It became a grim game to try to anticipate when one of these pyramidal waves would explode over the boat, and when we miscalculated, which was often, we would be drenched and the cabin below invaded with gallons of water.

Northern Magic was, as usual, handling the tough conditions with no difficulty, holding her course and bouncing back gamely from each onslaught. We had reduced our jib to a tiny size and were able to keep our speed around six knots, not daring to go any faster despite *Northern Magic*'s urging.

Inside, however, the motion had produced chaos. The cabin floor was covered with wet clothing, piles of steamy sheets, and a jumble of books, toys, and videotapes. In Jon's room, a large locker door had burst open, and its entire contents had spilled on the floor. But that violent sideways lurching prevented any of us from doing anything but hanging on to where we sat or lay.

Even Christopher, who had the toughest stomach of any of us, and who could jump around or play computer in the roughest of conditions, was affected. The poor little fellow threw up for the first time in years, soaking his beloved stuffed gibbon, Denny, named after his furry friend at Highland Farm. On a particularly hard lurch to starboard, bilge water would leak out of the edge of the galley floor, and toilet water would slop out of the toilet on the opposite site of the boat and slither under the door and across the floor to join it.

Eating was impossible, though none of us could stand the thought of it anyway. For me, sleep was impossible as well, and when Herbert relieved me at 1:00 a.m., I lay in my bunk, clenched stiff, eyes open in the darkness, my mind tense and anxious, and my body biliously rebelling against the motion, which was becoming increasingly uncomfortable as the wind and the waves shifted slowly forward.

Christopher had found it impossible to sleep in his bed, which was right at the bow of the boat, where the motion was the greatest. He had snuggled in beside me. In our entire trip, this was the first time he had ever found it necessary to do this. All night long, I cuddled my little one, who slept in my arms oblivious to the maelstrom around him. When morning came, sleep had still eluded me.

I was struggling, and Herbert was, too, with great misgivings about what we were doing. We had been in much worse conditions and we weren't in any imminent danger, but the awful fierceness of these waves and the howling of the wind spoke to our deepest insecurities and res- onated with all our fears and anxieties about this passage. We had always felt we were not taking an undue risk by bringing our children on this adventure, but now, in the middle of the black night, with those screaming waves rushing down upon us as if intent on doing us evil, we wondered whether we might have been wrong.

We endured the Indian Ocean gale for about twenty-four hours before the wind started to ease. Gradually, we began eating again and catching up on lost sleep. Herbert and I moved around like zombies. Because of the rough conditions, we exempted the kids from their watches. Cheerful and resilient as usual, they made hardly a word of complaint.

Not long after celebrating our midway point, our alternator failed. This was a brand-new one we had bought in Thailand. The alternator was what charged our batteries, so it was one of the most important pieces of equipment on the boat. We had spared no expense in purchasing a good one – twice, now.

Herbert had worked on the old alternator and gotten it working again to serve as a spare, although he didn't have much faith in it. Now would be its test, and Herbert's as well. Working upside down in the smelly engine room when the boat is bouncing was a sure recipe for nausea – even for a stomach as tough as our captain's. Herbert lay down on Michael's bunk a while, steeling himself.

The kids retreated to the front of the boat to let Dad work uninterrupted. I stationed myself between the tool locker, to hand him tools, and the rear hatch, to keep watch as he worked. As he emerged, asking for various wrenches, Herbert's face grew greyer and greyer and assumed an unhealthy sheen. I ran for a bowl, but he managed to continue his work, even with the boat lurching and spilling his tools from time to time into the dark abyss of the engine room.

It took an hour before everything was reassembled. When the motor came on, the kids emerged from their hiding places and watched keenly. They were vitally interested in the health of our charging system, because it affected whether they could play on the computer. We all watched as the green charging indicator lights lit up, and the kids and I joyfully burst into applause, recognition of our captain's efforts. Herbert just stood there, looking green and unsteady, supporting himself on handholds overhead as he, too, watched the line of lights come to life.

"Hail to the conquering hero!" sang Michael triumphantly.

But our accolades had barely died down when there was a disturbing sound from inside the engine room. Those cheerful little green lights flickered and went out. After only ten minutes of operation, the spare alternator had failed. It had all been for nothing. Herbert's face was the picture of despair. The kids slunk away. My head slumped. This was just too unfair.

We had one last spare alternator, but although Herbert made some motion to dig it out, I invoked my rights as ship's medical officer and sent him instead to bed. It was getting dark, he was now past the end of his six-hour shift, and he was sick and tired. It made more sense for him to get some sleep before facing that engine room again.

The kids washed and brushed up quickly and were also dispatched to their beds – no reading lights or fans allowed, to save electricity. After they were asleep, I snuck out my last hoarded bag of Hershey's Kisses from Thailand, spearing the pointy head of each Kiss into a marshmallow and savouring it in the darkness. I was entitled.

It was with a heavy heart that I woke Herbert at 2:00 a.m., knowing the ordeal that awaited him. I held the flashlight, handed over tools, and kept watch while Herbert installed our third and last alternator. But the minute he attached it, there was a spark. All power in the boat went out. An instant later, it felt as if the storm had returned, for the boat began bouncing wildly, followed by the sound of flogging sails. Without power going to the autopilot, *Northern Magic* was drifting, nose into the wind.

I leaped into the cockpit to take over steering. Down below, it was totally black, and I wondered how on earth Herbert was going to figure out what had gone wrong now. The compass light was, of course, out, so all I had to steer by was the position of the moon and the direction of the wind, which whipped past me, cold and biting on my bare arms and legs. I was angry, very angry, on Herbert's behalf. He didn't deserve this. I began to shiver. I hadn't thought to grab my jacket.

In about ten minutes the power came back on, and I gratefully returned inside, cold and wet. How Herbert had managed to re-establish power in pitch darkness, in a heaving boat, with only a half-dead flashlight for light, I have no idea. The short in the alternator had blown the main fuse, a big fuse Herbert had wisely installed himself as an extra precaution.

Grimly, he took out the alternator once again and opened it up, carefully checking all its connections one by one. I waited silently, not daring to speak, crouched beside him on the step. I prayed he could solve the problem before we ran out of power. I'd had enough of a taste of hand steering during those brief ten minutes to know I didn't want to spend the rest of the passage that way.

He worked and tested, and an hour crept by. Finally, he was ready to try again. We had our hearts in our mouths. To re-establish power, Herbert had been forced to bypass the blown fuse, so if there was still a short, we might really see fireworks. As he prepared to attach the wires, I stood by the switch to the battery bank, ready to turn it off at the first sign of trouble. My foul weather jacket was waiting this time at the cockpit entrance just in case.

This time, there was no short, and when he turned on the motor, the alternator actually worked! It was a small alternator, producing only a trickle of power, but it was better than nothing. Herbert wearily closed the engine-room hatch, and we watched the line of battery charging lights again grow brighter. I risked a smile. We'd once again need a new alternator, but at least this was enough to get us to Zanzibar, still a few days away.

But I smiled too soon. Within five minutes, charging had stopped. I'm not a good enough writer to describe exactly how this made us feel.

Summoning resolve from somewhere deep inside, Herbert threw open the engine-room hatch yet again, stuck his head down into that swaying black hole once more, and focused his attentions not on the alternator, but on the regulator. He had an idea that this last failure wasn't the alternator at all. Soon, he had hotwired the alternator directly to the batteries, and to our inexpressible relief, the charging lights flickered on again – and this time stayed on.

It was five in the morning. This time there was no chorus of admiring children to sing their father's praises, but the lack of applause made his feat no less heroic.

The rest of the passage was swift and uneventful. Eight days after setting out from the Seychelles, a dim, low outline materialized on the horizon. It was Zanzibar.

19

Africa Awakening

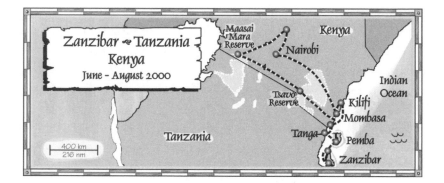

Zanzibar ◆ Tanzania
Kenya
June – August 2000

Maasai
Mara
Reserve
Nairobi
Kenya
Tsavo
Reserve
Kilifi
Mombasa
Indian
Ocean
Tanzania
Tanga
Pemba
Zanzibar
400 km
216 nm

ver since the day Herbert and I had noticed the island of
Zanzibar on our world atlas, not far off our planned course for
Kenya, we had looked at each other and said, "You can't be that
close and not go to a place with a name like Zanzibar." And so, without
knowing anything much about the place except the exotic appeal of its
name, it had been decided that to Zanzibar we must go.

Now before us was Zanzibar Town. It made a beautiful picture in the
late morning sun: large colonial-style buildings with ornate balconies, a
clock tower, and the remains of an old Portuguese fort. It looked mis-
placed in the twenty-first century, and its harbour, although containing a
few modern ships, was mainly filled with sailing dhows plying to and fro.
We anchored off a beach a mile or two away from the main town.

The next morning, all five of us set off eagerly in a taxi to Stonetown,
the oldest and most interesting part of Zanzibar Town, a small city of
100,000. We stepped out of the taxi into a world full of magic, mystery,

and a hint of danger. Tall, whitewashed stone buildings in varying states of decline lined a warren of twisting alleyways, so close that people in the second and third storeys on opposite sides of the street could practically touch hands. Most of the roads were much too narrow for cars, but well suited to pedestrians, bicycles, and the occasional donkey cart.

Some of the buildings were decrepit but still beautiful in the way of an elegant old woman who has lived long and well. Some were truly splendid, with ornate balustrades and the most fabulous entryways, ornately carved double doors lavishly decorated with stamped brass and studded with wickedly pointed brass knobs designed to prevent charging war elephants from knocking them down. Most of the doors also sported half a dozen heavy brass padlocks.

The people of Zanzibar are a mixture of African and Arab; for centuries, Zanzibar was under the influence of Oman, a country in the Persian Gulf. Today's Zanzibaris remain devoutly Muslim. The men wore beautifully embroidered skullcaps, and some wore long white shirt-dresses.

But it was the women of Zanzibar who made the greatest impression on us. Winding their silent way through these forbidding passageways in long black robes, called *bui buis*, that covered them from head to toe, they presented a picture straight out of *1001 Nights*. Even the fashionable platform sandals that peeked out from underneath their hems were not unlike those that might have been worn by Scheherezade herself. The effect – the enticing and faintly menacing labyrinth of decaying buildings, the smell of exotic spices, the unfamiliar sound of the Swahili language, the mysterious robed women, the feeling that at any moment you might come around a corner and be confronted by Ali Baba, or a slave trader, or a sultan, or a genie – was intoxicating. Zanzibar was one of those rare and elemental places, first glimpsed long ago in some fantastic, half-forgotten dream. But it was for real, and now we had found it.

At the end of our first day, a man stood waiting for us on shore near where *Northern Magic* lay at anchor. His clothes were slightly tattered and his white Zanzibari hat more battered than most, but his face broke into a broad smile as soon as he saw us. This was Mr. Suleiman, our *askari*. He would spend the next eight nights in our cockpit, protecting us from night-borne thieves. Mr. Suleiman didn't speak a word of English, and so we had had to use an interpreter to communicate with him and describe the terms of work. We agreed to pay him three thousand Tanzanian shillings a day, or about six dollars.

When everything had been explained, Mr. Suleiman smiled, nodded, and answered with two words "*hakuna matata*," which means "no problem" in Swahili. Over the next week, we were to hear these words often, always spoken with a smile.

Mr. Suleiman, who looked to be in his fifties, was gracious and good-natured. He thanked me extravagantly for the smallest consideration, such as a glass of water or a raincoat when the weather turned bad. Every day, he tried to teach me a few words of Swahili, and I learned that he was married and had five children. I went to sleep at night reassured by his presence.

Herbert, on the other hand, felt uncomfortable about the whole arrangement. He felt we were paying him too little, even though we were, in fact, paying him extremely well by Tanzanian standards. But it happened to be quite cold and rainy during the week, and the idea of this nice fellow having to sit all alone in the drizzling dark, right outside where we were comfortably sleeping, bothered Herbert a great deal.

But there was no point whatsoever in having him sit inside, and I reasoned that obviously our contribution to his family income, as meagre as it might have seemed, was enough to make it worthwhile for him. But the many holes in his old sweatshirt tugged at my heartstrings, too, so I gathered half a dozen old shirts Herbert was no longer using and presented them to Mr. Suleiman. He rewarded me with a dazzling smile and a very heartfelt "*Asante sana!*"

Almost every day, we made the short trip to Zanzibar Town, jumping onto a kind of overcrowded local bus called a *dala dala*. Once in Stonetown, we'd wander through the maze of small streets, buying fruit in the open market or browsing through small shops selling carvings and antiques. Invariably, we would lose our way and wander, hopelessly disoriented, through the warren of alleyways, an absolutely essential Zanzibar experience.

Other days, we toured spice plantations and Persian baths and roamed through the palaces of the great sultans of Zanzibar and Oman, including one mighty ruler who had ninety-nine wives in his harem and sired more than 130 children. One of his palaces was just a short walk away from where we were anchored. It was in ruins, with most of its roof gone and part of the second floor collapsed. Enough of it remained that the boys were inspired to play hide and seek within its massive, crumbling walls. While one of them counted, his face pressed against a stone pillar in the Sultan's great audience chamber, the other two ran off to hide in small anterooms or hidden alcoves. We explored with unalloyed delight, feeling as if we were the first to discover this treasure, for there was no one else around: no watchmen, no tourists, no local people. I sat back and watched with delight – who would ever have imagined that my own children would be playing hide and seek in the palace of the Sultan of Zanzibar? Even today, it seems hard to believe.

In the evening, we would find our way to the night market, where a huge variety of mouthwatering Zanzibar foods was laid out in outdoor stalls at the waterfront – samosas, potato cakes, shish kebabs, naan and chapatti, and delicious Zanzibari pizzas, which were something like a fajita. All five of us could eat a plate heaped with these treats for eight dollars. We ate on rough benches, with paper plates in our laps, and as soon as we finished, a flock of ragged young boys would swoop down and run off with our leftovers, gobbling as they ran.

On our final day in Zanzibar, we marched through the market one more time, passing the spot where slaves used to be sold, buying our last tiny loaves of fluffy Zanzibar bread, haggling over the price of pineapples and passionfruits. We had seen what we came to see, but Zanzibar still had a hold on us and it was hard to leave. Everywhere we went, people greeted us, as always, with a smile and a hearty *"Jambo!"*

We headed over to where we knew our favourite taxi driver would be to drive us back to *Northern Magic*. Mr. David had two (concurrent) wives and fourteen children to support, so we always gave him our business. This was our last chance to breathe the Zanzibar air, redolent of spices, sultans, and slaves. The sense of nostalgia was already growing.

"When you stop getting lost in the streets of Zanzibar, you know it's time to go," remarked Michael.

And so, reluctantly, we went.

After leaving Zanzibar Town, we made short hops up the island, stopping at ancient caves where slaves were hidden to escape detection by British warships, and exploring mysterious coral-stone villages whose shy inhabitants did not want their pictures taken. We then sailed to Pemba Island, which was considerably poorer than Zanzibar. We saw several boys of ten or twelve pushing around little homemade wooden trucks on the end of a stick. The ragged children really had nothing, and these pitiful little toys made Herbert and me cringe. Our kids didn't have the same reaction, instead admiring their counterparts' resourcefulness.

We went for a walk out of town, followed like the Pied Piper by a rapidly swelling group of children. Our boys found some sticks and engaged themselves in Star Wars light-sabre duels while the Pemba kids stood by and giggled. I enjoyed observing the girls, who, unlike most we had seen, were not robed from head to toe and could therefore play freely. They had very short hair on their bare heads, just a little bed of springy black whorls. It was surprisingly attractive, and certainly practical. These little girls, although they wore dresses, were as athletic and gregarious as their brothers, and I liked them for that.

I decided to offer a small bag of cookies, which was disappointingly crumbled when I opened it. I held it out and the kids, as soon as they realized what it was, dived into it *en masse*, about twenty grubby hands reducing it instantly to a pile of brown cookie dust. In seconds even the dust was gone, but there were lots of smiling faces.

＋

We headed across the channel to the mainland Tanzanian city of Tanga, arriving in mainland Africa at last. This was a tired old town whose buildings, sad reminders of more glorious colonial days, were quietly crumbling into disrepair. You could walk down the middle of its main street and not be inconvenienced too often by the passing of a car – although a bicycle once made us jump by issuing the surprisingly loud bleat of a goat, the source of which turned out to be trussed up and tied to a basket on the rear wheel.

We anchored in a quiet bay in front of the Tanga Yacht Club, the local hangout for an expatriate community made up mostly of foreign aid workers. Virtually all of Tanga's industries had beaten a hasty retreat years before, when many businesses were nationalized. Now it was a shell of its former prosperous self. Tanga was a welfare community whose entire cash flow was derived from foreign aid and the money brought in by the three hundred or so expats who administered it. Within a minute of landing ashore, we were adopted by Rob Jurgens, a big South African in his forties. Rob was in charge of renovating Tanga's water filtration plant and installing new water mains. Everywhere we went, we could see evidence of his team at work. He had about four hundred local employees reporting to him, making the German construction company for which he worked by far the largest employer in the region.

Rob brought us back to his home for showers and dinner. He had several staff – a cook, a housekeeper, a watchman or two – but lived in his simply furnished four-bedroom house alone. "I can't find a woman who will share this kind of life with me," he explained. "I've tried, but no one wants to live in places like this and move every few years."

Rob's casual clothes, baseball cap, and shoulder-length hair couldn't disguise the fact that he was very smart and *very* good at his job. It was his business to get things done in the most backward of places and for this, he earned about double what he might in North America.

"If you've worked in Africa for ten years and don't have at least half a million dollars in the bank, you're doing something wrong," he explained. But the price of financial success was high. Rob had suffered malaria fourteen times in five years – was quite ill from malaria, in fact, that very day – and the medications that controlled the potentially deadly disease had taken a terrible toll on his liver.

It was soon apparent that we had landed on the pinnacle of a three-tiered colonial-style society. Our gracious host and his European friends were on the very top, living a servant-supported lifestyle we thought had died with the end of the British empire.

"It was this way in South Africa until recently," Rob told us. "If you were white and had any kind of skill, you lived like this. Even a car mechanic could afford to live in a big house and have his own gardeners, maids, and cooks."

On the second tier were the second- and third-generation Indians, who owned the smattering of little stores and workshops in town. There were a few educated blacks who fell into this reasonably prosperous, tiny middle class, but very few.

At the bottom of the heap were the vast majority of native Tanzanians, who considered themselves lucky if they found jobs digging water pipes for Rob with their own shovels for three dollars a day. The women tended little plots of land, raised and buried many children, and grew their own maize, a kind of corn that is the staple food here. Most of them were barely literate. Jonathan, who was in grade six and a voracious reader, was stunned to learn that he probably had more education than the average village schoolteacher.

The next day, Rob, although feverish and bleary-eyed with malaria, took us on a tour of the countryside. We left town on a track that was more pothole than road, and our boys, in the open back of Rob's pick-up truck, had a wild and bouncy ride. After leaving town, we didn't see a single other motorized vehicle.

We passed through small villages that looked as if they had barely emerged from the stone age – tiny huts made of mud and sticks with thatched roofs, no water, and no electricity. We saw lines of women walking miles with large jugs of water on their heads and others trudging under heavy stacks of firewood. The villages weren't dirty or squalid, in fact they appeared quite clean and cheerful. The women looked wonderful in their colourful robes and turbans, and the children invariably waved and called "*Jambo!*" as we went by. Tanzanians are a beautiful people, and their faces lit up in brilliant smiles when they saw us, especially if we smiled first.

But these little collections of hovels were achingly primitive. As we travelled through them, we were seized by the terrible knowledge that these people were living much as their ancestors had for centuries, perhaps millennia past – and worse, that there was little prospect of this changing. Tanzania ranked near the very bottom of the UN's list of countries, ranked by standard of living, the one in which Canada often places first. Life expectancy was a shocking forty-seven years.

Rob brought us to a river, the source of Tanga's water supply. It was a fantastically beautiful scene, with tall mountains mistily rising up on the horizon, grassy countryside interrupted by clusters of flat-topped trees, and this enchanting river tumbling over a myriad of cascades. "Isn't this great?" said Rob, his arms outstretched. "*This* is why I love Africa."

He pointed out white kingfishers hovering like giant hummingbirds over the water, waiting to dive for fish. Other water predators – storks, egrets, and ibises – stalked around in the shallows. Great golden ospreys circled in the sky. Earlier, Herbert had seen one of these raptors plunge down and narrowly miss catching a mongoose, which scurried back into the undergrowth.

"Don't go near the water," Rob warned the boys. "There are lots of crocs here. Big ones, eight metres long, and also white Nile crocodiles."

We watched as a man with a bicycle, barely visible under a giant green haystack of grass, pushed his way down the dirt path to ford the river. He stood and paused for a full minute before he entered the water.

"He's checking for crocs," Rob told us. We held our breath and were pleased when he made it safely across.

On the way back to town, Rob stopped at a roadside sisal rope maker. Sisal is a large plant that looks like the top of a huge pineapple, with stiff spiny leaves. Its fibres are woven into ropes and mats. These men were making rope by hand. They had strung along the field a series of metal stakes to hold the strands off the ground, and at the end was a crank that they turned to make the rough twisted rope.

Rob negotiated to buy a spool, the biggest they had. The rope maker looked as if he couldn't believe his luck – the forty-dollar order was a big one by his standards – and ran around to make sure he had enough fibre to produce the rope by the next afternoon.

"If not tomorrow, then sometime later in the week," Rob said breezily, to the man's evident relief. As we climbed back into the car, the man energetically waved us goodbye, a huge grin on his face, Rob's cash deposit in his hand.

"I don't actually need the rope," Rob confessed as we drove off. "But there are so few businesses here, it's important to support those people who are trying to get something going. These are good people; they're hard workers, but they just can't get ahead."

We spent a lovely week in Tanga, our experience memorable because of Rob's extraordinary friendliness and hospitality. But the impression made by our first glimpse of mainland Africa was even greater. Everywhere we turned, we were confronted by the sheer size of the gulf between the haves and the have-nots. For the first time, we saw a leper. We met a beggar with elephantitis, a disease that had so deformed this poor man's legs and feet that they looked just like those of the animal after which the disease is named. At the supper table, we found ourselves debating ways the Western world could help. In the middle of the night, we would wake up troubled, our brains grappling even in sleep with the immensity of the problems and the scarcity of answers. Try as we might, we could see no solutions that wouldn't require generations to take effect.

These people had so little – not enough money, not enough education, and, most importantly, not enough hope that it could ever be otherwise. We liked Tanga and its smiling villagers very much, but what we saw hurt. Once again, we felt shame at our unearned, undeserved, and mostly unreturned good fortune.

+

After leaving Tanga, we sailed north, crossing the border with Kenya. A few days later, we were anchored securely in Kilifi Creek, north of Mombasa.

One day, not long after we arrived, two friendly young men approached us as we disembarked from our dinghy. They were carrying a small, tattered plastic bag, and inside it were dozens of beautiful fossilized shark teeth in hues of copper and black. They were hoping to sell us some. We had a better idea, however, and asked them to take us fossil hunting ourselves. We offered to pay them, but they refused to suggest a price, saying we could decide.

The next day our two new friends, Boniface, age sixteen, and Hamisi, eighteen, showed us how to search out the shiny fossilized teeth, about twenty million years old, which washed up on the pebbly beach every high tide. It took some practice to get good at spotting them, and our eagle-eyed experts found ten for every one we did. Boniface and Hamisi gave us all the teeth they found that morning, several dozen in all. Sometimes, I caught them planting teeth conspicuously in the sand so that we would all experience the thrill of discovery.

Both of them were finished school, Hamisi having only gone as far as primary grades and Boniface confessing that he had been forced to leave his secondary school a few months before. His family could no longer afford the fees. But they were both intelligent young men who spoke English well, and we enjoyed their company.

The next day, Boniface and Hamisi brought us down a cashew-tree-lined path to their villages. Hamisi's family compound was mainly empty, because his mother and sisters were away at the family *shamba*, or fields, some thirty kilometres distant. Like most rural families in Kenya, Hamisi's family were subsistence farmers who grew maize, the staple food of Africa.

The compound was a circle of a dozen tiny huts made entirely from thin mangrove poles and mud, each one measuring perhaps three by four metres. Everything in the homes was hand-made by Hamisi's family, including the thatch on the roofs. All the materials were from things that were locally available, and free. Not a single nail was used in their construction. The family owned virtually no possessions at all – each house was furnished only with a bed and a mud bench built against a wall. There was, of course, no electricity or plumbing, in fact no latrines of any kind.

Hamisi proudly showed us the house he was building for himself, something every young man does as a teenager. Nearby, he showed us the deep pit he had dug to find the thick red mud for the walls, filling in the gaps between a crude latticework of sticks. While we walked through it, Jonathan said enthusiastically, "This is really nice! It's big!" But later he confessed to me that he had said this only to make Hamisi feel good. Herbert and I were doubly glad we had paid the boys generously for their services the day before. It was dawning on us that these people – like most people in Kenya – lived virtually outside the cash economy, growing all the food they consumed and purchasing almost nothing.

Hamisi was eager to show us a special place at the edge of his village, a holy tree where his brother, a medicine man, performed his craft. He ushered us into a tree-shrouded grove where, at that very moment, his brother was performing a ceremony for a local woman.

The middle-aged woman was crouching at the foot of a giant baobab tree, whose grey, cigar-shaped trunk was draped with several lengths of bright cloth. All around the tree were hundreds of old bottles, some of them half-filled with liquids of various colours. Incense was burning. The woman's eyes were closed. She was chanting a long monologue. Hamisi explained that she was speaking to the spirits that resided in this holy place, asking for their help in solving a personal problem.

As the woman spoke, Hamisi's oldest brother, a thin man in his early forties, stood beside her. He was holding a weakly struggling white hen by the feet, just inches over the woman's bowed head. It looked like a large, feathery bouquet. Hamisi told us that his father had been a medicine man and had passed on his knowledge to his oldest son before he had died. Hamisi, too, had been instructed in the craft.

The woman rambled on for a long time. When she finally finished her plea, the medicine man carried the chicken to the side of the tree, held it over a plate, and, just as we had feared, slit its throat. He expertly caught the spurting blood in a bowl. He tossed the chicken aside and it landed, feebly moving, just a few feet in front of us. Ignoring the dying chicken, the medicine man mixed its blood with some of the mysterious potions contained in the forest of bottles that surrounded the tree, and began sprinkling the crimson liquid all around. The woman departed, pleased and smiling. She paused to thank us for watching.

We couldn't believe we had been permitted to witness this, or that this type of ceremony was still openly practised at all. When it was over, at Hamisi's suggestion, we contributed a hundred shillings, or two dollars, to the medicine man, as the woman had done.

Of Hamisi's ten brothers, only three, which included the medicine man, were employed. The other two earned sixty dollars a month working at distant hotels. Hamisi's family of about thirty people survived on two hundred dollars a month. We began to understand why Hamisi had not been able to continue his schooling, since secondary school cost about five hundred dollars per child a year.

We continued on to Boniface's family compound, a short walk away. The village was virtually identical to Hamisi's. We sat in the centre of a tidy collection of red mud huts, surrounded by young children in torn clothing, talking to Boniface's brothers. Boniface's family seemed to be better educated than Hamisi's, although their standard of living was the same. And in Boniface's family, too, three employed men were financially supporting all the rest. As in all of Africa, the women were working hardest of all, providing the food and the necessities of life.

I was making my usual effort to keep my English simple. Suddenly, Boniface's oldest brother, Andrew, leaned forward and said something like this: "I think it's time we stakeholders understood clearly that further education is anathema to the continuation of poverty in Africa."

Stakeholders? Anathema? I couldn't believe my ears! Most of the people I know don't even know what anathema means, much less being able to toss it casually into conversation. The contrast – between the blood-sprinkling medicine man and the confident young man saying *anathema* – left our heads were spinning.

Herbert and I leaned forward and began to study this man more carefully. Soon, we became engaged with him in a long and vigorous discussion about the Kenyan political system, corruption, tribalism, and the importance of education. "Ensuring transparency in our public institutions is paramount," he was saying. "Also the eradication of tribalism and the establishment of the merit principle."

Here we were, confronted with a man who was at least our intellectual equal, but who, like millions of other Africans no matter how gifted or capable, was still bringing up his children in a mud hut with no running water or electricity. Suddenly, we realized that if we had been born in an African village, it would have been us sitting in Andrew's place. We would have been just as helpless to do anything about it.

The oldest son of a polygamous, illiterate father, Andrew Thuva had begun school under a baobab tree, without even a roof over his head or textbooks. But from the start, he had been determined to succeed. He had heard that the best student in his school would qualify for a YMCA scholarship to continue into high school. Secondary school was an ambitious dream that could only be achieved with hard work and outside help. His father earned almost nothing and could never have hoped to send him. Andrew's ultimate ambition, to work in an office and one day drive back to his village in a car, seemed as far away as the moon.

Andrew not only won that scholarship, but went on to become the best student in his high school as well. He won another scholarship, which enabled him to attend college. He told us the story of how he had gone to Nairobi, with his school fees paid for but nothing more, with only ten dollars to his name and the clothes on his back. He had literally starved, sleeping on the dangerous streets while attending classes and earning good marks. The only thing he could think of was to write a European couple he had once met on vacation. They sent him enough money to pay for food and shelter during his three years in college.

Now, thanks to his education and ambition, thirty-two-year-old Andrew was earning two hundred dollars per month at a hotel. But instead of using the money to increase his own standard of living, he was doing his best to put his younger siblings through secondary school. He understood that nothing was as important to their future as education. He had already succeeded with two of them, Ngumbao and Mark, who used the word "hero" when he described the sacrifices his older brother had made for him. The next oldest, Katana, was also in high school. But the next in line, our friend Boniface, was out of luck. Andrew's resources had run out. This is why we had found Boniface hawking shark teeth on the beach.

Once again, Africa had clobbered us and shaken us up. Every night our dinner table conversation was dominated by the problem of African poverty. Meeting Andrew was another turning point in our trip, and in our lives. He helped us understand that a ragged young man living in a poor mud hut was just like us.

Gradually, painfully, we came to one unavoidable realization. If we turned our backs on these people – whose needs were both so modest and so great – if we left without making some kind of significant contribution, we would fail our test as human beings.

20

Plinking Stones
Down a Mountain

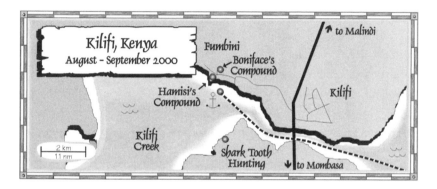

Kilifi, Kenya
August – September 2000

Fumbini

Boniface's
Compound

to Malindi

Hamisi's
Compound

Kilifi

Kilifi
Creek

Shark Tooth
Hunting

to Mombasa

2 km
11 nm

W e knew we couldn't solve all of Africa's problems, but we realized that we did have the power to help Boniface. We decided that the minimum our family could do would be to support Boniface through the rest of his schooling. It was no longer possible to watch Africa as spectators; decency required that we do something. If we provided an education for Boniface, one that would enable him to get a decent job and pull his future children out of poverty, we would, in fact, have changed the world: Boniface's world, and the world of those who would follow him. It was only a small act of kindness, one small pebble being tossed down a mountainside, but at least it was something.

We went away for two weeks on a safari to inland Kenya. During that time, we couldn't help but reflect that the money we spent on the safari could have fed Boniface's entire family for years. A few days after we returned, before we had a chance to tell Boniface about our intentions, he mentioned that his father, who had been ill, had taken a turn for the worse. Although he didn't ask directly, implicit in Boniface's statement seemed to be a request for help. Uncertain what was the right thing to do, a little nervous that we might be getting taken advantage of, we asked Boniface to take us to see his father.

We walked to Boniface's village. Boniface's father, Kitsao, was lying on his side on a woven mat on the swept dirt of the family compound, a shrivelled-up shell of a man wrapped in a piece of cloth. His eyes were closed, his head cradled on bony arms. He was only fifty-five, but looked seventy. His emaciated body was shaking violently, even though it was a warm day and he was lying in the sun. There was no question he was very sick.

We helped take Kitsao to a doctor, who informed us that the immediate threat was a severe case of malaria. Kitsao's underlying problem, however, was even more serious: a large and growing tumour in his prostate gland was blocking his urinary duct. The doctor put a temporary catheter in place to drain the urine, but this was only a stopgap measure. Kitsao was in urgent need of surgery, which would cost at least 50,000 Kenya shillings.

My mind was reeling as I tried to translate Kenya shillings into dollars without misplacing any zeros. I double-checked my arithmetic with Herbert. He confirmed my fear: the cost was a thousand dollars. This family could never come up with that kind of outlay. They didn't even have the ten dollars required to see the doctor that day. My heart sank into the pit of my stomach, and lay there, heavy as a rock.

While Kitsao was having his malaria injections, I whispered to Herbert what the doctor had told me. For a moment, Herbert and I debated in whispers whether we would be willing to assume the cost of the operation. It was our first instinct; how could we deny this man his life? But then we realized that we could not take on all of this family's burden. Kitsao was already an old man by Kenyan standards. We had to establish priorities. That same money would go much further if invested in Boniface.

As we stood there, we realized we had just come to a decision not to help the sick man who sat slumped in a chair before us. Both Herbert and I had to struggle hard to control tears so Mark and Boniface wouldn't see our anguish. For a moment, we wished we hadn't got involved, hadn't brought Kitsao to the doctor at all. It was like biting into an apple from the Tree of Knowledge – now there was no escaping the terrible knowledge, or its consequences.

"This is the price we have to pay for bringing these people into our lives," Herbert said sadly. It was a heavy price indeed.

That night we lost sleep again – our Africa sleep, we were beginning to call it. We decided it was crucial that we talk to Andrew to make sure he understood the severity of the situation and began tapping into all available resources as soon as possible. We suspected no one in this family really understood what their father was facing. Mark had listened to the doctor along with me, but I wasn't sure he had clearly understood the message, buried under medical terminology, that without surgery his father was going to die. Andrew worked at a hotel near Mombasa, and only came back to his wife and children on Sundays. The following Sunday, Boniface brought Andrew to the beach where we were anchored.

We had guessed correctly; Andrew had no idea. When we told him how badly his father needed the operation, and the cost of it, his face receded deeper into the shadows of the mangrove tree under which we were standing, and he was quiet for a long moment. We could see that he was crying.

In a minute, Andrew regained his composure, and thanked us for letting him know. He began making plans to see whether his father qualified for some kind of medical fund that would at least pay part of the cost. But we had delivered a difficult blow.

It was hard to be the bearers of bad news, but we had good news for Andrew as well. We explained that we had come to a decision to sponsor Boniface to complete secondary school, provided he agreed to do everything possible to ensure that his own children would have the same advantage – and this meant not having more children than he could afford. Herbert also explained that one of the conditions was that in future, if Boniface was able, he also sponsor another child to go to school, and place upon that child the same conditions we were outlining today.

Boniface stood gravely as we spoke, looking very shy, almost as if afraid to speak. Andrew's eyes were glistening again as he listened; then he turned to his brother.

"Do you understand the obligations you would be assuming?" he said to his younger brother in a severe tone. "This is a tremendous opportunity they are offering you. But if you accept, you will have to abide by these conditions. And you are going to have to work very hard. They are not going to invest this money in you unless you get very good marks. This is a lot of money. This is not the kind of money people throw away for nothing."

Boniface nodded mutely. His eyes were huge.

"You don't need to answer today," said Herbert. "You take some time to think this over, and decide whether you are prepared to meet these conditions."

Andrew shook our hands with an extra squeeze and we promised to meet again in a week.

As the brothers walked away down the beach, we could hear Andrew continuing his fatherly tirade. Andrew was a small man, but so very large inside. Our admiration for him went up another notch. Herbert and I climbed in our dinghy and returned to *Northern Magic*, carrying our own curiously heavy mixture of grief and hope.

+

It was time to get *Northern Magic* ready for her long slog up the Red Sea. We asked Boniface, Hamisi, and Mark to help us with painting her bottom. On the appointed day, another of Boniface's many brothers, Katana, appeared as well. Katana was an extremely dark and handsome young man of nineteen, quiet, polite, intelligent, and unusually mature like the rest. Since we didn't have the heart to send him away, he joined the paid work crew as well.

At high tide, we drove *Northern Magic* alongside some old cement pilings from a long-since-disappeared dock, tying up securely so that we wouldn't tip over. As the tide fell, Herbert and the African boys scraped and painted her hull. Mark and Katana offered to stay awake in our cockpit overnight to guard against thieves. They appeared after dinner armed with crossbows and fishing line, and we slept securely knowing they were on watch.

In the morning I was faced with the question of what to feed them for breakfast. Being fresh out of maize meal, the African staple, I decided to make oatmeal porridge instead.

Porridge sweetened with milk and sugar was a luxury our friends had never experienced. But what was most interesting was Katana's reaction to raisins. He just couldn't get enough – so much so that after finishing his second huge bowl of porridge he began spooning raisins directly into his mouth. I finally gave him the whole pack, and he gobbled them all down. He'd never seen nor even heard of such a food before. I had, in fact, bought the raisins in Mombasa, but of course our friends did not shop at supermarkets.

The four of them worked hard and got *Northern Magic* scraped and sanded at low tide on the first day, and totally repainted on the second. I cooked a giant batch of chili, which, at the end of the day, we all wolfed down together in the cockpit. The meat as well as the bread with butter were more rare treats for our team of hungry, paint-splattered young men. A whole loaf disappeared in a flash.

As we sat there together, chatting, satisfied, and tired, Mark turned to me and said with a very big and grateful smile, "It's amazing that people like us can sit here and just be friends with people like you."

"What do you mean?" said Herbert.

"You are different from us," Mark replied, "and we're not used to people like you treating us as friends."

"And what is the difference between us?" asked Herbert, although he knew full well what Mark meant.

There was a pause and it was Katana who answered, saying softly, "Our skin is black."

"Well that's the only difference," replied Herbert, "and it's no difference at all."

All four of our guests nodded, but not with much assurance. There was something in this exchange that made my heart crumble. Why should these four intelligent, capable, and nice young men feel so grateful for the ordinary friendship we had offered them? It was because, for them, receiving hospitality from a white person, a *mzungu*, was unheard of.

The community of Kilifi consisted of a few relatively wealthy retired whites, mostly of British background, living in palatial homes, and a large number of extremely poor black people living hand-to-mouth. There is no fault in being rich, but it's quite another thing to treat the rest as if they are just a little less than human. Yet this is what we saw, over and over again.

It would not be fair to suggest that the examples we saw are representative of all white people in Kilifi. There were people who treated everyone with consideration, and these were the same ones who were making other substantial contributions to the community. But Mark had been raised to feel that there was something insufficient and offensive about him, some mysterious rule of the universe that dictated that if you had white skin, you were automatically rich, and if you had black skin, you were poor and liable to be yelled at, kicked, or chased away.

I can't forget how Mark looked after he saw the cramped interior of *Northern Magic* for the first time. After the painting was done, our boys had taught Mark, Boniface, Katana, and Hamisi how to play computer games, the first time the Africans had ever used a computer. Mark looked around in wonder at everything we had inside the boat – books, running water, toilet, stove, TV, VCR, stereo CD player, two computers, and so much more. Mark himself owned very little more than the clothes on his back.

"I can't believe you ever leave this boat," he said. "You have everything you need right here. Why would you ever want to come ashore?"

Boniface and Hamisi had treated us to a cashew nut roast, so we decided to hold a marshmallow roast on the beach. None of them had ever seen marshmallows before. We used up five whole bags that day – the marshmallows being grabbed, roasted, and gobbled as fast as I could liberate them from the bag.

But we had something even better in store. A few days earlier we had made our weekly visit to Mombasa, one and a half lurching hours away by bus, to send our e-mails and buy groceries. And there we had discovered the most wonderful news: three other *Ottawa Citizen* readers, moved by my earlier dispatch about the struggles of Boniface and Hamisi and their families, were offering to send money to help them. We were blown away. The amount that had been pledged totalled nine hundred dollars.

One donor wrote, "I realize that this donation may seem like little more than a token gesture of kindness, particularly since poverty affects many families in Africa, but I feel inwardly compelled to do something. I have many things to be thankful for in my life – a healthy family and the privilege of a higher education. Please offer my best wishes to these two families. Tell them that there is someone on the other side of the world that is thinking about them."

We showed that message to Mark and Andrew, and each of them got tears in their eyes when they read it.

Over the course of the next week, we met with Andrew and other family members several times to listen to their proposals of how best to use the money. Education was a high priority, and there were many more ideas than could be accommodated in the funds available. It was our job now to sift through all the possibilities and find the best plan to make a permanent change in these people's lives.

Our job was time consuming, yet very satisfying. How lucky we were, to have been given an opportunity to make a difference, however small. How much easier it was to sleep at night, knowing that at last we were doing something! How wonderful that our own small pebble had caused a few more to roll down that mountainside with it!

Herbert and I neglected our own children over the next few weeks, while we traipsed all over the countryside checking out prospects, visiting high schools, cow farms, training schools, and colleges. Usually, these trips involved long rides in a *matatu*, a hugely overloaded minivan. We'd generally try to bring along one of our three boys, although they weren't too keen about making that long walk into Kilifi and then spending an hour or more on some bumping, grinding *matatu* with someone's bare armpit pressed into their face. "You ride in a *matatu*?" several different white Kenyans said to us in tones of disgust and incredulity when they found out this was our regular mode of travel. But this, too, was part of the Kenya experience.

We were on our way to another distant country school: Herbert and I, Christopher, Boniface, and Mark. The *matatu*, as always, was hopelessly overcrowded, filled with about twenty people, the ladies wrapped in colourful skirts with babies slung on their backs, some with an intricate pattern of raised ornamental scars on their faces. One or two men hung out the door.

As the crowd thinned out, Christopher suddenly realized that he had lost track of Boniface. Our boys had by now grown incredibly fond of

Boniface and Mark, both of whom had the patience and the good nature to engage them endlessly in stick fights, wrestling matches, and games of catch on the beach. The minute Christopher saw one of them, he would automatically launch himself into their arms. Somehow, I was finding myself turning into a mother of five.

"Mom! Where's Bonnyboy?" Christopher had said in alarm, as if his special friend had gotten irretrievably lost among the throng in the *matatu*.

"He's sitting right beside us," I answered, flicking my head to the right.

Christopher looked over and saw, to his relief, that Boniface was indeed there, safe and sound. What happened next engraved itself forever into my memory.

Christopher's soft little white hand had quickly and quietly nestled itself into Boniface's big brown one. It was the most natural gesture in the world. As everyone else in the *matatu* stared at this unaccustomed sight, I had the feeling that for that one tiny snapshot in time, all was right in the universe.

+

We were down to our last days before setting off on the ocean once more, with only a few items remaining on our to-do list, such things as "do oil change," "tune rigging," and "buy cow."

Yes, we were in the cow business. Now that Boniface's school fees were taken care of, we were seeking ways to help Hamisi earn an income. We set him up in a shark-tooth jewellery business, turning those precious fossils into jewellery that he could sell for a much higher price. During one of our weekly trips to Mombasa, Herbert and I had found a bead shop, where we rubbed shoulders with brightly robed, long-eared, and bead-bedecked Maasai tribeswomen who were, like us, stocking up.

We had a great time choosing a variety of beads, clasps, and earring-making supplies. Boniface and Hamisi wasted not a moment putting them to use. Resourcefully, they used old shoe leather and glue made from sap of the cashew tree to attach tiny rings to the stone fossils and turn them into smashing necklaces and earrings. I donated my old sandals to the cause. We printed up and photocopied little cards to accompany the shark teeth, explaining that they were real, rare fossils. We bought some other presentation materials so that the treasures could be better displayed.

Hamisi, who was serious and quiet, seemed ready to burst with pride as his new business took off. After the first batch of earrings sold out – to tourists as well as to Africans – he predicted that one day he would be travelling all over Kenya selling his jewellery to shops. We launched the little business for a total investment of one hundred dollars. In the first week, Hamisi earned almost thirty dollars.

But with the extra funds that had poured in from *Citizen* readers, we found ourselves in a position to do something more substantial. Hamisi wasn't interested in school, and we figured there was no point in imposing it on a family that wasn't already convinced of its value. Maybe in a generation or two, they would be ready. After many meetings and days of deliberations, including advice from aid workers at the local office of Plan International (Foster Parent's Plan), who had spent days showing us their excellent programs and helping us develop similar ones for our friends, we decided to buy Hamisi a cow. It would be the start of a dairy cow herd that would provide him with capital growth and a steady income base. There was a big market for milk in Kilifi, and Plan International was already doing similar projects with their foster families, so we all agreed that it was a good plan.

Early one Sunday morning, we surprised Hamisi by walking into his village unannounced to ask whether he wanted to buy a cow that day. We were very pleased to see him already up and outside his hut, working diligently on making more shark-tooth jewellery. Hamisi packed up his jewellery-making supplies, and we all marched purposefully to the Plan office, where Kenneth Muriithi, the head of the Plan office, and Kalimbo, Plan's professional farm adviser, were waiting for us on their day off. Kenneth had made the facilities of his office available to us, even though Hamisi lived outside Plan's boundaries. "We're happy to help," Kenneth had said, "after all, your objectives and ours are exactly the same." Kalimbo had gone all over the countryside on his own motorbike to find the perfect cow.

Just as we were turning down the road to the Plan office, Herbert turned abruptly to Hamisi and said, "You do know the money is only a loan, don't you?"

Hamisi's jaw dropped and his eyes opened wide. This is the first time anybody had said anything about a loan. He thought he was getting the cow for free.

"Well, there's nothing free in this world," Herbert continued. I didn't dare look at Hamisi, for fear of cracking into a grin and messing it all up. Hamisi couldn't see what I could, which was that Herbert's eyes were twinkling wickedly.

"Oh yes," said Herbert mercilessly, "this is a loan. And I'll tell you how you have to repay it. You will repay it by taking good care of this cow, growing a herd, and making enough money from selling the milk to send your future children to school. You only went to grade eight, but the condition of accepting this cow is that you send your own children at least to the end of high school. If you do that, we will consider this loan repaid."

Hamisi's relief was palpable, and he nodded his head vigorously. He was a young man of few words with puppy dog eyes, one droopy eyelid giving him a rather sad look except when he smiled his big, bright smile. He was smiling now.

"Oh yes, I agree," he said eagerly. "I'm planning to have a herd of thirty cows. When you come back to visit next time, you will see." We had become very fond of Hamisi, who, it seemed to us, had much untapped potential and ambition underneath his shy and unassuming exterior. To the end, he remained quite deferential to us, continually referring to me as "Madam." Even though we'd shared chili in the cockpit of Northern Magic, he couldn't quite bring himself to address me by my first name. We had settled on having him call me "Mamma Michael" in the traditional fashion of his tribe, where women are identified by the name of their firstborn child.

Two days later, we all hiked over to see the new cow. Hamisi and a brother had walked for six hours the day before to lead the heifer to her new home. She was eighteen months old, not quite fully grown. The cow gave us a great moo of welcome and followed us faithfully around. Perhaps we were partial, but she seemed to be a very attractive animal, as cows go, with great big liquid eyes and a pleasing light brown hide. In fact, I'd go so far as to say this was the nicest cow we had ever bought. We asked Hamisi what her name was, and he looked at us queerly. So we grabbed the chance and dubbed her *Magic*, a name she shared with a certain little gibbon in the wilds of Borneo.

By buying Hamisi's cow, some veterinary supplies, and the jewellery supplies, we had used up almost half of the contributions that had come in, which now totalled $1,070. We decided the most effective use of the remaining money was to establish a scholarship fund for Boniface's family to give him and his brothers access to post-secondary education. Within a few weeks, Mark began attending a hairdressing college.

We were now at the end of our intense, often heart-breaking, and ultimately rewarding experience in the village of Kilifi. As we said our final goodbyes to our friends, who assembled on the beach to see us off, hugs were exchanged, tears were shed on both sides, and promises made for letters, e-mails, and future visits.

But this was only the beginning. Within a few weeks, even more people sent in money, more than six thousand dollars in total. Among them was a contribution from one young Ottawa family who, after reading about the plight of Kitsao, couriered a cheque for a thousand dollars so that he would not be deprived of the life-saving surgery he needed. A warm-hearted Ottawa hairdresser also responded to the challenge and sent in more than enough to cover the cost. "I cannot get their father's plight out of my mind," she wrote, "and with Christmas coming, I find it hard to justify buying presents when his life might be saved."

Thanks to their generosity, Kitsao did get the life-saving surgery he needed. Those tears we had shed in the hospital had not been in vain.

We were overwhelmed, awed, and humbled by the faith and generosity of these strangers who saved Boniface's father's life. Our having come to Africa could not have produced a better result. I believe it was in Kenya that we discovered the very purpose of our trip, the reason why our magnificent dream had pulled at us so powerfully to leave our home behind and come so far in our little boat. Maybe we were meant to find ourselves in that dusty little African village. Maybe we were meant to leave a part of ourselves behind.

Perhaps that is why, when we finally made our way back out into the ocean, our hearts, once so weighed down by all we had seen in Africa, no longer felt quite as heavy. All we did was plink one little stone down a mountain. Maybe it would help start an avalanche.

21

Pirates and Terrorists
in a Lawless Sea

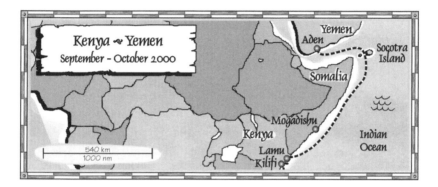

Kenya ❧ Yemen
September – October 2000

Yemen
Aden
Socotra Island
Somalia
Mogadishu
Kenya
Lamu
Kilifi
Indian Ocean
540 km
1000 nm

I t was several months since we had last been at sea. We set out for
Lamu, a town on the northern Kenyan coast. To our dismay, however, we discovered that we had all lost our sea legs. Every hour on
this overnight passage trudged by as slowly and ponderously as a day.
We couldn't help but think about our next long passage, coming up so
quickly, along the entire coast of Somalia. How would we ever survive
days and days of this?

We arrived at the entrance to Lamu Island exhausted, bilious, and
feeling as though we had come through a storm. This was depressingly
far from the truth, which was that the passage had gone very well.
Northern Magic had fairly flown through the water. Our sturdy boat was
ready for anything; it was her crew, too long at anchor, that was lacking.

As we closed on the coast, we found ourselves in what looked like
Arabia, with undulating brown sand dunes and hardly a tree to be found.
A heavily loaded train of donkeys trotted along the base of the dunes,
flogged mercilessly by their whip-wielding driver.

The next day we went ashore among the huge gleaming houses that dotted the shoreline, looking like Arabian palaces with onion-shaped arches and shining white façades. Lamu was very similar to Zanzibar, both of them being old Arab towns. It featured the same warren of two- and three-storey buildings, seemingly leaning towards each other so as to almost meet over the narrow alleyways. The women were robed in black, and covered their faces if they saw you looking at them. There were no cars, so people went by dhow, on foot, or by donkey. We loved the donkeys, with their silly floppy ears and their attempts, mostly ineffectual, to go more slowly than their drivers wanted. It was up to you to keep an eye out for some heavily whipped donkey appearing unexpectedly over your shoulder as it made its way at high speed through the tangle of narrow streets.

We were captivated by Lamu. But somehow we didn't enjoy it as much as we should have. It was because something was hanging over us, something we dreaded but couldn't escape. With each passing day, the prospect of our next passage loomed larger and larger until it seemed our emotions became entirely tied up worrying about it.

We had more than one reason to dread this passage. The first was the sheer size of it: 1,600 nautical miles, the second longest voyage of our circumnavigation. Our recent experience with that rough and uncomfortable Indian Ocean had not led us to look forward to that ordeal.

Another reason was weather: the winds where we were heading were notoriously strong, especially around the Horn of Africa. There was even a slight chance of encountering a cyclone.

But what really had us spooked were the pirates. We'd gone through pirate country before, in Indonesia and the Malacca Straits, but those poor Indonesian fishermen armed with knives seemed like kindergarten pupils compared to desperate Somalis armed with AK-47s lurking near the coast and at the bottom of the Red Sea. There had been at least eight attacks on private yachts in the previous twelve months, two of which had involved machine-gun fire. Some years earlier, a yacht had actually faced a barrage of mortar fire and only escaped unscathed thanks to a last-minute rescue by the Canadian naval ship *Fredericton*. Attacks on merchant ships were virtually a daily event. More than once, we wondered whether we had made the right decision in going so far off the beaten path, on a route that forced us to trace a thousand miles along the lawless Somali coast. If we had followed the more traditional route, we would have gone up the Red Sea in company with other sailboats, would not have had to sail along Somalia, and would not have had to face these dangers alone.

But no matter how we looked at it, we had no choice now but to go right through the ominous collection of "x"s I had been marking on a map, one "x" for each recent attack on a yacht or a commercial ship, which were reported to us daily by the International Piracy Centre via Inmarsat. We just had to run the gauntlet and hope for the best.

So our minds were preoccupied with preparing for a voyage that scared us more than any other had before. We made the decision to remove our radar reflector and not to use our VHF radio or our navigation lights in order to make ourselves as invisible as possible. We devised plans to protect the most important equipment on the boat. We found a little cubbyhole under Michael's bunk that the pirates would be unlikely to find and stashed in it our handheld GPS, our handheld VHF, and our camera. We made room there for our laptop computer and satellite e-mail system. We had a dry run to see how long it would take to stow these things away if danger threatened. We removed our wedding rings, gathered most of our cash, and hid them in another place no one would ever find. We hid a smaller stash of cash and traveller's cheques somewhere else, to sacrifice if need be.

Finally, we all wanted to leave, just to get it over with. So, when every contingency had been thought of, prepared for and fretted over, when we were as ready as we ever would be, we set off. All we could do now was pray.

✦

Our route to Yemen and the Red Sea forced us to make a frustratingly long easterly backtrack around Somalia and the Horn of Africa. The Piracy Reporting Centre in Malaysia was advising all ships to avoid Somalia like the plague and stay a minimum of fifty miles – and preferably a hundred miles – off the coast. Anyone venturing nearer was in danger of being looted or taken hostage by armed Somalis who had lived the previous ten years without benefit of law and order.

On the other hand, the nearer we stayed to the coast, the more we would receive the helping push of the north-going Somali current, which would shorten the number of days we would have to stay in these troubled waters. In the end, we decided that a sixty-mile buffer would provide both a measure of safety and one to two knots of current helping us on our way. As we sailed, we kept a wary and watchful eye in the direction of that unseen and unhappy country to our west.

On our first day out, Herbert broke the little toe on his left foot. He stubbed it viciously, and the poor toe was bent right over on top of the next one and twisted grotesquely so the nail faced the outside. We weren't sure whether we ought to attempt to straighten it ourselves or wait until we got to Aden in two weeks and have it seen by a doctor. We considered turning around, but it would have been several days of struggle back to Lamu against wind and current, so this was not an option.

Over the next day, the little toe gradually worked itself back into a more normal position, and by the time we received e-mailed instructions on setting it, it had practically done the job itself. Herbert finally gathered the courage to make the final adjustment, twisting the toe so that its nail faced upwards instead of sideways. Later, he had it x-rayed, and the doctor pronounced the break cleanly set. But it hurt him for weeks afterwards, something we noticed most keenly by the volume of Herbert's yell when one of us accidentally stepped on it.

The wind was at our back, and the waves as well, so we flew up the coast. *Northern Magic* heaved effortlessly up and over the waves as they rolled under our keel, giving us the rush of a powerful forward shove each time. The winds were light, around ten to fifteen knots, but still we made great time, especially as we sailed north of Mogadishu, over the equator and in the northern hemisphere again.

On our sixth night on passage, we spotted a big south-going ship, heading on a collision course. Taking evasive action, we were highly conscious that we would be invisible to the ship until it was close at hand, since we were travelling without lights. The onus of watchkeeping was entirely on us.

The ship was safely abeam, a mile and a half away, when suddenly a huge spotlight burst awake on its mast and began sweeping the ocean until it settled accusingly upon us. Clearly, the ship's radar operator had discovered us and been alarmed at finding an unlit boat just off their beam. We switched on our masthead lights, which clearly identified us as a sailboat. The searchlight went off. It seemed they were just as twitchy about pirates as we were. We felt a little sheepish, being responsible for their scare, but considering that we were so much more vulnerable to attack, we felt our strategy of cloaking ourselves in darkness was more than justified. We continued on our northbound track, silent and invisible.

As the days went by, the wind grew stronger, and *Northern Magic* continued to heave effortlessly up and over increasingly large following seas as they rolled under our keel. On Day Eight, sailing wing and wing, we logged 184 nautical miles, a record for us.

On Day Nine, we were nearing Socotra Island, our first real danger point. Lying off the tip of the Horn of Africa, 235 kilometres from the Somali coast, Socotra had a long-established reputation as a hotbed of piracy. We had debated for months whether to head inside Socotra or outside, a detour which would have added at least four days to our passage and expose us to the North Indian Ocean's most notoriously windy stretch of ocean. Most of the cruising wisdom suggested it was better to head outside rather than risk being spotted by pirates.

Following the advice of people who knew these waters well, however, we elected to go inside Socotra. It had been a long time since there had actually been an attack there. We timed our arrival so we could slip through in darkness and be well clear by morning. We drew near late in the afternoon, catching only the haziest glimpse of Socotra's small neighbouring islands before darkness fell. Our nerves were jangling as we approached this infamous place.

The wind, surprisingly, died down completely, forcing us to motor. Earlier that day, however, the pump feeding cooling water to the engine had failed, causing the engine to overheat. Herbert had quickly replaced it with a spare, but within a few miles of Socotra we discovered that the spare pump had developed a significant leak. This meant we were pumping seawater directly into our engine room. We didn't discover it until the steady spray of water had filled the huge aft bilge and risen right to the bottom of our engine. This was not the place to mess around with a further repair, which would have left us floundering around in the water in this most dangerous of places like a wounded duck. We decided to leave the leaky pump in place. For the rest of the passage, as long as the motor was on, we had to remember to empty the bilge every thirty minutes.

As darkness fell, and our twin anxieties about pirates and water leaks rose, we discovered a small visitor on board. It was a tiny grey and white wagtail, an endearing swallow-like bird with a long tail. The jaunty little bird landed on our deck and proceeded to give the entire boat a walking inspection, ignoring our presence and boldly marching right over our bare feet. Then it flew inside and did the same, tip-tip-tipping around and checking out each room.

We called our new friend Popeye. His presence was very welcome, a vote of confidence. If rats desert a sinking ship, surely a little bird throwing in his lot with us at our point of maximum danger had to be a good sign.

Soon, Popeye was landing right on top of our heads, walking along our arms and onto our outstretched hands. We couldn't get him to eat – not bread, nor fruit, nor even the little squid and flying fish we collected for him on deck. He wanted insects, but we were all out of those, so he settled for a sip of water. Popeye kept us entertained for hours before darkness fell and he chose a spot to sleep for the night. It was in Michael's berth, which we used as a navigation station on passage, on the floor beside the ladder leading into the cockpit. Our little feathered friend slept very trustingly with his head tucked under his wing, oblivious to us entirely.

That night, we permitted no lights at all inside the boat – no reading in bed, no games, only brief use of a flashlight for the brushing of teeth. We didn't want to chance betraying our presence with as much as a glimmer of light.

As Jon fell asleep, he suddenly had an urgent request: "Mom, could you take the CD out of Biggie [our big computer]?"

"Why, love?" I asked, puzzled.

"Because I was playing Baldur's Gate, the one Grandpa bought us, and I love that game so much. I just remembered that I left the CD inside Biggie. If the pirates come tonight and take Biggie, at least I don't want to lose that game."

At around midnight, we passed Socotra less than ten miles to our starboard. Like a thief in the night we tiptoed through, masked in darkness.

When morning's golden light illuminated the sea, there was no land in sight. Popeye, our guardian angel, woke up late, and after a further inspection of the boat, including a walking tour over my sleeping body, he flew off. We never saw our dear little friend again.

The closer we got to Aden, the more shipping traffic we encountered on their way to and from the Suez Canal. Huge tankers, container ships, and ocean-going cargo ships of every kind were charging up and down the Gulf of Aden as it narrowed into the southern neck of the Red Sea. We were an insect in comparison, doodling along at the outer edge of the shipping lanes. We kept strict watch. At night, this was particularly important, because we still weren't using lights. Just because we were getting close to our goal didn't mean the danger of piracy was over. Not long before, an Australian yacht had received machine-gun fire and been boarded by pirates just four miles from the Yemen shore.

Two days away from Aden, in the middle of a stinky-hot, inky-black night, a large tanker was one of several converging on us from the west, once again on a collision course. Our radar had enabled me to see this coming, and I was slowly moving us out of the tanker's way. At the point at which the ship passed us, only a quarter of a mile away, suddenly its searchlights burst on. Just as before, the spotlight settled upon us, illuminating us as if on a stage. Our VHF radio sprang to life.

"Put on your lights!" roared someone on that ship. "You should not be travelling without navigation lights! Put on your lights! Put on your lights!"

I switched on our lights, but did not answer. I didn't know who might be listening to the radio. My preoccupation was still invisibility. Yes, if we were inattentive, we might be run over and killed. That was our responsibility, but also a risk we could at least control. Against pirates, invisibility was our only hope.

As soon as the angry tanker was out of sight, I turned our lights off again and we continued on our way, dark as the Arabian Sea night. We only turned on our lights the final night, with the glow of Aden already in view. We arrived in Yemen after thirteen and a half nerve-racking days at sea. It had been, for me, the most frightening passage of our trip.

While we'd been on the passage, the Middle East tinderbox had exploded into flames. On September 28, just a few days before we landed in Yemen, a provocative visit by Ariel Sharon to Jerusalem's holiest Muslim site had sparked a renewal of the *intifada*, the Palestinian uprising against Israel's occupation of their homeland. Riots erupted across the West Bank and Gaza. Israel responded with deadly force. Over the next weeks, hundreds of Palestinians would be killed. A new wave of violence had engulfed the Middle East, and displaced Palestinians all over the Arab world rose up in anger. Suicide bombers in terrorist training camps sharpened their skills. One of the places many of these Palestinians and terrorists were centred was Yemen.

But we knew none of this when we landed. Everything I knew about Yemen had come from collecting exotic stamps as a twelve-year-old. We saw dusty brown buildings crowded between the sea and tall, craggy volcanic peaks in hues of faded pink, mauve, or sepia, depending on the time of day. No plant life found a foothold on these steep, inhospitable slopes; it was not hard to imagine that Lawrence of Arabia might appear out of the desert at any time, galloping at the head of a bunch of sword-swinging brigands.

Upon going ashore to go through the immigration formalities, Herbert was met by a helpful taxi driver named Salem, who drove him around in an old jalopy to the various offices and even lent him local currency to buy the necessary stamps. Salem, a cheerful father of two in his late thirties, had a more African-looking face than most of the hawk-nosed Arabs who filled the streets, but he was dressed as they were, with a checkered turban wound loosely around his head and a wrap-around skirt.

We grew to love Salem, another one of those special people we seemed to come across so often in our travels. He had waved off Herbert's attempts to pay him that first day, saying there was no rush, that it would all be straightened out later. The next day, after spending the whole afternoon driving us around, he again refused to discuss payment, saying it was entirely up to us.

"And if we say we want to pay you nothing?" I asked.

"Then that's fine, too!" he said. "I just want to help. Smile, you're in Yemen!"

Salem became our constant companion, driving us everywhere, running errands, finding us the freshest bread, the cheapest and most delicious fresh orange juice (ten cents a glass), the meanest-looking ornamental daggers, the most beautiful antique silver jewellery.

Salem took us in his steaming-hot car to Arab Town, where cart-pulling camels competed with cars in the narrow streets. As we walked around, we tried not to stare at the Yemeni men, whose cheeks were puffed out like a squirrel's with the mild narcotic leaf called *qat*, the national addiction. I was fascinated by the women, the very modern ones daring to show their faces underneath black head coverings and head-to-toe black robes, but most of them revealing nothing but dark eyes peering through a narrow slit. The very modest ones showed not an inch of skin, even in forty-degree heat, with semi-transparent veils over their eyes, black gloves covering their hands, and opaque black stockings covering their feet. I didn't go so far as to cover my face, but I did make a point of wearing long skirts and full-length sleeves whenever I left the boat.

When Salem brought us to an air-conditioned ice cream parlour, we ate in the men's room at the front. I was the only woman. Tucked away at the back, behind a curtain, was the women's room, where ladies with black robes and henna-died hands could take off their veils and eat without fear that a man might glimpse their faces.

Everywhere we went, we attracted hordes of curious people and smiling admirers, as well as beggars. These were mostly poor Somali refugees, women who looked at us imploringly through the tiny slits in their veils with sad, long-lashed eyes. Aden was full of these ghostly figures, clad from head to toe in black. Sometimes, it seemed there were outstretched hands facing us everywhere we turned. Michael in particular really hated that. I wanted to take pictures of the veiled women, but they were shy of the camera. I offered to pay some of the beggar women for permission to take their photo, but most of them shook their heads and moved away.

As we drove around Aden, we twice came across large mobs of marching, demonstrating men. It was hard to tell whether the hundred or so men were violent or happy – sometimes it looked like a party, sometimes like the beginning of a brawl. We learned they were Palestinians, but since we knew nothing about the renewal of the *intifada*, or the growing hostility towards Israel and its Western allies, or about someone named Osama Bin Laden telling his followers it was their duty to kill Americans wherever they might find them, we viewed these demonstrations with innocent curiosity.

Two days later, on October 12, 2000, we were walking up a dusty brown mountain with Salem, exploring a five-hundred-year-old fortress. Christopher was walking beside Salem, holding his hand as we climbed and chatted with him non-stop – those two had developed a mutual adoration society. Michael and Jonathan had brought their laser tag game with them and had been noisily playing shoot-'em-up among the ruins, running in and out of dungeons and dark chambers, scattering bats, and raising sweat in the thirty-five-degree heat. We were just heading up to the highest ruin when we heard an enormous explosion.

"What's that?" we asked, wondering whether the civil war might have started up again. It sounded just like the mortar fire we had heard a few months before on a mountaintop in war-torn Sri Lanka.

"It's nothing. . . . Smile, you're in Yemen!" But Salem's own smile was uncertain.

When we returned to the harbour two hours later, it was full of uniformed men. Several soldiers armed with machine guns blocked our way. By then we had heard that there had been some kind of explosion on an American ship, but that's all we knew. Salem had heard it was some kind of internal malfunction.

We stood there in confusion, with our three hungry, tired children and an armful of baguettes. "We have to go to our boat," we said over and over again to the nervous young soldiers, who spoke no English but were determined not to let us through. Finally, after fifteen or twenty minutes, someone more senior let us pass. But no sooner had we climbed into our dinghy than two more soldiers confronted us. They made it extremely clear, even without benefit of a common language, that we were not to proceed.

"That is my boat! I have to go back to my boat!" Herbert kept repeating. But we dared not leave without permission, not when our antagonists were carrying machine guns. After five or ten minutes more, the stand-off ended and to our relief we were waved through.

A container ship was filling up with fuel beside us, partly blocking our view of the rest of the harbour. We were curious to see the ship involved in the explosion. Michael shinnied up the main mast and from the spreaders reported that he could see a large grey warship with a huge blackened hole in its hull. We didn't know more until some hours later when we received a surprising e-mail by satellite from my parents. "*Are you OK?*" the e-mail said. "*There's been an explosion.*"

We couldn't imagine how my parents had heard about the blast. It was only in Dad's next e-mail early the following morning that we learned what had happened. The name of the American ship was USS *Cole*. Two suicide bombers in a dinghy had come alongside as though they were harbour employees, taken the *Cole's* mooring lines, stood to attention beside the ship, saluted, and blown themselves up. Seventeen American sailors had died. Yemen, this strange and exotic backwater, had just been forced onto the world stage. There were, of course, no reporters there yet, no TV cameras, no CNN. We had no reliable source of news other than Salem, and my father.

At that time, we had never heard the name Osama Bin Laden, who is widely accepted to have been responsible for this attack. But bin Laden's path and ours had just crossed, for his bombers had gone right past *Northern Magic* in order to destroy the *Cole*. They might, in fact, have used the very same dock at which *Northern Magic Junior* had been tied.

Early the next morning, Michael and I set out in *Junior* to get a better view of the damage. The ship that had earlier blocked our view had moved, and we could now see the *Cole* clearly, only a few hundred metres away. A giant hole, nine by twelve metres, was blasted through the hull, extending well below the waterline. The ship's pumps were working hard to eject water as quickly as it was pouring in; water was streaming out of an outlet beside the hole at a tremendous rate, like an open city water main. The ship was listing to one side. To us, it looked like a mortal wound. We learned later that the *Cole* had, in fact, been in imminent danger of sinking.

We stopped at a nearby sailboat and spoke to her Swiss captain, who had been on deck the morning before and had a clear view of the huge billowing cloud of black smoke that had risen into the air right after the blast. Although he hadn't seen the suicide bombers, he did watch in puzzlement as three large pieces of an inflatable Zodiac dinghy had floated by our boats, perhaps the remains of the dinghy used in the attack. He pointed the pieces out to me. Through my binoculars I could see them on the beach.

I decided to radio the *Cole* and ask for permission to approach it to take photographs and possibly interview crewmembers for the *Citizen*. "I don't think you'll get permission anytime soon," the radio officer answered. "But I'll ask my Charlie Oscar."

I called back later and asked again for permission to approach. It was denied, the officer said, because divers were at that moment working underwater to assess the damage. We spent the rest of the day listening to our VHF radio as the *Cole* communicated with other arriving naval vessels. Another two warships, USS *Donald Cook* and HMS *Marlborough*, which was either Australian or British, judging from its name and the accent of its radio officer, were circling in the harbour entrance. For security reasons, they didn't come inside the harbour.

The *Donald Cook* and the *Marlborough* began assisting the *Cole*, sending boatloads of crew carrying huge awnings to cover the *Cole*'s open deck. With all electrical, water, and air-conditioning systems down, the *Cole*'s crew had to abandon their cabins and sleep in the open. They were still fighting hard to save their ship from sinking. We could see lots of activity and what looked like many bundles lying on the huge aft deck of the ship. We watched them hold some kind of service or ceremony.

We continued to eavesdrop shamelessly on VHF radio, listening to the *Cole* coordinate repair efforts. The internal damage was tremendous. They seemed to have few electrical systems still operating, problems feeding and housing their remaining crew, and a big struggle to keep the water level from rising. Day after day, we heard them ordering supplies: hose connectors, batteries, flashlights, laundry bags, paper cups, food, water, ice, and – oh, yes – duct tape. They were coordinating the sending of e-mails to the families of crew. Most of the ship's computers had been destroyed or rendered non-functional by the blast.

At the end of the afternoon, still with no permission from the *Cole* to approach, I returned with Jonathan to the spot from where Michael and I had taken photographs and videos earlier in the day. The big container ship that had partially obscured the view from our own boat was now gone, and the tarpaulin covering the blast site had blown aside, revealing the extent of the damage. We wanted to get a bit closer, to get a better view.

We had scrambled up on a huge mooring buoy. I had snapped but a single shot when we were approached by a fast-moving pilot boat. "No photos," they said. "Not allowed. Police are coming. Go away now!" They continued on to *Northern Magic* and yelled at Herbert that I should stop taking pictures, that I was crazy and would be taken away to jail. With their hands, they pantomimed handcuffs.

Jon and I nervously scrambled back into the dinghy and returned to *Northern Magic.* A motorboat driven by a single Yemeni naval officer in a sparkling white uniform passed us. I waved gaily to him, for lack of anything better to do. Fortunately, he just waved back and didn't confiscate my camera, put me under arrest, or worse.

We didn't venture forth to take any more photos. Herbert was now looking particularly grey and stressed about my journalistic exuberance. My first-hand report on the incident did, however, play on the front page of the *Ottawa Citizen* and was reprinted across the United States on the Associated Press wire service.

We had intended to go that night to a dancing demonstration, but news that the British Embassy in Sana'a, Yemen's capital, had also been bombed, and that threats had been made against all Westerners in Yemen, made us change those plans. A close associate of bin Laden was urging Muslims worldwide to attack U.S. and Israeli targets wherever they might find them. As North Americans, we no longer felt welcome, or safe. The Canadian department of foreign affairs contacted my family and told them to advise us to leave immediately, that we were at high risk of being kidnapped.

Leaving the kids on the boat, Herbert and I went to an Internet café to send messages to worried family and friends. On the way, we spoke to another yacht owner, a Serbian with his own stridently anti-American views, who told us he had been making lots of friends among the angry Palestinians. He told Herbert he had met a taxi driver who boasted that he had known that the embassy in Sana'a was going to be bombed a day before it happened. There were many people in Yemen who had known what was going on; those suicide bombers had certainly not acted alone. It's unlikely, in fact, they could have carried out their plan without the connivance of harbour employees, the same ones we chatted with every time we came ashore. Indeed, Herbert was taken aside by the port captain, who talked to him at length about the explosion, trying hard to convince him that there had been no terrorism, that the explosion was an internal malfunction, maybe even sabotage from inside the *Cole*. There had certainly been no suicide attack, he said. Even though pieces of that exploded inflatable dinghy were still visible on the beach, he told Herbert that no such dinghies existed in Aden.

As he drove us to the Internet café, Salem told us that glass in his house, and many others, had been broken from the concussion of the blast. Yemenis were very afraid, he told us, because even during the civil war six years ago, they had never heard a blast like that one. The government was telling the people the explosion had come from a malfunction inside the ship. But he had heard otherwise on CNN.

"Life is going to get very difficult here again," he told us with regret. "It was just recovering from the war, and now this. This is crazy."

That night, I sat on the deck of *Northern Magic*, looking into the night. A full moon had a risen over the jagged mountain peaks. Strings of lights, put up in honour of the Yemeni Independence Day long weekend, glittered festively on tall buildings and along the major boulevards. From loudspeakers, long drawn-out chants from the muezzin, calling the faithful to prayer, competed discordantly with each other from various tall slender minarets. The streets were full of men wearing tasselled skirts and Arab headdresses, laughing and clasping hands with each other. Some wore wickedly curved daggers thrust through wide belts. It was Friday, the close of a holy day. One would never know that disaster had struck just a few hundred metres away.

Across the calm water of the harbour, the scene was anything but festive. Here, the stricken American warship lay, listing to one side, its floodlights drawing attention to the gaping blackened hole in its side. It looked like a mortal wound.

We had liked Yemen, with its smiling, roguish-looking men and its silent, black-robed women. We hadn't felt the least bit threatened during our six days here. In fact, we had felt quite welcome. Even the filth, the garbage-strewn streets, the flocks of beggars, and the piles of concrete rubble – whether from demolition or the remnants of civil war, we were never quite certain – hadn't obscured the curious charm of this undeniably exotic place.

But tonight, with that benevolent full moon rising and those falsely festive lights winking, the knowledge that kidnappings and further terrorist action against Westerners like us had been promised, made Aden no longer seem the friendly place it had been one day before.

We departed three days after the explosion. For those three days, as Herbert and I went about our final chores in town, we didn't let the kids off the boat. We felt conspicuous everywhere we went, even though, in truth, we had always stood out on the streets like bright red poppies in a sea of buttercups.

We stopped by the Movenpick Hotel, which had by now been taken over by flocks of reporters and U.S. investigators. Yemeni soldiers were posted outside, armed with machine guns, questioning anyone who wanted to enter. Inside the compound, U.S. marines carried automatic rifles and also watched everyone coming in. We saw huge crates of bottled water, destined for the *Cole*, whose crew was afraid to drink any water supplied by local people. It felt as if we were in a war zone.

None of the reporters was allowed within the harbour area. They were forced to take their pictures of the *Cole* from the upper floors of buildings in town. It seemed strange that we were still coming and going inside a zone forbidden to everybody else. Herbert was interviewed for CBS TV, which had spotted our friendly looking Canadian flag flying in the middle of what now seemed like a hostile place.

And yet, there remained a soft spot in our hearts for Yemen, messy, chaotic, overrun with beggars, and yet also in many ways friendly, warm, and full of unexpected delights. Yemen was like rummaging through a dusty old second-hand store – you got your hands a little soiled, sifting through the junk, but you never knew what treasures you might find. At any moment, you might end up with Aladdin's magic lamp. Or with a good man like Salem.

22

Out of the Frying Pan and Into the Fire

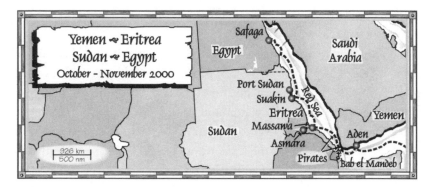

Yemen ↝ Eritrea
Sudan ↝ Egypt
October - November 2000

Safaga
Egypt
Saudi Arabia
Port Sudan
Suakin
Red Sea
Eritrea
Massawa
Sudan
Asmara
Yemen
Aden
Pirates
Bab el Mandeb

926 km
500 nm

uelled and watered up, we prepared to head into the Red Sea. First we had to pass through a narrow channel called the Bab el Mandeb, or the Gate of Sorrows – an apt name, considering the difficulties with strong headwinds and vicious seas that awaited every northbound mariner travelling beyond it.

Our immediate concern, however, was not the wind or the waves, or even terrorists – it was, once again, pirates. The very morning of our departure, I had downloaded all our Inmarsat weather forecasts. Among them was a piracy report. To my horror, there had been no fewer than five new incidents of piracy around the Bab el Mandeb and the southern Red Sea – all in the previous few days, and all exactly on our path.

Suddenly, it felt as if we might be jumping out of the frying pan and into the fire.

It grew dark as we made our way through the harbour, past *Cole* and the gaping hole that leered blackly in its hull, past container ships, oil tankers, and battleships. The mournful sound of the muezzin echoed from the cliffs as we left. Once clear of the busy shipping lanes, we again turned off our navigation lights and were hidden by the night, as dark and concealing as the robes worn by the sad Somali beggarwomen who had refused to be photographed.

The wind was unexpectedly good, or perhaps it was a favourable current, because we somehow ended up at the Bab el Mandeb the next afternoon six hours earlier than planned. Our strategy, now ruined, had been to slip through the high-risk area in darkness. Now we would have to do it at high noon.

I was actually asleep as we approached the Gate of Sorrows, but the urgency of Herbert's call from the cockpit roused me instantly. "Get up!" he barked, and I leapt out of bed, instantly awake.

"Where are we?" I asked.

"We're right at Bab el Mandeb," he answered curtly, "and there's a speedboat heading for us." We were, in fact, precisely at the point where armed pirates in a speedboat had attacked a ship three days before.

Dead ahead, still a mile or two away, I could see the small boat, leaving a plume of spray behind it. It had altered course to put itself on an interception path.

We swung into action – the kids shut down Happy Lappy, the laptop computer, and moved it into Michael's cabin along with our precious video and still cameras. As I kept watch in the cockpit, Herbert quickly stashed them away in our secret hiding place. Michael turned on the big computer and began entering our position in a distress message, leaving it on the screen ready to send by satellite at the touch of a button. I held the VHF radio in my hand in the cockpit. Luckily, there was a large ship coming down the strait; if we got into trouble, our first call would be to it.

The rapidly approaching boat contained six men. It was a small, fast speedboat, just like the kind mentioned in the reports. There was no point in altering course; the lane was narrow, with Yemen bordering us on one side and Djibouti on the other, both shores clearly visible. The speedboat was making at least twenty knots. There was no way we could evade it, and nowhere for us to hide.

We watched silently as the boat approached, feeling strangely calm and alert. There was absolutely no question it was trying to intercept us.

With the two older boys popping their heads through the hatch and Herbert and me in the cockpit, all we could do was wait.

We had heard about another yacht with children on board that had been attacked by pirates the year before. Apparently, the pirates, upon entering the boat, had looked dismayed to find children inside. If this report was true, we figured there was no harm in displaying the fact that we were a family. Maybe the presence of our young boys would dissuade them from boarding us.

As the small boat came closer, we could see the faces of the men within. Two of them were young, maybe eighteen years old. The older ones looked like typical scruffy Yemenis with their dark moustaches and their skirts and flapping turbans, the kind that might indeed have blown up railroads with Lawrence of Arabia. Or prey on vulnerable sailboats.

The boat slowed and came alongside. The men didn't look hostile; in fact they looked curious, so we waved. Two of them waved back. Then they circled us. There was no sign of any weapons, but it didn't look as if they were fishermen, either; the small boat was entirely full of men, no nets.

As they circled behind us, they stopped unexpectedly. There was something caught in their propeller, and two men began working to disentangle it. We couldn't help but grin; they had run afoul of the fishing line we were towing. It took them a minute or two to clear their prop. Once free, they started their powerful outboard engine again, and turned around, back toward us! Our hearts, having calmed down a bit during this almost comical interlude, jumped right back into our throats.

As they approached for the second time, one of the men rummaged around in the bottom of the boat and came up with something. Was it an automatic weapon? No, it was a plump fish. What a relief! It wasn't pillaging or looting that had brought them out to intercept us; it was entrepreneurism.

We shook our heads to say no, we didn't want a fish. The men seemed certain we would want to buy the nice tuna they displayed, but we kept on shaking our heads, no, no, no. We just wanted to get rid of them as quickly as we could. Finally, they left, speeding off in the direction of the desolate and treeless Yemen shore.

Were these pirates who had decided we weren't worth bothering with? Did showing the kids' faces really dissuade them? Or was this just a boatload of men making a detour to take a quick look at a foreign yacht and maybe make a few dollars selling a fish? We will never know, although the last possibility seems unlikely, as these were clearly not fishermen. We continued deeper into the throat of the Bab el Mandeb, nervously laughing, adrenalin pumping. Inside the cabin, flickering patiently on the computer screen, our distress message was still waiting, unneeded and unsent.

A couple of hours passed. Happy Lappy was retrieved from its pirate-proof hiding place and the kids were playing computer games on it once more. Herbert and I were both in the cockpit, our eyes peeled, still on edge. We were almost through the narrow strait, looking forward to the Red Sea opening up so we could lose ourselves in it. Here, visible from both shores, trapped in a bottleneck, we felt incredibly conspicuous, a floating advertisement that shouted, "Lone yacht! Rich foreigners on board! Come, check us out!" How we wished we had other boats with which to travel.

We still had to pass through one last area of high risk. "Persons in small fast boats have been trying to board several ships off Bab el Mandeb in the southern tip of Red Sea," the piracy advisory had warned. "Masters have reported that small boats wait at the northern end of traffic lane where ships slow down to make a turn."

We were at that very spot now. And, lo and behold, there in the distance was the exact thing we had most been dreading – not one, but two small speedboats, at the northern end of the traffic lane. And they were coming for us.

It was an instant replay of the earlier scene: Lappy quickly turned off and stowed away, radio in cockpit. We resurrected our previous distress e-mail, modifying it to show our new position. As before, we left the message on the screen ready to send.

The two boats approached from ahead, one well in front of the other. The first was packed full of men, seven of them. It cut across our bow and slowed down as it came alongside. Two of the men stood up and looked us over. Again, we could see these were not fishermen.

"Cigarettes! Cigarettes!" they yelled, pantomiming smoking. "You have cigarettes?"

"No smoking, no cigarettes!" Herbert yelled back, shaking his head and shrugging his shoulders. Some of the other pirate attacks we'd heard about also began with a request for cigarettes, giving the pirates a chance to check the boat out. Again, the innocent and friendly faces of our boys popped out of the hatch.

The boat stayed beside us while the men scrutinized us for a few minutes more. Then, without further ado, they sped off. The second boat continued by without even stopping. Once again, we'd had a scare, but again it was nothing. It's extremely rare to be approached by another boat while underway, but to be intercepted twice within a few hours, and right at the number one spot on the pirate hit list, was enough to lay us panting on the floor. All we could assume was that these were pirates, and that perhaps, because they saw we were a family, they decided not to bother us.

When the two boats had safely receded into the distance, the kids asked for Lappy back. We parents, however, still weak in the knees, thought it better to leave Lappy where it was, just in case anyone else in a small, fast boat wanted to solicit something from us. Who was it going to be next: a vacuum-cleaner salesman, perhaps? The Avon Lady?

✦

After we made it through the notorious Gate of Sorrows and into the southern Red Sea, we faced a number of choices about our route. The first choice was whether to sail east or west around the Hanish Islands. We couldn't approach the islands too closely; they were under dispute between Yemen and Eritrea, and many yachts blundering into that zone had found themselves being shot at. We had enough on our minds dealing with pirates, real or imaginary, to want to tackle trigger-happy soldiers as well.

The previous spring, renewed fighting had broken out in the ongoing war between Eritrea and Ethiopia over the Eritrean port of Assab, just to our west. Although open hostilities were over, Assab was still reputed to be a rather lawless place. We had been warned by numerous people to stay well clear. So we decided to take the slightly longer route around the islands to the east, closer to the Yemeni coast.

Even still, we had two more troubling spots to negotiate.

Our route took us across the first of these later that night, after successfully passing the Hanish Islands. Now we had to cross the shipping lanes and make for the Eritrean coast. It was my shift, on a dark and moonless night. It felt good to be swallowed up in the blackness of the night, to know that we would be safely invisible until morning. Weather-wise, we were having a nice passage. Apart from being keyed up and nervous, things were going well.

I was particularly watchful, because not only were we in the shipping lanes, we also happened to be within a few miles of the site of yet another recent pirate attack. I could see a few ships' lights, and was tracking them on radar. Then, unexpectedly, two small blips appeared on the radar screen. They were very near, less than two miles away. Obviously, since they hadn't shown up earlier, these green specks represented two small boats.

I jumped into the cockpit and peered into the darkness. Nothing. At this distance, lit boats should have been easily visible. What possible reason could two small boats have to be loitering around the shipping lanes, unlit, in the middle of the night? There was only one reason I could think of, and the Avon Lady wasn't it.

I altered course sixty degrees, taking us away from those menacing green blips. Then I roused Herbert from bed. Once again, he rummaged around performing what were now sadly familiar and well-rehearsed actions, concealing valuables in their hiding places. I turned on Biggie and once more typed a distress message. There was something surreal about the whole exercise, repeated now for the third time – but that made this threat no less worrisome. In fact, of all the potential pirates we faced on the voyage, those two green blips were likely the most dangerous of all.

Together, we stood vigil – Herbert outside, straining his eyes to peer into the blackness, and me inside, eyes glued to the radar image, our nerves keyed to the maximum. As far as we could tell, the two unknown vessels were unaware of our presence. We would be just as invisible to their eyes as they were to ours. We snuck behind their stern with half a mile to spare.

In the morning, the kids wondered why Happy Lappy wasn't in its usual spot. "Another pirate attack, Mom?" Michael inquired in the blasé manner of one who has endured many such crises, a hint of sarcasm evident in that single raised eyebrow.

There was just one more "x" left on our chart for us to cross, denoting the place where the last of the recent spate of pirate encounters had occurred. It had been at midnight, five days before. "A ship detected two high speed unlit boats approaching on radar," the report had said. "When the ship fired three rockets, the boats retreated."

It was half past midnight, once again my shift (naturally, all close encounters of the nighttime kind took place on my shift). Unavoidably, we were travelling right over that last "x" marked on our chart, and I was more fretful than usual because of it. I was hating the Red Sea.

My eyes were focused on two ships in the vicinity that didn't seem to be moving, which concerned me. Then two more sets of lights suddenly popped up, which really confused me, because they didn't seem to be matched by the appropriate blips on radar. I couldn't figure out whether I was seeing a really huge, distant ship, or two small boats very close up.

I woke up Herbert and altered course to take us away from the new lights. Soon, we ascertained that they belonged to two boats less than two miles away. Unfortunately, it turned out that they were heading the same direction, which meant that unless we made a big course correction, we had to try and outrace them, slipping in front of them before they crossed our path. A hundred times, Herbert had told me, "Never try to cross a ship on its bow; always go behind it," but here we were, breaking his cardinal rule.

Committed to our path, perhaps foolishly so, we revved up our engine and charged forward under full power. We were going to make it, but it would be close. The other boats still couldn't see us, and in our desire to remain undetected we decided to stay unlit and try to evade them without them ever knowing we were there.

Just as we were passing its bow, the outline of the first small ship loomed up in the darkness. We were less than a quarter mile away.

"If we can see them, they can see us," Herbert muttered.

Seconds later, the sky above was illuminated with a shocking bright light; the nearest boat had shot up a white flare, which soared fifty metres up, cast a brief and unearthly light, and fizzled out.

To my rattled brain, there was something unspeakably ominous about the launching of this flare. My first, horrified, thought was that it might be marking our position, signalling the start of a multi-boat assault. Then I realized, with great embarrassment, that the reverse was more likely true. We were the ones, after all, travelling unlit, like thieves in the night. This was a probably just a simple fishing boat, launching the flare out of panic to summon help and scare away evil-doers, just as the ship in the piracy report had. How shocking it must have been for them to suddenly discover an unlit vessel right under their bow – and in a place known to be frequented by pirates, where no honest person travels without lights.

Thank goodness we were anonymous. We steamed away into the welcoming darkness, the night hiding our red faces. We could only imagine the fright we had given them.

"Well," I said a few minutes later as we collected ourselves in the cockpit, feeling more than a little foolish, "there we go. We have survived yet another attack by pirates."

"No," said Herbert, looking over his shoulder at the lights of the boats receding behind us, "*they* have."

✦

We arrived at Massawa, Eritrea, four stressful days after leaving Yemen. Massawa's harbour was amazingly clean, tidy, and modern, with giant new cranes busily offloading goods from several large ships. The Eritreans are a handsome people – dark skin like Africans, but with fine facial features like Arabs or Indians. The women are incredibly beautiful, tall and slender with colourful translucent robes. After the uniformly repressive and monotonous head-to-toe black of the Yemeni women, these diaphanous Eritrean beauties were a real treat.

We anchored the boat near a once-magnificent silver-domed palace that looked like – and was – the victim of a bomb attack. This used to be the governor's palace, but it was badly damaged in the fierce fighting that almost destroyed Massawa in 1990. Several other buildings at the harbourfront – including a glorious pillared bank that looked magnificent enough to have been a palace in its own right – were similarly destroyed, full of bullet holes and larger wounds from shells.

Once ashore, we gravitated automatically to that magnificent domed palace. We climbed up the great curving double staircase that led to its grand second-floor entrance. We shuffled through shards of shattered ceramic tile that used to face the palace, along with broken pieces of marble. The big silver dome had huge holes in it and was three-quarters gone. Pockmarks from bullet fire were everywhere. Several ornately carved wooden doors hung limply inwards on rusted hinges. We peeked in one of the shuttered windows and were surprised to see fancy dining-room furniture still inside – velvet upholstered chairs, china cabinets, serving tables, all covered with dust. This palace, a passing man told us, used to belong to Haile Selassie, the last great emperor of Ethiopia. Herbert and the boys scrambled in through a half-boarded up window, but just as I was about to climb in, someone came by. I pretended I was just looking around, inspecting my shoes and the broken tiles on the ground until the others returned. Inside the dusty ruins, they had found a squatter sleeping.

Massawa had once been, and will be again, a lovely town. It was the victim of a misguided policy of colonialism when the British, only the last in a series of rulers, had drawn political boundaries without much consideration of ethnic and cultural ones. Eritrea had been handed over on a platter to Ethiopia, a much larger neighbour that didn't share the same culture. Ethiopia had been ruthless in its suppression and control of Eritrea, even going so far as to make its language illegal.

Beginning in the 1960s, Eritrea had waged a bloody but successful popular revolt that had liberated its territory bit by bit. Finally, in 1993, the population virtually unanimously voted in a referendum to separate from Ethiopia, which finally resulted in Eritrea's acceptance as a nation by the world community. But for each of the previous three years, Ethiopia had attacked Eritrea, trying at least to regain its valuable Red Sea ports, Assab and Massawa, where we now were. The last fighting had taken place just a few months before our visit, the latest ceasefire signed only weeks before.

"Doesn't it scare you that Massawa is one of the targeted cities?" I asked one man, whose nineteen-year-old son was now serving his compulsory duty in the armed forces.

"Our fighters are very good, and they are fighting for their own homeland," he explained. "The Ethiopian soldiers don't really want to fight. They bring them here, and if they don't fight, they get shot. They will never defeat us."

Our friend in Massawa was a man named Weldemicael, or Mike for short. Mike, in his late forties with a sprinkling of grey in his tightly curled hair, travelled by bicycle and lived in a typical crumbling stone house built by the Turks a century before, with twenty-foot ceilings and lots of gaps. He was quite well off by African standards, with electricity, TV, a fridge, and even a washing machine, with which he ran a laundry service. He took it upon himself to be our guide and friend, taking us to the market, showing us around, letting us use his phone, and arranging a driver to take us to Asmara, the capital of Eritrea.

We were anxious to make that overnight trip as quickly as possible, because there was one thing we hated about Massawa – it was hot! We felt like lobsters boiled alive. No wonder all the stores closed up between noon and 4:00 p.m. But whereas the Massawans had their nice cool high-ceilinged houses in which to take their afternoon siestas, we had only our steaming steel lobster pot. Once we heard that Asmara was up in the mountains and cool, all we could think about was getting there. The Canadian embassy had been frantically e-mailing us, telling us not to stop anywhere in Eritrea on account of the war and undiscovered land-mines, but they confirmed at least that the road from Massawa to Asmara was clear, the only safe road in the country.

The scenery along that road was spectacular. Before we arrived at the mountains, we drove through an area of desert and low scrub brush. Sometimes, we passed camels grazing in the sparse grass of a wadi, a dried riverbed chiselled out of the surrounding rocky sand. There were many bleached bones of long-dead animals, and once or twice the rusted carcass of a tank.

As we left the arid coastal lowlands behind, the cool air embraced us. Nothing had prepared us for the beauty of these mountains. Each peak was covered with innumerable terraces. They had been created by gener-ations of farmers painstakingly collecting the rocks that entirely covered the steep mountain faces and building them up into low walls. Looking at the work that went to build these hundreds of thousands of terraces, miles from any village or evidence of human habitation, made us consider how long it must have been that people were scratching out a living in this seemingly inhospitable place. This was one of the oldest states in the world, spanning more than two millennia.

We passed many simple mountain villages, the inhabitants living in stone houses and looking picturesque in their swirling robes and with their working camels and donkeys alongside. There were hilltop monasteries that you could get to only by a steep, seven-kilometre walk – and only if you were a man. Eritrea has a population of about 3.5 million, about 1.5 million of whom are displaced refugees on account of the war, or victims of drought. A full 40 per cent of this struggling country's population is barely clinging to life. We saw countless victims of the war, men missing arms or legs and hobbling around on wooden crutches.

After two and a half hours of driving on this steep and winding new road, we arrived in Asmara, perched near the top of this mountain chain, on hills noticeably greener than those that had preceded. Asmara was a clean, charming, and quiet little city, with a broad central avenue and many cafés opening up onto a main street dominated by a huge cathedral. The feeling was peaceful and cheerful. In the evening, it seemed as if the entire population was on the streets, promenading around, men holding hands, women linking arms, people chattering and laughing and enthusiastically greeting each other with a strange repetitious bumping of shoulders. Our friend Mike had told us that we could walk around in Asmara all night with pockets full of money and nothing would happen to us.

Instead of staying in our usual ten dollar flea-bag room, we had splurged on a decent hotel for the night. We were feeling a little wrung out from all our recent experiences and felt we deserved a break. We were also starved for news – so much was happening in the world, and in the Middle East in particular, that we knew nothing about. Once ensconced in our suite, flopped on a big bed with the TV on, we could hardly be persuaded to move. What a treat! On *Northern Magic*, we were sleeping without pyjamas or even a top sheet, our beds soaking wet with sweat each morning. Here, we actually needed blankets! Here, we had a bathtub! Here, we had CNN!

I got up only once during the night to check the anchor chain, and was reassured to find the hotel very securely anchored.

We reluctantly checked out next morning for the trek back down the mountains, pleased with our interlude and with Eritreans in general, who impressed us as honest, civilized, decent people. It felt as if Eritrea was on the right track and, if given a chance, its people would build a fine country, well deserved after thirty years of desperate struggle.

$$+$$

We continued on our way up the Red Sea, but our progress was disappointing. Something was wrong with the boat. After a slow overnight sail, we decided to stop at Difnein Island, about forty miles away from Massawa, where Herbert and Michael dove to see what was going on. They were dismayed to find a forest of algae and barnacles sprouting on our bottom. Our Kenyan antifouling paint was no good. In places it had peeled off, and the remnants of our old antifouling underneath, even half sanded off, repelled growth better than the brand-new paint we had so carefully applied with the help of Boniface and Hamisi just weeks before.

All that work and money had been for nothing – no, not even for nothing, for we were far worse off than if we had just let the old paint be. Now, once a week, Herbert would have to dive down and scrape the bottom of the boat, an arduous and unpleasant task. Every time he had to do this, he emerged panting, dizzy, and in a bad mood.

Arriving at Suakin, Sudan, we entered a narrow channel that was bounded by watchtowers, machine guns, and Howitzer gun emplacements. Not a very appealing welcome. There were tall brown mountains in the hazy distance, but the immediate surrounding was sandy desert. As we made our way down the channel, a flock of seven gangly pink flamingos flew overhead.

Then we saw the ruins of old Suakin, an entire abandoned city made of coral stone, standing on a small island in the middle of the harbour. In the golden light of the afternoon sun, it looked spectacular and mysterious, with its crumbing minarets and half-collapsed buildings, mounds of rubble, and the odd lone wall holding out bravely. We shared the harbour with just one incredibly smelly fishing boat that was festooned with strings of drying fish and dozens of reeking shark fins. Originally, we had anchored ourselves downwind of that boat, but one whiff changed that plan.

It was if we were the first foreigners ever to seek entry. Dozens of customs and immigration officers floated around in the dusty, mostly empty government buildings at the harbour, but no one seemed to know exactly what to do with us. Eventually, we got connected to an agent, a man named Mohammed, and with his help gained our shore passes. The next day, we were finally allowed to come ashore.

Mohammed, a friendly black giant of a man in a long white robe and with size 15 feet, kindly showed us around the market. By now, we had seen hundreds of colourful outdoor markets, but none was quite like this. It wasn't the food on display that was so impressive – in fact, the selection was disappointing, only the most basic vegetables and fruits – it was the people and animals of the Suakin market that spun our heads in a whirl.

The transition from Eritrea to Sudan seemed to have thrown us back a thousand years. There were donkeys everywhere, braying their ineffectual rebellion against whip-wielding drivers. There were shaggy goat-sheep with funny long ears that hung down beside their heads and flopped around when they trotted, like a little girl's pigtails. Some of the goats were skilled thieves, running through the market and snatching bites of the grains that were displayed on the ground in low wide baskets, grabbing one quick guilty mouthful before being beaten off by angry shopkeepers.

There were women robed from head to toe in the colours of precious gems: ruby and topaz and sapphire. Some had masks over their lower faces the size and shape of a surgeon's, ornamented with a beautiful and delicate tracery of tiny silver beads. Their hands were painted in fanciful designs in the dark red of henna, and from their wrists hung many bangles of gold and silver. Mohammed told us they belonged to a tribe from Saudi Arabia and were not really Sudanese, having arrived only some four hundred years ago.

And there were tall, majestic black men in robes, long swords at their sides and nests of cloth on their heads. Most of them had decorative scars, three parallel lines, etched into their cheeks. Some of them were actually riding camels. If I looked hard enough, I was certain I would find the Three Kings around a corner somewhere, selecting the best frankincense and myrrh, both of which were on offer and whose perfume wafted pungently through the market.

And the flies! They covered everything, clustering all over the pile of discarded sheep shins, hooves still attached, that lay rotting in front of the leathermaker, with his three types of whips on offer. Flies scrambled over the piles of garbage strewn everywhere amid the shabby shanties tacked together from burlap and tin from old fuel drums. Flies swarmed around the rubble of the ancient coral buildings. Flies crawled over the faces and even the lips of the Sudanese, who seemed hardly to notice their presence.

Flies crawled by the hundreds over the piles of pita breads, the open baskets of dates, the bunches of blackening bananas, and the gory sides of mutton hanging in the butcher's stall, whose rows of gleaming red and white ribs shimmered with clusters of moving, glistening black bodies. Many of the hanging carcasses had head, hooves, gonads, and long furry tail still attached. No doubt the stringy meat was being nicely tenderized by the ministrations of all these eager insects. It was also receiving an extra marinating, thanks to that unceasing north wind, in a piquant mixture of desert sand, camel dung, and pulverized donkey poop. All this at no extra charge, special price for you, today, my friend.

Suakin was unlike any place we had ever seen before. Surrounded by the throngs of scar-faced men, the shy masked women, the curious young boys, the renegade sheep, the cacophonous donkeys, the belligerent camels, and the swarms of questing flies, our home in Canada had never seemed so far away.

On our first afternoon, we grabbed the chance to explore those mysterious ruins. The three-thousand-year-old city had been abandoned since the Second World War, when it had ceased to serve its traditional purpose as a slave-trading centre – the last slave market in the world. Now its buildings were falling down, most of them already transformed into piles of coral stone rubble. Among the hundreds of mounds, however, there were still many standing houses, two mosques with tall minarets, and a small palace.

The hills of rubble were tall enough that within minutes the five of us were having trouble keeping track of each other. I tried to keep up with

Christopher, who was clambering over the four-metre-tall piles of stones with the ease of a mountain goat. I trailed behind, hampered by my modest floor-length skirt, worn in deference to the proprieties of this strict Muslim society in which most of the women kept at least their heads, if not their entire faces, covered. Finally, I was forced to hoist my voluminous skirts somewhat immodestly over one arm. But there was no one around to gawk; we had this fabulous abandoned city entirely to ourselves. Here and there, we stepped over the hooves, woolly skin, and bones of long-dead sheep.

I had stopped to admire a single wall of what must have once been a beautiful house, because an ornately carved wooden window frame was still standing. Somewhere in the distance, I heard a call from Michael, and looking up I spotted him, waving from the top of the tallest point in the entire city, the slender, slightly leaning minaret of an ancient ruined mosque.

I caught my breath, for he was standing on the outer rim of the tower, a slanted ledge with no railings. Abandoning my contemplation of the lone wall, I clambered over the obstacle course to where my son was perched high above. Long before I arrived, Jonathan had joined his brother on the top of the tipsy minaret.

Soon, all of us had clambered in through a small window, climbed up the narrow spiral staircase, and from inside the tower enjoyed an eagle's-eye view of the entire ruined city and *Northern Magic* anchored far below. We convinced the boys to climb down, whereupon they immediately launched themselves into a game of laser tag in the labyrinth of streets and ruined buildings. Christopher sketched out a map. By the time Herbert and I collected the three of them from the far-flung corners of their empire and returned to the boat, the boys were hot, panting, and satisfied.

✦

Our departure from Suakin was delayed by two things. The first was the failure of our transmission, which required us to take a bus ride into Port Sudan, where Herbert spent a day supervising the construction of a replacement part made out of welded-together bits and springs from old car transmissions. We named this strange contraption Frankenstein, and prayed it would bring us to Egypt, where we could have a new part delivered.

The second thing that delayed us was a bout of the worst illness ever to visit us on *Northern Magic*. I was the first to be hit. Chills, fever, violent shaking, bloody diarrhea that became virtually continuous, vomiting, dizziness, and tremendous jolts of electric pain in my head, creating an uncontrollable spasm in my body every ten minutes, all left me sicker than I have ever been. Twice, while waiting in the bathroom to vomit, freezing cold even in the extreme heat, I passed out and woke up on the floor.

At some point in my fog of absolute misery, I slowly came to the realization that I might not be able to fight this off on my own. I had gotten much worse overnight, so nobody else was really aware of the seriousness of my situation. In the back of my mind the frightening word "dysentery" began floating around. For a few hours in the darkness, in between electric spasms, my muddled brain blearily tried to figure out what to do.

Then, the name Cipro popped into my head. Ciprofloxacin is a very powerful and expensive antibiotic, the same one for which people were clamouring during the anthrax scare. We carried a supply on board. As soon as it was light, I managed to stagger over to our medicine drawer and find a bottle. Within a few hours, I began to feel its blessed effects. Within forty-eight hours, I was at least shakily back on my feet and able to keep down some thin chicken broth. It felt to me as if the Cipro had saved my life.

Unbeknownst to me, that first night Michael had also succumbed to the same violent bug. Feverish and hot, he had crawled into the cockpit, where he vomited overboard and suffered alone and unnoticed. Because his ordeal began twelve hours later than mine did, however, we intercepted it more quickly with antibiotics, and he and I recovered at the same time. When, half a day later, Herbert got walloped with the same ton of bricks, he got the benefit of the Cipro almost immediately and recovered most quickly of all.

After eating nothing for three days, both Michael and I were noticeably thinner. In my case this was a decided bonus, but it wasn't good for

Michael. Our fourteen-year-old was very slim to start out with, and now was positively skeletal. Seeing him from behind, the outline of his pelvis and every bone in his back sticking out starkly, made me gasp. For the next few days, it became my mission to fatten him back up.

We finally left Suakin with three of us feeling weak, but eager to get on our way. As we glided past the ruined city, which was glowing golden in the early morning light, Herbert and I both paused to admire it one last time.

Complacency is a sailor's worst enemy. On our way in, our attention fully engaged, we had observed a reef sticking into the narrow channel and avoided it. But now, in the slanted light, not only was that reef invisible, in our last-minute contemplation of that enchanted ruined city, we had forgotten all about it. Before we knew it, we were hard aground – embarrassingly, unnecessarily, stupidly aground.

Our captain, still feeling woozy and weak, his nerves already taut from the affair with the transmission, our failed bottom paint, his sickness, and the general frustrations of fly-ridden Sudan, lost it. In a flash, genial Captain Herbert was transformed into wrathful Captain Bligh. We, his mutinous crew, were forced to scurry around resentfully under the lash of his tongue. After sailing three-quarters around the world without so much as touching a reef, to get ourselves stuck here was mortifying. And after much useless roaring of our motor, it was clear we were not going to get off without a lot of effort.

But at least our fuming Captain Bligh had not lost his resourcefulness. He curtly ordered a couple of young midshipmen to launch a longboat. Setting off, cursing, to the shore of the ruined city, he attached a sturdy anchor rope to some huge half-submerged rocks that had once been pillars. We all held our breaths as he attempted, using the electric anchor winch, to pull us sideways off the coral into deeper water.

Luckily, we were right on the edge of the reef, so by pulling against those ancient toppled blocks of stone we were able to slide ourselves off sideways. The whole rescue operation took only about twenty minutes, but Herbert was still stressed and angry, his cup overflowing from the week's overly generous share of frustration. He had not enjoyed Sudan, and this was the final straw.

"Why don't you just shoot me and put me out of my misery?" he asked.

"That's one of the options I've been considering," I muttered back.

✦

After three days of sailing north, violent winds forced us to seek shelter within a lagoon in the middle of the sea, formed by a U-shaped submerged reef. But now, several days' difficult sailing later, we were finally nearing the Egyptian port of Safaga. By ten o'clock that night, we were four and a half miles, or about an hour away, from a reef at which we had to make a course adjustment for our final run in. But once again, the wind was increasing.

At ten thirty, we were about three miles away, but now we were only making three knots, so it was still an hour to go.

Half an hour later, our speed had dropped further, to just over two knots. We had 2.2 miles to go – *still* an hour.

By eleven thirty, we had a mile and a half to go to reach our waypoint, but our speed had now dropped under two knots. It seemed as if we were on a treadmill; the closer we came to the reef, the more slowly we sailed, so that it remained ever beyond our grasp, like a carrot dangling in front of the nose of a patiently plodding donkey.

By now the wind was really howling, and *Northern Magic* was hobby-horsing into a marching row of almost vertical waves. We would ride high over the first wave, our bow rearing up into the night sky, and come crashing down with a thump that sent two fluorescent white waves of foam streaming out from our bows. Spray blanketed the boat.

Coming down, we would slam our nose, *wham!* right into the next wave. This time, instead of leaping over, we would dive right into it. The force of that impact would drive us to a shuddering stop, often slewing us sideways. Our faithful autopilot, TMQ, had to work mightily to keep us on course as wave after wave battered us. But both it and *Northern Magic* soldiered on.

Inside, although I hadn't noticed it, seawater was being forced into various waterproof vents. The water was finding its way underneath our fibreglass dinghy and around the lip of an overhead hatch that wasn't screwed down tightly enough. Large amounts had also been forced into the chain locker near the head of Christopher's bed. Luckily, Christopher had tucked himself into our bunk with Herbert and so was unaware that most of his books, toys, sheets, and even his pillow were soaked.

The motor was roaring, and its sound reminded me of the stresses we were placing on Frankenstein, the patched-up transmission damper we had cobbled together in Port Sudan. Would it hold together with all this jarring? What would we do if it failed?

Finally, our GPS showed us to be at our waypoint, but to be safe I waited another achingly long ten minutes (three hundred more metres!) before setting us on a course closer to shore, where, I hoped, we would get some respite from this pounding.

Herbert appeared to take his watch, and we traded places. I snuggled in beside Christopher, who opened his eyes and bestowed upon me an angelic smile that he wouldn't remember in the morning. I can't imagine how he slept with the boat rearing up beneath him like an angry bull. It was now wet at the foot of our bed.

Sleep certainly evaded me. The sound of water trying to infiltrate itself into the boat infiltrated my brain as well. From time to time, a deluge forced its way in through the galley vents, and I could hear it cascading in and sloshing around on the floor before it made its way into the bilge. Dishes rattled around inside the cupboards. We were beating into a full gale now, and the wind was screaming against the rigging, halyards hammering loudly against the aluminum masts.

I caught snatches of sleep, but three hours later I was again wide awake. By five thirty, I decided it was stupid to stay in bed and went to relieve Herbert, whose hair was pasted to his head with salt water. The reef we passed at the end of my shift, four and a half hours earlier, was only seven miles astern. We still had thirteen miles to go.

The sun rose, and one by one the kids awoke. The night before, we had promised to be there by morning, so they were surprised we weren't in calm water.

The Egyptian coast, as the sun rose, was magnificent. Tall mountains revealed themselves, breathtakingly near. I knew they would look dusty brown in the middle of the day, but now they were part of a Martian landscape, dazzling in hues of mauve, rose, and orange. I kept snatching hungry looks at this scene, although I had to squint against the blasting wind and the dollops of spray slapping my face.

The sea was wild, sparkling, and beautiful in its ferocity. Marching ranks of waves – not extraordinarily high, perhaps two metres from crest to trough, but standing straight and proud like row upon row of soldiers – stretched ahead as far as the eye can see. Their breaking crests shone a brilliant white. As a wavelet reared up, the wind snatched its top right away and threw it like a handful of twinkling diamonds across the water. Every square inch of *Northern Magic* was shedding water in a continuous glittering cascade as we continued to see-saw slowly forward. Now that it was light and I could see what the motor and autopilot had been struggling against, I marvelled that we were making progress at all.

Eventually, we did arrive, although it was in early afternoon, not at dawn as we had thought. It had taken us fifteen gruelling hours to cover these final twenty-four miles. As we set anchor in Safaga harbour, our faces were gritty with salt, our stomachs screaming for nourishment, our eyes heavy with fatigue, and the inside of the boat sticky and damp. The entire outside was covered with a coating of salt so thick that you couldn't touch anything without having lumps of it rub off on you, feeling slightly caustic and slimy. In the upper parts of the rigging, salt granules had formed tiny stalactites. It felt as if we had been at sea for twenty-two days, not twenty-two hours.

But all this didn't matter any more. We were safe, most of the Red Sea was now behind us, and we had arrived at last in Egypt.

23

The Trouble with Egypt

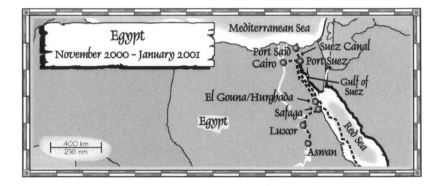

Egypt
November 2000 – January 2001

Mediterranean Sea
Port Said
Suez Canal
Cairo
Port Suez
Gulf of Suez
El Gouna/Hurghada
Safaga
Egypt
Luxor
Aswan
Red Sea

400 km
216 nm

When you enter a country by boat, you have to jump through a series of hoops. Sometimes it's easy, a boatload of officials coming out to stamp your passports, gone again within ten minutes. Usually you have to visit the officials in their offices. But nowhere did we ever experience anything as tortuous, inefficient, or frustrating as clearing into Egypt.

We had visas for Egypt already, which ought to have eased things somewhat. We had conscientiously obtained them in advance from a very unfriendly Egyptian embassy in Asmara, Eritrea. It was our first experience with Egyptian officials on this trip, and it was not a good one. Jonathan, who was in the midst of a severe attack of vomiting, had not come in with us, but the official had insisted on all three children being present. We returned with a stumbling, green-looking Jonathan in tow, and as soon as we entered the waiting area – a sumptuous room with marble floor and a lovely Persian carpet – poor Jon turned to me and said, biliously, "Mom, I'm going to throw up!"

I jumped up and found the sour-looking official, who was back in another room, shuffling his papers. "My boy is sick," I said urgently. "Is there a toilet we can use?"

He looked up at me for a moment before saying, "No." Then he looked back down at his work. I was dismissed.

I returned to Jon, told him to do his best to hold it in, and sat there stewing. In the back of my mind was a wish that my son would empty his stomach all over the carpet. Somehow, Jon managed to contain himself until we got back outside, but I was a little sorry that he did.

That was just the beginning of our adventures with Egyptian officialdom.

I'm now going to condense our first day in Safaga. You might call it our Safaga Saga. All we were trying to do was get our passports stamped and clear through Customs. It took four and a half hours.

Here we go: tie up to official dock, speak to officials who say to go to immigration, in yellow building. Stop at yellow building: wrong one. Stop at another yellow building: wrong one. Stop at another yellow building: right one, but the guards there don't know it and send us on, outside the port gate. Go through security checks one and two. Walk three more kilometres. Stop at many yellow buildings. None of them is the right one. No one knows where it is. Walk into bank to change money: they don't know where yellow building is. Ask policemen: they don't know. Ask taxi drivers: they know. It's in Hurghada, forty kilometres away. They will take us there. Ask more people. One man seems to know. He walks us back three kilometres, through security checks two and one. Stop for second time at yellow building number three. Man talks to same guards who told us before to go away, convinces them this is the right building. We thank helpful man and walk up three floors. Wait in office, receive multiple forms. Go to second office, fill out forms. Go to third office, speak to Grand Poobah with gold epaulettes, show him forms. Forms are no good. Back to office one, amend forms, then again to office three again (Grand Poobah). Passports are stamped.

Now to Customs – wherever that is. Grand Poobah's helper points to window in building far away. No one can really describe which building. Walk down three floors, back one kilometre, study buildings. All signs are in Arabic. Take a chance on one. It's Customs, but wrong office. Walk to another building. It's also Customs, but still wrong office. Official walks us right back to yellow building number three, taking short cut through filthy back way. Find correct Customs Office on first floor (two floors below Grand Poobah's helper who told us to find it in far away building). Fill out forms. Wait. Need photocopies of visas – they have photocopy machine, but won't allow us to use it. Walk almost all the way back to Customs building number two, get photocopies at public machine, return. Hand over copies. Receive forms. Tell kids we're almost done. Walk all the way back beyond Customs building number two, to cashier. Enter giant Customs Hall, fight through a swarm of pilgrims returning from Mecca, carrying half of Saudi Arabia all bundled up in Persian carpets. Stand in line, wait, pay money. Get forms stamped. Tell kids we're almost done. Walk all the way back to yellow building number three. Get more stamps. Then retrace our steps back to Customs building number two for even more signatures. Tell kids we're almost done. Try to take same short cut we took before, but this time guards with machine guns stop us. Take long way instead. Return to Customs building number two for fourth time. Get more signatures. Walk back to Customs building number one (sixth time) for more signatures and stamps. Tell kids we're almost done. Return to Customs building number two (fifth time) with yet another form for more signatures and stamps. Tell kids we're almost done (seventh time). Return to cashier (second time), dodge pilgrims to get another stamp (twelfth time). Tell kids we're done. Whew!

✦

We stayed in Safaga for two more days, replenishing our provisions, filling up with diesel, and stretching our legs after our long spell on the boat. Then it was a short hop of about fifty miles to get to a little marina where we could dock the boat safely while we made an overland trip to Luxor.

The trip to Luxor didn't start out too well. Even though we had tickets, there were no seats for us on the bus from the town of Hurghada, near our marina, and we were left standing in the empty bus station, disappointed and forlorn, surrounded by our baggage.

We had, however, a great idea of what to do with this unexpected free time. There was, in Hurghada, a most special monument. It didn't date back quite as far as the time of the Pharaohs, but it was a symbol of a mighty civilization, nonetheless. Its two elegant and massive gilded parabola were, in fact, famous the world over. We had spent the last eleven months dreaming of the day when we would stand under them at last.

And now we were here. Muslims may make their pilgrimages to Mecca, but we were required – indeed it was our destiny – to pay homage to the fabled Golden Arches. So, on the first day of our Egyptian over-land trip, instead of marvelling at Pharaonic monuments, magnificent temples, or ancient tombs, we found ourselves delightedly oohing and aahing at Big Macs, French fries, and Chicken McNuggets.

After our feed, we jostled our way onto the next bus, which took us through mountainous desert, across the spine of the range of steep brown mountains that runs along the Red Sea. You could tell exactly when we entered the Nile Valley, because suddenly luxuriant fields of crops began springing out of the desert. The vast majority of Egypt's population, now and in antiquity, has flourished within a few miles of the life-giving Nile.

A few more adventures by car, mini-bus, and horse-drawn carriage brought us to Luxor, site of the ancient and fabled city of Thebes. This is one of those elemental places you can return to again and again, and of which you will never see enough. Standing in awe at the bottom of a forest of gigantic stone pillars, gazing upon ancient tomb paintings whose colours still throb with life, touching with our very own fingers the inscribed name of a Pharaoh dead three thousand years, but whose ambition and power stand before you still, is to be made fully conscious of the extraordinary history of human kind. Everyone should go there, if they can.

Returning to Luxor was in many ways a pilgrimage for Herbert and me. At last we stood at the same ancient avenue of sphinxes where, in a very real way, our voyage had begun five years before. It was there that our hearts had thrilled and resonated with the spirit of the place and those who had built it. It was there that our passion for life had been reborn. Now we delighted in sharing it with our children: the tombs of famous kings, the temple-city of Karnak, where in darkness we once again heard the voices of long-dead Pharaohs speak to us from the ages, and the magnificent rock temple of Queen Hatshepsut, who was forced to depict herself as a man, since no woman had ever before been Pharaoh. After her death, her successor had removed her face from temple paintings and replaced them with his own. ("Now that's what I call being defaced," remarked Jonathan.)

We continued south to the city of Aswan, located in a beautiful spot at the first cataract of the Nile, not far from Sudan. There, we stood at the actual quarries from which came the granite used in the many monuments of Luxor and the pyramids themselves. There was a massive unfinished obelisk still in the quarry, abandoned because of an internal flaw. Jonathan declared that finding out how the Egyptians had raised those giant monuments would become his life's quest. We visited tombs of ancient noblemen, some of which had human bones inside them. We noticed more strewn about outside the tombs and actually picked up several pieces of human skull, including a piece of jawbone that included a tooth.

The camel ride into the desert to explore an ancient monastery was the biggest hit of all. Christopher giggled non-stop atop the mount he and I shared, especially so on the way back, when we persuaded our camel to break into a trot. As we passed Michael, his camel swung out and gave us a little hip check to slow us down. But we laughed in the face of adversity, got our mount racing again, and began gaining ground on Jonathan, whose animal we had named Rogue because of his tendency to go his own way. Christopher was filling the air with so much laughter that the rest of us had no choice but to join in.

As soon as Jon's Rogue noticed we were gaining on him, he entered the race, the camel's huge knobby legs swinging. Michael's camel was now trotting as well, and our poor camel drivers, on foot, had to run to keep up. It was tremendous fun, and we gave our good-natured young helpers an extra tip at the end of it all. (My rear end and thighs suffered for the next two days, and Michael's back, too, because he had been imitating the grand vizier of Egypt and was sitting cross-legged when the trotting began.)

There is no country in the world with as many magnificent sights as Egypt. There is also no country in the world, in our experience, with such an immense ability to frustrate and anger you. Tourism, like power, tends to corrupt, and as Egypt is the greatest tourism destination in the world, it is, perhaps, no wonder that it also contains the worst class of scoundrels – mostly shopkeepers, felucca and taxi drivers, tour guides, and generally corrupt baksheesh-grabbers – we've ever come across. Walking through the tourist market in Aswan or Luxor was like running a gauntlet. The stall owners were so desperate for our money, they clung to us like Velcro.

Walking along the Nile, we had to face the unscrupulous touts offering sailboat rides in a felucca, and they were the worst of all. Like the taxi drivers who, every time they saw us waiting for a local bus, ran up and explained that the buses weren't running today – only giving up grinningly when the bus actually pulled up – the felucca drivers were shameless in their lies. Although we still loved Egypt, it seemed to us that the Egyptians who had the most to gain from tourism were doing their utmost to wreck it. To our dismay, we noticed ourselves losing our normal friendly outlook and turning surly and suspicious of virtually anyone who tried to initiate a conversation.

One of the most important objectives for our trip to Luxor had been to pick up a package from home that contained Christmas presents: a digital camera donated by a reader, some desperately yearned-for chocolate, as well as our badly needed new transmission damper. The package had been shipped from Canada with a promise that we would receive it in four to five days. That had been two and a half weeks before. In that time, the courier company had led us on a merry chase that involved them inventing a new story each day to explain the absence of the package. It was just like 1001 Nights, but even more creative. Every time we called (and each phone call required an hour of walking to get to the public phone and as much as half an hour awaiting our turn), there was a new and different story. The waybill was lost. The declaration was lost. The entire package was lost. No, it really was the waybill that was lost. It was our Safaga Saga all over again, but worse. Eventually, we decided the only way to unsnarl this mess would be for Herbert to travel twelve hours to Cairo to try to clear the problem up in person.

He travelled overnight to Cairo, where the package was being held at the airport. There the unhelpful courier company agent – who wouldn't even come out of his office to see Herbert – directed him to take a two-hour bus ride to Port Suez to sort it all out. A brilliant diversionary tactic.

Herbert dutifully got back on the bus and travelled to Port Suez, but there he wasn't even permitted to enter the Customs compound or talk to a single official. After two days of intense frustration and no progress whatsoever, Herbert returned to the boat in despair.

After this debacle, we debated long and hard about whether to continue in *Northern Magic* to Suez. But we had already motored six hundred difficult miles from Sudan with our strange Frankenstein transmission and had grave doubts about how much longer it would hold out. We decided the whole family would take the long ride to Cairo by bus instead. Our last hope was to call the Canadian embassy.

Soon, we were sitting at a big boardroom table ("Wow! This table is as big as our boat," Michael marvelled), being given a very warm welcome by embassy staff, including the ambassador herself. The embassy swung into action immediately. By the next day they had managed to free our transmission part, and the day after that even got Customs to release the kids' Christmas presents, my mother's home-baked Christmas cake, and, most important of all, my chocolate. The only thing Customs refused to release was a used digital camera, sent by one of our readers so that we could transmit digital pictures to our Web site.

In the end, the digital camera was sent off to Cyprus, to wait for us there. The rest of the package, in all its despoiled glory, was delivered to us, after six whole weeks of trying. By now mice had eaten through some of the precious marzipan, and money included in one letter was missing. But the most important things: the Magic Cards, the books, Grandma's Christmas cake, the bag of Fudgee-O cookies (double creme), and, of course, the Hershey's Kisses, were all intact and just days later sitting, rewrapped, under our little Christmas tree back on the boat. All, that is, except Grandma's Christmas cake, which was mainly devoured in our Cairo hotel room. I didn't touch the Hershey's, though, I swear.

Okay, okay, just one little taste.

✦

Our weeks of continuing struggles in Egypt had, in truth, been getting us down. The cumulative effect of so many aggressive people trying to cheat us, plus our troubles getting the package, had been made worse by the fact that the people who had been currently renting our house back in Ottawa, who also happened to be Egyptian, had just broken their lease and done a midnight move. This deprived us of our main source of income. Finding a replacement tenant for the seven months that remained before we came home would be difficult and costly. The burden of this impending financial disaster was weighing on us heavily.

Our time in Cairo had been further complicated by Ramadan. We had been in Muslim Malaysia during Ramadan and had hardly noticed it. But in Egypt, this holy month totally circumscribed our day. Most restaurants closed between dawn and 5:00 p.m. If we didn't join the hungry throngs right at the stroke of 5:00 p.m., we would risk not being able to find food at all. As the month of Ramadan proceeded, especially late in the day, people became extremely crabby – understandably so, since they were hungry, thirsty, and needed their nicotine fix. If this is anything like how I am when I need a chocolate fix, I sympathize entirely. However, it made it all the less enjoyable for us, and I'm sure contributed to some of the problems we had with shopkeepers and taxi drivers.

In Cairo, we were invited to the home of Vice-Consul Nikki Dunn, where, along with other embassy staff and their families, we celebrated their success in getting our package released. That night, Canadian warmth and hospitality surrounded us like a warm blanket, a blanket we really needed. Nikki even presented us with a real, honest-to-goodness Butterball turkey for our Christmas dinner. For the first time, it felt as if Christmas really might be coming after all.

We spent two more days marvelling at the sights of Cairo. Christopher's highlight was seeing the glorious golden mask of Tutankhamun at the Cairo museum, which contained enough treasures to stock half a dozen institutions. Jonathan's favourite was gazing upon the face of Pharaoh Ramses II, preserved well enough over 3,200 years that you could still see the colour of his hair. As Michael finally stood in the shadow of the Great Pyramid of Cheops, he put his hand reverently upon the giant stone blocks and said, "Mom and Dad, you can do what you want for the rest of the trip; now I've achieved my dream."

There was truth in Michael's words for Herbert and me as well. Standing once again beneath the pyramids was, for each one of us, an awesome moment.

We spent our last day in Cairo trying to do our Christmas shopping at the Khan el Khalili bazaar. It's amazing how many different forms of Tutankhamun, the pyramids, and statues of the Egyptian god Anubis appeared under our little Christmas tree that year. On December 23, we caught the bus back to the boat, carrying our hard-won care package. A bus official looked suspiciously at the box, which was covered with large stickers and stamps from Customs. Frowning, he demanded to know what was in it, and whether we had paid the duty. One Hairy Eyeball from Herbert, and he didn't dare ask another thing.

On the bus, we met an Egyptian woman who was also on her way to El Gouna, the small resort town where *Northern Magic* had been berthed. Her name was Ekbal El Asyouti, and it turned out she had lived in Ottawa for twenty-three years. We were still smarting over weeks of problems with shopkeepers, touts, taxi drivers, officials, and courier company employees, so when Ekbal said, "Everyone loves coming to Egypt, because Egyptians are so friendly," I simply couldn't stay quiet.

"Well," I said, trying not to offend but needing to be honest, "I don't think most tourists really feel that way," and proceeded to tell her some of our experiences.

She was shocked. "Real Egyptians aren't like that," she said. "If only you would come to Cairo again – you could stay at my house and I'd introduce you to my friends. You'd have a completely different view." As we parted at the bus station, she pulled a lovely long sequinned robe out of her bag and gave it to me. A few days later, she and two friends visited us on the boat, carrying a load of additional presents – chocolates, wine, souvenirs for the kids. It was her way of demonstrating that not all Egyptians were as grasping as we'd been led to believe. We really appreciated her friendship.

Preparations for our fourth, and final Christmas on board *Northern Magic* were hurried. We began wrapping and decorating only on Christmas Eve, after our long bus ride through the desert the day before. Yet somehow or other, despite our frustrations, Christmas arrived just the same.

"Take a look at this," said Herbert two days later, emerging from the engine room carrying Frankenstein, our old, jury-rigged transmission damper. "Now I'm really glad we got that package."

Frankenstein was falling apart. The driving disc was already cracked, and several of its mismatched springs were wearing against the flanges that had been welded in to hold them in place. It was only a matter of time before it all would have burst into pieces. If we had continued without the new part, as we had seriously considered doing, disaster would certainly have awaited.

We dubbed Frankenstein's replacement Frank, in honour of my father. "What an honour to have a transmission damper actually named after you!!!" Dad wrote in his next e-mail. "Few, if any, ground crew have ever been so honoured!! I am a happy NM crewman!" A few days later, thanks to both Franks, we were on our way again.

✛

We entered the Strait of Gubal, the narrow entrance to the Gulf of Suez, and joined the parade of massive ships moving in stately procession on their way to and from the Suez Canal. Manoeuvring in the Suez shipping lanes at night, trying to make sense out of the thousands of lights surrounding us, was quite an experience. There was the continuous procession of red, green, and white lights from passing ships, which, if we didn't watch out, would run us down without even knowing. There's a wonderful story – probably true – of a supertanker arriving in Suez with an entire sailboat mast and sail unknowingly snagged on its bow anchor. There were the small, garishly lit fishing boats that bobbed around, trawling for prawns. A row of flashing buoys marked the channel. Then there were the lights from the different settlements and winking headlights from passing cars, visible on both shores.

But the most impressive of all were the rigs pumping oil out from under the Red Sea. Thousands of white lights illuminated their towering superstructures, making them look like science fiction cities of the future. Scattered within this galaxy of lights were huge orange flames of burning natural gas, spouting out directly from the sea floor like torches at the gates to Hell. As we sailed close to these infernos, surrounded by so many confusing lights, our nerves were taut. So it was with a tremendous sense of exhilaration that we arrived at Port Suez by mid-afternoon the next day.

Virtually every yacht making the two-day transit of the Suez Canal has bad experiences to report. The problem is the canal pilots you are required to have on board. Sometimes it's a matter of unwelcome advances to female crew, but most typically the problem is the pilots' aggressive demands for "gifts." There are even instances of pilots retaliating in various unpleasant ways if they don't get what they want.

The day before our transit, an official of the Suez Canal authority arrived. After he finished measuring our boat to assess our fees, he asked whether we had been having any problems with Egyptian officials. Herbert, smiling, just rolled his eyes. In Suez we'd already been pestered to death by requests for money from people doing nothing more than their jobs – including, just minutes before, the man who had brought this very official to our boat.

"I've heard," said Herbert delicately, "that many boats have problems with the canal pilots."

The official went into a long and reassuring speech, saying that we were under no obligation to provide any gifts whatsoever to the pilots.

"So," he said, when he was finished, his eyes darting around our salon, "do you have any sunglasses you can give me? Any souvenirs?"

Ah, Egypt.

The next day, when our first Suez Canal pilot, Atia, jumped on board, we were all on our guard. Although we were not in the gift-giving mood, we had, in fact, purchased the traditional cartons of Marlboros to facilitate our transit through the canal. But Atia proved to be a real gentleman. He was friendly and helpful, thanking me effusively for the simple lunch I served him. By the end of our first day motoring along the featureless sandy-sided canal, punctuated only by decrepit-looking military outposts, we were feeling positively warm towards him. Best of all, he didn't ask for a thing.

So I happily prepared a bag containing small gifts and treats for him and his children, as well as one of our two cartons of cigarettes. He accepted these with delight. Herbert and I giggled to see him trying to hide the bulky carton under his jacket, tucked inside his pants, to avoid having to share it once he got off our boat.

"Well, if our second pilot is as good as this one," said Herbert, heaving a sigh of relief as we anchored at Ismailia, our halfway point, "that will be great. I'd really like to leave Egypt on a good note."

The next morning, ninety minutes late, our second pilot, named Mohammed, appeared. He was a small, wiry man with a thin moustache. The first thing he said when he jumped on board was that we needed to give something to the three men on the boat who had delivered him. Gritting our teeth, for we had heard that if you refuse to pay the pilot boat they may ram you, we put three Cokes in a plastic bag and reluctantly handed them over as ransom.

Mohammed's very next words were: "And what gifts do you have for me?"

"Don't talk to me about gifts," said Herbert, shaking his head. "You haven't even done anything yet." We weren't off to a very good start.

But Mohammed didn't take the hint. He continued his pestering. Throughout the next eight hours, between his insistent requests for gifts, he was overly friendly in an obsequious, pushy way. Twice, he made unnecessary physical contact with me, once actually lying right down in my lap as I sat, cross-legged, on deck. Eventually, the kids and I fled inside the cabin to avoid further contact with this odious man.

About an hour before we arrived at Port Said, Mohammed asked for a letter of reference. Herbert wasted no time in turning that task over to me. Nice guy. For a while I puzzled over what I could possibly write. Finally, I put pen to paper and then silently showed my efforts to Herbert, who nodded and signed the document with an official flourish. Mohammed took the letter and glowed with satisfaction as he read it. Then he carefully folded it, thanked us, and tucked it into his pocket.

At Port Said, a boat came to pick him up, but we were handing out no goodie bags at the end of this party. Herbert whispered that he had told Mohammed we didn't carry any cigarettes on board. There was no way he was going to give this slimy fellow a thing.

"So, do you have any gifts for me?" Mohammed asked once more in his thin, wheedling voice.

"No," our captain said. "We paid a lot of money for this transit, so you have already been paid for your work."

"You have nothing for me?" Mohammed asked in disbelief.

"No, nothing."

Four more times he asked. Four more times Herbert shook his head, standing impassively, an immovable rock at the wheel.

"Don't you have anything for the pilot boat?" Mohammed asked despairingly, as it drew alongside. Again, Herbert shook his head – he would risk a ramming rather than reward this man's greediness with so much as a toothpick.

Finally, Mohammed, no longer smiling, jumped onto the pilot boat and left without looking back or even answering our goodbyes. "Is he gone?" the boys asked, poking their heads into the cockpit. "Good riddance!"

Herbert's eyes met mine and we shared a secret grin.

As the pilot boat receded into the distance and a wonderful flood of relief rushed over us, I pulled out a copy of the letter I had written. It was our parting gift to Mohammed and to Egypt. It read:

> Mohammed was certainly a good representative of the type of professional pilot we had expected to meet, based on the experiences of other yacht captains in the Suez Canal. He was friendly, eager and acquisitive, and we found his behaviour on our boat to be utterly dependable in this regard. Certainly he conducted himself in a manner befitting so many of the other Egyptians we have had the privilege of meeting during our weeks in this lovely country. We are grateful for such an appropriate send-off and look forward with trepidation to a repeat visit in future.

And with that, we left Egypt behind and steamed out into the waiting Mediterranean Sea.

24

Culture Shock in Reverse

Israel ❧ Cyprus
Turkey
January - March 2001

Istanbul · Ankara · Turkey
Izmir · Goreme (Cappadocia)
Marmaris · Kaş
Mediterranean Sea · Cyprus · Larnaca
Ashkelon · Israel · Jerusalem
Egypt
300 km
162 nm

The sea was calm as we motored on an overnight hop to Israel, 120 miles away. Because of the delicate political situation between Israel and its surrounding, mostly hostile, neighbours, we hadn't told anybody in Egypt that we were going there; we had said instead that we were heading for Cyprus.

Even the kids had been told not to mention anything about Israel, for fear that we might stir up bad feelings or an unpleasant confrontation with Arabs, who, clearly, blamed Israel for the recent upsurge in violence. Many times we had heard Egyptians refer to "those Israelis who are killing our children." From the Arab point of view, there was only one way of looking at this conflict. It was an issue we wanted to stay as far away from as possible. As we were leaving Port Said and out of earshot of anybody in Egypt, however, Michael – who just couldn't hold the secret in any longer – stood at our stern, raised his clenched fists in the air, and shouted defiantly, "We're going to Israel!"

About twenty-five miles away from the Israeli coast, we heard a call on the radio. It said, "Would any ship or yacht in the position 31 degrees 32 minutes north, and 34 degrees, 12 minutes east, please call Israeli Navy." I checked our GPS and discovered they were talking about us. They had picked us up on their powerful radar and wanted to know who we were.

About ten minutes later, I detected a white plume on the horizon. Soon the big rolling bow wave revealed itself to be a naval gunboat, heading for us at tremendous speed. The boat circled and came within twenty metres of us, its two big deck-mounted machine guns trained directly on us by soldiers in black baseball caps and flak jackets. We came under the scrutiny of large binoculars. I resisted the urge to grin and wave.

After about five minutes, the men at the machine guns relaxed and turned their guns away. Then one of the soldiers gave us a little wave. On the radio, we heard the men on the gunboat address us for the first time.

"Thank you very much, *Northern Magic*," a voice said. "Welcome to Israel."

Once safely at the dock, having been escorted in for the last few miles by a police speedboat, we were boarded by a beautiful young security officer who looked all of twenty years old. She subjected us to a barrage of polite but pointed questions. Her main concern was whether we had met any local people in any of the Muslim countries we had visited, even as far back as Malaysia, and whether any of them had come on board. Of course, we had spent most of the previous eighteen months in Muslim countries. She questioned us carefully and noted the names of all the friends we had made in these places, especially those who had given us gifts. Obviously, she was screening us in case we were inadvertent carriers of a bomb. She nodded when we told her we hadn't told anyone we were coming to Israel. "That was wise," she said.

After she was finished, three police officers came on board and insisted that we watch as they made a search of the boat. Everyone seemed almost apologetic that we had to be subjected to all this searching and questioning, but with shootings and bombings a daily occurrence, we weren't upset in the least. I think Michael was probably wishing, in fact, that our interrogation by the lovely security officer had lasted even longer.

At noon the next day, we were expecting a visitor, a friend of my father's who had business in Israel. Dad had been pressing rather hard to see whether we would be arriving in time to meet his friend in person, and Herbert and I had wondered whether the deliverer of this package might in fact be Dad himself. But we didn't say a thing to the kids, lest we get their hopes up for nothing.

At ten minutes to noon on January 8, Jonathan came to me and said, "Hey, Mom, do you think the man coming to see us might really be Gramps?"

"Oh, no, I don't think so," I said, not quite believing my own words.

But Jon began keeping an extra good lookout on the dock, and exactly ten minutes later triumphantly shouted, "I was right! It's Gramps!"

At first I thought he was kidding. But it was true, and in a flash Jon had jumped off the boat and was running down the dock. He launched himself bodily at his grandfather, whose slim, athletic frame absorbed the shock of that joyful greeting quite well.

Michael was hot on Jon's tail, and he, too, leapt into the air, wrapping his long legs around my dad's body. Michael was now a good inch taller than me, but Dad didn't flinch.

Christopher was next, but his soon-to-be-nine-year-old body, even flying through the air, was no problem.

Now it was my turn. Yep, I did it too. Dad gamely withstood even this onslaught.

Next it was . . . oh no . . . Herbert's turn. Would he really? No . . . he wouldn't, would he? But, yes, he did. You'll just have to use your imagination to picture two hundred pounds of captain hurtling himself down the dock and jumping onto my poor father. That's the last time he would pull a surprise visit on us. Dad did stagger a bit, but, to his credit, even this didn't take him down. He didn't rupture even a single internal organ.

Soon, we were all on our way to have lunch, my dad flanked by grandsons, who skipped and jumped, jostled for position, and chattered non-stop with their beloved Gramps. This trip had really brought us so much closer to Dad, who had been an unceasing source of support.

Dad had rented a car, and the next day, Christopher's birthday, we drove to Jerusalem. We had a wonderful guided tour of the city and returned to the boat just in time to eat Christopher's favourite meal and a birthday cake. Then Gramps rolled out his suitcase. Not only were there presents for Christopher, there were special things for the rest of us as well.

On the dock that night, we hugged hard and shed tears in the darkness as we said goodbye to my father. It was an emotional farewell. We had the Mediterranean Sea and the Atlantic Ocean to cross before we would see him again.

As we continued our sightseeing in Israel – two more visits to Jerusalem, floating in the Dead Sea, and climbing up to the mountaintop fort of Masada – evidence of the escalating conflict between Palestinians and Israelis was all around us. Khaki-clad, rifle-toting soldiers were everywhere. Every time we entered any public place, like a shopping mall or a grocery store, we were asked to submit our bags to armed security guards for inspection. Even to approach the Western Wall, an outer wall of Temple Mount where Jews have prayed for centuries, we had to be searched and pass through a metal detector. On our earlier trip to Jerusalem, when we had driven through Arab neighbourhoods, our guide had ostentatiously placed an Arab headdress on the dashboard and Muslim prayer beads dangling from the rear-view mirror, to deter any fanatics from vandalizing our Israeli rental car, or worse.

In the skies, the evidence of a high state of alert was even more obvious. Our marina was close to the Gaza Strip, an area controlled by Palestinians that served as the headquarters for the Palestinian Liberation Organization (PLO) and many of those carrying out the *intifada*, the uprising against Israel. While we were there, the Israeli army had closed the Gaza Strip, penning in the Palestinians as a security measure. Israeli warplanes zoomed past every hour or so. When there were shootings or demonstrations by Palestinians, this Israeli show of force was increased, and for days many low-flying helicopters raced by on their way to fly over Yassar Arafat's headquarters just twenty-five kilometres away. Huge missiles hung ominously from the belly of gunships that flew so low over the marina we were deafened by the noise and wondered whether they would scrape the top of our mast.

In the newspaper, there was a daily list of the various snipings and shootings. The list was not short. One time, a street was blockaded, and we watched as a bomb-squad robot investigated a duffle bag that had been left unattended by a bus stop. It was a small yellow robot on wheels, mounted with video cameras, controlled from a police van fifty metres away. Luckily, the duffle bag contained nothing more hazardous than a pair of old cowboy boots.

Although signs of danger were all around us, we quickly got used to them and began automatically offering up our backpacks for inspection half a dozen times a day without needing to be asked. After a while, we hardly noticed the soldiers. Once, there was a whole busload of them, guns slung casually over their shoulders, waiting in line with us at McDonald's.

We found Israel congenial, but time was flying by, and so, reluctantly, on a fine clear day, we left this fascinating, troubled land behind. We were once again picked up on long-range radar by the Israeli navy, who, as we were passing Tel Aviv in darkness, suddenly seemed to notice us and required us to spend fifteen minutes on the radio explaining exactly who we were and giving our departure time from Ashkelon, right down to the minute. But this time they didn't bother sending any gunboats to check us out.

+

We were on our way to Cyprus, a country we knew practically nothing about. I had some distant memories of a Canadian United Nations peacekeeping force being stationed there, but until we arrived, we had no idea that this was still very much a divided country, with Greek Cypriots controlling the south of the island, and Turkish Cypriots the north. In between, there was a UN-patrolled buffer zone keeping the two sides apart.

We anchored at Larnaca, in southern Cyprus, the part controlled by Greeks. It was a beautiful little town, very European and full of chic boutiques. More importantly, it had a real supermarket! I have to confess, I made a fool of myself there, raving over products we hadn't seen for a very long time. In particular, I got all worked up over pork, having been hoarding our last precious scraps of Kenya bacon through a long succession of Muslim countries and then through Israel.

"Oh, look! Ham!" I said, triumphantly, hoisting up a great pink haunch like Wayne Gretzky holding the Stanley Cup. "I can't believe it! And look – pork chops! And nacho chips! Ooh, Shreddies! And Gummi

Bears! Fresh milk! And . . . and . . . and . . .!" Eventually, to save himself further embarrassment, Herbert left my side to prowl the aisles on his own.

We took a trip to Nicosia, and explored both sides of that strange city, the last divided capital in the world. We also had a chance to catch our breath and recover from a year of travel in difficult places. Ever since leaving Kenya, we had been travelling hard, often accompanied by a sense of danger. We were beginning to recognize how much all this, especially our six frustrating weeks fighting for our package in Egypt, had affected us. We realized we had stopped laughing as much as we used to, that we were not as friendly to strangers. We had a new, hard edge. Now we consciously began trying to shed those defences.

In most of the countries we had visited over the previous three years, we had looked and felt sophisticated compared to the local people, many of whom regarded us with a certain awe. But in Cyprus we were no longer extraordinary. Herbert, wearing the battered old Greek captain's hat he had worn everywhere around the world, looked so much like a local that people often tried to strike up conversations with him in Greek. The same didn't happen to me. With my lack of make-up and coiffure, my unfashionable shoes and pants, I looked nothing like the elegant painted Greek women around me. I had no body-conscious clothing, no henna highlights in my hair, no high-heeled shoes, no lipstick carefully outlined with just the right shade of lip liner. People addressed me in English.

I stood, gazing in amazement at dainty crocodile-skin handbags, as foreign to me as if they were artifacts from another planet. I had only my well-worn backpack, slung over my shoulders as always, stitched and re-stitched half a dozen times by shoemakers in dusty African towns. How many hundreds of kilos of potatoes had it carried? But in Indonesia, in Thailand, in Kenya, in the Sudan, we had been *rich*. The fact that in Europe we were no longer important and prosperous, but instead anonymous and slightly shabby, hit us surprisingly hard. Now, suddenly, we felt like poor cousins. Those fancy handbags and silk suits had no more place in our lives than they did for a Bedouin camel driver. They were vaguely troubling, these status symbols of modern life. They reminded us of who we used to be. They looked enticing, but like the song of the Sirens that tempted Odysseus in this very sea, they were more than simply beguiling. Their faint but persistent call was a warning about what was waiting for us ahead, the financial and material pressures we would soon be facing once again. We couldn't help but wonder how we would re-adapt to a life in which we would be thinking of taxes and business suits and meetings rather than whether we'd be able to find fresh pineapples for our breakfast or whether the clouds looked good for an early-morning departure. Or whether that one particular twinkling light amidst a myriad of others in the brilliantly spangled night sky was a planet, a star, or the *ka* of a long dead Pharaoh.

Now that we were back in the Western world after being away so long, we couldn't ignore the fact that our trip would soon come to an end, that more big changes would soon be facing us. We began to get the feeling that maybe we were no longer the same people who had set out on this adventure almost four years before. Would we do better, we wondered, once back at home, at keeping a balance in our lives, at being generous, at remembering the things we had learned, at living our lives with passion?

+

Eventually our weather window appeared, the fluffy white cumulus clouds beckoned us to leave, and we were ready to sail onwards. We had to hurry in order to reach a safe harbour in mainland Turkey before the next winter depression swooped down. And so, on a fine sunny day, we left our explorations, our musings, and the baubles and finery of those lovely, troubling shops behind, we closed our ears to the call of the Sirens, and once again turned our bow west.

Dawn found us sailing past the western tip of Cyprus. Clearly visible behind the last of Cyprus's low green hills, the tall mountains of Turkey were already looming up over the horizon, only about eighty miles away. As we motored through the day, Cyprus disappeared from view and the mountains grew taller and more breathtaking with each passing hour. When Herbert woke me up for my early-morning watch after our second night at sea, he whispered, "Take a look outside. You can see snow!"

I could scarcely believe my ears. Snow? But off our port bow, there it was, a solid cap of snow on the highest mountain peaks. Half an hour later, when Jonathan woke up, he poked his head out of the cockpit and yelled, "Snow ho!" It had been nearly four years.

We arrived at a town named Kaş, an astonishingly beautiful place, with picturesque multi-storey houses cascading down the steep sides of a green valley. With the shining white buildings, the gleaming wooden fishing boats, the lone, pencil-shaped minaret, and the deep green forest, we had found ourselves a perfect little paradise. But we had no more than two days to explore lovely Kaş and its well-preserved ancient Greek amphitheatre. We had to move on, or be stuck there in bad weather.

We left in late morning, sailing behind the shelter of the Greek island of Nisos Kastellorizon, which was just three miles offshore from mainland Turkey. The island protected us beautifully from the waves of the open sea, allowing us to scoot along in perfectly flat seas at almost seven knots.

"When people think about cruising in the Mediterranean," I commented as we sailed exhilaratingly quickly, with Kastellorizon just fifty metres away on one side and the mountains of Turkey towering on the other, "this is what they're imagining."

"That's right," said Herbert, "and if sailing around the world were always like this, everybody would be doing it!"

We approached the island of Rhodes after nightfall. It felt as if we were back in the Singapore Strait or the Gulf of Suez, for we began encountering an immense amount of shipping traffic, all of it apparently heading directly for us. The small cargo ships were all coming through the bottleneck around the northern tip of Rhodes, and so we found ourselves on a collision course with an oncoming ship at least half a dozen times during the night. All this dodging and weaving made for very wakeful night watches, with no urge to doze off whatsoever.

We motor-sailed around Rhodes in darkness, never seeing more of this fabled Greek island than its myriad lights. There was still no sign of the approaching storm, but ominous gale warnings were beginning to be broadcast every few hours on VHF radio. By morning, we had passed Rhodes and turned north into a labyrinth of bays of ever-diminishing size, at the end of which was our destination, near the tiny village of Orhaniye. Around us, closing in more and more closely as we glided through calm, protected waters, were tall hills lightly covered with pine forest. I half expected to see the Mongol hordes, with bushy eyebrows and curved scimitars, rushing down the slopes at any minute.

That night, our halyards began slapping, our rigging howled out a mournful song, and our masts shivered as they were lashed by cold wind and rain. But we didn't care. We were all tucked into our beds, snuggling under warm blankets and feeling very pleased to be tied up, safe and secure.

+

Within two days of arriving at our new home base in Turkey, *Northern Magic* was lifted out of the water and set ashore near the walls of an intriguing ancient ruin located right within the marina. Day after day, our captain sanded off layers of old paint and applied layers of new. To get onto the boat we had to clamber up a tall metal scaffold.

With ready access to land, the kids took to playing soccer inside the walls of the old ruin during their breaks from schoolwork. The boys were outside on one of these breaks, while I was helping Herbert do something or other in the engine room, when there was a clatter just outside the boat, followed by a scream. It was such an intense, unbroken shriek that I couldn't immediately recognize which of the boys was producing it. Whatever had caused that wail must have been something bad.

Swinging over the abyss of the engine room using overhead hand-holds – Herbert was deep inside, bent over, and so was slower to extricate himself – I burst outside through Michael's hatch to discover that the boy in distress was Jonathan. He was lying on his back motionless on the ground beside *Northern Magic*, his terrible scream still piercing the air. He had fallen off the ladder.

With one hand on the boat, I leaned over and grabbed the metal scaffolding to climb down. The instant I did, my body sizzled and jumped with a powerful electric shock. I released the scaffold reflexively and cradled the hand that had grabbed it, zinging with pain up to the wrist. Now I realized what had happened to poor Jon, and it was more serious than just a fall. An electric shock had thrown him from the top of the ladder.

"Honey! Get here right away! The boat's electrified! Get here right NOW!" I yelled. There had to be a short circuit in the boat's power. The instant anyone connected the boat with the ground, through the metal ladder, they completed the circuit, using their own body to conduct 240 volts of electricity. As long as the power was still surging through the boat's metal decks, stanchions, and lifelines, I had no way of getting down to help Jon.

By now, Michael had sprinted up. Seeing me jump back from the shock, he had the presence of mind to run over to the outlet that connected us to external power. As soon as he pulled the plug, I gingerly touched the ladder. This time receiving no voltage, I climbed down as quickly as I could and finally knelt beside poor Jonathan.

"Mom, I got shocked," was all he could say.

The whole marina had heard the commotion and we were now surrounded by a ring of ten or fifteen concerned people. Without moving Jon from the wet ground, Herbert and I carefully touched and prodded, saw that toes were wiggling and all body parts working, before helping him up. After grabbing the metal stanchions of the boat and getting the shock, he had fallen three metres, landing flat on his back. But nothing was broken, and the shock itself seemed not to have hurt him.

"When I grabbed the boat and got shocked, it seemed to hold me there for five seconds," he told me a few hours later, his eyes glistening and his lips trembling just a bit in response to the painful memory. "I couldn't move. My whole body was on fire. Then when I was falling, it seemed like slow motion, like I was twirling through the air."

But Jon bravely got up, climbed that ladder again, and got to eat jelly-beans in bed for the next hour. In short order, he was back on his feet, sore, but none the worse for wear. His guardian angel must have been standing over him that day, because it could have been so much worse. "You mean his angel was standing *under* him," corrected Michael. "He'd better not fall again, because his angel probably got squashed."

While Jon was recuperating, Herbert got to work finding out what had caused the short circuit. Even with a metal rod connecting the boat to the ground, the instant external power was reconnected, the hull of the boat was electrified again. After ten minutes of experimentation, the culprit turned out to be our battery charger, which we had bought brand new just two weeks before. Herbert threw it away without attempting to repair it. The next day Jonathan was back playing soccer, climbing up and down that ladder like a monkey, as if nothing had ever happened. But now, before grabbing the stanchion on the boat, he gave it a little tap first.

✦

Soon *Northern Magic*'s hull was smooth and newly painted once again, and we were just about ready to get her back into the water. But a number of huge lows were churning their way across the Mediterranean. We were attempting to cross this difficult sea in winter, a season when few other sailors left their cosy marinas. Our entire purpose was to avoid these winter storms. The nasty weather system was just the excuse we needed to explore Turkey. So, instead of sailing to Greece, we rented a car and found our way to the vast inland plains of Asia Minor.

We saw many wonders and marvels on our trip, more than I can write about here. The best of them, however, were the underground cities and cave dwellings of Cappadocia. Virtually invisible from ground level, these four-thousand-year-old underground cities had hundreds of chambers on multiple levels, large enough to accommodate tens of thousands of inhabitants in a labyrinth of interconnected rooms: stables, wineries, kitchens, storerooms, living rooms, baths. We explored two of the more than forty that exist, clambering up and down claustrophobic passageways and tunnels, narrow ramps and winding stairways, getting lost in a maze of chambers that led us eight storeys and fifty-five metres underground. This was surely the stuff of childhood fantasies.

We continued into the heart of Cappadocia, with its bizarre badlands landscape becoming more and more weirdly eroded. Soon we came upon the first fairy chimneys, strange natural pillars with peaked caps. Upon arriving at a hilltop and taking our first look down at the small town of Goreme, I simply had to throw my head back and burst into peals of laughter. Arrayed before us was a perfect little goblin village of troglodyte cave houses, carved right into a forest of fairy chimneys. Smurfville!

The Smurf houses of Goreme were sprouting out of the earth everywhere, like mushrooms. It was as if God's giant landscape architects, busy at their serious work of sculpting the majestic mountain peaks to the north and south, had shooed their kids away with giant blobs of Play-doh and instructions to amuse themselves. The resulting creation surely had to be the neatest, cutest, most delightful place we had ever seen. The fairy chimneys created by these fanciful kid-giants came in all shapes and sizes: tall, thin ones, short, stubby ones, straight ones, tipsy ones, even really silly ones with three caps sprouting out from a single base like a jester's cap. And the Cappadocians had further refined these wacky and wonderful formations by hollowing them out, cutting little doors and windows in them, and turning them into houses that are still in use today.

Down into the valley we descended, still periodically chortling as we meandered through narrow, winding streets with Smurf houses on every side. We gigglingly found ourselves a wonderful small hotel constructed right inside a fairy chimney, and then went horseback riding among the strange goblinesque cave houses, monasteries, and churches.

We put thousands of miles on our car, touring most of Turkey's most memorable sights. What an under-appreciated jewel of a country! At Istanbul's Grand Bazaar, we endured the requisite pestering by innumerable carpet salesmen, all of whom had special deals for us. I couldn't help but remember what a very nice carpet salesman in Goreme had told us after taking us through his factory's excellent demonstration of silk making and weaving. He had paused over one traditional design that represented the five times each day Muslims are called to prayer. "Good Muslims pray five times a day," he had told us with a grin. "Bad Muslims sell carpets."

From Istanbul we continued on the European side of the Sea of Marmara, driving towards the battlefields of Gallipoli and on to Troy, the site of the Trojan wars, and Ephesus, Turkey's greatest archaeological site. The stunning façade of the Library of Ephesus blew us away. I was reluctant to take my eyes off it, so taken was I by its beauty, even two thousand years after being built.

We drove into the exotically named city of Izmir to find a hotel for the night. Somehow we took a wrong turn and found ourselves driving down a tiny pedestrian shopping street crowded with stalls and shoppers. That cobblestoned street led to another, even smaller, and then to an even smaller one, just about as wide as our car. As we drove through the maze, the only car in sight, we were like Moses parting the Red Sea – only the Red Sea was made up of mildly annoyed people wondering just what we thought we were doing. We eventually got out, but not before having collapsed with laughter.

We were back in good form again, laughing a lot and playing silly pranks. But after we returned to *Northern Magic*, I was struck by a melancholy sense of finality – that the ending of this last wonderful overland excursion in some way symbolized the end of our journey. The next time we would use those well-travelled backpacks would be to pack up our things and take them home. It would have been easier, perhaps, had we not loved Turkey quite so much.

$$\bf{\div}$$

We were now spending many hours discussing our return to regular life. Herbert was more eager to get home than I was, more tired of living in the cramped confines of the boat and dealing with the constant worries and repairs. My feelings were much more mixed. While it would be nice not to have greasy engine repairs constantly done in the middle of my living room, for four years I had been surrounded by the four people I loved most, while doing what I loved best – exploring the world, sharing our discoveries through my writing, making a small difference where we could. I was more than a little nervous about having that magical bubble burst.

The night after we returned from our overland trip, this gloomy sense of finality somehow brought to the surface a much deeper fear. In the darkness, a great black horror of death came over me. I had experienced a feeling of pure, sharp fear like this only once before, the day I learned I had cancer. Perhaps it was because I had been blessed with so much that the knowledge that one day I would have to give it up felt so terrifying.

My moment of darkness redoubled my urge to make sure I made the most of my brief time on earth. I realized I could never stop living my life with passion, that I would never be content with going back to the life we had lived before. Herbert and I had already made a promise to ourselves not to forget the dying rainforest and its creatures in Indonesia, nor the struggling people of Africa. We had somehow to find a way to make a contribution. What was the point of going through all we had experienced, of learning all we had learned, if not to use it?

The next morning I looked at our three precious children with a painful lump in my heart, feeling so proud of them and at the same time dreading the moment I would have to give them up. Soon I would have to share them with school, friends, and girlfriends. Some day I would have to say goodbye to them forever. How would I ever be able to bear not having them with me, not being the most important person in their lives? How could I bear losing the togetherness we shared in our tiny, water-borne home?

Michael had surely grown up on the trip. He was turning into a man right in front of my eyes. This trip had given him confidence. By now he had survived storms, piloted us through reefs from the top of the mast, and had taken charge when we were hit by lightning. He was dreaming big dreams for the future. Yet this was also a young man who brought me flowers, told me regularly that I was beautiful, and gave me back scratches when I was having a bad day. He even gallantly lied about the all-too evident effect the chocolate I consumed on this voyage was having on my tummy.

He could be argumentative and still needled his little brothers, but Michael was a magnet to small children and stray animals, who instinctively recognized his large heart.

Underneath the playful persona, which Michael performed to perfection, of a self-absorbed egotist named Magnum Opus – or sometimes the equally narcissistic Gloateus Maximus – was a sensitive, loving, and articulate young man. What a wonderful husband and father he would make some day. I could already visualize a flock of grandchildren.

Of all of us, Michael was by far the most eager to get home. We had known from the beginning that Michael, who was now almost fifteen, was the boy on whom we had the most tenuous grip. How right we were to have pushed the trip forward so quickly. If we'd waited even another year, it would have been too late. The call of approaching adulthood would have been too powerful for even this magnificent adventure to overcome. Mike often wished that he was biking around our old neighbourhood with his friends (and girls – oh yes, there was always something about girls), but just a few weeks earlier, in an unguarded moment, he had told me, "Confidentially, Mom, this trip hasn't been too bad."

As for Jonathan, who was about to turn thirteen, he had developed a strong sense of compassion and a desire to do something to help the rest of the world. Jon, the real traveller of our three boys, had probably learned the most about the world. He had been greatly moved by our experiences in Asia and Africa. Where Michael had been depressed by the poverty, Jon had been able to appreciate the things he had in common with the people living in it. Many a time Jon would be the one to hand out treats in an Indonesian village, or give up his toys or even the hat off his head for a poor African child. He was always the first to extend his hand in friendship. He had no trouble overcoming any barrier of culture, age, or language. Jon had a great big smile, which he used often, and a heart to match.

Hard-working, responsible, cheerful, eager to please, Jon, when asked to help around the boat, invariably replied, "Sure, Dad!" Jon's alter ego was the obnoxious Thunderbear, a stuffed bear he impersonated who'd been given to us early on the trip by someone who'd turned out to be a scoundrel. But in reality compassionate, responsible Jon was just the opposite.

Christopher was still something of an enigma, smart as a whip but as stubborn and as bull-headed as . . . well, his father. (Herbert feels that I, too, had something to do with it. In fact, he argues that I am *solely* responsible for the trait. But he's wrong.) Christopher was nine now. Super competent in some things, helpless in others, he hadn't yet quite learned that he was capable of anything. One day, when he figures that out, he'll be unstoppable.

Christopher was still my sunshine boy, a bit babyish for his age, exploiting his role of lastborn child to the hilt. He really needed to be back in school, learning how to play with children his own age. And yet how I dreaded losing his constant loving, even if he sometimes made my head spin with his never-ending stream of talk!

Where Michael played at being the self-absorbed Magnum Opus, and Jon the boorish Thunderbear, Christopher had a number of alter egos. Sometimes he transformed himself into Baelog the Fearless, a mighty Viking warrior, brandishing a sword made from the nearest stick. He and Michael engaged in stick fights on the beach by the hour.

After our experiences with gibbons, Christopher turned into Denny the Gibbon, a cheerful little soul who swung around our boat on his long arms, played silly pranks, and laughed a happy gibbon laugh. Christopher's plan was to find a cure for AIDS, win a Nobel Prize, and with the prize money go back to Borneo and establish a gibbon sanctuary.

But lately he had become enraptured by a popular kids' game called PokéMon, which had turned him into a loveable fuzzy yellow animal with a lightning tail named Pikachu. As I sat typing at my computer early one morning, Christopher climbed out of his bed with a furry yellow toy under his arm, and came over to whisper in my ear. "Mom," he said, "Pikachu would give up his life for you."

We did live on a cramped, often uncomfortable little boat that was smaller than our master bedroom at home, we did have to worry about storms and pirates, but I also had the constant companionship of a little mop-headed boy who, at least fifty times a day, snuggled up beside me to tell me that he loved me. How could I not feel sad our trip was coming to an end?

25

Captain George to the Rescue

Greece ~ Sicily ~ Sardinia
Mallorca ~ Gibraltar
March – June 2001

Spain
Italy
Mallorca
Sardinia
Greece
Gibraltar
Cagliary
Cefallonia
Delphi
Mediterranean Sea
Sicily
Athens
Siracusa

500 km
270 nm

S oon we were off, sailing west as always. Sadly, we didn't stop at any of the islands we passed in the Aegean Sea, each of them with its own niche in the fabulous history of ancient Greece. Our long, overland sojourn in Turkey had put us behind schedule, so we bypassed the many islands with alluring, half-familiar names and headed straight for the Greek mainland.

We had more than the usual assortment of minor mechanical problems on the two-day passage, starting with a broken fan belt, a baulky bilge pump, and a failing cooling-water pump. During our first night of the passage, our mainsail gave up as well. It parted completely along one seam, its two severed parts flapping limply. With the mainsail gone, we had to rely on the motor and its suspect cooling system even more.

After two days at sea, sailing across busy shipping lanes, dodging cargo ships and tankers, we approached the sprawling metropolis of Athens, where an endless field of low white buildings sprouted on tall, sparsely vegetated hills, capped by a halo of haze. By now, a flaky bearing in our water pump had completely flown apart. Somehow, Herbert had managed to patch things together sufficiently to keep us going, but he knew his repair wouldn't last long. We hoped it would buy us the two hours we needed to make it into harbour.

Two hours later, the pump was still hanging in there as we circled behind a breakwater at the port of Piræus. Marina staff hadn't answered our radio calls and, once we'd arrived, had been slow to direct us to a berth. As we hovered in the centre of the marina, motor idling, I thought briefly how funny it would be if the water pump gave up right now, when we were so close. Fifteen minutes later, just as we began to follow the marina skiff that was finally escorting us to our berth, I found out just how funny. The wobbly water pump fell apart, chewing up the new fan belt in the process, the engine overheated, and, in the end, the marina staff had to tow us, humiliatingly, into our berth. Hilarious.

After a two-day struggle to comply with official requirements to check into the country, we spent the next days attempting to find the parts we needed. But we grew more and more disillusioned. It seemed no one wanted to help us or even talk to us. When we attempted to ask people for directions in the street, they raised their shoulders like shields and marched the other way, pretending not to notice us. Shopkeepers ignored us. We felt like pariahs.

"It's probably not just Greece," Herbert kept reminding me, trying to convince himself as well. "All of Europe could be like this, especially in big cities. Europeans are just not that friendly." Whether this was true or not, we found ourselves more and more anxious to leave. Even a visit to the Acropolis and the architectural marvel of the Parthenon – for me, the fulfilment of a lifelong dream – failed to raise our spirits. In fact, after only a single tiring visit into central Athens, a long walk and subway ride away, we took a vote and decided not to go back.

But just when we were feeling most sick of Athens, everything changed.

In Turkey, we had been contacted by a *Citizen* reader, Paul Dole. He e-mailed us that we simply had to meet a friend of his, a "splendid captain" and "wonderful man" named Captain George Kotsovilis. Paul had even telephoned Captain George on our behalf.

It was a Sunday afternoon, and Herbert was doing a routine oil change. The simple procedure had turned into a marathon of frustrating and stupid problems involving the old oil filter, which had been completely stuck in place, and in the course of an hour's work trying to get it free, he had irreparably damaged some brass fittings. Now we had even more new parts to find, and wouldn't be leaving the next day after all.

Just as we were sitting down to a very belated lunch, with Herbert tired and crabby – all of us, in fact, tired and crabby – a gentleman with a pleasant face and white hair appeared on the dock and stood there, smiling. He was carrying several large gift baskets, wrapped up in sparkly cellophane and bows.

"Are you Captain George?" I asked.

"Yes, I am," he said. "And *you* have crossed *oceans* in this little boat?"

Thus, like a whirlwind, Captain George swept into our lives. For us, Greece would never be the same.

Captain George showered us with gifts. I don't mean a little wrapped bauble or two; I mean gifts – as in Christmas, as in Santa Claus. *Northern Magic* shuddered under the burden of things he had brought: not one, but three bottles of wine, a giant basket of fruit, some olive paste, a jar of gourmet pickles, a container of chocolate-covered almonds, a box of freshly baked cookies, a necklace, a brass treasure box, a beautiful full-colour book about Greece, and a giant bouquet of spring flowers. We had done nothing to deserve this bounty, and it was a little embarrassing. Plus, we were all in shabby clothes (Herbert had evidence of the just-completed oil change still in his hair) and were eating chicken-noodle soup at the time of his arrival. Captain George sat down at our salon table, already crowded with soup bowls, cracker crumbs, schoolbooks, toys, and a wrench or two, to chat.

George was a former ship's captain. He had worked for Aristotle Onassis before buying his own cargo ship, the first of many. After a few days with Captain George, our earlier impression of Greeks as being unfriendly had been completely wiped away. Our host was the personification of generosity, helpfulness, and hospitality. He put all his business affairs aside for us. Instead of feeling alone and shunned, we were being driven everywhere while George took care of finding our needed parts. Instead of gnashing our teeth, we were munching on delicious

Greek food with our gracious host at an outdoor *taverna* in the shadow of the Acropolis.

George never arrived at our boat empty-handed. "I think he must really be an enemy agent in disguise," said Jonathan one day, shaking his head in amazement, "his mission is to sink *Northern Magic* under the weight of all these presents."

+

After leaving Athens we sailed through the Corinth Canal, stopping to marvel at the ruins of Delphi, then sailed along Greece's Bay of Corinth, accompanied by troupes of dolphins. Eventually, we made our way to the beautiful island of Kefallonia, our last stop in Greece. There, we were punished by unremitting cold and rainy weather brought by an inexorable marching series of fronts, each one bearing storms and contrary winds. For ten days we waited, hoping each day for a respite. We celebrated Jonathan's birthday there with kids from a Belgian boat, playing "Pin the Tail on the Donkey" on a palm tree at the quayside.

First thing on Easter Monday morning, with foil Easter egg wrappers and a few un-found eggs still littering the boat, we got this message from Dad: "South wind is now in Sicily and Ionian Sea. Above 40 degrees N south winds 35–40 knots, forecast to decrease. New low is now forecast to be in north Italy in next 48 hours. It's a tight hole, but this is the best chance I've seen in the last 10 days. You make the call!"

Within three hours, we'd gulped down a fast lunch of canned ham and beans and hastily made *Northern Magic* shipshape. As soon as the last dishes were washed and the last few drying socks brought in, we cast off. We were already drifting away when there was a commotion near the Belgian boat. Two small figures were sprinting along the quay. One of these shapes was familiar. It was Jonathan. "Wait! Wait!" he was yelling as he ran frantically, hands waving.

In our rush to set off, we had completely forgotten that Jon had gone over to the other boat for one last chance to play with his friends. By the time he breathlessly arrived, we were already drifting a metre away from the quay. Poor Jon literally had to jump across the widening gap to get on board.

And so we set out, a little sheepishly, but with white puffy clouds and a blue sky corroborating Dad's promises of a good passage. Motoring into the Ionian Sea, we were hoping he was right and we could make the five hundred kilometres across to Sicily before the next batch of nasty weather arrived.

As the sun was setting on our second night at sea, still seventy miles away from our destination, we caught sight of the tip of Italy's boot, as well as the very top reaches of Mount Etna, Europe's largest active volcano, poking its smoky head into the low-lying clouds ahead of us. In ancient times, the often-fiery top of Etna served as a natural lighthouse for weary sailors seeking land.

We slowed down overnight, so as not to arrive before dawn, and motored into the harbour of Siracusa just as the sun rose over the castle that guarded the harbour entrance.

Siracusa turned out to be a great city. It was a beautiful warren of narrow alleyways and marvellous architecture, punctuated with cathedrals, plazas, fountains, outdoor cafés, and vivid bunches of blooming bougainvillea. Our feet always slowed down while passing the numerous *pasticcerias*, offering the most amazing selection of delectable pastries and marzipan fruits.

But we had chosen to stop in Siracusa for something other than its picturesque old city, its extensive Greek ruins, or even its pastries. Long before, in Australia, we'd met a Sicilian sailor named Peppino, along with his wife, Lucia, and his son, Blu, nine years old at the time. It had been two years since we'd seen them. Jonathan was especially excited to see Blu again, since they had been good friends.

Michael was the only one of us who was not so keen on going out of our way to visit Peppino. He hadn't liked Peppino much, since Peppino had been on his back almost daily about Michael's failure to greet him properly. In fact, the phrase "You forgot to say good morning!" barked out gruffly and with an Italian accent had assumed icon-like status in the *Northern Magic* pantheon of jokes.

The morning we arrived, we e-mailed Peppino to say we were moored in the Grand Harbour. No sooner were we back on the boat than Peppino himself was standing there, a muscular, robust fellow of fifty-three with a salt-and-pepper beard. It was definitely the same old Peppino – gregarious, voluble, almost overpowering in that passionate, uniquely Italian way. Within minutes he was whisking us away to his apartment for lunch. "I hate going to restaurants," he told us, "not because of the money, but because they don't know how to cook like I do."

As we sat at the table watching Peppino make spaghetti, we grabbed the chance to settle a longstanding Stuemer family feud on this very topic. To use knives, or not to use knives, that was the question. Jon and Herbert thought fork-twirling was the only way, while Christopher, Michael, and I felt knives and forks were much more efficient and civilized. So here we were, in Italy, with a real Italian making spaghetti for us, and it seemed appropriate to ask the question.

"Tell me, Peppino," I ventured, "do Italians use knives when they eat their spaghetti?"

Peppino whirled around from the stove, where he was cutting great chunks of garlic, his eyes ablaze. "Knives?" he bellowed.

The room went silent. Jonathan and his father looked smug. My lips were pressed together. But later, Michael, Christopher, and I defiantly used our knives just the same. What do Italians know about spaghetti, anyway?

Over the next days, Peppino whirled around us like a tornado. What was Peppino's was ours, including his car, which he insisted we take for the duration of our visit. We drove up the smoking flanks of Mount Etna, where the kids ran up and down volcanic craters. Peppino helped us with boat repairs, phoned and faxed to help track down another missing package sent from home, provided hot showers, laundry facilities, Internet access, and meals, and flooded us with wine and wonderful pastries named *cannoli*, filled with a cheesecakelike mixture of sweetened ricotta. Fantastic! If we'd asked for the shirt off his back, no doubt Peppino would instantly have peeled it off and asked whether we wanted his pants, too.

One night, Peppino came over to *Northern Magic* for dinner (fried chicken and potato salad – knives permitted). As we sat together in the salon, he brought up the subject of his confrontations with Michael back in Australia. "Do you remember when I used to correct him for not saying good morning?" he asked. We smiled and cast a secret look at each other. Oh yes, we remembered.

"And then one day," Peppino continued, "when Michael appeared carrying a huge poster with 'good morning' written all over it in different languages? I bet he thought I was a mean old Sicilian then, didn't he?"

"Yes, he did," I answered. "But now I think you've wrecked your mean old Sicilian act for good."

✦

A high-pressure system had moved over the central Mediterranean, giving us relief from the stormy weather and the perfect opportunity to make the two-day sail to the island of Sardinia. And so we left Sicily on a glorious day, watching the lovely architecture of Siracusa slide by as we made our way gently out of the harbour.

We had a good passage, and arrived at the southern tip of Sardinia, the Mediterranean's second-largest island, late in the afternoon. We anchored on a wild-looking shore beneath a sheer cliff. A small village teetered on the cliffside, a precarious track led along the precipice, and an ancient castle turret, half collapsed, gazed gloomily down at us through the ages. The craggy rock face was rugged, fissured, and glowing golden, almost as if alive. For a moment, I felt we'd arrived at another world entirely, an ancient elemental world full of fauns and satyrs, naiads and dryads.

We wandered through the medieval city of Cagliari, admiring the beautiful buildings, bastions, palaces, and cathedrals, and dodging the occasional car that was brave enough to venture into cobblestone streets that were barely wider than it was. We made several local friends.

But as beautiful as Sardinia was, we were really just putting in time. In truth, we were itching to leave. We were undergoing a transformation, and suddenly could hardly wait to continue our trip as quickly as possible. Although we had Spain and the Azores still ahead of us, it was the thought of Canada that made us chatter with excitement. I remember seeing Australian boats with the same syndrome in the South Pacific; while the rest of us were enjoying the fabulous islands of Polynesia, all the Aussies were racing through their last few thousand miles. Now the same feeling of urgency had come over us. It was time to go home.

We sailed for two more days to Mallorca, and then set off for Gibraltar, 350 nautical miles away. An increasingly large swell rose up, and Dad e-mailed us to keep sailing as fast as we could; thirty-five-knot winds were following right behind us. The two-, sometimes even three-metre swell rising up under our stern and throwing us forward with roaring force as it passed under made it clear he was right. On we went, rejoicing as we passed waypoint after waypoint without needing to seek shelter, coasting along at almost eight knots.

These were our last few days sailing on the Mediterranean, and they contained moments of pure enchantment. In the middle of the night, in total darkness, I was adjusting the jib when I noticed that as I grasped the jib sheet, or rope, it would emit tiny sparks of blue phosphorescent light, some of which briefly stayed, glowing, on my hands. It was like the sparkles of fairy dust from Tinkerbell's wand. As I coiled the sheet around a winch and tightened it, it sparkled merrily. Obviously, some of the waves washing over the deck had left wet fingerprints behind, in the form of tiny bioluminescent plankton.

Another time I was on deck at night when I heard dolphins right beside us in the darkness. I heard not only the splash of their leaping and the snuffy exhalation they made when they opened their breathing holes to grab a gulp of air, but I actually heard them squeaking to each other underwater. Their torpedo shapes were illuminated by bits of sparkling plankton, as if they, too, were sprinkling blue-white fairy dust behind them. We also had overnight visits from many friendly little birds who, to our delight, chose to rest inside our cabin.

After our third night at sea, I awoke with a start at 6:00 a.m. Herbert had sharply reduced the throttle, our longstanding signal to get to the cockpit, quickly. I bolted up. In fact, Herbert hadn't been calling me at all; he had been trying to avoid a container ship that was turning in front of us. But at the moment I emerged into the cockpit, I was transfixed. For there, right in front of us, loomed an unforgettable shape, large, even blacker than the black expanse of sky behind it, and unbelievably grand. The ancients knew this as one of the Pillars of Hercules. It was the Rock of Gibraltar.

The next day, the view from the top of The Rock was grand. There, to our left, through a cloud of squawking and circling seagulls, was the Mediterranean, the sea we had now successfully crossed. Ahead, on the far side of the Strait of Gibraltar, were the misty purple mountains of

Morocco. But our captain had his eyes fixed on the vastness of the North Atlantic to our right, stretching out into infinity.

Since the beginning of our trip, the North Atlantic was what had haunted Herbert in the middle of the night. Not the vast Pacific, not the Indian Ocean, not the dangerous Red Sea, not the unpredictable Mediterranean, but the North Atlantic. Now, every time I looked over at him, he was scrutinizing its ruffled grey surface – as if looking for a clue about what the deadliest of the world's oceans held in store.

It was time to get *Northern Magic* ready for her last big trial of our circumnavigation. Herbert went on a binge of inspecting, repairing, and adjusting. Each day we studied weather charts for the timing of our next passage to the Azores, a small group of islands in the middle of the Atlantic. Day after day, we frowned to see cold fronts, lows, isobars squeezing close together on our path, particularly around Newfoundland. Having just read *The Perfect Storm*, it made me feel pretty queasy. I began to understand why Herbert kept looking pensively west. Even when there were no lows, the wind invariably came from a bad direction.

We had felt pretty smug, upon arriving in Gibraltar, about having made it across the entire Mediterranean in the non-sailing season without a single day of bad weather at sea. We met only two or three others who had attempted it, and they all told horror stories. The reason for our success was more than luck; it was careful planning and Dad's assiduous weather forecasting. But now, facing an 1,100-mile passage of a week or more, it was a whole new game. Nobody could reliably predict what would happen four or five days out. We were prepared for a rough ride.

Finally, there was no longer any reason to wait; the boat was fixed up, rigging checked, bilge pump and coupling fixed, five meals prepared in advance. We'd all showered, and Christopher had taken his last bath in our laundry tub in the marina shower stall. Sixteen loads of laundry had been hand washed and dried, and all the linen on the boat was fresh and clean. Charts were organized and studied, waypoints plotted. We were ready as we'd ever be to tackle the North Atlantic.

26

Facing the North Atlantic

The first leg of our Atlantic crossing took us through the Strait of Gibraltar and west along the bottom of Spain, with the coastline of North Africa clearly visible. Once clear of the narrow strait, we angled northwest, creeping along the southern coast of Spain for another day. We sailed out on a helpful east wind that continued only until nightfall and then died, leaving us motoring into a light westerly breeze.

Not long after I came on duty in early evening, I noticed a strange cloud formation in the sky ahead. It was as if the low, flat clouds on the horizon were leaping up, arms outstretched, to pounce on us. A few minutes later, a little alarmingly, the same predatory clouds had closed their distance by half. I wasn't sure what this meant, although I didn't think it was a squall, because a squall line is usually hard, black, and well defined.

A minute later I learned. We were suddenly enveloped by a fog so dense you could barely see the end of the boat. Ghostly tentacles swirled around and obscured our masthead light from view. Within seconds, we were in pea-soup fog, still close to the shipping lanes, but now completely blind.

The most valuable instrument on our boat at that moment was the radar. All night we groped our way through the fog, looking for green blips on the radar screen, of which there were many. No matter how close they were, how much we strained our eyes, we never saw them.

The fog lasted for thirty-six hours, only dissipating completely days later when we were well offshore. But now a new challenge arrived in the form of the west winds we had been dreading. Soon, we were motoring into an increasingly strong wind and waves that began slapping us and showering *Northern Magic* with salty spray. We endured a whole day of pounding, and the lurching motion brought me – but only me, thank goodness – to my knees with retching. My body had learned to adapt to a lot of conditions on this trip, but motoring into the wind was not one of them. Eventually, it began to calm down, however, and on the third day of the passage the wind died away almost altogether, leaving us motoring in relative peace, glad to be away from land, that devilish wind, and the claustrophobic fog.

One day passed, then two days, three, and it became calmer and calmer. On Day Five of our passage we were treated to a North Atlantic that was as peaceful as a giant lake. We had not a breath of wind. Not even the tiniest ripples marred the glassy surface of the water. It was only the third time on the entire trip that we had seen an ocean so placid. Overhead, the blue sky was marked with the contrails of many jets, passing swiftly overhead on their way to Paris, Amsterdam, and London, while we churned slowly through the water below, invisible and unknown. In a matter of hours, they'd have crossed the Atlantic, something that would take us at least three weeks of non-stop sailing to do. By suppertime, those passengers would be eating in fancy restaurants on the Champs d'Élysées, while we'd still be on our small bobbing speck of a boat, scanning an empty horizon, wondering how long it would take before we'd see land again.

The monotony was relieved by a whale surfacing just a few metres away. It was a humpback, longer than *Northern Magic*, with a broad, glistening black back. We all got excitedly on deck and noticed that periodically we could see what looked like puffs of grey smoke on the horizon. Two of these puffs would appear simultaneously, sometimes three, as if from a steamship. *Thar she blows!* All day long, three whales kept pace with us, moving just slightly faster than we were. Our whale book showed us to be in the middle of the humpback migration route.

Most days we saw a ship or two, and twice during the middle part of the passage we had to take evasive action to avoid a collision. Once it was a sailboat travelling the other way that hadn't shown up on radar until we were almost upon it. Herbert changed course, and as we passed at uncomfortably close range, he couldn't detect any evidence that anyone in the other boat was keeping watch at all. If we had been a big ship relying mostly on radar, that little sailboat would simply have disappeared into the deep.

Tiny wavelets began ruffling the water's surface, like a ripple chip. The wind was picking up, right on the nose. We adjusted course a bit and managed to motorsail at an angle just sufficient to keep the mainsail filled. We were still reliant on our motor to keep us moving forward. This way we could continue ploughing steadily ahead, logging about 140 miles every twenty-four hours.

Over the next two days, the wind continued to build. The puffy white popcorn clouds were consumed by an evil-looking, amorphous grey mass. Our barometer began to drop. Dad, in his e-mails from Northern Magic Weather Forecasting Central, warned of a low front approaching that would bring even-stronger west winds with it. It now became a race to make it to the Azores before the front made it to us.

Bam! Bam! Bam! We slammed endlessly into the waves. Mostly, our bow parted them, and they peeled away to the sides like an extravagant moustache. But from time to time, our bow became buried in a particularly large wave, or one that we entered at a bad angle after see-sawing down into it from the wave before, and we'd be temporarily submerged in water. Christopher's hatch began letting in water. Soon, everything in his cabin – mattress, sheets, blankets, books, toys, all his clothes – was damp. Within a day, the boat began smelling of mildew.

We still had 350 miles to go to our destination, the island of Faial in the Azores. As the wind picked up, we had to keep revising our confident earlier predictions of our day and time of arrival. Gradually, we began to discuss ending our voyage prematurely, at the island of São Miguel, about 150 miles closer.

It became impossible to eat or sleep. Herbert and the boys lived off small munchable junk foods after my chili dinner, painfully reheated at great personal cost, remained mostly uneaten. My stomach decided to evacuate itself no matter what I attempted to put into it. The lurching motion caused a small African mask mounted on Jonathan's wall to fly right across the cabin. Michael's bunk, directly under the hatch used by the person on watch, got soaked, as did the person on watch. Our hair was constantly wet, thick with salt, and plastered against our heads. It began to rain, forcing more salty water down the backs of our necks. It was pure misery.

After receiving an e-mail from Dad that the weather was going to get even worse, it took us all of five seconds to decide to head for São Miguel, even though it meant a southerly detour of twenty or thirty miles. Not long after we adjusted course, the wind switched to the southwest as well so it could continue to blast directly against us.

Focused as we were on wind, waves, water, and fatigue, we were completely unprepared for the jewel-like beauty of São Miguel. When it finally, slowly emerged from the low-lying clouds, it revealed itself to be a tall volcanic island completely draped in emerald green. Every surface of the bold, upward-thrusting shoreline was draped in this soft, living green velvet cloth. It looked like paradise. It was as welcome to our eyes as a cool spring in the desert. A giant outcrop guarded the tiny harbour, looking like the paws and haunches of a headless Sphinx, loosely draped in a luxurious mantle of green. Hundreds of circling, plunging, gluttonous boobies greeted us from the air, while in the water, dozens of skipping dolphins did the same.

We entered the harbour, which was surrounded by towering rock cliffs with an old windmill at the very top. Fishermen had pulled ashore their small wooden boats and were cleaning their nets while young boys jumped from boulders and splashed in the water. A sprinkling of tidy white houses was visible at the top of the cliff. But we didn't need all this superfluous beauty. The simple prospect of a calm anchorage, a hot meal, and a good night's rest was all the paradise we required.

After a meal, our first in thirty hours, we collapsed into bed, looking forward to a good sleep at last after seven nights at sea. The boobies and seagulls, returning to their crevices in the cliffside for the night, made a cacophony of squawks all night long. But at least we were safe from the battering waves. Safe, that is, as long as the wind didn't shift to the north, because our tiny harbour was totally unprotected from that direction. Of course, overnight, that's exactly what it did.

By the middle of the night, a large swell was rolling into the harbour, tossing us around mercilessly. "I had a terrible sleep," said a bleary-eyed Michael as he staggered out of bed before dawn. "It was worse than being on the ocean."

As much as we hated to face the sea again, the direction of the wind left us no choice but to leave. We cast off at 6:00 a.m. to motor thirty-five miles around the southern tip of the island to the town of Ponta Delgada.

+

Ponta Delgada was a tidy collection of white buildings, whose red tile roofs contrasted pleasingly with the vibrant green of the surrounding fields. São Miguel was certainly one of the three most beautiful islands we visited on our entire trip. Most of these volcanic mounds had long since been tamed by humans, and had been turned into lush pastures separated by dark green hedges. The whole effect was spectacular. The many natural domes around Ponta Delgada had a distinctly mammarian shape, as if you really were looking at the living body of Mother Earth herself.

The next day a man with the extravagant name of Felipe Le Velly de Sousa Lima arrived at the dock. He was a slim, articulate, casually dressed, native Azorean whose family controlled many of the island's businesses: grocery stores, a vegetable oil factory, a chicken farm, hotels. He was also the honorary Canadian consul, whose office on a quaint cobblestone street we'd already noticed because of its billowing Canadian flag. He worked there every day, helping travelling Canadians with their problems.

Felipe had been alerted to our arrival by our ally, Paul Dole, who had introduced us to Captain George. Friendly, voluble Felipe and his beautiful wife, Ana, whisked us away and brought us to the top of one of the huge volcanoes, Sete Cidades, that dominates the island. They wanted to show us two famous lakes inside the caldera. The lakes, although side by side, are different colours – one blue and one green – because of the way they reflect the light of the sky and the surrounding vegetation.

On the way down through a cloud to the inside of the crater, Felipe told us the legend of why the two lakes have different colours. A grieving princess, he explained, had been exiled to the top of the mountain by her father the king, because of a forbidden love. This princess had one blue eye and one green, and as she cried, her tears transformed the lakes into different colours.

We emerged from the mist and stopped by the shore of Green Lake. From one angle it looked quite green, but from another the water plants around its edge and the dark sunless sky overhead made it look yellowish, even brown.

"I wonder," Michael whispered into my ear, "what did the princess do to make the lake turn yellow and brown?"

Felipe stopped at the end of Blue Lake, where the air filled our lungs with the invigorating scent of living green. Flowering hydrangeas, azaleas, lilies, Norfolk pines, maple trees, a carpet of grass, and small flowering plants – everything was bursting into life, lush and verdant. It could have been the Garden of Eden. We were blown away.

"Can't you see why I love this island?" murmured Felipe, his arms opened wide.

✦

As usual, we were monitoring the weather carefully. One day Dad alerted us to a small, two-day window, just big enough to jump to a more westerly island. We grabbed the chance and motor-sailed the 140 miles to the island of Faial in twenty hours. As we arrived, we were greeted by fifty or more dolphins who leapt for joy and came rushing at us from all directions. In dolphin language, they were shouting, "They're here! They're here!" They took turns riding along beside us, leaping in our bow wave, five and ten at a time. A quarter-mile away we spotted the spouting of sperm whales, followed by four whale-spotting tour boats.

The pavement of the quay at Horta was covered with creative paintings made by yachts that had stopped before us. We had wanted to make our own, but we didn't get the chance. Within two days of our arrival, the weather charts suggested another opportunity to go, this time all the way to Canada.

We were eager, very eager, to get going. That's not to say we weren't nervous about this, our last long passage across the Atlantic. We were mightily nervous. But there comes a point when you're so tired about dreading something that you just want to get it over with.

We were attempting a very unusual route west across the North Atlantic. The definitive book for sailboats crossing the Atlantic said only something like, "It is rare for boats to travel west to the northern U.S., but not unheard of." It didn't even mention the possibility of a passage to Newfoundland, which we were contemplating. Our route, although shorter, was against the prevailing winds as well as the strong Gulf Stream current, and went through an area notorious for weather, fog, and often icebergs. Yet we felt this was the only choice for us; it would take us a whole extra year to get home on the traditional southerly route. Somehow, we were going to have to drag ourselves across the North Atlantic, by willpower alone if need be.

And so we headed out, feeling a strange combination of anxiety and excitement, eager to get the 1,280-mile passage over with. It was a relief to finally be facing our fears. Every mile, we kept telling ourselves, was one mile we wouldn't have to do ever again.

During the afternoon of the next day, we saw Flores and its neighbour island of Corvo, which had a flying saucer of cloud over its volcano. The wind was picking up as we pushed along, hitting us at twenty knots. We began getting slammed by steep seas two and three metres high, topped with frothy whitecaps. The large swell suggested even stronger winds ahead. We lay in our bunks and counted out the miles. When that became too slow, we began counting out the minutes.

I told the others it was like having a baby: hard at the time, but later the pain would be forgotten. I began singing the old Helen Reddy song, "I am Woman." This probably had the opposite of its intended effect on the rest of the crew. "I don't wanna have a baby!" Herbert lamented.

Our engine hissed and bubbled and began to overheat. For the moment, we just turned it off and left it, because it was hopeless trying to motor into that strong a wind anyway. On a northerly tack at a forty-five-degree angle to the wind, our speed dropped dramatically, down to four, three, sometimes even two, knots. The motion at the bow of the boat, rearing up into the air at the crest of a wave and then plunging down with a mighty thud into its trough, was horrendous. We all competed for space in the aft cabins, where the motion was the least. Christopher wedged himself beside me into Michael's tiny bunk, a space barely wider than my shoulders, where we snuggled together and sang songs.

We slowly hobby-horsed past Corvo as the sun started to fall. Both Herbert and I privately wondered if we were stupid not to be stopping there in the face of the rising wind. But we just wanted to go home. Every mile was bringing us closer . . . every mile was bringing us closer . . .

Herbert was steeling himself for the horrendous job of coaxing our engine back into life. He, like the rest of us, was queasy and weak, but he now had to hang head-down in the stinky fuel-smelling engine room to try to find out why we were overheating. Half a day earlier, he'd already had to replace a failing cooling-water pump, which in the process of spraying seawater all over the engine room had also temporarily disabled the charging system. This repair had exacted a terrible price on our poor captain's stomach and made it even tougher for him to begin anew. Every time he sat up, he emitted huge belchy sounds that in happier times might have encouraged Michael to respond with an indignant "Is that a challenge?" But no one dared engage in any belching contests right now.

Three times over the next day and a half, Herbert attempted to fix the overheating problem. Each time, he came up from the engine room trembling and greener than the time before. Finally, he had no choice but to rest.

By the middle of the night, we had winds against us of up to thirty knots. In one particularly bad lurch, our bathroom vanity mirror, fixed permanently to the wall, crashed down and shattered against the sink just inches from my head as I was on the toilet. We were barely making one knot of westerly progress, two kilometres per hour. At this rate, it would take us forty-three days to get to Newfoundland and we would run out of fuel.

The next morning, with Herbert sicker than ever, the motor still not fixed, the wind still blasting the tops off the whitecaps, we got another e-mail. "New low advancing with heavy thunderstorms," it read, ominously. "Suggest Flores for R&R, fuel and better weather."

We knew Dad wouldn't have suggested turning around for nothing. In a day and a half of tough sailing, we'd advanced only fifty miles beyond Flores Island. Still, it was painful to admit defeat. We had struggled so hard for those miles, it broke our hearts to give them back up. We had never abandoned a passage before. But we did it now.

We arrived back at Flores Island almost two days after we had first passed it.

+

Refuelled with the first good food and sleep we'd had in three days, we set out to explore the town of Santa Cruz. It was small but very pretty, with cobblestone streets, narrow sidewalks, attractive white houses with red tile roofs, all perched on the cliff side overlooking the ocean, with cultivated green hills behind. Flamboyant lilies, azaleas, and hydrangeas bloomed everywhere. *Northern Magic* was snugly moored in a tiny rock-bound harbour barely larger than she was.

Every day we walked to the Internet café, and every day we left it stressed by what we had seen on the weather charts. The entire North Atlantic, from Newfoundland to the Azores, was convulsed in a series of gales. At least we could congratulate ourselves on having made the difficult but correct decision to turn around

During our period of enforced waiting, we developed a new strategy for getting to Canada. Instead of trying to buck the prevailing winds on the direct route to Newfoundland, as we had on our first attempt, this time we'd head south on a much longer, indirect path. This would give us a chance at better winds. We would cross the Atlantic a few hundred miles south of our original route, make as much westing as we could while those wild northwesterlies raged farther north. We'd head north to Canada only at the last minute. With this new strategy, landing in Newfoundland was no longer the obvious choice. Coming from our southerly path, Nova Scotia was a possibility as well. While underway, the wind would make the choice for us.

Soon the first gale swept over us, knocking us around in our tiny harbour. Luckily, Herbert had reinforced the lines holding us off the rocks, so we were restrained by a spiderlike web of criss-crossing lines, like Gulliver tied down by the Lilliputians.

We were still tossing, two days later, when an even worse storm hit. Wind bullets of fifty knots or more shot down the mountainside, making *Northern Magic* shudder in a way she had done only once or twice before. Rain drove at us horizontally from the hillside. We were now not only bucking fiercely, but rolling as well. The motion inside the harbour was worse than on many ocean passages. I hated to think what it was like in the open ocean beyond the protection of the island. We could so easily have been out there, instead.

Worst of all was the shrieking of the wind. That unholy sound – the sound of death, of evil spirits, of people being torn limb from limb – just about made me go crazy. With the shuddering, the bucking, the rolling, the slamming of our halyards against our masts, the fear that if our lines broke we'd be cast upon the rocks that hemmed us in on all sides, it was impossible to sleep, or even close our eyes. At one point in the middle of the night, I thought I just couldn't stand it another minute. I jumped out of bed and paced around the boat like a tiger imprisoned in a cage. I did sit-ups, tried some deep knee bends, stared outside. I prayed for that evil wind and its insane shrieking to stop. I prayed for our lines to hold. I prayed for just a few hours of rest. I prayed to be safe and sound back at home.

By morning the storm was passed, and the sky was blue and friendly again.

The next day, the thought hit us like a lightning bolt. Perhaps we, ourselves, were accountable for this spell of foul weather. The wind gods always demand their due, and we had not paid it. We'd ignored the long-time sailors' tradition in Horta by leaving without painting a picture on the harbour pavement. Until we paid homage in this way, we'd surely be doomed to stay.

We started on our painting project immediately. We decided two murals on the harbour wall would be even better than one. Herbert painted a black square with a picture of *Northern Magic* similar to one he'd painted in Cuba three and a half years earlier. The boys and I painted a map of the world, showing the path of our voyage. The line we had completed was so long compared to the tiny dotted line that still remained. How close and yet how far Canada seemed!

Our homage thus paid to the fickle and jealous wind gods, we waited for the gales to ease so we could at last begin our final voyage home.

On our final night before facing the ocean once more, yet another gale swept through. This time we slept more securely, figuring that if our web of lines had protected us from the last two storms, we would be safe this time. We shouldn't have been so complacent. Morning's light revealed that the main rope holding us in place on the breakwater, a thick anchor rode, had parted. One of our brand new fenders had also chafed through its line and was now on its way to Ireland.

At least, we said, our spare anchor rode was still holding us in place. Herbert stood at the bow and raised the anchor while I prepared to pilot us out of the narrow rock opening to the harbour. With that windward shoreline having parted in the night, all our safety had been resting on that anchor. But when he pulled it up, he blanched in horror: only a single strand of its heavy rope was still intact. The rest had chafed away overnight. The next big blow would have snapped the line entirely. Heaving sighs of relief at having survived this close call, we were at last on our way.

+

Duly placated by our wall art, the wind gods rewarded us by providing the nicest weather we'd seen in a month. We travelled southwest under the benevolent protection of a lovely high-pressure system that obliged us by mirroring our path. With our thousand-litre fuel tank and extra jerry cans of fuel, we happily motored along for four days in mostly calm seas. Our strategy was working. Each easy mile west was a gift.

On our fifth day at sea, the high was beginning to depart. Now the southwesterlies began to set in. It was getting to be tougher slogging.

On our sixth day at sea, we passed the halfway point of our journey.

We were motor-sailing closehauled into the wind, bucking into increasingly nasty waves. The motion on the boat was beginning to clench up in our guts, making eating and sleeping difficult. My legs were feeling trembly and weak. The halfway point had seemed to take forever to come, and Canada was still seven hundred long miles away. We couldn't help but consider that things were only likely to get worse from here.

We had been sailing southwest, and were now more than a hundred miles south of the latitude at which we had started. Although Canada was six hundred miles to the north and west of us, we didn't want to head north too soon. That was where the fierce weather usually was, and we also wanted to save our northing in case the southwesterly winds became too strong to allow us to continue straight west. This took a lot of faith and self-discipline that our strategy was correct, because it increased the distance we had to travel by many hundreds of miles.

Dad began warning about a front coming, high winds and rain that we'd have to force our way though. Then he sent a strange e-mail. It looked as if the front was splitting in two, he said, and we just might squeak through between the two parts. Sure enough, just an hour or two later, I saw a big dark arc in the sky – rain and bad weather ahead of us on both sides, with a little bit of clear sky in the middle. Somehow we were able to sail through that arc, right into the patch of sunny blue sky ahead. My mom had established a praying circle among her friends, and it seemed then as if we really were the beneficiaries of divine intervention.

By July 8, Michael's fifteenth birthday, Dad's e-mailed weather forecasts were again making us nervous. A front was on its way, bringing strong winds of twenty-seven knots and twelve-foot seas. I had only enough time to bake a batch of Aunt Linda's Excellent Oatmeal Chocolate Chip Cookies and stick a candle in one of them for a rather pitiful celebration before the waves picked up and made our lives miserable. It was the best we could do.

As the day went on, the waves became steeper and closer together, slapping us from two angles. Those chocolate chip cookies were virtually all we ate that day. Overnight the wind picked up more, until we were getting the howling winds Dad had predicted. "Well, at least we'll have a nice fast sail," I consoled myself.

The morning of July 9 broke, and the grey ocean stretching end-lessly around us was fierce and ugly. The night before, Herbert had double-reefed the mainsail in expectation of the strong winds to come. It was good that he did. The wind was now hitting us at close to thirty knots, with steep waves rearing up and smacking us around, making the boat shudder and veer. Our stalwart TMQ autopilot, which had served us so faithfully since Australia, muscled us back on course, even though our steering wheel was groaning with each swing. Waves were breaking over the boat, drenching the decks and the cockpit. The windows on the lee side were submerged each time an especially large wave tipped us sharply and then overran us. The wooden grates on the floor of the cockpit floated up as the cockpit filled with deluge after deluge. The lashings and grommets holding our weathercloths gave way under the vicious onslaught of rushing waves, leaving the lee side cloth flapping.

The three- to four-metre seas were not only unusually steep and close, they were also coming from two different directions. Every now and then two opposing waves would meet to form one large triangular wave that would violently bash into us. We were living inside a piñata, swinging wildly around in the branches of a wind-whipped tree. Every now and then a cruel and malicious boy would come by with a baseball bat and take a whack at us. Mostly we just braced ourselves lying in our beds. But when we managed to move our nauseated bodies around, it was a pathetic little shuffle – three baby steps forward, using two hand-holds all the time, pausing while the next wave reared up under us and tipped us sharply to the side, then three more little baby steps before the next wave hit. And if we got bashed by that giant baseball bat in the meantime – well, we just clung on for dear life.

But what was worse than everything else – the shrieking of the wind, the deluge of waves, the slamming and jarring – was the fact that for all our suffering, and with all that wind, we were still getting nowhere. As the morning progressed, our speed was inexplicably but steadily declin-ing. From six to five, to four, to three, finally to two, and even, some-times, to one and a half nautical miles per hour. What was going on? From inside the boat, *Northern Magic* was vibrating with speed. Her sails were taut. It felt and sounded like we were on a freight train racing out of control. Yet the GPS proved we had slowed down to a crawl. Why were we not ticking down the miles?

I clambered outside and discovered that our knotmeter showed that we were indeed speeding along at between seven and eight knots through the water. We had entered the Gulf Stream, that powerful current of warm water that speeds along the eastern coast of North America and then veers eastward towards Europe. The current was stopping us dead.

Now our engine began overheating. Every time we tried to turn it on to charge our batteries, we'd have to turn it off after only a few minutes. The breaking waves were forcing air into our seawater intake and stopping the flow of cooling water. When Herbert had to descend into the engine room, he came up vomiting. Trying to make the motion easier while Herbert worked to solve the problem, I tried temporarily turning the boat north so that we would have a following wind and take the waves and swell on our stern. The motion was much better, and we instantly doubled our speed over the ground to a hardly impressive, but much improved, three knots.

Up until then, we'd been heading for the Nova Scotia town of Canso. It was farther than Newfoundland, but the weather promised to be more reliable there. But as we turned north, with Newfoundland almost directly over us, Herbert and I had a serious discussion about whether we should abandon Canso and head for Newfoundland instead. That way we'd be able to stay on this more comfortable course.

I e-mailed Dad, hopefully asking what the weather was like in that notorious stretch ahead of us, towards the Grand Banks. I was praying he'd say that this was a great idea. But his return e-mail destroyed all my hopes. No, he said, if we sailed north we'd just sail along the front that was causing the unsettled weather and strong winds rather than cutting across it. Better to stick to our original plan. The wind was forecast to be even worse the next morning; we had to stay strong for two more days.

Two more days of this? At that moment it seemed hopeless. I lost it. I stuck my head out of the hatch, turned my salty face into that terrible wind, and wept tears of misery. I didn't want the boys to see me cry. The wind whipped the tears across my cheeks, and the spray added some briny splashes of its own. I just couldn't keep my spirits up any longer. It felt like we'd been at sea forever and were doomed never to arrive.

The instant I came down from that hatch, I vomited. I hadn't been sick before, although my empty stomach had been tightly knotted. I realized then that the cramping in my stomach was simply my self-control willing the seasickness away. The instant I had lost it, even for a moment, the nausea took over. After I finished, I promised myself I would not – could not – lose my composure again.

Night fell and the wind howled even louder. We had gone eighteen hours now without a meal. We continued screaming along at high speed through the water and going almost nowhere. At that speed, you feel tense and frantic, as if something is about to break. We ought to have been covering 170 miles a day, which would have made up for all our suffering. Instead, we were only twenty or so miles ahead of our position in the morning. Our bodies felt bruised and tender from too much lying down. Our ears ached from being whammed into the pillow with each downward thump.

Then another e-mail came from Dad. "Good news! They just updated the forecast, and if you head straight north, the wind will drop to ten knots tomorrow. And then, the day after, east winds. Yes! EAST WINDS! Then you can turn the corner and head straight for Canso."

I didn't even wake Herbert up to consult with him; I just headed starboard forty degrees. Instantly, the motion improved. An indication of how powerful the current was, however, was the fact that although we were trying to head straight north, I had to point our bow northwest in order not to go east. That east-bound current was sweeping us along so strongly our bow was pointed a full forty-five degrees to the west of our actual course. We were basically sailing sideways.

By mid-morning, just as Dad had promised, the wind began to drop. The knots in our stomachs loosened at bit. By noon, our appetites had returned. We even began to smile again. And just as suddenly as it had come, as if by magic, the current disappeared as well. Three knots, four, five, soon we were sailing happily along at a wonderful seven knots of speed. We were going home!

We kept our bow pointed northwest, heading once again for Canso, Nova Scotia. "I think I Canso, I think I Canso," e-mailed Dad. "Yes we Canso!" I e-mailed back. On July 10, our tenth day at sea, we were sailing fast and true on our correct course. But nature had more tricks in store.

"I think the wind's going to take one last kick at you," said Dad's next e-mail. We took out a blank map of the North Atlantic and began pencilling in the lows and fronts described on our Inmarsat weather forecast. As I graphed it onto the page, my jaw dropped with horror.

There were two new lows ahead of us, one slightly to the north, one to the south, both moving in our direction. I sketched out the position of the two lows and the jaggedy evil cold front ahead of them, spanning a full two thousand miles of ocean and kicking up a froth of wind and waves. The front was just ahead. To the north: twenty to thirty knots of wind, eight- to thirteen-foot seas. To the south: thirty to thirty-five knots of wind, eleven- to nineteen-foot seas. We were right in the middle, where my sketched semi-circles collided. By all rights, we should have had at least twenty-five knots of wind.

Instead we had – dead calm.

"How could it be?" we asked ourselves. According to the coordinates, we should be in a near gale. All we could figure was that we were behind the front and right between the two lows. If Dad hadn't told us to turn north, we would have been in the middle of a North Atlantic gale. Instead, we seemed to be sneaking through the goalposts.

"This isn't a window we're sailing through," Herbert muttered uneasily, "this is a crack."

Our stomachs contorted again with anxiety. Herbert turned up the motor, thrusting us forward at seven knots. We were now only three hundred miles from Nova Scotia. That we'd outraced the bad weather was just too good to be true. We didn't dare count on it. That front might still hit us any time.

July 11 dawned, but we never saw the sun. Where the sun should have been, there was only an indistinct glow. A thick grey fog draped the ocean like a fuzzy blanket. It was so dense you could see it wafting through the cockpit a few metres away. When you stuck your head out into it, the fog left droplets of condensation, like a gentle rain, on your face. The entire boat began sweating humidity. All our clothing and bedding felt damp. Outside, we couldn't see a thing. We navigated solely by radar.

That day's weather forecast was even more frightening than that of the day before. A brand-new front was right ahead of us. A new, deeper low was coming fast. The "x" showing our present position was plotted within a big rectangle containing thirty to forty knots of wind – a full gale – and seas of eleven to sixteen feet. For hundreds of miles north and east, thirty knots. For hundreds of miles south and east, twenty-five to thirty-five knots. The North Atlantic around us for a thousand miles was a maelstrom.

Astonishingly, unbelievably, impossibly, we were still motoring through a dead calm.

We were riding up and down a glassy, oily swell that increased rapidly in size as the morning went on. The three- and four-metre swell was ample proof that there were strong winds raging behind us not far away. But we continued motoring along in the fog, up and down, up and down those glassy hills of rolling water, with not a breath of wind. "I think all those people who are praying for us really are making a difference," said Herbert reverently. "How else can you explain this?"

We didn't know whether this ominous, oily, fog-shrouded calm was a sign of our deliverance or simply the calm before the storm. It was unnerving. We were now heading over the shallow banks off Nova Scotia only 150 miles from land, practically close enough to smell it. According to the weather chart, the front was still ahead of us. We held our breaths, awaiting any sign of stormy weather, waiting for the shoe to drop.

But the wind we dreaded and feared and fretted over and prayed about never came.

The next morning, the fog lifted briefly, just long enough for us to catch a glimpse of the Nova Scotia shore, now only five miles away. After that enticing glimpse, the fog returned to smother us again just as quickly as it had lifted.

The last few miles were the most dangerous part of our approach. The shoreline around Canso was littered with small islands and rocky reefs. Plenty of ships had foundered there within sight of shore. We didn't want to be one of them, but just when we needed maximum visibility, there we were, once again blundering sightlessly in the middle of a thick, claustrophobic cloud.

We'd been told by radio that there was a boat containing an *Ottawa Citizen* reporter and photographer waiting for us near the lighthouse. But the closer we got to shore, the deeper the fog became, until there was nothing – no lighthouse, no boat, absolutely nothing – to be seen. We were unnerved first to hear, and then finally to see, a breaking reef just off our starboard side.

"I see a dot on the radar three-quarters of a mile ahead of us," called out Herbert in a voice of alarm. He was sitting in the navigation station, plotting our position on the computer screen, watching the GPS and the radar. "I don't know whether it's the lighthouse, a rock, or that boat. We'd better slow down."

We all got into battle stations. I moved to the bow of the boat, armed with a horn, trying to see ahead. Herbert stayed down below at the all-important radar. Michael stood at the wheel. Jonathan ran back and forth amidships to help me watch and to relay instructions.

I peered myopically into the fog. "Whatever it is, it's now half a mile away," yelled Herbert. Jonathan stood beside me and cocked his ears like an attentive German Shepherd. There was a roaring sound like a train, or a helicopter. "I think it's waves," he said. He was right.

Jon ran back to relay the troubling news. Breaking waves was bad news: another reef close enough to hear. Too close. The fog thinned a bit, and in a minute we could see it: a disturbing line of foamy white water, this time to port. Reefs on either side of us. Our bodies were tense. We were only a mile away from shore, but between us and safety it was an invisible rocky obstacle course.

Suddenly Jon shouted, "There's the boat!" We had almost passed each other in the fog. Soon the familiar face of Wayne Cuddington, the same photographer who had been there for our departure, was smiling up at us. A few minutes later the fog cleared. And there before us was Canada.

It was July 12, 2001: twenty-five years to the day since Herbert and I had met each other at the Calgary Stampede. It was twelve days since we had left the Azores. And it was three years and ten months since we had set out from Ottawa in a boat we had never sailed, filled with hopes and dreams. My throat grew tight while tears rolled down my cheeks. We were home.

The Best Maple Doughnut Ever

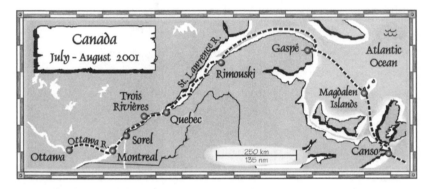

*H*ands waving. People smiling. Cameras pointing. Joy. Relief. Tears. A beautiful little church and steeple beckon from the crown of a grassy hill. Nova Scotia! Canada! Home! A second boat is arriving to escort us in. We've done it! We have really done it! Kleenex – need more Kleenex. All the boys out on deck, eating cheesies and chips. Fenders in place! Lines ready! We follow the boats in.

Competent hands take our lines, secure us to the dock. Northern Magic gently comes to rest, in Canada again at last. Michael springs off the boat, running to kiss the ground. Jon and I follow, doing the same. A small stone, a piece of Canada, actually sticks briefly to my lips. Then I notice: grass! The smell of freshly cut grass! It's the smell of summer, summer in Canada.

We take a walk. Like young colts we kick up our heels in the soft, sweet-smelling grass. It's the best, the greenest, the most fragrant grass ever. "Can I roll down the hill, Mom?" asks Jon. Christopher is jumping *up and down, skipping and leaping like an impala, saying over and over, "I'm supercharged!"*

Oh, look – a convenience store! We make a beeline for it. It's only a small corner store, but better than what passes for a supermarket in most of the countries we've seen. Oh joy! Look! Bits 'n Bites! Caramilk bars! Fudgee-Os! Oh – Cherry Blossoms! I haven't given a single thought to Cherry Blossom chocolates for four years, but the minute I see those familiar little square yellow boxes, containing a miniature volcano oozing thick cherry syrup, I absolutely must have one, can't wait another minute. Bliss!

Jonathan and I discover a wonderful nature trail through a swamp and find that it's an exotic wonderland. Perfectly formed balsam trees with fresh green branch-tips. Glossy yellow buttercups, looking good enough to eat. Maple trees, actual maple trees. Cheeky red squirrels, chittering and chattering to us from the treetops. Cattails. A bubbling, burbling stream. Oh, look at the chickadee! And a robin! Oh, a loon, a loon! All of these things familiar yet strangely exotic. All of them Canada.

Friendly people. People who look just like us, who watch the same TV shows, laugh at the same jokes. We no longer stand out. The bank machines work. The grocery store aisles are unbelievably wide and open and clean and well stocked. Oh – blueberries! Beef-a-roni! Eggo waffles! Butter tarts! The check-out girls smile! A young man is actually bagging our groceries for us and wheeling our cart outside. This is efficiency! This is great!

For breakfast we eat Eggo waffles with real Aunt Jemima Syrup. The best Eggos ever. We drive to a Walmart! It's the best Walmart ever! Cherry Blossom chocolates, four to a pack! And they have Wheat Thins, and Breton Crackers, and Cheez Whiz and . . . and . . .

We find a payphone and make a call. Miracle! The phone works! Hey, there's even a telephone book. This is the best payphone ever!

We find a Tim Hortons. Christopher chooses a chocolate-covered doughnut, something he's had before but has no memory of. I savour the best, absolutely the best maple-flavoured doughnut I've ever had.

Isn't this country great?

$+$

We had now left all three of the world's great oceans in our wake. Soon the rising and falling of the restless surface of the sea, our constant companion over the past four years, would be only a dim memory. We said our goodbyes to the Atlantic with a mixture of nostalgia and satisfaction. Then we turned our eyes ahead, to the St. Lawrence, the great river that would take us almost all the rest of the way home.

The mouth of the St. Lawrence was a wonderland of sealife. Funny, curious seals, harbour porpoises, herring gulls, graceful, long-winged gannets, stubby little dovekies, long-necked black cormorants, all diving from the air or from the water and coming up with fish. Often they bobbed on the water in contented little groups, taking off in flight only at the last minute, just as we were upon them, their webbed feet churning hard on top of the water as they approached lift-off.

But we reserved our greatest enthusiasm for the whales. Fin whales, minke whales, smiling white beluga whales by the dozen, we loved them all. We could see the fin whales spouting from far away, their blows reaching up into the sky in a tall, long-lasting plume of what looked like white smoke. At first we all craned our necks and shouted with excitement when some far away black shape emerged out of the water like a giant floating rock. Soon, however, these sightings became so commonplace we would pay attention only if the whale surfaced right by our boat. We saw more whales in one day on the St. Lawrence than we'd seen on the entire circumnavigation.

The sky was blue, a warm breeze ruffled our hair, and we were all exclaiming in delight and rushing from one part of the deck to another as various seals and whales made their appearances. For months, we had found it so hard not to think about getting back home. It had been almost a year since we had left Kenya, and since then we'd been travelling hard, mostly against hostile seas and contrary winds. Long gone were those peaceful days in the South Pacific when the wind was always at our backs and we never had to check a weather report. While crossing the Atlantic, we had actually posted a picture of our house on a bulletin board in our salon, to inspire us and remind us what of was waiting for us, just ahead.

But here, surrounded by nature at her most bountiful, I was thinking not about what was at home, but about the things we were soon to lose.

Here on our little boat we had found adventure, new experiences, a better understanding of the world and our place in it, closeness as a family, personal growth, warm friendships, and the chance to appreciate the wonder of our glorious Earth. Somehow, on this trip, we found the freedom to reinvent ourselves, to laugh more, to become more the people we would like to be.

As much as I looked forward to the comforts of home, it was hard, and more than a little scary, to give this up. Watching the whales swimming free in the St. Lawrence River, all of a sudden I was jealous of them. I realized, with more than a touch of sadness, that our own golden days of freedom were rapidly coming to an end.

+

We continued pressing onwards, forty or fifty miles each day, timing our trips to coincide with the rising tide. As we approached the spot at Sorel where the Richelieu River branched off the St. Lawrence, where we had turned off towards New York four years before, another great swell of emotion filled my throat. This constant crying of mine was getting tiresome. But I had good reason: this was it. Even though it was not the end of our trip, this was the end of our circumnavigation.

We had always had faith that we would circle the globe, no matter what. And here we were, at a simple river branching off another – and for us it was the culmination of a dream, a dream so powerful it had let nothing stand in our way. As Herbert led a countdown to the moment when we would cross our path, I couldn't help but think back over the crazy year of preparation in which we had cast aside our land life and begun turning ourselves into sailors, with no experience, nothing but a grand vision to sustain us. I thought of the storms in the Pacific, the waterspout in Indonesia, the endless mechanical failures, of seventeen days of fearful sailing through pirate-filled waters off Somalia, the misery of sickness in Sudan, of fighting our way across the North Atlantic. I thought of the endless days at sea we'd spent, pushing, pushing, pushing always westward. We'd had far more wonderful experiences on our trip than bad ones – but at that moment, all I could think of were the struggles we'd overcome to reach this milestone. Now, no matter what happened to us in future, this achievement could never be taken away. We were circumnavigators.

The next day we continued on to Montreal with the flags of all thirty-four countries we had visited waving proudly from our rigging. We had worked hard for every one of those flags: thirty-four countries, twenty-two languages, one by one we had sailed through the world's time zones until now we were back where we started. Every time a ship passed us, someone in the pilothouse would scrutinize us with binoculars. Then, invariably, a small uniformed figure would appear on the upper deck and wave down at us. The captains of these mighty ships understood exactly what those flags meant. Rarely had our insignificant presence been acknowledged by one of these floating behemoths, but now our own captain stood proudly at the helm as passing ships saluted his achievement.

We stopped in Montreal, and for two days Herbert worked hard, with the help of our boys and crews from other boats, to take down our masts. They wouldn't fit under the bridges ahead. The walkways on *Northern Magic* were now filled with wooden booms, displaced bicycles, and other clutter. Two large aluminum masts and all the associated tangle of rigging now bisected our cockpit, making it very difficult to move or see. As we worked, both Herbert and I got lumps in our throat. The dismantling of our proud and beautiful ship made it only too obvious that the end of our trip was just around the corner. Even Michael, who was so enthusiastic about getting home, was saddened. "I hate *Northern Magic* this way," he complained. "She doesn't look right at all." More than once did the thought cross our minds that maybe we should just put those masts back where they belonged and turn ourselves around.

We navigated carefully through the shallow waters on the way to the lock at Ste Anne de Bellevue. A few people were waiting there to see us. We were also pleased to meet the same helpful lockmaster who had so kindly driven us to buy groceries and radio parts when we had passed through four years before. He had been only the first of hundreds of people we had met during our travels who had offered their help.

We continued to our last lock, at Carillon. There were more people, sixteen of them in fact, waiting for us with gifts at the lock as we arrived.

("There are giggling girls!" exclaimed Michael, a sly grin on his face.)

The next day we continued on. Every now and then we would notice people waving, honking, and flashing lights at us on the shore. Seeing these little welcoming committees never failed to surprise and delight us. We were slowly discovering that we had a lot more friends waiting for us to return home than we had when we left.

Yet the closer we were coming to home, the more our hearts – Herbert's and mine at least – were feeling wrenched with nostalgia over the ending of our trip. There were a hundred things about home we had missed – our waterbed always came first on the list, but also long, hot showers, the washer and dryer, our own car, TV news, Christmas Eve with friends, and big rooms you could whirl around in. There were plenty of times, especially on difficult passages, that we had practically obsessed about those missing comforts and couldn't wait to be back.

But as Christopher, my sunshine boy, came up onto the deck to snuggle in my arms, as he still did at least a dozen times a day, tears rose up in my eyes. This was happening to me with increasing frequency the closer we got to home.

It was not the loss of the adventures I was grieving, nor even the loss of our freedom to go wherever and do whatever we wanted. It was the prospect of losing the tremendous closeness we had developed as a family that seemed, in the end, to be the most bitter pill to swallow. To have had all this time together, enjoying each other's company, laughing at silly jokes, playing card games together in the evenings, holding each other when we were queasy or scared, working together, suffering together, talking about life and love under bright stars in the middle of the ocean – the loss of these simple but profound moments was what saddened me most.

Once we were home we would all begin moving our separate ways. It was good and right that we should do so; our boys were growing up. But for four precious years we had held our children close and watched them develop, selfishly enjoying them and having them all to ourselves. We had lived as fully and as well as we knew how, and had shown them, we hoped, something about the meaning of life and of love. The boys – the confident and capable young men – we were bringing back home were a source of such pride and joy to us that it was looking at them, not at the oceans and adventures and wonderful experiences receding behind us, that brought the biggest lump to my throat as we covered those last few miles.

The penultimate stop on our voyage was at the tiny town of Papineauville, Quebec, just about twenty miles from Ottawa. There was a friendly marina there with a small crane to help us put our masts back up. We wanted to arrive back home with our heads held high and flags flying.

On the last evening of our trip, Herbert, Michael, Jonathan, Christopher, and I sat together in *Northern Magic*'s tiny, crowded salon – where we had shared so many close times, so many frustrations, so many discussions, jokes, laughs, and tears. The air was charged with a strange and potent mixture of excitement, joy, pride, nervousness, and fear. Our new life was about to start, a life in which we had to invent brand-new roles for ourselves, as people, as members of a close-knit family, as public figures, and as citizens of the world.

As I prepared to go to bed, I stopped and looked at a small card on our bulletin board, a card from Dad that seemed so perfectly to sum up how we had actually managed, against all odds, to make it around the world. The card said:

NEVER

NEVER

NEVER

GIVE

UP

The next morning we left on the final twenty miles of our 35,000-mile, 1,445-day journey. Fern Beauvais, the kind marina manager who'd taken us under his wing, wept almost as much as I did as we hugged goodbye. On board with us were reporter Bev Wake and photographer Wayne Cuddington from the *Ottawa Citizen*, both of whom had by now become our friends. (Wayne was developing a bald spot on the top of his head from all the noogies the kids were giving him.) CBC-TV journalist Steve Fischer rounded out our crew, bringing with him a gourmet lunch for all. "I just knew if I didn't bring this," he said, "you wouldn't eat today at all."

As we made our way upriver, accompanied by two escort vessels from the Navy League of Canada, we began to see people, hundreds of people, lining the shores. They were honking and waving at us and holding up giant banners saying, "Welcome Home *Northern Magic.*" Even today, many months later, my eyes fill up and my throat chokes at the memory of all those beautiful hand-painted signs, held up for us so bravely as a heavy rain began to fall. Small boats began joining us, some falling away to be replaced by others, but many of them staying on and on. Soon we had a flotilla of three dozen boats following in our wake. Sailboats, motor cruisers, dinghies, and even kayaks joined us in the rain.

As we saw all these people, my eyes, already well primed and practised, filled yet again with tears. We'd been hugged and loved and protected and helped by so many people for so long, there was just no place left for all that swelling emotion to stay inside. I was not the only person on board *Northern Magic* with moist eyes.

We didn't know exactly what might have been planned for our actual arrival – Diane King, who, along with her husband, Paul Couch, had established the *Northern Magic* Web site three years before, had been working on some kind of homecoming party, but she had been evasive about the details. As the skies opened up and began to pour with rain at noon, an hour before our scheduled arrival time, I became worried the torrential rainfall would have wrecked her plans. We sped up, not knowing what might await us ahead.

Long, long before, Michael had made a vow that he was going to abandon ship and jump into the water as soon as we approached Petrie Island, where our trip had begun. Wayne Cuddington had gotten wind of this, and was determined to capture the event on film. This became a bit of a contest, because Michael was just as determined to foil Wayne's attempts to photograph him. We'd shared the plan with my father, and had told him where to wait for Michael ashore with a towel and a change of clothes. Michael had decided to dive from the boat while we were still moving. He figured Wayne wouldn't be expecting it until we were anchored.

"*Go! Go!*" Herbert said, at a moment when Wayne had his camera down.

Michael did a beautiful dive over the lifelines from the cabin top, but somehow Wayne nonetheless managed to capture it in three frames, shooting from the hip even before he pulled the camera up to his face. Virtually no one in the flotilla, or ashore, noticed Michael's small figure pulling smoothly through the water, leaving *Northern Magic* behind. It was Michael's final act of the voyage, his symbolic gesture of independence.

Meanwhile, on the highway above, there was a traffic jam as cars slowed down or stopped to watch our arrival. The air was filled with honking. But what was most amazing was what lay ahead, on the sandy banks of Petrie Island. Waiting for us – *for us!* – was a sea of people. Twenty-five hundred people were there, standing in the rain, covering the sandy beach and the hill above, pressing towards the shore to catch a glimpse of our arrival. "In your wildest fantasies, if you would dream about the perfect homecoming," I said to Steve Fischer, my face crumpling up with emotion, "it would look like this."

We anchored *Northern Magic* and, taking a deep breath, stepped into our dinghy and headed off ashore.

As we bumped up against the sandy shore of Petrie Island, a solid wall of people pressed forward. One by one, we jumped into a forest of waiting arms. Television cameras and radio microphones were pushed in front of us. People pressed in to touch us.

The instant they landed, Jonathan and Christopher were completely swallowed by the crowd. I lost sight of them. Luckily, my Mom had grabbed them and began propelling them through the cheering people to the stage. Michael had arrived from his swim ten minutes ahead of the rest of us and was already towelled dry, shaking hands and signing autographs like a real celebrity.

Now Herbert, Michael, and I began a long, slow walk I will never forget – never want to forget. In a thousand lifetimes, I could never duplicate the feeling. I'm not even capable of describing what it was like to be the recipient of a giant group hug, 2,500-people strong. As I made my way through the throng, my wad of Kleenex got larger and larger – helped by kindly ladies with tears in their own eyes, who added their spare tissues to mine. It was like a beautiful slow-motion dream. We'll still be feasting on that memory when we're ninety years old. Look at me – I'm crying again even now.

We went up on the stage, which was lined by RCMP officers in crimson red dress uniform. Hearing the national anthem just about broke me apart. Christopher stood by my side and hugged me. We were even given the flag off the top of Parliament Hill. The Hershey Factory had sent the Hershey Kissmobile, which showered us with chocolate and Gummi Bears. ("Next time you do a circumnavigation, you should tell everyone how much you love diamonds," whispered Paul Couch in my ear.)

The whole crowd sang a song to us, the story of our voyage put to the tune of *Gilligan's Island*. We were presented with a huge cake. Then we descended from the stage to meet once again the hundreds of people who wanted to speak to us. Dozens of volunteers were there, selling *Northern Magic* T-shirts and food donated by local merchants, all the proceeds going towards our special projects in Indonesia and Kenya.

Nothing in the previous four years, nothing in our lives, had prepared us for the enormity of this welcome. Our voyage might have been over, but the magic of our journey was not. In truth, a whole new adventure was just beginning.

Epilogue

"What you can do or think you can do, begin it.
For boldness has magic, power, and genius in it."
– Johann Wolfgang von Goethe

I'm sitting under a canopy of rustling pine trees on a rocky shore in Ontario's Algonquin Park, listening to the music of loons and bullfrogs. The taste of wild blueberries picked earlier in the afternoon still lingers on my tongue. We've come by canoe, our long-awaited repeat of what had always been a cherished annual family pilgrimage. We reminisced often about this very place while travelling over seas much larger than this secluded, tree-rimmed lake.

Almost a year has passed since our return home. The boys have resumed their appropriate grade levels at school, and are appreciating the comforts and privileges of Canada. They've had their fill of travelling for a while, and are just enjoying being regular kids again – although Michael does talk about backpacking to Tibet, and Jonathan anticipates a return visit to Cappadocia, and Christopher still pretends he's a gibbon. When we returned home, little Chris had no recollection whatsoever of our house – all of his life's memories had been formed on a boat.

Thanks to the trip, a few more wonderful young men have become a part of our lives, these ones halfway around the world. Every week or so we receive an e-mail from a Balinese veterinarian who's dedicated his life to the creatures of Borneo. He tells us about ambitious and worthy projects in fish farming and tree planting, helping animals and fighting logging. We continue to send funds to his group, the Friends of the National Parks, to help make a difference in their precious corner of the world. Their path, since we left, has been a difficult one. Tanjung Puting remains under siege from a variety of threats. I made a trip back to Borneo, only to discover that the situation was even more troubling than we had thought. They need help more than ever. The battle they're waging is ours, too.

We also get regular e-mails from Andrew Thuva in Kenya, who's overseeing our growing list of affairs in his country. (Andrew and his brothers, Mark and Boniface, all have *Yahoo!* e-mail accounts now, something that tickles us pink!) Andrew tells us that his neighbour and our friend, Hamisi, is busily crafting shark-tooth jewellery (we've placed a large order), and Magic the Cow has borne a calf and is producing milk.

The news from Andrew's family is also good. Boniface's father, Kitsao, has recovered well from his surgery, and Boniface has begun his second year at high school. The people who welcomed us home at Petrie Island contributed eleven thousand dollars for our projects, and donations from generous people from all over North America continue to come in. As a result, we are now supporting Boniface's brother, Katana, and twelve other students at a local high school in Kilifi. We will soon be adding to that number, and expanding our program in other ways.

We're also collecting money to permit one or more of these students, among the top scholars in their school, to attend university. One ambitious young man's dream is to become a physician. We've discovered there's no better feeling in life than to help make someone's dream come true. Although this aspiring young doctor doesn't know it yet, his future is looking pretty good.

Another of Boniface and Andrew's brothers, Mark, has now completed his hair-stylist course. The friends of *Northern Magic* – led by a phenomenal Ottawa hair salon owner, Karen Sharp, who's been donating the profits from her shop one day each month to this project – have just provided Mark with a loan to establish his own salon in the

Kenyan village of Mtwapa. He plans to call it Mark's Magic Hair &
Beauty Center.

We recently received an e-mail from Mark that brought tears to our
eyes. He wrote this message not only to us, but to all the friends he's
never met, whose generosity and faith have given him a chance to pull his
entire family out of poverty.

"When we first met," Mark wrote, "it didn't occur to me that you
would change my life. I still hold fond memories of our talks and strolls
in Kilifi. This is a time when I wish we were together to share my joy of
life changing for the better, because of caring friends who at one time
were simple strangers. Again I appreciate your kindness and your great
support. With you in support I see my dreams come true. May God bless
you all."

People often ask Herbert and me how we've adjusted to being back
in the real world. I don't know how to answer that question, because in
many ways this world, with its rather artificial pressures, feels less real
than the one we left behind. A large part of us is still out there. We're
very conscious that as westerners we live within a very tiny, exclusive and
privileged enclave. We're painfully aware that if our African friends ever
came to visit and saw our large suburban home, we'd feel embarrassment
and shame that we aren't doing more.

We haven't resumed regular jobs, but have instead focussed on the
things that have sprung out of our journey – sharing our story through
writing and public speaking, helping others realize that they, too, are citizens of the world, and, best and most important of all, raising money
for our projects in Indonesia and Kenya. Certainly, our love of travel has
not been quenched – if anything, it's grown. We spend a lot of time
dreaming up our next big trip, wondering what adventures are in store,
what twists and turns our life may take in the next ten years.

All I know for sure is that Herbert was right when he threw a photo
of a small blue and white sloop on the kitchen table that day and said
God wanted us to buy that boat. It's clear to me now that our family was
meant to take this journey. We learned that ordinary people can dream
big dreams and make them happen, whether they are ready or not. We
learned that the world is full of good people, who are just like us in all
the ways that matter. And we learned that those of us who have been for-

tunate enough to make a living and thereby build ourselves a life, have the power – and also the duty – to help build a better world, even if only by changing the world of one single person.

I hear a little animal noise beside me, and glance up to see the face of Magic – not Magic the Gibbon or Magic the Cow, but a brand new Magic who's bounded into our lives. It's Magic the Puppy, who looks up at me with adoring brown eyes, one ear up and one ear down. She's imploring me to take her for another swim. The boys are playing Magic Cards beside the tent, and Herbert, by the water's edge, is busily improvising a repair to our ancient cedar-strip canoe – newly dubbed the *Leaky Tiki* – using medical gauze and candle wax. Some things never change.

But I don't oblige Magic with a swim, for my mind is elsewhere – whether in the past or the future, it's hard to say. To be surrounded by family and trees and water and the sounds of nature has brought a certain magical feeling back with tremendous and unexpected force. Where might I be, right now, if I close my eyes? On a river in Borneo? Hunting for shark teeth on a beach in Kenya? Or maybe embarking on a camel trek to Timbuktu? What new places and friends are out there, awaiting our discovery?

Life – as Michael would say – is glorious. There's still so much to do, and not a moment to waste.

Diane Stuemer
Stratton Lake, Algonquin Park, Ontario
July 20, 2002

If you want to become part of the journey of *Northern Magic*, or simply want to find out more about our past and future adventures, this book is only the beginning! Visit us at: www.northernmagic.com.

Acknowledgements

The true story of *Northern Magic* is the story of people everywhere, helping and giving to others. We thank you all, whether we had the space to acknowledge you by name, or not.

Some of the people who helped us during our hectic pre-departure phase were: **Marco Heinrich**, **Shawn Murphy**, **Shawn Hooper**, **Ghaffar Ahmed**, **Ali Al Aldein**, **Robert Alain**, **Maureen Scale**, **Dr. David Edmison**, **Dr. Chiam-Vimonvat**, **Marilyn Dow**, **Mina King**, and **Carole Chenier**.

We'd also like to thank:

Michael Mitchell, for his songs of the sea and songs of Canada, which accompanied us and inspired us around the world; **Joanne Griffin** and other teachers and students of Fallingbrook School, who supported us in many ways before, during, and after our trip; **Gina Nichols** and **Sandy Mountford**, for hosting us in Washington, and especially Gina for rescuing us during the last-minute scramble to move out of the house; **Betty** and **Sam Switzer** in Ft. Lauderdale, for permitting us to stay at your marina; **Merita Zuñiga**, and her husband, **Francisco Bauta**, in Jaimanitas, Cuba, for the feast and for sharing what you had; **Amanda**, **Kaspar**, **Greg**, and **Oliver**, who helped us through the Panama Canal at the last minute; **Delphine Barsinas** in Tahuata Island, Marquesas, for showing us Marquesan hospitality; **Ambrose** and **Natacha Colombani** in Tahiti, for the tour of the island and for showing us the giant eels; **Bob** and **Tupou Marsters**, **Bill Marsters**, and especially **Metua Atuatika**, Palmerston Island, for treating us like kings; **Petiola Maratu'u** in Tonga, for sharing your niece's wedding and much more; **Joeli** and **Kasanita Lau** in Suva, Fiji, for making an underground feast for us, whether we could stay to eat it or not; **Bobby** and **Niru Kumar** in Suva, Fiji, for taking us under your wing, and especially Niru, for your tears; **Ed McLaughlin** from Hawaii, on *Aka*, for helping Herbert earn his Ph.D. in refrigeration mechanics and only accepting three cookies in return.

Many members of the Rotary Club of Kippa Ring, Scarborough, Australia, but especially **Brian Shoobert**, and **Steve** and **Melissa Griffith**, who gave us a home away from home; all the *Ottawa Citizen* readers who sent us letters, and to **Laura Robin** who delivered them, just when we needed it; **Brian** and **Beth Winterburn** in Bowen, for adopting our family like stray cats; **Yves Matson**, our sixth crewmember for a month, for engaging us in endless philosophical discussions and teaching us truly how to laugh, even though some of your jokes were pretty rude; **Andy Schinner** and **Lana Cherkasova** on *Futuna*, and **Jim** and **Dianne Carlin** on *September Song*, for your lasting friendship; the **Dodge family** on *Nanamuk*, for sharing some wonderful adventures with us; the many other cruising friends from many boats and many countries whose help and friendship enriched us.

Ketut, a young waiter in northern Bali, for opening our eyes and really making us think; **"Mr. Ambon"** in Kalimantan, for caring enough to ask important questions; **Andi, Ferry, Anang**, and **Pak Susiantoro**, for being our guides and our friends and especially for your help during my second research trip back to Borneo; **Wanto, Dr. Gede Suarsadana**, and **Dr. Bayu Wirayuda** in Kalimantan and Bali, for showing us your dedication to helping protect something important on behalf of all of us; **Sin Boon Lim** in Malaysia, for a real Chinese meal and much computer help; **Bill** and **Connie Price** in Kuala Lumpur, Malaysia, for more favours and hospitality than I can list; **Dr. Harry Heckel**, single-handedly circumnavigating in his 80s, for living life with passion; **Pharanee Deters** and the late **Bill Deters** of Mae Sot, Thailand, for sharing your precious gibbons with us; **Kodah Chotung** in Thailand, for the boat tour and visit to your village, and for not using perfume containing alcohol; **Ma Chok**, a young woman of the Karen (Long-Neck) Tribe near Mae Hong Son, Thailand, for your curiosity and beauty; **Police Chief Amangiri** of the Nicobar Islands, for arresting us and thus giving us a great story to tell our grandchildren; **Ekka Kehelkaduwa Withan Darmasena** and his beautiful wife, **Shavanthi**, in Sri Lanka, for friendship, hospitality, and smiles when we needed it; **Ahmed Mohmed** in the Maldives, for saying "yes" to everything; **Captain Ilyas Hassan** and his crew, Addu Atoll, Maldives, for a birthday party none of us will ever forget; **Rob Jurgens** in Tanga, Tanzania, for unbelievable hospitality and for buying a roll of handmade sisal rope; **Tony** and **Daphne Britchford** of Kilifi, Kenya, for providing a home away from home.

Kenneth Muriithi of Plan International in Kilifi, Kenya, for showing us how it ought to be done, for arranging so many tours of villages and schools, and especially for helping make our own project happen; **Andrew Thuva** of Kilifi, for being probably the most important person we've ever met; **Boniface Kitsao, Katana Kitsao, Hamisi Mwanadoro,** and **Mark Thuva,** for your friendship and helping us grow; **Kalimbo** and **Dr. Kate** of Plan International, for helping us buy a milk cow; **Alice** and **Don Williams,** for hosting us at Lewa Downs and for making the first contribution to the Boniface and Hamisi Project; the incomparable **Karimosho,** our first Maasai friend, for walking slowly enough that we could keep up; **Ron Beaton** and his family and staff at Rekero, Kenya, especially **Jackson Saigilu Ole Looseyia,** for helping children in need and turning down a tip; **Valens John,** brave schoolteacher of Maasai children; the Maasai grandmother **Deeay,** for inviting us into your smoky mud hut and warming Christopher in your robe; **Salem Yeslam** in Aden, Yemen, for not caring whether you got paid; **Weldemicael Habtezian** in Massawa, Eritrea, for your friendship and for letting us cool off in your high-ceilinged home; **Abu Mohammed Hamed** in Suakin, Sudan, for taking care of us and bringing us back carrots from Port Sudan; **Nageeb Mostafa** in Safaga, Egypt, for your endless great stories, all of which ended up "Boom! Kalaboush!"; **Ekbal El Asyouti** from Cairo, for your gifts and friendship; the mighty **Ahmed** of Cairo, for protecting us from the evil Ali Baba; many Canadian embassy staff in Cairo, including **Stuart Bale, Nicola Dunn,** and "Smooth Sammy" **Samir Kader,** for defeating the Grinch and bringing Christmas to us, far from home; **Customs officials** and **DHL** delivery company staff in Egypt and Italy, for giving us an endless fund of dramatic and exciting stories of triumph over adversity; **Don Amoore** on *Lutana* in Turkey, for sharing his brain teasers with all of us, especially Jonathan.

The amazing **Captain George Kotsovilis** and his wonderful wife, **Georgia,** for more favours, gifts, and outstanding Greek hospitality than anyone could ever dream of, and especially for caring about Africa; **Peppino, Lucia,** and **Blu Falabella** in Sicily, for endless help and extraordinary hospitality, even though you all eat spaghetti the wrong way; **Teresa** and **James Peralta,** for helping us understand Gibraltar; **Ana Maria Albuquerque Taviera** and **Filipe de Sousa Lima,** for your tours, gifts, and hospitality, and for your continuing friendship; **Paul Dole** of Ottawa for connecting us with so many wonderful new friends; many prayer groups in different cities, who prayed for us when we crossed the Atlantic; **Wayne Cuddington** and **Bev Wake** of the *Ottawa Citizen,* for being there in Nova Scotia when we finally emerged from the fog; **Joanne Sams, Steve Morden, Anita Paeglis,** and **Delton Sams** in Gaspé, for all your friendship and hospitality; **Commander Tom Turnbull, Lt. Commander "Godd" Pierre Godin,** and **Maryanik LeGoff** and the rest of the Sea Cadets in Trois Rivières, for everything you did to make our stay there memorable; **Fern Beauvais** of Papineauville Marina, for making me feel like Julia Roberts and for crying along with me when we left; **Bob, Judy,** and **Lady** from *Catch the Sun,* for your help in Montreal; **Douglas Thomas** and others from the Navy League of Canada, for the escort to Petrie Island in the rain and for making us laugh about you-know-what; **Steve Fischer** of CBC-TV, for signing on as crew and for bringing out the best in all of us; **Laurent Blanchet,** for caring about our boys; **Graham Vokey,** alias Jean Big Foot, The Pirate of Petrie Island, for your gifts, your friendship, and for help moving into our home; **Bruce Johnston,** who also helped us move and whose friendship has enriched our lives; our many neighbours on Brookridge Crescent, who helped us unpack and who yanked man-sized weeds out of our front garden.

We also have a very special place in our hearts for the late **Emily Acton,** who showed us the meaning of true courage; **Karen Sharp,** who demonstrated extraordinary generosity to our African friends, and continues to do so; **David Villeneuve,** for more favours than we can count, including driving all the way to Montreal to pick up a shipment of Balinese souvenirs; **Diane King** and **Paul Couch,** and **Aimee** and **Jeremy King,** for establishing and maintaining the *Northern Magic* Web site, for supporting all our special projects in many ways, for organizing the Petrie Island homecoming party, and for becoming our friends; everyone who donated food, supplies, services and gifts at our wonderful Petrie Island home-coming, resulting in $11,000 raised for our projects and my gaining five pounds; and a big thanks and hug to all the people who stood in the rain along the shore at Petrie Island and at various docks and marinas on the way, greeting us as we arrived home.

We need to thank **Neil Reynolds**, former editor of the *Ottawa Citizen*, for believing in us and giving us a chance to share our experiences and growth; everyone else at the *Ottawa Citizen*, including **Wendy Warburton**, who permitted us to share our story and who supported our efforts to publicize important causes; all the readers of the *Ottawa Citizen*, other newspapers, and the Web site, who travelled along with us and who became an important part of our adventure; and especially all those who contributed money and services to our projects in Palmerston Island, Indonesia, and Kenya, especially the Friends of Boniface and Hamisi, who transformed our journey and our lives.

We also have to make special mention of **Mike** and **Karen Hooper** of Orleans, and **Shawn** and **Kevin Hooper**, who did so much for us over many years, including endless overseeing and maintenance of our house and a midnight chase after lease-breaking tenants. Kevin, your instruction of Michael in the art of burpalese was a major contribution to our trip as well.

I also sincerely thank **Douglas Gibson, Jonathan Webb, Alex Schultz**, and the rest of the great people at McClelland & Stewart, for making it possible to share our story with a wider audience. You not only made me feel this project was very important to you, you also somehow convinced me to cut my manuscript to 40 per cent of its original size. It's been a great privilege and honour working with you. **Linda, Mom**, and **Dad, Aunt Ethel, Debbie Black, Bruce Johnston**, and **Diane King**, thank you as well for your valuable advice and help with the manuscript.

I don't have the words to thank my family adequately: my mother, **Jeanette King**, my father, **Frank King**, and my sister, **Linda Maslechko**, for the many hours of work you devoted daily to making this trip possible and to keeping us afloat and safe. You are the true sixth, seventh, and eighth crewmembers of *Northern Magic*. Your love and support reached over the miles to us every day, and still does.

Michael, Jonathan, and **Christopher**, thank you, my precious boys, for leaving your comfortable home, your bikes, and your friends for four years; for putting up with uncomfortable conditions without complaint; for finding your own granola bars when I couldn't manage a meal; for liking Kraft dinner made with mouldy noodles and rancid powdered milk; for gleefully keeping track of how many times I barfed; for making me share my Hershey's Kisses with you in the middle of the night; for teaching me to play Magic Cards; for making me laugh; for being resourceful and cheerful no matter what; for countless snuggles and back-scratches; for giving me the incredible privilege of watching you grow up with the entire world as your playground. Thank you for being a part of this dream, even though it wasn't always yours.

And my final thanks goes to my brilliant, stubborn, resourceful, sometimes infuriating, and always devoted husband, **Herbert**, who first dared to dream, and then made it all happen, no matter what.

Photo Credits

All photos are copyright © Herbert and Diane Stuemer, except for the following:

p. 1, photo on front page of *Ottawa Citizen*, courtesy Wayne Cuddington, *Ottawa Citizen*;

p. 8, photos of kelotok, loggers' camp, Rosemary and babies, and young gold miners, courtesy Andy Schinner; photo of Magic the gibbon, courtesy Grace Dodge;

p. 12, photo of Maasai boy, courtesy Linda Maslechko;

p. 13, large photo of Maasai grandmother, courtesy Linda Maslechko;

p. 16, photos of arrival in Nova Scotia, Mike diving, Herbert hoisting sail, Diane and family, and Diane on *Citizen* front page, courtesy Wayne Cuddington, *Ottawa Citizen*; photo of crowd, Aug. 26, 2001, courtesy Bruce Johnston.

I am a part of all that I have met;
Yet all experience is an arch wherethrough
Gleams that untravelled world, whose margin fades
For ever and for ever when I move.
How dull it is to pause, to make an end,
To rust unburnished, not to shine in use!
As though to breathe were life.

Alfred, Lord Tennyson,
Ulysses

Diane Stuemer's journal of her family's voyage appeared weekly in the *Ottawa Citizen* from September 1997 to August 2001. The articles enjoyed phenomenal success and the Stuemers appeared on the newspaper's front page on nine occasions.

On March 15, 2003, five months after *The Voyage of the Northern Magic* was first published, Diane lost her battle with melanoma. Her husband, Herbert, and their three boys, Michael, Jonathan, and Christopher, continue their commitment to activism and humanitarian work. They live in Ottawa.

To learn more about the Stuemers, their voyage, and the family's ongoing international projects, visit www.northernmagic.com.